Managing in Construction Supply Chains and Markets

Managing in Construction Supply Chains and Markets

Reactive and Proactive Options for Improving Performance and Relationship Management

Andrew Cox, Paul Ireland and Mike Townsend

thomas telford

Published by Thomas Telford Publishing, Thomas Telford Ltd,
1 Heron Quay, London E14 4JD.
www.thomastelford.com

Distributors for Thomas Telford books are
USA: ASCE Press, 1801 Alexander Bell Drive, Reston, VA 20191-4400
Japan: Maruzen Co. Ltd, Book Department, 3–10 Nihonbashi 2-chome,
Chuo-ku, Tokyo 103
Australia: DA Books and Journals, 648 Whitehorse Road, Mitcham 3132,
Victoria

First published 2006

Also available from Thomas Telford Books

A catalogue record for this book is available from the British Library

ISBN: 0 7277 3001 0

Typeset by Academic + Technical, Bristol
Printed and bound in Great Britain by MPG Books, Bodmin, Cornwall

Contents

Preface

This is the third book about relationship and performance optimisation in construction supply chains and markets in a series undertaken as part of a continuous collaboration between researchers at the Centre for Business Strategy and Procurement (CBSP) at Birmingham Business School and Newpoint Consulting Ltd. This collaboration commenced in 1994 when Mike Townsend, the CEO of Newpoint Consulting, began work with Andrew Cox at the CBSP to investigate the benefits of partnering approaches in the construction industry as part of a British Airports Authority (BAA)-funded project. That research led to the publication by Thomas Telford of *Strategic Procurement in Construction* (Cox and Townsend, 1998) and a companion piece, funded by a research grant from London Underground and Railtrack, entitled *Contracting for Business Success* (Cox and Thompson, 1998). In the intervening years work on construction, as well as other relationship and performance management issues, has continued both at the CBSP and in Newpoint Consulting.

Now, due to this extensive experience by Newpoint Consulting in the construction industry, and the generous funding over the last three years by the Chartered Institute of Purchasing and Supply of more detailed research into construction supply chains and markets, it has been possible to produce a third book. In this book, it has been possible to provide a much more detailed insight into the full range of relationship and performance management outcomes that are feasible in construction supply chains and markets, as well as a more detailed understanding of the appropriateness of different ways of working under specific supply chain and market conditions.

The primary focus of this book is on how buyers and suppliers in construction relationships can optimise their own performance. The optimisation of the performance of exchange partners is also considered. This is, however, a secondary concern because, while the performance of exchange partners is obviously an issue for both buyers and suppliers in all business relationships, their primary concern must always be with their own performance. In this sense, assisting the performance of an exchange partner may be important for the performance of the other, but, in the end, it may not be.

We recognise that this may not be the current dominant thinking in the industry, where the attachment to partnering principles in recent years has generated an enthusiasm for considering the optimisation of everyone's performance in construction supply chains and markets. Our view is that while optimising the performance of exchange partners may be a legitimate concern for actors involved in supply chains and markets, it is not the best way to think about performance optimisation. This is because, while it can be a sensible approach if relationships need to be sustained over the long-term, it may be sub-optimal in the short-term when relationships do not need to be sustained.

This implies, as we shall see in what follows, that in construction – where long-term relationships based on high levels of bilateral dependency are not always necessary for either the buyer or the supplier to achieve their commercial goals – achieving outcomes that are equally beneficial to both parties may, but they may not, be essential. If this is the case then the management problem in construction supply chains and markets must be to decide whether it is essential to develop long-term and highly collaborative (partnering) relationship management approaches, or whether these should be replaced by relatively short-term and arm's-length (opportunistic) buyer and supplier interactions.

This way of thinking clearly takes issue with those writers who argue that 'best practice' in construction relationship management is *always* to develop highly collaborative approaches based on high levels of trust and transparency in preference to opportunistic and adversarial approaches. These approaches – sometimes referred to as partnership sourcing, project partnering and relationship marketing – have been the dominant ways of thinking about construction 'best practice' since the publication of the Latham and Egan Reports (Latham, 1994; DETR, 1998) into the problems facing the industry. This book, while not rejecting these approaches, argues that they can only be appropriate ways of working for particular actors under specific construction supply chain and market circumstances. When these circumstances do not occur then alternative supply chain and market management approaches will be appropriate.

The central premise of this book is, therefore, that, while there may be opportunities for some buyers and suppliers to develop highly collaborative exchange relationships in construction, the majority of relationships will continue to be managed on a short-term and relatively opportunistic, arm's-length basis. Furthermore, it is argued that there is nothing fundamentally flawed in the management of construction relationships using highly opportunistic and arm's-length ways of working. In practice, the performance and relationship optimisation problem in construction supply chains and markets is about appropriateness. This means that buyers and suppliers both have to choose wisely from a range of relationship management approaches – some of which may be commercially adversarial or non-adversarial, and some of which may be operationally collaborative or arm's-length.

It is also argued that, when making appropriateness choices, while the idea of developing win–win outcomes in which both parties fully achieve all that they ideally desire is an appealing idea, it has no basis in reality when an objective (economically rational) view is taken of commercial exchange between buyers and suppliers. This means that *positive-sum* (win–win) outcomes are not objectively feasible, and that only more restricted forms of *mutuality (nonzero-sum* or mutually beneficial) outcomes (based on win–partial win and partial win–partial win), or *zero-sum* outcomes (based on win–lose and partial win–lose) are achievable in buyer and supplier exchange (Cox, 2004a, b). As a result, the desire to achieve outcomes that optimise the performance of both parties in an exchange relationship may represent a serious misunderstanding of buyer and supplier exchange – both in construction specifically, and in business relationship management in general.

This is, however, to run ahead of the discussion presented here. In Part A, Chapter 1 provides an introduction to the performance and relationship optimisation problem in construction supply chains and markets. It is argued that, even though writers from the *relational* school of writing contend that developing trusting and transparent, non-adversarial and highly collaborative approaches to relationship management is the best way to optimise performance, construction supply chains and markets have unique and distinct demand and supply characteristics that often militate against the development of longer-term and highly collaborative ways of working.

Given this, most construction supply chain and market relationships will remain essentially short-term and operationally arm's-length, whatever proponents of more collaborative relationship management approaches may desire. This chapter shows that the optimisation problem for buyers and sellers in construction supply chains is, as a result, one in which there is an inherent tendency for most relationships to be managed by both parties in a commercially opportunistic manner. This does not mean that such an approach is always necessary, but that it is inherently likely because of the power structures that exist in a mainly project environment rather than process supply chain environment.

Following this discussion of the inherent problems facing managers in construction supply chains and markets, Chapter 2 outlines the *power and leverage* perspective on relationship and performance management. This school argues that while collaborative ways of working may be appropriate for some actors in some construction supply chains and markets they are not appropriate ways of optimising performance for all actors. On the contrary, it is argued that only a limited number of actors, who possess key power resources in construction supply chains and markets, will be able to undertake collaborative approaches effectively. Furthermore, this school contends that when undertaking collaborative relationships unconditional trust and absolute transparency of operational and commercial trade-offs may be naïve, and also that, in the absence of collaboration, opportunistic arm's-length relationship management may be a highly desirable way of working for either the buyer or the seller.

This discussion is informed by an analysis of the range of relationship management and performance optimisation approaches that are available to buyers and suppliers. This provides a way of thinking about the relationship management and performance optimisation choices that may be more or less appropriate for managers to utilise when they act as buyers or as suppliers in construction supply chains and markets. It is argued that buyers and suppliers can interact using essentially reactive or proactive ways of working, and that there are essentially two reactive (*supplier selection* or *supply chain sourcing*) and two proactive (*supplier development* and *supply chain management*) approaches that are feasible in buyer and supplier exchange (Cox et al., 2003).

Unfortunately, as Chapter 3 shows, it is not always possible for both parties to an exchange to fully achieve their ideal commercial and/or operational goals when they operate within these four relationship management approaches. Sometimes the buyer will achieve much more than the supplier and vice versa, or the buyer or supplier will win and their exchange partner will lose operationally and commercially. This is essentially because exchange is contested and win–win outcomes are not feasible in relationships between buyers and suppliers (Cox, 2004a, b).

Given these conclusions, sixteen short empirical case studies (in Chapters 4 to 19 in Parts B1 and B2) provide an overview of the relationship management and performance optimisation outcomes that can occur in construction supply chains and markets. These case studies show that it is possible for buyers and suppliers to operate using highly proactive and collaborative, as well as highly reactive and arm's-length ways of operational and collaborative working. Furthermore, as the cases show, when either proactive or reactive ways of working are selected, while it may be impossible for *positive-sum* (win–win) outcomes to occur, it is possible for *nonzero-sum* (win–partial win and partial win–partial win) and *zero-sum* (win–lose and partial win–lose) outcomes to occur. This demonstrates that when managers make decisions about relationship management approaches there can be very different performance optimisation outcomes within them for the buyer and the supplier.

The sixteen cases demonstrate, therefore, that, when it comes to optimising individual performance, some relationship management choices may be operationally and commercially superior to others for both buyers and suppliers. This means that making choices about different ways of working for construction buyers and suppliers is not just a simple choice between proactive and collaborative or reactive and arms-length. On the contrary, although the Latham and Egan Reports have tended to coach the choice in these simplistic terms, it is clear from the analysis presented here that buyers and suppliers sometimes have reactive options that are superior to all of the proactive choices available to them, and vice versa. Furthermore, the analysis shows that when making decisions about proactive and reactive options there are also options available that provide buyers and suppliers with involvement only at the first tier (market-only) or throughout the whole supply chain. In making decisions about reactive or proactive relationship management, therefore, buyers and suppliers also have to consider their market and supply chain options.

This more comprehensive understanding of the complexity of available relationship management choices for buyers and suppliers in construction supply chains and markets provides the basis for a final discussion in Part C (Chapter 20) of the implication for relationship management and performance optimisation. The final chapter demonstrates that although there are sixteen broad relationship and performance optimisation outcomes that are feasible in buyer and supplier exchange, the majority of outcomes in construction, as in all other forms of business-to-business exchange, occur in the *nonzero-sum* (partial win–partial win) category. Despite this, even when *nonzero-sum* or *mutuality* outcomes occur it is not the case that both parties in an exchange relationship will be equally satisfied with the performance outcome.

In the final chapter the essentially contested nature of exchange in construction is explained by reference to the fact that, given the nature of the demand and supply characteristics of this industry and the power structures it creates, opportunism and reactive arm's-length relationship management rather than proactive collaborative options are often preferable for most exchange partners. This means that in the project-based side of construction *zero-sum* outcomes are likely to be more frequent than is the case in many other industries. As a result, while there is scope for proactive relationship management approaches based on trust, transparency and collaboration, these may not be feasible for all actors in the industry.

The final chapter also provides some pointers for managers when they think about appropriateness in selecting relationship management options. It is hoped that this will assist managers in construction to understand when it is, and when it is not, appropriate to utilise reactive or proactive approaches, and how they should think about performance optimisation for themselves and their exchange partners. It is hoped that, by presenting this more detailed account of the types of relationship and performance approaches and outcomes that can occur in construction supply chains and markets, practitioners will be able to select more wisely from alternative ways of working. In doing so it is also hoped that they can achieve far more success in their relationship and performance management approaches than appears to be the case given the high level of sub-optimality that is currently endemic throughout the industry.

If this book provides an opportunity for practitioners to understand the full range of relationship choices available to them – whether these are reactive or proactive – to leverage improvements in performance then it will have served its purpose. We are grateful for the forbearance of Thomas Telford Publishing and its editors in granting many extensions to a gestation process that has been longer than we would have preferred. We would also like to thank Jackie Potter and Michelle Donovan for their invaluable support in putting this manuscript together. Any sins of omission or commission are, of course, ours alone.

References

Cox, A. (2004a), 'Business relationship alignment: on the commensurability of value capture and mutuality in business exchange', *Supply Chain Management: An International Journal*, **9**(5), pp. 410–420.

Cox, A. (2004b), *Win–Win? The Paradox of Value and Interests in Business Relationships*, Earlsgate Press, Stratford-upon-Avon.

Cox, A., Ireland, P., Lonsdale, C., Sanderson, J. and Watson, G. (2003), *Supply Chain Management: A Guide to Best Practice*, Financial Times–Prentice Hall, London.

Cox, A. and Thompson, I. (1998), *Contracting for Business Success*, Thomas Telford, London.

Cox, A. and Townsend, M. (1998), *Strategic Procurement in Construction*, Thomas Telford, London.

DETR (1998), *Rethinking Construction*, Department for the Environment, Transport and the Regions, London.

Latham, M. (1994), *Constructing the Team*, HMSO, London.

Part A

Introduction

The performance and relationship optimisation problem in construction

1.1 Introduction

In this chapter the major relationship management and performance optimisation problems faced by actors in the construction industry are outlined. In particular, the discussion focuses on the unique demand and supply characteristics that comprise construction supply chains and markets. These demand and supply characteristics are relatively unique when compared with other industries because the construction industry tends to experience a high level of short-term, *ad hoc* and highly differentiated demand with highly contested, small-scale supply markets that have relatively low barriers to entry.

Whether these demand and supply characteristics occur in the UK or in other countries does not really matter. This is because the underlying power circumstances that are generated by them are similar everywhere. Despite this, in some construction supply chains and markets longer-term, more regular and standardised demand and supply requirements occur, which generate different power structures and alternative relationship management choices for buyers and sellers. Nevertheless, the industry as a whole is dominated by one-off, small-scale, highly differentiated project demand rather than process or serial project demand, with highly fragmented and heavily contested supply markets, often with low barriers to market entry and limited scope for suppliers to create sustainable differentiation.

These circumstances have ensured that the construction industry has been prey to a continuous culture of short-term opportunism historically. As a result, many academic writers and practitioners, and in the UK the authors of government sponsored industry reports, have attempted to find solutions to these problems by encouraging industry players to adopt more relational approaches. Relational approaches are normally predicated on the need for buyers and sellers to enter into more long-term, trusting and transparent collaborative relationships to seek mutual advantage. These partnering or relationship marketing ideas have normally been copied from other industries – in particular from Japanese and Western automotive supply chains and markets.

Unfortunately, as the discussion here shows, much of this thinking is simplistic and fails to understand the constraints imposed upon action by the power structures that arise internally and externally for construction buyers and suppliers from the unique properties of demand and supply in their supply chains and markets. Most relational writers are, therefore, guilty of willing an 'end' – mutual benefit

– without properly understanding whether the 'means' are available to achieve this in all circumstances, or whether this is always the most favourable approach for all buyers and all suppliers in all circumstances. The argument here is that in construction these types of approach will rarely be the most appropriate for buyers or suppliers, although when they are they should be adopted vigorously.

In this first chapter, therefore, the unique demand and supply structures that occur in construction are described, with a discussion of how this affects performance and relationship optimisation for both buyers and suppliers. This is followed, in Chapter 2, by a discussion of the strengths and weaknesses of the *relational* and *power and leverage* perspectives, as mechanisms for improving performance and relationship management outcomes. Chapter 3 provides an overview of the problem of achieving win–win outcomes in business in general, and in construction in particular. This chapter demonstrates that only some outcomes are feasible and that win–win is an unattainable ideal between buyers and suppliers, although it is feasible in other types of business relationships.

1.2 Demand and supply structures in construction supply chains and markets

The construction industry covers all aspects of building, civil engineering and the process plant industry and encompasses the planning, regulation, design, construction and maintenance of buildings and other physical structures. It includes projects of dramatically different types, sizes and complexities and requires extensive professional and trade skills. The importance of construction cannot be understated. Regardless of their primary business, organisations always require interaction with the construction industry to source the physical assets to house their operations. This requirement ranges from the construction of major industrial units for the manufacturing operations of large organisations, to minor repair and maintenance work for the offices of small organisations. The size of an organisation and nature of its business, therefore, determine the extent and regularity to which an organisation sources from construction supply chains and markets.

There is no doubt that construction remains a key economic activity. Within the UK economy it contributes approximately 7% to GDP[1]. However, despite the importance of the construction sector in terms of revenues and number of firms, construction supply chains and markets remain highly adversarial, fragmented and contested. This has resulted in the emergence and development of complicated structures of power and leverage in the materials, labour, equipment and professional services marketplaces. There are suppliers who occupy smaller, more specialised niches in order to survive through the avoidance of the direct competitive battle with the established market-leaders. There are also firms who span these 'niches' by providing complete 'solutions' to large first-tier organisations who act as 'integrators'. The end result is a very large number of suppliers with which any firm may do business in the delivery of their construction requirements. However, the number of firms is not the only factor that has increased the inherent difficulties facing procurement professionals when managing construction requirements.

---

[1] In the UK, the total volume of all construction work in 2000 was valued at over £68 billion (throughout this book, billion means one thousand million).

Despite the low levels of expenditure on innovation there have been significant technological advances with actual construction products and services. This has opened up a wide range of different sourcing and relationship management possibilities. From the continuum of construction products and services (routine commodity components to highly specialised and critical services), the gamut of possible buyer and supplier relationships ranges from purely independent trans-actional, short-term price-based interactions, to highly interdependent relationships that may involve a considerable long-term investment by both parties.

Within the UK construction industry, therefore, a myriad of construction supply chains and markets need to be integrated by any construction firm when it delivers a solution to an end customer (client). Figure 1.1 suggests that the key generic supply chains required for a typical solution are rather simple and linear but the reality is quite different. The ultimate level of complexity involved with the management of a construction project will be determined by the extensive requirements of the end customer as defined in the design and specification. It is difficult to quantify the exact number of constituent material, equipment and labour supply chains that have to be integrated into a 'typical' project because such a project does not exist, due to the ubiquity of its unique project-specific requirements.

During the construction process, the end customer (the client) often requires professional services to ensure a level of professionalism and to guard against supplier opportunism that is rife within the industry. These professional services may include a wide range of capabilities: project management, design and architec-ture, civil engineering, structural engineering, services engineering, quantity surveying and independent cost consultancy. These services provide the detailed design, planning and project management expertise that is fundamental to a successful project and the avoidance of the problems widely experienced by clients.

Within the generic supply chain the first-tier construction firm plays the major 'integrating' role for all upstream supply chains. There is, however, a high degree of subcontracting within the industry, with main (first-tier) contractors, faced with irregular demands from clients, appointing second-tier companies to deliver 'packages' that can be easily integrated within the final solutions. These packages may include groundworks, steel fabrication or mechanical and electrical products and services. For each of these elements there will be a requirement to source from additional upstream labour, materials and equipment supply chains.

Throughout the project procurement process little control or management of the entire supply chain is normally taken up by the focal organisation – the client (London et al., 1998; London and Kenley, 1999). As a result, each organisation in a tier is able to manage its supply relationships in such a way that it can effectively act as a procurement gatekeeper. The first-tier organisation typically acts as a gate-keeper to the subcontractors' tiers of suppliers and each trade subcontractor subsequently acts as a gatekeeper to the materials suppliers operating at the third-tier. Furthermore, the relatively unmanaged use of subcontracting within the industry increases the endemic problems associated with opportunism.

One of the primary reasons given for opportunism in the industry is related to the one-off nature of demand that characterises relationships between buyers and suppliers. It is often argued that the construction industry is unique in the way that it establishes projects to deliver one-off products (Burbridge and Fulster, 1993; Cutting-Decelle, 1997; Cox and Thompson, 1998; Cox and Townsend, 1998; Cox and Ireland, 2001, 2002a, b). It is the client who takes the initiative to start a construction project, and this leads to the frequent conceptualisation of

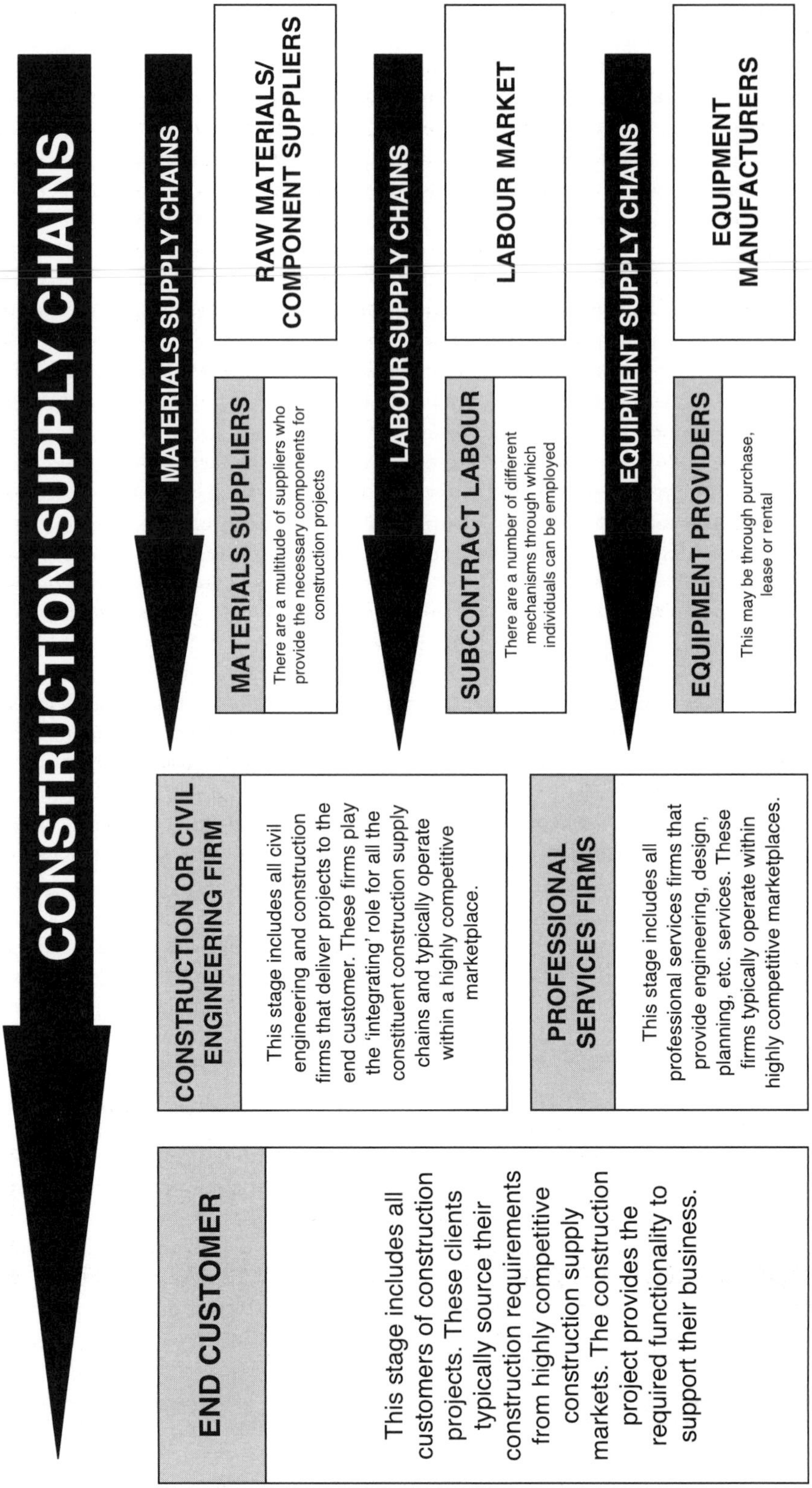

CONSTRUCTION SUPPLY CHAINS

MATERIALS SUPPLY CHAINS

RAW MATERIALS/ COMPONENT SUPPLIERS

MATERIALS SUPPLIERS

There are a multitude of suppliers who provide the necessary components for construction projects

LABOUR SUPPLY CHAINS

LABOUR MARKET

SUBCONTRACT LABOUR

There are a number of different mechanisms through which individuals can be employed

EQUIPMENT SUPPLY CHAINS

EQUIPMENT MANUFACTURERS

EQUIPMENT PROVIDERS

This may be through purchase, lease or rental

CONSTRUCTION OR CIVIL ENGINEERING FIRM

This stage includes all civil engineering and construction firms that deliver projects to the end customer. These firms play the 'integrating' role for all the constituent construction supply chains and typically operate within a highly competitive marketplace.

PROFESSIONAL SERVICES FIRMS

This stage includes all professional services firms that provide engineering, design, planning, etc. services. These firms typically operate within highly competitive marketplaces.

END CUSTOMER

This stage includes all customers of construction projects. These clients typically source their construction requirements from highly competitive construction supply markets. The construction project provides the required functionality to support their business.

Figure 1.1 The myriad of construction supply chains (Source: Cox and Ireland (2001), p. 221)

the construction supply chain as a process explicitly starting and ending with the end user.

A common representation of the construction process, as shown in Figure 1.2, starts with an initiative by the client to demand a constructed asset, for example a factory or office complex. After establishing a construction project organisation to provide the necessary competence and expertise to finalise the design and specification, the client will undertake a tendering process to select a main contractor. In most cases, the main contractor will take care of employment of subcontractors and the procurement of materials. When contracts are formalised, and a sufficient amount of information is available, the physical execution of the construction project can start. This includes production of materials, manufacturing, engineering and assembly of elements, and final construction on site. After the successful completion of the project, there will be the hand-over and use of the completed asset by the end user (Hughes, 1991; Luhtala *et al.*, 1994; Potts, 1995; Vrijhoef, 1998; Alarcón *et al.*, 1999; Kagioglou *et al.*, 2000).

The final project-specific construction supply chain that arises is, however, a system of multiple supply chains delivering all raw materials, human resources and information required for the successful completion of a project to the place where the specific end product must arise. With limited prefabrication, construction is largely a site operation, confined to the specific location where the final assembly takes place (Nam and Tatum, 1988; Westling, 1991). Construction often takes place, therefore, at the place of consumption, as opposed to the wide and less-specific end market of manufacturing industry.

For this reason construction projects tend to be temporary (Cleland and King, 1983; Cleland and Kurzner, 1985; Turner, 1993a, b; Morris, 1997; Murray-Webster and Thiry, 2000; Turner and Keegan, 2001; Turner and Simister, 2001; Turner and Müller, 2003). In contrast to manufacturing, this implies a temporary organisation of production for each project characterised by a short-term coalition of participants with frequent changes of membership, often termed 'temporary

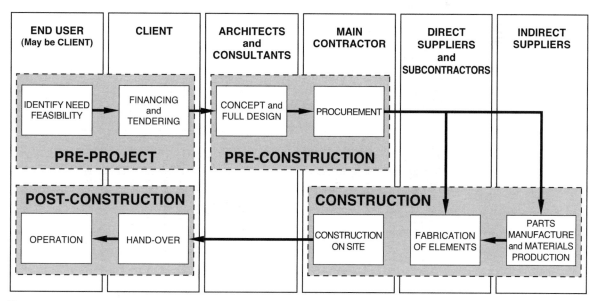

Figure 1.2 Typical representation of the construction process (Adapted from: Vrijhoef (1998) and Luhtala et al. (1994))

multi-organisation' (Cherns and Bryant, 1984; Luck and Newcombe, 1996; Koskela, 1997). The participants operate through a variety of contractual arrangements and specific procedures with considerable fluctuations in productivity (Westling, 1991; Hellard, 1995; Mohamed, 1997).

While this literature argues that a construction project is unique and temporary, there is a literature that argues that this is not the case for all construction projects (Cox and Townsend, 1997, 1998; Cox and Thompson, 1998; Cox and Ireland, 2002a). This literature highlights that while unique, temporary and one-off projects constitute a large percentage[2] of the market, there are a number of major construction clients whose construction portfolio may be classified as regular and process-based (Cox and Townsend, 1998). The regular nature of their construction demand means that it is relatively standardised and capable of being managed in a similar manner to a manufacturing process. In such circumstances, it can be argued that different performance optimisation and relationship management approaches may be appropriate to those that might be appropriate in circumstances where the client's spend is short-term, *ad hoc* and project-based.

1.3 Inherent problems of performance optimisation in construction supply chains and markets

While it is essential to recognise the characteristics that differentiate the construction industry from more process-based manufacturing industries, what is perhaps more important is to understand the implications of this for effective relationship management and performance optimisation in the construction environment. As the majority (if not all) of demand is for relatively unique, one-off projects that are delivered through highly fragmented and adversarial supply markets, this can lead to optimisation problems for all actors (buyers and suppliers) within construction supply chains and markets.

A key problem surrounds the inability of clients to achieve their business objectives (Alarcón, 1997). Since the majority of clients do not procure construction on a regular basis, their lack of understanding of the industry often results in an inability to leverage the supply market effectively. This infrequency, combined with the low criticality of construction spend to the overall business, often means that the client does not approach the sourcing of construction in the most appropriate manner. Clients may be unaware that, if they changed the way that they procured construction, they could achieve significant improvements in relation to cost, quality and project time. To avoid the high costs, poor quality and late delivery of typical construction projects, clients require an understanding of the different value proposition trade-offs that are available. These are illustrated in Figure 1.3.

Figure 1.3 illustrates the trade-off that construction clients have to make in relation to the key project variables of cost, quality and delivery (time). It is the balance between these variables that leads to the alternative value propositions outlined in Table 1.1. This is somewhat simplified, but it is critical that the

---

[2] The nature of demand for construction can be segmented in a number of ways. Cox and Townsend (1998) differentiate between clients who have a regular requirement for construction work of similar value and content (process spenders), and infrequent purchase clients (commodity spenders). Cox and Thompson (1998) contend that clients that possess regular process spends are unlikely to constitute more than 25% of the total UK market, while Blismas (2001) contends that multi-projects accounted for 10% of the entire industry's output and as much as 30% of contractors' output in 1999.

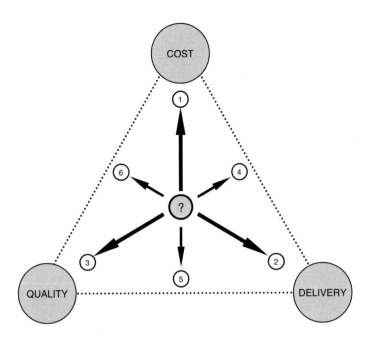

*Figure 1.3 Trade-offs
between project variables*

Table 1.1 The different value propositions available to clients

Value Proposition	Primary Factor	Secondary Factor
1	Cost is of overriding importance and the key variable on which the project is assessed. It is argued that cost is always the factor upon which project success is ultimately judged	Quality and delivery are of equal status but only of secondary importance. Clients may make sacrifices with these factors to achieve objectives with cost
2	Delivery is the primary factor upon which the client is selecting the project team	Quality and cost are of equal secondary importance to the client who may pay higher costs or accept a lower quality if delivery is guaranteed
3	Quality is of primary importance to the client's objectives. This may be the case in a risk-averse environment	Delivery and cost are of equal secondary importance to the client who may trade higher costs or later delivery for an agreed quality standard
4	Cost and delivery are of equal primary importance to the client	Quality is only of secondary importance to the client and may be forgone for the other factors
5	Quality and delivery are of equal primary importance to the client	Cost is a secondary consideration and the client may accept higher costs to guarantee certain levels of quality and a timely delivery
6	Cost and quality are of equal primary importance to the client when defining project objectives	Delivery is of lower importance and the client may opt for later delivery if lower costs and/or higher quality can be attained from the supply market

alternative trade-offs are recognised and fully understood by all individuals undertaking the procurement activity within construction supply chains. This is a fundamental prerequisite to the development of appropriate relationship management approaches to optimise desired performance and business objectives.

In addition to the problems stemming from a lack of understanding of the structure and characteristics of the industry and poor specification of value propositions by clients, there are many other problems within the practice of construction. A summary of some of the common problems that occur during the life of a typical construction project is provided in Table 1.2. In summary, the main problems that arise include (Abrahamson, 1991, 1996; Gann, 1996, 2001; Crowley, 1998; Bresnen and Marshall, 2001):

- low rates of productivity and considerable cost inefficiency and waste;
- frequent time-overruns and high rates of quality defects;
- considerable complexity and non-transparency of processes;
- high variability and uncertainty during the project making effective project planning and management difficult;
- poor quality information exchange that is hindered by obsolete information systems and self-interest from key players;
- lack of co-operation and communication between key project players;
- inability of firms to develop (and invest in) long-term relationships; and
- high rates of insolvency brought on by late payment and cash-flow problems.

In attempting to resolve these problems there are always two key relationships that can be identified. First, there is the relationship between the client and the first-tier main contractor. This is considered to be the main relationship that establishes the project in the first instance. This relationship may also incorporate the association between the main contractor and the client's design team (i.e. architects and consultants). The second primary relationship is that between the first-tier construction firm and second-tier parties in the supply chain (i.e. subcontractors and suppliers of materials).

In these two relationships the main contractor plays a fundamental and central role, managing downstream demand and upstream supply. In such a position, the main contractor may act as a 'facilitator' or 'inhibitor' to any relationship management and performance optimisation approach desired by either downstream clients or upstream suppliers. At the same time, it is possible that, even if the client and main contractor have decided upon the most appropriate relationship management and performance optimisation approach for themselves, their upstream suppliers may not be competent and/or congruent partners (Cox, 1999a; Cox et al., 2003). Upstream suppliers may lack the competence to do what is necessary, fail to understand the relationship management approach that they are expected to adopt, or (even if they do understand) they may wish to sabotage implementation in order to achieve their own operational and/or commercial goals.

This short discussion demonstrates that, just because there are longer-term and highly collaborative relationship management and performance optimisation approaches available in construction supply chains and markets, this does not mean that all actors in the industry will be equally committed to their implementation. This equivalence of commitment would only arise, it can be argued, if the benefits arising operationally and commercially for all of the parties that must be involved in the supply chain are worth the necessary investments of time, resources and money that they must make, and that this investment leads to performance

Table 1.2 Common problems in construction supply chains and markets (Adapted from: Vrijhoef (1998), p. 49)

Stage	Problems
Conception, Feasibility and Initiation	Misunderstanding of required value proposition and customer requirements Misunderstanding of technical and financial viability of project Customer demands very likely to change during project Poor demand management by clients adversely affecting their leverage
Financing and Tendering	Inappropriate funding strategy, budgeting and/or cost–benefit analysis Inappropriate contract strategy and tender procedures Unclear, ambiguous and adversarial tender documentation and contracts Different use of performance terminology (needs to be linked to client's requirements) Unclear distribution of roles, responsibilities, authority and accountability Failure to select competent and congruent suppliers for tender list Lack of robust supplier selection methodology
Design	Incomplete and/or inappropriate design information and documentation Failure to undertake adequate geotechnical and site investigation Limited appreciation of potential standardisation or prefabrication/assembly No or little scheduling of design work into project programme Design work is separated from (value) engineering and construction planning
Procurement	Delayed involvement of procurement Adversarial procurement methods focusing on lowest cost Adversarial post-tender negotiation Selection of incompetent or incongruent suppliers and subcontractors Selection of suppliers and subcontractors not linked to performance criteria
Fabrication of elements	Limited consideration of prefabrication or pre-assembly Unrealistic timescales for engineering and fabrication Deliveries neglecting necessary site handling Inappropriate time buffers built into programme Different order of delivery than site installation Restricted possibility to change designs after order placed
Parts and Materials manufacture	Inappropriate time buffers built into programme Deliveries not conforming to requirements and neglecting site handling Inflexible reaction to variations in design Unfeasible long delivery times
Construction on site	Poor site preparation and problems with wayleaves and approvals Poor quality products and workmanship Inappropriate project management and poor scheduling of work Inappropriate time buffers built into programme Inappropriate site supervision, coordination and management of work Inefficient operations and improper handling of materials Inappropriate contract for nature of work Unsystematic feedback and updating of contract information Incompatible or inappropriate equipment Unexpected and variability of ground and site conditions Poor communication between key players involving very late variations to work Insufficient skills and knowledge of workforce Poor levels of profitability for the construction firm
Hand-over	Unexpected delays in completion, exceeded cost price and/or delivery and quality problems Disputes regarding claims and variations Problems with (late) payment and cash-flows Subsequent arbitration and legal action
Use	Functionality and usability problems as client requirements are not met

outcomes that are better than any alternative relationship management approaches and performance outcomes that are currently feasible (Cox *et al.*, 2003). In the absence of this benign trade-off between investments and incentives it is highly unlikely that the problems that are endemic to construction supply chains can ever be eradicated.

This means that attempts to adopt highly collaborative relationship management approaches based on trust and transparency in construction must be capable of supporting performance outcomes that consistently improve on the outcomes that clients and their suppliers could achieve by using alternative and more opportunistic short-term relationship management approaches. But, if demand is project-specific and one-off or irregular, as well as non-standard, and supply markets are highly fragmented and subject to low levels of supplier differentiation, then it is unlikely that there will be many incentives for either buyers or suppliers to adopt long-term collaborative relationship management approaches.

This is because there are few incentives available beyond the one-off relationship to induce the necessary investments by buyers or suppliers in the relationship-specific adaptations and dedicated investments that would be necessary to create even higher levels of performance (Cannon and Perreault, 1999). Unless there is continuous demand from the buyer, and some scope for market closure or improvement in commercial returns for the supplier, there is nothing in the relationship that warrants such high levels of investment and, in the absence of these incentives, relationship management approaches are likely to remain opportunistic and arm's-length.

It is this problem of relationship management investments and incentives that much of the recent literature on construction 'best practice' does not address. As we shall see below, the current ideas on 'best practice' in construction appear to be based on a desire to replicate collaborative partnering approaches in other industries in general, and specifically those in the automotive sector. Unfortunately, these arguments are based on two misunderstandings. First, there is only a rudimentary understanding of the demand and supply characteristics and commercial motivations that underpin relationships in the automotive industry – especially those of Japanese automakers. Second, there is a failure to understand the problem of relationship and performance choices from the perspective of two actors (the buyer and the supplier) who operate within an environment in which exchange is contested and win–win outcomes are not feasible.

This has led some academics, practitioners and sponsors of industry reports to take the relationship management approaches that are feasible for actors in some industry supply chains and markets (especially the automotive) and recommend them for all actors in the construction industry. Unfortunately, these long-term collaborative relationship management approaches, based on trust and transparency, are feasible for only a minority of the actors within construction supply chains and markets. As we shall see, only for those clients with high levels of regular and standardised demand, or those suppliers with scope for supply market differentiation and/or above normal industry returns is such an approach feasible. To recommend that everyone within the industry should adopt exactly the same relationship management and performance optimisation approach, even though they are experiencing very different demand and supply circumstances (one-off or irregular demand and highly contested supply markets with low or normal returns), is a recipe for inappropriate relationship management and sub-optimal performance outcomes.

1.4 Recent recommendations to resolve the endemic problems in construction supply chains and markets

The first major industry report reviewing the performance of the UK construction industry appeared in 1929. Since then, a catalogue of reports have bemoaned the current levels of performance of the industry and advocated change (Simon, 1944; Philips, 1950; Emmerson, 1962; Bowley, 1963, 1966; Banwell, 1964; Higgin and Jessop, 1965; Bishop, 1972; NEDO, 1978; Munday, 1979; Ball, 1980, 1983; NEDO, 1983, 1988; Latham, 1994; DETR, 1998; NAO, 2001). All of these reports were inspired by clients' concerns about the impact of inefficiency and waste in the construction industry on their commercial performance and focused on similar problems: fragmentation, a short-term focus, adversarial attitudes and a lack of trust. It has been argued consistently that these shortfalls lead to low levels of performance in cost, time, quality, running costs and fitness-for-purpose for the end user, and in profitability for the contractor.

It is interesting to note that, although the industry has seen considerable innovation with construction materials and techniques, the industry has failed to address its major relationship and performance management problems, with the contractual relationship between client and contractor remaining highly short-term, adversarial and lacking in trust. It may well be, as we shall argue here, that there are structural reasons for this failure that have very little to do with a lack of willingness of actors in the industry to find solutions to their problems. On the contrary, the failure to resolve these problems arises not because actors are malicious or ignorant (an implicit view in many reports), but rather that they are logically and rationally pursuing their own economic self-interests in an environment that is only rarely conducive to the long-term and collaborative relationship management and performance optimisation approaches that industry reports (and their supporters) argue are essential.

In recent years, the Banwell Report (Banwell, 1964), the Latham Report (Latham, 1994), the Egan Report (DETR, 1998) and the Accelerating Change Report (Strategic Forum for Construction, 2002) have all focused on the inherent problems that are endemic to the industry. The discussion here focuses primarily on the Latham and Egan Reports. These reports are widely recognised by industry practitioners and it is within them that the ideas of adopting the same relationship management and performance optimisation approaches as those adopted in the automotive sector have been most comprehensively articulated.

The Latham and Egan Reports challenged the UK construction industry to look at what it does and do it entirely differently. The ultimate challenge to the industry was for it to deliver its products to its customers in the same way as the best consumer-led manufacturing and service industries. Table 1.3 summarises a number of the recommendations within the two reports to achieve this objective. The reports clearly adopt the logic of integrated supply chain management as developed in the automotive sector as the leitmotif for reform in construction. It is argued that supply chain management approaches based on partnering may lead to 30% cost reduction and 20% improvement in cycle times, with improved profitability for both buyers and suppliers. As we shall see, however, one of the major criticisms that can be made of these reports is that the vast majority of clients source construction on an irregular basis and are unable to offer construction firms or suppliers the ongoing revenue in the long-term that is essential for these partnering and supply chain management approaches to work effectively.

Table 1.3 Comparison of Latham and Egan Reports in key areas (Adapted from: Murray and Langford (2003), pp. 202–212)

Theme	Latham Report, 1994	Egan Report, 1998
Key Procurement Issues		
Contractor selection	States that tender list arrangements need rationalising. Argues that tenders should be assessed on quality as well as price	States that the industry complains about the difficulty in obtaining quality when selection is on basis of lowest cost and not VFM. Argues that clients do not benefit from having a new team on each project
Partnering	Argues that partnering with a 'win–win' approach may be beneficial and provides an example (Sizewell NP) that was delivered on time and budget. States that partners must be sought through a competitive tender process	States that tools to tackle fragmentation such as partnering increasingly used instead of traditional approaches. Argues that partnering may lead to 30% cost savings and 20% in time. Argues that integrated teams are critical to continuous learning
Key Parties in Relationships		
Client	Argues that clients are at the core of the process and their needs must be identified and met. Argues that Government should become a best practice client	Argues that clients fail to get value for money projects that are free from defects and delivered on time. States that clients' immediate concern is to reduce capital and running costs while improving quality
Main Contractor (MC)	No direct finding or recommendation mentioned	Argues that cutthroat competition and inadequate profitability is harming all especially the MC. Wishes to create culture of radical and sustained improvement to end the debilitating cycle of competitive tendering, conflict, low margins and dissatisfied clients
Subcontractors (SC) and suppliers	Argues that a joint code of conduct for SCs based on fair tendering and teamwork is needed. States that SCs complain about onerous contract conditions	Argues that fully integrated supply chains are needed to drive innovation. Argues that suppliers and subcontractors have to be involved in design process
Teamwork, trust and co-operation	States that relationships between MCs and SCs are very poor, with Dutch auctioning common. Most SC requirements deemed incompatible with those of the MC, yet its performance is recognised as critical to the success of projects	Argues that supply chain relationships should be based on trust. Argues that designers should work collaboratively with others in the design process. States that partnering relationships require interdependence to bring about long-term satisfactory arrangements
Project Performance		
Design	Argues that effective management in the design process is crucial for the success of the project	States that clients believe significant value improvements in cost are achievable where the majority of design work is complete before construction phase starts
Prefabrication and standardisation	States that McDonald's have reduced costs and time in the UK by 60% in the previous five years by using modular techniques	Using the McDonald's example, argues that standardised components and pre-assembly will improve quality and performance

Table 1.3 Continued

Theme	Latham Report, 1994	Egan Report, 1998
Quality	Argues that clients have the right to expect high quality on projects. Argues that defects or failure in design costs industry £1000m per annum	States that 30% of construction is rework. Argues that quality increases and cost decreases will not occur until workforce embraces culture of teamwork
Value for money	States that methods for establishing what is best value for money need to be identified along with how to implement them	States that clients need better value from projects. Argues that value management can reduce costs by 10% through the removal of non-value-added activities

There has been significant academic literature advocating the implementation of supply chain tools, such as lean thinking or partnering, in the construction industry prior to the calls for their introduction in recent industry reports. Rather than acting as forerunners for leading-edge best practices, the authors of the industry reports were merely introducing these academic ideas to a wider audience. The Egan Report (DETR, 1998) in particular suggested a number of ways to improve the way the construction industry performs. Based on evidence from a number of case studies, where construction performance was improved by the adoption of these techniques, conclusions were drawn that lean thinking should be applied to the UK construction industry.

> 'Lean thinking presents a powerful and coherent synthesis of the most effective techniques for eliminating waste and delivering significant sustained improvements in efficiency and quality ... [The Report] recommends that the UK construction industry should also adopt lean thinking as a means of sustaining performance improvement.'
>
> (DETR, 1998, pp. 25 and 26)

Prior to this endorsement, considerable lean construction literature had emerged (Koskela, 1992, 1997; Ballard and Howell, 1994, 1997; Akintoye, 1995; Koskela *et al.*, 1996, 1997; Smook *et al.*, 1996; Alarcón, 1997; Melles, 1997; O'Brien, 1997; Tanskanen *et al.*, 1997). Since the publication of the Egan Report, the application of lean principles to construction has grown rapidly (Howell and Ballard, 1998, 1999; Green, 1999, 2000; Koskela, 1999, 2000; Naim *et al.*, 1999; Common *et al.*, 2000; Ballard *et al.*, 2001, 2002; Conte and Gransberg, 2001; Vrijhoef *et al.*, 2001, 2002; Bertelsen, 2002; Bertelsen and Koskela, 2002; Johansen *et al.*, 2002). However, this literature has largely applied the lean concept without empirical exploration of the specific market and supply chain structures within the construction industry and without a rigorous understanding of the appropriateness of these practices for all construction supply chain and market relationships.

As a result, in recent years there has been an empiricist backlash against lean thinking based on an alternative approach – agile construction. Proponents of this view argue that a responsive and agile approach is more appropriate than a lean approach to relationship and performance management because of the dynamic (*ad hoc*, one-off, irregular, unpredictable and non-standard demand and supply) characteristics of the industry. The agile school also argues that, while a lean approach makes sense under conditions where demand is predictable, the requirement for variety is low and volume is high (as in typical manufacturing), an alternative is needed in unpredictable, volatile, highly customised and low volume markets (such as construction). In response to this, the agile manufacturing paradigm has been highlighted as an alternative to leanness[3] (Richards, 1996; Harrison et al., 1999; Mason-Jones and Towill, 1999; Naylor et al., 1999; Towill and McCullen, 1999; Christopher, 2000; Christopher and Towill, 2000a, b, 2002).

Despite having a very independent body of literature that states that a lean approach does not always make sense, the agile school does not, however, take issue with the presumption within the lean supply school of thought in favour of longer-term collaborative relationships between buyers and suppliers based on trust, transparency and a requirement for coordinated and integrated supply chain activity. The disagreement with the lean approach to partnering is not about the general management philosophy and way that relationships should be managed, but rather with what they should be focusing on and how they deal with different demand conditions. Although the term 'agile' has not surfaced in the industry reports, it may only be a matter of time before it does. It should be noted that the first real mention of lean construction was in the Egan Report (DETR, 1998) a considerable length of time after it first emerged in the business and supply chain management literature.

The previous discussion has highlighted how the focus of most of the academic and practitioner literature on supply chain management in the construction industry is focused on the development of a new 'industry culture'. This new 'culture' is to be based on long-term relationships, mutual competitive advantage, shared learning, greater transparency and trust (Saad et al., 2002). This has led to the emergence of 'partnering' or the development of long-term collaborative relationships founded on 'co-operation and collaboration instead of adversarial conflict and litigation' (Bresnen and Marshall, 2000, p. 230).

Close collaborative ways of working are not, however, a recent phenomenon within the construction industry; it has existed in various guises for many years, although it was not explicitly referred to as partnering (Loraine, 1994). The use of partnering nowadays, as advocated by Latham and Egan, 'attempt(s) to address a fundamental characteristic of the [construction] industry . . . that it is fragmented, as individuals from different organisations which are geographically and temporally dispersed are involved in the construction process' (Luck, 1996, p. 1). The aim is to achieve win–win or mutually beneficial outcomes through joint working.

To achieve mutually beneficial outcomes – as identified in Table 1.4 – a partnering approach encompasses collaboration, commitment, open communication and information, trust, co-operation, equity, respect, customer focus, fairness, empowerment, innovation, joint risk sharing and problem solving (CII, 1989, 1991; NEDO, 1991; Loraine, 1994; Baden-Hellard, 1995; Bennett and Jayes, 1995, 1998; Infante, 1995; Larson, 1995, 1997; Barlow and Cohen, 1996; Godfrey, 1996; Hinks et al., 1996a, b; Rackham et al., 1996; Bresnen and Marshall, 2000; Lazar, 2000).

A reading of the literature confirms that there is no shortage of advocates of partnering. The difficulty comes when one compares rhetoric with the achievement of mutual benefits that is supported by hard evidence. A consistent theme within the

---

[3] There is considerable confusion within the literature about a distinction between a lean and agile approach. While many authors use the terms interchangeably (Graves, 2000), others make a clear distinction.

Table 1.4 The stated benefits of a partnering approach (Sources: Matthews et al. (1996), Bennett and Jayes (1998), Bresnen and Marshall (2000), Black et al. (2001), Ng et al. (2002))

	Benefits
Clients	Reduced exposure to litigation through open communication and development of issue-resolution strategies. This will also reduce post-contract legal expenses and associated administration costs
	Lower risk of cost overruns through improved cost control of projects
	Increased opportunity for a financially successful project because of non-adversarial 'win–win' attitude from all players
	Lower risk of time overruns because of better control over the efficient scheduling of the project. There is also a potential to expedite the project through efficient implementation of the contract
	Better quality product because attention is focused on the ultimate objectives of all parties (including the needs of the client) and not affected by adversarial concerns. This also leads to a better quality product through reduction of defects and rework and higher levels of safety
	Established team finds time to develop techniques that may provide better quality information. This information combined with open communication allows more efficient resolution of problems
	Increased opportunity for innovation through open communication and the element of trust, especially in the development of value engineering changes and constructability improvements
	Partnering helps reduce client's staff time to go through the necessary learning curve. This is particularly important for less regular clients who have developed a team for future projects
	Partnering reduces costly and time consuming selection processes leading to shorter design times, quicker start times and shorter construction times
	Partnering firms are more responsive to short-term emergencies and to changing project or business needs or market conditions
	Increased market share and profitability
Contractors and Specialist Contractors	Reduced exposure to litigation through communication and development of issue-resolution strategies thus reducing post-contract legal expenses. This also leads to increased productivity because of elimination of defensive case building
	Improved cost control of projects leading to greater certainty and likelihood of meeting business objectives. There is also an increased opportunity for a financially successful project because of a non-adversarial 'win–win' attitude from all players
	Enhanced repeat business opportunity as well as an opportunity to increase margin through more efficient post-tender value management procedure
	Improved control of duration because of improved project management. There is also a potential to expedite the project through efficient implementation of the contract and improved decision making with issue resolution strategies and agreed approaches to deal with variations
	Better quality product because attention is focused on the ultimate objectives of all parties and not affected by adversarial concerns
	Established team finds time to develop processes that may provide better quality information. This information combined with open communication allows more efficient resolution of problems and improved materials management
	Increased opportunity for innovation in the supply market through open communication and the element of trust, especially in the development of value engineering changes and constructability improvements
	More efficient selection processes leading to shorter design times, quicker start times and shorter construction times
	The guarantee of a regular workload leads to improved long-term management of demand, the elimination of the costs associated with bidding on a project basis and lower marketing costs
	Faster payments reducing problems with cash flow

Table 1.4 Continued

	Benefits
Professional Service and Design Firms	Reduced exposure to litigation through open communication and presence of issue-resolution strategies thus reducing post-contract legal and administration costs Minimised exposure to liability for document deficiencies through early identification of problems, and co-operative resolution that minimises cost impact Increased opportunity for a financially successful project because of non-adversarial 'win–win' attitude from all players Opportunity to develop and refine skills that can be transferred to future projects. This includes an understanding of others' approach so that they can propose and develop designs in ways that are similar and aligned
Subcontractors and Suppliers	Reduced exposure to litigation through open communication and presence of issue-resolution strategies thus reducing post-contract legal and administration costs Equity involvement in project increases opportunity for innovation and implementation of value engineering work Potential to improve cash-flow position as fewer disputes occur and payments are faster Increased opportunity for a financially successful project because of non-adversarial 'win–win' attitude from all players The guarantee of a regular workload leads to better long-term management of demand (and the benefits associated with this), the elimination of the costs associated with bidding on a project basis and lower marketing costs Established team finds time to develop techniques that provide better quality information. This information combined with open communication allows more efficient resolution of problems and better integration and materials management

literature is that traditional construction contracting is characterised by an adversarial relationship between client and contractor, and that adversarialism is closely linked to the competitive nature of the industry, creating conflicting objectives, suspicion and contempt (Ng *et al.*, 2002). Partnering is seen as a way of replacing traditional contracting practice with a more efficient way of working.

Much of the current partnering literature examines the conditions that encourage or inhibit collaboration between clients and their contractors (Bennett and Jayes, 1995, 1998; Barlow and Cohen, 1996; Holti and Standing, 1996; Barlow *et al.*, 1997). At the same time, there is still considerable disagreement about precisely what form partnering can or should take, under what conditions it is likely to develop and how such ways of working can be fostered and developed (Barlow *et al.*, 1997; Cox and Townsend, 1997, 1998; Cox and Thompson, 1998; Thompson and Sanders, 1998).

1.5 Have collaborative and partnering relationship management approaches achieved what was expected in performance improvement terms?

Notwithstanding these esoteric academic debates about the efficacy of partnering or of lean or agile forms of collaboration, recent industry reports have argued that the adoption of 'best practice' collaborative relationship and performance management would deliver major commercial improvements to both the demand and supply-side of the industry. On the demand-side, it has been argued that simple descriptions of client objectives in construction are being re-evaluated and that to deliver 'core objectives' experienced clients are frequently pursuing best value as opposed to lowest cost, and are becoming more proactive in their implementation of 'best practice' construction supply chain approaches (Blockley and Godfrey, 2000; Green, 2000; Kelly and Male, 2001; Tookey *et al.*, 2001; Green *et al.*, 2002). In this pursuit, it is argued that in an attempt to drive change, clients frequently select construction firms on their ability to undertake the project using such approaches as supply chain management and partnering[4].

According to Tookey *et al.* (2001) and Cain (2003), construction now stands at a decision nexus between two approaches to procurement selection. If the traditional approach was largely based on tender cost and contract type, Figure 1.4 indicates that a post-Latham and Egan approach, based on lean construction, partnering and collaborative supply chain approaches, may be available to 'expert' clients.

This conclusion implicitly suggests that success with this type of approach may be related to the regularity of sourcing. An 'expert' client approach, involving the adoption of 'best practice' supply chain management techniques may, therefore, only be available to those clients with a continuous and high level of construction spend. This is a major conclusion since it indicates that highly collaborative relationship and performance management approaches may not be feasible for very many clients or contractors within construction supply chains and markets. This conclusion is reinforced by recent criticisms from the National Audit Office (NAO) about the lack of clear evidence that the adoption of lean and partnering approaches in construction has resulted in any real improvements in value for money (NAO, 2001).

The discussion so far shows that in recent years there has been a growing consensus among academics, practitioners and industry-sponsored reports about the efficacy of longer-term collaborative and partnering relationship management approaches based on the principles of relationship marketing (Gummesson, 1999), integrated supply chain management (whether lean or agile-based) and high levels of trust and transparency between relationship partners. The promotion of these approaches is also supported by a considerable academic literature that suggests that 'world-class' companies in construction need to develop similar construction procurement and supply strategies.

It can be argued, however, that it is simply not possible to provide construction practitioners with a generic solution, such as partnering or collaboration, to the problems inherent within the industry. This is because the demand and supply (and therefore power and leverage) circumstances in which firms operate as buyers and suppliers vary all the time (Cox, 1997a, b; Cox and Townsend, 1997, 1998; Cox and Thompson, 1998; London and Kenley, 2000a, b, 2001; Tookey *et al.*, 2001; Walker and Hampson, 2003). As a result, the major problem in the industry is that far too much time and effort is devoted to finding 'the solution' and insufficient attention is being paid to what is 'fit for purpose' (Cox and Thompson, 1998; Cox and Townsend, 1998). The stream of industry reports and academic prescriptions may, therefore, contain a methodologically flawed pursuit of a 'best practice' approach and/or a simplistic view that it will be possible to find an exemplar company in construction to show everyone in the industry how to be more efficient and effective.

---

[4] The UK Ministry of Defence (MOD)'s 'Building Down Barriers' initiative, also known as prime contracting, is perhaps the best-known current example of the newly discovered client power and how clients need to select contractors on the basis of capability rather than cost.

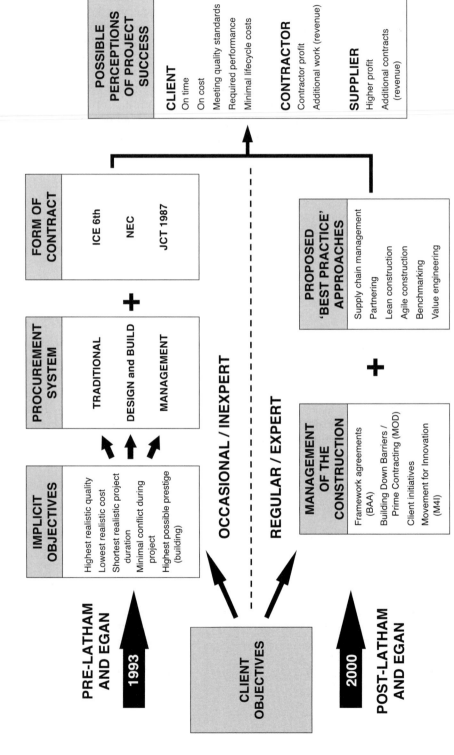

Figure 1.4 The alternative procurement routes for clients (Adapted from: Tookey et al. (2001), p. 23)

It can be argued that such thinking is misguided, because it fails to recognise that the construction industry encompasses a range of structurally diverse supply chains delivering different products and services to different clients. The anecdotal evidence of the successes of long-term collaborative relationships for some players does not constitute grounds for arguing that everyone in the industry should operate in the same way. On the contrary, 'better practice' relationship and performance management may actually be about understanding under which supply chain and market circumstances it is appropriate to use particular operational tools and techniques (Cox *et al.*, 2002, 2003, 2004a).

Firms and managers must, therefore, acquire knowledge of the full range of operational tools and techniques that are available to them to manage relationships and optimise performance. This may include concepts such as partnering (adversarial and non-adversarial collaborative relationships) as well as 'traditional' (adversarial and non-adversarial arm's-length relationships) contracting – the latter of which is now often seen as obsolete. Second, firms must understand the business circumstances that confront them. This is a difficult task, but is critical, as some relationship and performance management tools and techniques are only likely to be appropriate under certain supply chain and market circumstances (Cox *et al.*, 2004b).

This appropriateness approach also requires that construction firms understand the resources that augment power and leverage in business relationships. The *power and leverage* approach contends, therefore, that a firm will have relative power if it is able to own and control critical resources in markets and supply chains that allow it to sustain its ability to appropriate and accumulate value for itself by leveraging its customers, competitors and suppliers (Cox, 1997a, b, 1999b; Cox *et al.*, 2000, 2002, 2004a). Only when a firm has understood the power resources that are available, and also those that are available to its exchange partners in supply chains and markets, is it possible for the correct relationship management and performance optimisation approaches to be selected. In the next chapter we discuss the relational and power and leverage approaches and then explain in more detail the full range of relationship management and performance optimisation approaches that are feasible for managing in construction supply chains and markets.

References

Abrahamson, E. (1991), 'Managerial fads and fashions: the diffusion and rejection of innovations', *Academy of Management Review*, **16**(3), pp. 586–612.

Abrahamson, E. (1996), 'Management fashion', *Academy of Management Review*, **21**(2), pp. 254–285.

Akintoye, A. (1995), 'Just-in-time application and implementation for building materials management', *Construction Management and Economics*, **13**(2), March, pp. 105–113.

Alarcón, L. (ed.) (1997), *Lean Construction*, AA Balkema, Rotterdam, Netherlands.

Alarcón, L., Rivas, R. and Serpell, A. (1999), 'Evaluation and improvement of the procurement process in construction projects', *Proceedings of the 7th Conference of the International Group for Lean Construction*, 26–28 July, Berkeley, CA, USA, pp. 219–230.

Baden-Hellard, R. (1995), *Project Partnering: Principle and Practice*, Thomas Telford, London.

Ball, M. J. (1980), *The Contracting System in the Construction Industry*, Birkbeck College Discussion Paper, Number 86, London.

Ball, M. J. (1983), *Housing Policy and Economic Power*, Methuen, London.

Ballard, G. and Howell, G. A. (1994), 'Implementing lean construction: improving downstream performance', *Proceedings of the 2nd Annual Conference of the International Group for Lean Construction*, 28–30 September, Santiago de Chile, Chile, pp. 13–22.

Ballard, G. and Howell, G. A. (1997), 'Towards construction JIT', in Alarcón, L. (ed.), *Lean Construction*, AA Balkema, Rotterdam, Netherlands, pp. 291–300.

Ballard, G., Koskela, L., Howell, G. and Zabelle, T. (2001), 'Production system design in construction', *Proceedings of the 9th Conference of the International Group for Lean Construction*, 6–8 August, Singapore.

Ballard, G., Tommelein, I., Koskela, L. and Howell, G. (2002), 'Lean construction tools and techniques', in Best, R. and de Valence, G. (eds.), *Building in Value: Project Delivery*, John Wiley & Sons, New York.

Banwell, Sir H. (1964), *The Placing and Management of Contracts for Building and Civil Engineering Works*, HMSO, London.

Barlow, J. and Cohen, M. (1996), 'Implementing partnering: some common red herrings in the literature', *EPSRC Workshop on Partnering in Construction*, 13 May, University of Salford.

Barlow, J., Cohen, M., Jashapara, A. and Simpson, Y. (1997), *Towards Positive Partnering*, The Policy Press, Bristol.

Bennett, J. and Jayes, S. (1995), *Trusting the Team: The Best Practice Guide to Partnering in Construction*, Reading Construction Forum, Reading.

Bennett, J. and Jayes, S. (1998), *The Seven Pillars of Partnering*, Thomas Telford, London.

Bertelsen, S. (2002), 'Bridging the gaps: towards a comprehensive understanding of lean construction', *Proceedings of the 10th Annual Conference of the International Group for Lean Construction*, 6–8 August, Gramado, Brazil, pp. 23–34.

Bertelsen, S. and Koskela, L. (2002), 'Managing the three aspects of production in construction', *Proceedings of the 10th Annual Conference of the International Group for Lean Construction*, 6–8 August, Gramado, Brazil, pp. 13–22.

Bishop, D. (1972), *Building Technology in the 1980s*, Phil. Transaction Royal Society, London, pp. 533–563.

Black, C., Akintoye, A. and Fitzgerald, E. (2001), 'An analysis of success factors and benefits of partnering in construction', *International Journal of Project Management*, **18**, pp. 423–434.

Blismas, N. G. (2001), *Multi-project Environments of Construction Clients*, Unpublished PhD Thesis, Loughborough University, Loughborough.

Blockley, D. and Godfrey, P. (2000), *Doing it Differently: Systems for Rethinking Construction*, Thomas Telford, London.

Bowley, M. E. A. (1963), *The British Building Industry*, Cambridge University Press, Cambridge.

Bowley, M. E. A. (1966), *The British Building Industry: Four Studies in Response and Resistance to Change*, Cambridge University Press, Cambridge.

Bresnen, M. and Marshall, N. (2000), 'Partnering in construction: a critical review of issues, problems and dilemmas', *Construction Management and Economics*, **18**(2), pp. 229–237.

Bresnen, M. and Marshall, N. (2001), 'Understanding the diffusion and application of new management ideas in construction', *Engineering, Construction and Architectural Management*, **8**(5/6), pp. 335–345.

Burbridge, J. L. and Falster, P. (1993), 'Reducing delivery times for OKP products', *Production Planning and Control*, **4**(1), pp. 77–83.

Cain, C. T. (2003), *Building Down Barriers: A Guide to Construction Best Practice*, Spon Press, London.

Cannon, J. and Perreault, W. (1999), 'Buyer–seller relationships in business markets', *Journal of Marketing Research*, **36**(4), pp. 439–460.

Cherns, A. B. and Bryant, D. T. (1984), 'Studying the client's role in construction management', *Construction Management and Economics*, **2**(2), pp. 177–184.

Christopher, M. (2000), 'The agile supply chain', *Industrial Marketing Management*, **29**(1), pp. 37–44.

Christopher, M. and Towill, D. R. (2000a), 'Supply chain migration from lean and functional to agile and customised', *Supply Chain Management: An International Journal*, **5**(4), pp. 206–215.

Christopher, M. and Towill, D. R. (2000b), 'Marrying the lean and agile paradigms', *Proceedings of the 7th EurOMA Conference*, 4–7 June, Ghent, Belgium.

Christopher, M. and Towill, D. R. (2002), 'The supply chain strategy conundrum: to be lean or agile or to be lean and agile', *International Journal of Logistics: Research and Applications*, **5**(3), pp. 299–309.

CII (1989), *Partnering: Meeting the Challenges of the Future*, CII Special Publication, Construction Industry Institute, Austin, TX, USA.

CII (1991), *In Search of Partnering Excellence*, CII Special Publication, Construction Industry Institute, Austin, TX, USA.

Cleland, D. I. and Kerzner, H. (1985), *A Project Management Dictionary of Terms*, Van Nostrand Reinhold, New York, NY, USA.

Cleland, D. I. and King, W. R. (1983), *Systems Analysis and Project Management*, McGraw Hill, New York, NY, USA.

Common, G., Johansen, E. and Greenwood, D. (2000), 'A survey of the take-up of lean concepts among UK construction companies', *Proceedings of the 8th Conference of the International Group for Lean Construction*, 17–19 July, Brighton, 10 pages.

Conte, A. S. and Gransberg, D. D. (2001), 'Lean construction: from theory to practice', *AACE International Transactions*, pp. CSC 10.1–10.5.

Cox, A. (1997a), *Business Success: A Way of Thinking about Strategy, Critical Supply Chain Assets and Operational Best Practice*, Earlsgate Press, Stratford-upon-Avon.

Cox, A. (1997b), 'On power, appropriateness and procurement competence', *Supply Management*, October, pp. 24–27.

Cox, A. (1999a), 'Improving procurement and supply competence: on the appropriate use of reactive and proactive tools and techniques in the public and private sectors', in Lamming, R. and Cox, A. (eds.), *Strategic Procurement Management: Concepts and Cases*, Earlsgate Press, Stratford-upon-Avon.

Cox, A. (1999b), 'Power, value and supply chain management', *Supply Chain Management: An International Journal*, **9**(5), pp. 167–175.

Cox, A. and Ireland, P. (2001), 'Managing construction supply chains: the common-sense approach for project-based procurement', *Proceedings of the 10th International Annual IPSERA Conference*, 9–11 April, Jönkoping, Sweden, pp. 201–214.

Cox, A. and Ireland, P. (2002a), 'Effective supply chain management in a project-based environment: evidence from the UK construction industry', *Proceedings of the Logistics Research Network Conference*, 4–6 September, Birmingham, pp. 391–398.

Cox, A. and Ireland, P. (2002b), 'Managing construction supply chains: a common sense approach', *Engineering, Construction and Architectural Management*, **9**(5/6), pp. 409–418.

Cox, A., Ireland, P., Lonsdale, C., Sanderson, J. and Watson, G. (2002), *Supply Chains, Markets and Power: Mapping Buyer and Supplier Power Regimes*, Routledge, London.

Cox, A., Ireland, P., Lonsdale, C., Sanderson, J. and Watson, G. (2003), *Supply Chain Management: A Guide to Best Practice*, Financial Times-Prentice Hall, London.

Cox, A., Lonsdale, C., Sanderson, J. and Watson, G. (2004a), *Business Relationships for Competitive Advantage: Managing Alignment and Misalignment in Buyer and Supplier Transactions*, Palgrave Macmillan, Basingstoke.

Cox, A., Lonsdale, C., Sanderson, J. and Watson, G. (2004b), 'Managing appropriately in power regimes: relationship and performance management in 12 supply chain cases', *Supply Chain Management: An International Journal*, **9**(5), pp. 357–371.

Cox, A., Sanderson, J. and Watson, G. (2000), *Power Regimes: Mapping the DNA of Business and Supply Chain Relationships*, Earlsgate Press, Stratford-upon-Avon.

Cox, A. and Thompson, I. (1998), *Contracting for Business Success*, Thomas Telford, London.

Cox, A. and Townsend, M. (1997), 'Latham as a half-way house: a relational competence approach to better practice in construction practice', *Engineering, Construction and Architectural Management*, **4**(2), pp. 143–158.

Cox, A. and Townsend, M. (1998), *Strategic Procurement in Construction*, Thomas Telford, London.

Crowley, A. (1998), 'Construction as a manufacturing process: lessons from the automotive industry', *Computers and Structures*, **67**(5), pp. 387–400.

Cutting-Decelle, A. F. (1997), 'The use of industrial management methods and tools in the construction industry: application to the construction process', in Annumba, C. J. and Evbuomwan, N. F. O. (eds.), *Concurrent Engineering in Construction: Papers Presented at the First International Conference*, Institution of Structural Engineers, London, pp. 306–318.

DETR (1998), *Rethinking Construction*, Department for the Environment, Transport and the Regions, London.

Emmerson, Sir H. (1962), *Study of Problems Before the Construction Industries*, Report for the Ministry of Works, HMSO, London.

Gann, D. M. (1996), 'Construction as a manufacturing process? Similarities and differences between industrialized housing and car production in Japan', *Construction Management and Economics*, **14**(5), pp. 437–450.

Gann, D. M. (2001), 'Putting academic ideas in practice: technological progress and the absorptive capacity of construction organisations', *Construction Management and Economics*, **19**(4), pp. 321–330.

Godfrey, K. A. Jnr (ed.) (1996), *Partnering in Design and Construction*, McGraw-Hill, New York, NY, USA.

Graves, A. (2000), *Agile Construction Initiative*, University of Bath, Bath.

Green, S. D. (1999), 'The dark side of lean construction: exploitation and ideology', *Proceedings of the 7th Conference of the International Group for Lean Construction*, 26–28 July, University of California, Berkeley, CA, USA, pp. 21–32.

Green, S. D. (2000), 'The future of lean construction: a brave new world', *Proceedings of the 8th Conference of the International Group for Lean Construction*, 17–19 July, Brighton, 11 pages.

Green, S. D., Newcombe, R., Williams, M., Fernie, S. and Weller, S. (2002), 'Supply chain management: a contextual analysis of aerospace and construction', in Lewis, T. (ed.), *CIB W92 Procurement Systems Symposium – Information and Communication in Construction Procurement*, University of West Indies, Trinidad and Tobago, pp. 245–261.

Gummesson, E. (1999), *Total Relationship Marketing*, Butterworth-Heinemann, Oxford.

Harrison, A., Christopher, M. and van Hoek, R. (1999), 'Creating the agile supply chain', *School of Management Working Paper*, Cranfield University, Cranfield.

Hellard, R. B. (1995), *Project Partnering; Principles and Practice*, Thomas Telford, London.

Higgin, G. and Jessop, N. K. (1965), *Communications in the Building Industry*, Tavistock Publications, London.

Hinks, A. J., Allen, S. and Cooper, R. D. (1996a), 'Adversaries or partners? Developing best practice for construction industry relationships', in Langford, D. A. and Retik, A. (eds.), *The Organisation and Management of Construction: Shaping Theory and Practice*, E & FN Spon, London, pp. 222–228.

Hinks, A. J., Cooper, R., Allen, S. and Carmichael, S. (1996b), 'Adversaries or partners? A case study of an established long-term relationship between a client and main contractor', *Proceedings of the 4th Conference of the International Group for Lean Construction*, University of Birmingham, Birmingham, 26–27 August, 10 pages.

Holti, R. and Standing H. (1996), *Partnering as Inter-related Technical and Organisational Change*, Tavistock, London.

Howell, G. A. and Ballard, G. (1998), 'Implementing lean construction: understanding and action', *Proceedings of the 6th Conference of the International Group for Lean Construction*, 13–15 August, Guarujá, Brazil, 9 pages.

Howell, G. A. and Ballard, G. (1999), 'Bringing light to the dark side of lean construction: a response to Stuart Green', *Proceedings of the 7th Conference of the International Group for Lean Construction*, 26–28 July, University of California, Berkeley, CA, USA, pp. 33–38.

Hughes, W. (1991), 'Modelling the construction process using plans of work: construction project modelling and productivity', *Proceedings of CIB W65 International Conference*, Dubrovnik, Croatia.

Infante, J. (1995), 'The relative merits of term partnering and project specific partnering', *Construction Productivity Workshop Report 18: Project Specific Partnering*, November, European Construction Institute, Loughborough University, pp. 2–4.

Johansen, E., Glimmerveen, H. and Vrijhoef, R. (2002), 'Understanding lean construction and how it penetrates the industry: a comparison of the dissemination of lean within the UK and the Netherlands', *Proceedings of the 10th Conference of the International Group for Lean Construction*, 6–8 August, Gramado, Brazil, pp. 415–426.

Kagioglou, M., Cooper, R., Aouad, G. and Sexton, M. (2000), 'Rethinking construction: the generic design and construction process protocol', *Engineering, Construction and Architectural Management*, **7**(2), June, pp. 141–154.

Kelly, J. and Male, S. (2001), 'A value management approach to aligning the team to the client's value system', *Proceedings of the RICS Foundation Construction and Building Research Conference*, Volume 1, pp. 107–116.

Koskela, L. (1992), *Application of the New Production Philosophy to Construction*, Technical Report 72, Department of Civil Engineering, Stanford University, CA, USA, 75 pages.

Koskela, L. (1997), 'Lean production in construction', in Alarcón, L. F. (ed.), *Lean Construction*, AA Balkema, Rotterdam, pp. 1–9.

Koskela, L. (1999), 'Management of production construction: a theoretical view, *Proceedings of the 7th Annual Conference of the International Group for Lean Construction*, University of California, Berkeley, CA, USA, July 26–28, pp. 241–252.

Koskela, L. (2000), *An Exploration into a Theory of Production and its Application to Construction*, VTT Publication 408, VTT Building Technology, Helsinki University of Technology, Espoo, Finland.

Koskela, L., Lahdenperä, P. and Tanhuanpää, V.-P. (1996), 'Sounding the potential of lean construction: a case study', *Proceedings of the 4th Conference of the International Group for Lean Construction*, University of Birmingham, 26–27 August, 11 pages.

Koskela, L., Ballard, G. and Tanhuanpää, V.-P. (1997), 'Towards lean design management', *Proceedings of the 5th Conference of the International Group for Lean Construction*, Gold Coast, Australia, 16–17 July, pp. 241–252.

Larson, E. (1995), 'Project partnering: results of 280 construction projects', *Journal of Management in Engineering*, **11**(2), pp. 30–35.

Larson, E. (1997), 'Partnering on construction projects: a study of the relationship between partnering activities and project success', *IEEE Transactions on Engineering Management*, **44**(2), pp. 188–195.

Latham, M. (1994), *Constructing the Team*, HMSO, London.

Lazar, F. D. (2000), 'Project partnering: improving the likelihood of win/win outcomes', *Journal of Management in Engineering*, **16**(2), pp. 71–83.

London, K., Kenley, R. and Agapiou, A. (1998), 'Theoretical supply chain network modelling in the building industry', *Association of Researchers in Construction Management (ARCOM) Conference*, Reading.

London, K. and Kenley, R. (1999), 'Client's role in construction supply chains – a theoretical discussion', *Proceedings CIB Triennial World Symposium W92*, Cape Town, South Africa.

London, K. and Kenley, R. (2000a), 'Mapping construction supply chains: widening the traditional perspective of the industry', *Proceedings of the 7th Annual European Association of Research in Industrial Economics*, EARIE Conference, Lausanne, Switzerland, 21 pages.

London, K. and Kenley, R. (2000b), 'The development of a neo-industrial organisation methodology for describing and comparing supply chains', *Proceedings of the 8th Conference of the International Group for Lean Construction*, 17–19 July, Brighton.

London, K. and Kenley, R. (2001), 'An industrial organization economic supply chain approach for the construction industry: a review', *Construction Management and Economics*, **19**(8), pp. 777–788.

Loraine, R. K. (1994), 'Project-specific partnering', *Engineering, Construction and Architectural Management*, **1**(1), pp. 5–16.

Luck, R. (1996), Construction project integration strategies, Working Paper, Department of Construction Management and Engineering, University of Reading.

Luck, R. and Newcombe, R. (1996), 'The case for integration of the project participants' activities within a construction project environment', in Langford, D. A. and Retik, A. (eds.), *The Organisation and Management of Construction: Shaping Theory and Practice*, E & FN Spon, Glasgow, pp. 458–470.

Luhtala, M., Kilpinen, E. and Anttila, P. (1994), *LOGI: Managing Make-To-Order Supply Chains*, Helsinki University of Technology, Espoo, Finland.

Mason-Jones, R. and Towill, D. R. (1999), 'Total cycle time compression and the agile supply chain', *International Journal of Production Economics*, **62**(1/2), pp. 61–73.

Matthews, J., Tyler, A. and Thorpe, A. (1996), 'Pre-construction project partnering: developing the process', *Engineering Construction and Architectural Management*, **18**(1/2), pp. 117–131.

Melles, B. (1997), 'What do we mean by lean production in construction?', in Alarcón, L. F. (ed.), *Lean Construction*, AA Balkema, Rotterdam, Netherlands, pp. 11–16.

Mohamed, S. (1997), 'Benchmarking, best practice – and all that', in Alarcón, L. F. (ed.), *Lean Construction*, AA Balkema, Rotterdam, Netherlands, pp. 427–436.

Morris, P. W. G. (1997), *The Management of Projects*, Thomas Telford, London.

Munday, M. (1979), *Education for Information Management in the Construction Industry*, CIIE Bulletin, Number 3.

Murray, M. and Langford, D. A. (eds.) (2003), *Construction Reports*, Blackwell Science, London.

Murray-Webster, R. and Thiry, M. (2000), 'Managing programmes of projects', in Turner, J. R. and Simister, S. J. (eds.), *The Gower Handbook of Project Management*, 3rd Edition, Gower, Aldershot, pp. 46–64.

Naim, M., Naylor, J. and Barlow, J. (1999), 'Developing lean and agile supply chains in the UK housebuilding industry', *Proceedings of the 7th Conference of the International Group for Lean Construction*, 26–28 July, University of California, Berkeley, CA, USA, pp. 159–170.

Nam, C. H. and Tatum, C. B. (1988), 'Major characteristic of constructed products and resulting limitations of construction technology', *Construction Management and Economics*, **6**(2), pp. 133–148.

NAO (2001), *Modernising Construction: Report by the Comptroller and Auditor General*, National Audit Office, HMSO, London.

Naylor, J., Naim, M. M. and Berry, D. (1999), 'Leagility: integrating the lean and agile supply chain', *International Journal of Production Economics*, **62**(1/2), pp. 107–118.

NEDO (1978), *How Flexible is Construction?*, HMSO, London.

NEDO (1983), *Faster Building for Industry*, HMSO, London.

NEDO (1988), *Faster Building for Commerce*, HMSO, London.

NEDO (1991), *Partnering: Contracting without Conflict*, HMSO, London.

Ng, S. T., Rose, T. M., Mak, M. and Chen, S. E. (2002), 'Problematic issues associated with project partnering – the contractor perspective', *International Journal of Project Management*, **20**(6), pp. 437–449.

O'Brien, W. J. (1997), 'Construction supply chains: case study, integrated cost and performance analysis', in L. Alarcón, (ed.), *Lean Construction*, AA Balkema, Rotterdam, Netherlands, pp. 187–222.

Philips, Sir (1950), *Philips Report on Building: Working Group Report to the Minister of Works*, HMSO, London.

Potts, K. (1995), *Major Construction Works: Contractual and Financial Management*, Longman, London.

Rackham, N., Friedman, L. and Ruff, R. (1996), *Getting Partnering Right: How Market Leaders are Creating Long-term Competitive Advantage*, McGraw-Hill, New York, NY, USA.

Richards, C. W. (1996), 'Agile manufacturing: beyond lean?', *Production and Inventory Management Journal*, **37**(2), pp. 60–64.

Saad, M., Jones, M. and James, P. (2002), 'A review of the progress towards the adoption of supply chain management (SCM) in construction', *European Journal of Purchasing and Supply Management*, **8**(3), pp. 173–183.

Simon, Sir E. (1944), *The Placing and Management of Contracts*, HMSO, London.

Smook, R. A. F., Melles, B. and Welling, D. (1996), 'Co-ordinating the supply chain: diffusing lean production in construction', *Proceedings of the 4th Conference of the International Group for Lean Construction*, 26–27 August, University of Birmingham, Birmingham, 8 pages.

Strategic Forum for Construction (2002), *Accelerating Change: A Report by the Strategic Forum for Construction Chaired by Sir John Egan*, Rethinking Construction, Construction Industry Council, London.

Tanskanen, K., Wegelius, T. and Nyman, H. (1997), 'New tools for lean construction', in Alarcón, L. F. (ed.), *Lean Construction*, AA Balkema, Rotterdam, Netherlands, pp. 335–341.

Thompson, P. J. and Sanders, S. R. (1998), 'Partnering continuum', *Journal of Management in Engineering*, **14**(5), pp. 73–78.

Tookey, J. E., Murray, M., Hardcastle, C. and Langford, D. (2001), 'Construction procurement routes: redefining the contours of construction procurement', *Engineering, Construction and Architectural Management*, **8**(1), pp. 20–30.

Towill, D. R. and McCullen, P. (1999), 'The impact of an agile manufacturing programme on supply chain dynamics', *International Journal of Logistics in Manufacturing*, **10**(1), pp. 83–96.

Turner, J. R. (1993a), *The Handbook of Project Based Management*, McGraw-Hill, London.

Turner, J. R. (1993b), 'Integrated supply chain management: what's wrong with this picture?', *Industrial Engineering*, **25**(12), pp. 52–55.

Turner, J. R. and Keegan, A. E. (2001), 'Mechanisms of governance in the project-based organisation: a transaction cost economics', *European Management Journal*, **19**(3), pp. 254–267.

Turner, J. R. and Müller, R. (2003), 'On the nature of the project as a temporary organisation', *International Journal of Project Management*, **21**(1), pp. 1–8.

Turner, J. R. and Simister, S. J. (2001), 'Project contract management and a theory of organisation', *International Journal of Project Management*, **19**(8), pp. 457–464.

Vrijhoef, R. (1998), *Co-makership in Construction: Towards Construction Supply Chain Management*, Thesis of Graduate Studies, Delft University of Technology/VTT Building Technology, Espoo, Finland.

Vrijhoef, R., Koskela, L. and Howell, G. A. (2001), 'Understanding construction supply chains: an alternative interpretation', *Proceedings of the 9th Conference of the International Group for Lean Construction*, 6–8 August, Singapore, 15 pages.

Vrijhoef, R., Cuperus, Y. and Voordijk, H. (2002), 'Exploring the connection between open building and lean construction: defining a postponement strategy for supply chain management', *Proceedings of the 10th Conference of the International Group for Lean Construction*, 6–8 August, Gramado, Brazil, pp. 149–182.

Walker, D. H. T. and Hampson, K. (eds.) (2003), *Procurement Strategies: A Relationship-based Approach*, Blackwell Publishing, Oxford.

Westling, H. (1991), *Technology Procurement: For Innovation in Swedish Construction*, Swedish Council for Building Research, Stockholm, Sweden.

The power and leverage perspective: an alternative view of relationship and performance management

2.1 Introduction

Having outlined the basic problem as a lack of understanding about appropriateness in business relationship and performance optimisation, this chapter focuses specifically on the topic of what is the most 'appropriate' way for a buyer and a supplier to manage commercial transactions with each other. There has historically been considerable debate about the best way for buyers to manage business relationships with suppliers, and vice versa. At one extreme, some argue for the adoption of transparent win–win partnering; at the other is the diametrically opposed zero-sum approach associated with win–lose outcomes. Given this diversity of opinion about what buyers and suppliers should do, it is somewhat surprising that there has not been more emphasis in the literature about 'appropriateness' (Cox and Thompson, 1998; Cox and Townsend, 1998; Cox and Ireland, 2002; Cox, 2004b; Cox *et al.*, 2004a, b; Ireland, 2004).

In this book it is argued, however, that what is 'appropriate' for a construction buyer or supplier to do depends on the power and leverage circumstance in which it finds itself. In other words, there is no single way of managing business relationships for a buyer or a supplier in construction that is always appropriate in all circumstances. Managerial competence must, therefore, rest on buyers and suppliers understanding not only what is 'ideal', but also what is possible (or 'optimal') given the circumstances they are in.

The chapter demonstrates, therefore, that while there may be 'ideal' situations for buyers and suppliers in construction, they both have to manage business relationships in a range of very different circumstances that are far from ideal. This implies that relationship management and performance optimisation competence requires a detailed knowledge and understanding of both the buyer and supplier exchange circumstances that can exist, as well as the full range of relationship management choices available to use, when working in any of these circumstances. This is another way of saying that buyers and suppliers need a guide to action when they confront the universe of real world circumstances that can occur when managing relationships in construction.

The chapter first outlines the *power and leverage* perspective and shows how it differs from the *relational* approach that has dominated most recent thinking about 'best practice' in construction. This is followed by an analysis of the different relationship and performance management choices available for buyers and suppliers when they enter into transactions. This discussion is then linked to an understanding of the contingent (changing) power and leverage circumstances that confront buyers in relationships with suppliers, and vice versa. From this starting point it is then possible to explain why it is only by analysing supply chain networks (and the power regimes operating within them) that buyers and suppliers can fully understand the relationship management and performance optimisation choices available to them, and make appropriate choices between alternatives.

2.2 The power and leverage perspective on relationship management and performance optimisation

The *power and leverage* perspective on relationship and performance management has a long history based on fundamental analyses in economic theory about market imperfection (Bain, 1956; Marx, 1967; Bowles and Gintis, 1988); in sociology about resource dependency (Emerson, 1962); and in business management about asymmetric resource endowments (Pfeffer and Salancik, 1978; Porter, 1980; Campbell and Cunningham, 1983; Cox *et al.*, 2000, 2002; Cox, 2004d). The central premise of this perspective is that business relationships between buyers and suppliers are essentially contested. This means that, while it is perfectly possible for buyers and suppliers to engage in long-term and highly collaborative operational relationships, the commercial performance that results will always remain a bone of contention between the two parties. The reason for this resides in the essential conflict over objective commercial interests between buyers and suppliers about ideal and feasible outcomes (Cox, 2004c, d).

Given this starting point, it is obvious that there is a major theoretical and intellectual disagreement between writers from the *relational* perspective. In this school of writing one can include those who espouse the value of partnering or partnership sourcing, in which short-term adversarial relationships are rejected in favour of commercially non-adversarial and highly collaborative operational ways of working based on trust and transparency. This school of writing has a more contemporary lineage and includes recent writers from business, marketing and construction management backgrounds such as: Gummesson, 1987, 1997, 1999; Carlisle and Parker, 1989; CII, 1989, 1991, 1994; Womack *et al.*, 1990; Christopher *et al.*, 1991; Sako, 1992; Lamming, 1993; Hines, 1994; Latham, 1994; Macbeth and Ferguson, 1994; Bennett and Jayes, 1995, 1998; Hellard, 1995; Godfrey, 1996; Hinks *et al.*, 1996; Holti and Standing, 1996; Womack and Jones, 1996; Barlow, 1997; Koskela, 1997; McGeorge and Palmer, 1997; DETR, 1998; Thompson and Sanders, 1998; Christopher, 2000; Vrijhoef and Koskela, 2000; Lamming *et al.*, 2001; Ng *et al.*, 2002; Saad *et al.*, 2002; Turner and Müller, 2003; Smyth, 2005).

Essentially, the *relational* perspective argues that the most appropriate way for buyers and suppliers to work together operationally and commercially in any exchange relationship is to develop close and highly trusting and transparent collaborative relationships, in which both sides seek to increase 'the size of the pie' that may be created and then share it relatively equally. Following on from this logic about dyadic exchange between buyers and suppliers is the related argument that, since companies have to compete against one another, it is best if buyers and suppliers entering into these longer-term collaborative relationships extend the same thinking throughout their supply chains. This means that the client in the construction environment must (if necessary) select a design and engineering supplier, as well as a main contractor, with whom to have long-term partnering relationships. The main contractor, in particular, is then encouraged to extend these types of open and transparent relationships all of the way through the supply chain with its suppliers and its suppliers' suppliers.

The mantra that has been developed by proponents of the *relational* perspective is that in the future competition will be about supply chain against supply chain, and that those who do not create partnership-based efficiencies will be competed away by those that do. It takes only a moment's reflection about the reality of demand and supply structures in construction (and it may be said in many other industrial supply chains and markets) to realise that these recommendations are simplistic and potentially dangerous for the unwary.

In construction, as we saw in Chapter 1, most buyers and suppliers are not involved in continuous repeat games with one another in which there are high levels of bilateral operational dependency on one another beyond the one-off project that is required by the client. While there are clients – such as utilities companies, major housebuilders, major retailers, insurance companies, oil and gas companies, and Government Departments – that do have a requirement for continuous project work, or for continuous repair and maintenance of their infrastructure and facilities, the majority of demand for construction work is *ad hoc*, non-standard and does not involve a high level of continuous bilateral dependency between buyers and suppliers.

Given this, it is obvious that, if one segments construction demand, there are only a limited number of clients that have a regular process and highly standardised demand, and within these the regularity of demand may not always be for exactly the same standard design and construction activity. This means that a high percentage of construction work is from clients that may only ever enter the market once in their lifetime and, even if they return, they may have project requirements that are unique when compared with the last time they used construction supply chains and markets.

The underlying demand and supply structures that exist in construction, therefore, while not always inimical to the development of long-term collaborative relationships, are not always conducive for them. The underlying demand and supply structures within construction are, for most clients although not all, markedly dissimilar to those that exist in automotive manufacturing where there are high levels of regular and highly standardised demand for the same supply products and services. In this particular circumstance the opportunities to use bilateral dependency to drive efficiencies over the long-term are very high indeed, and when similar conditions exist in construction similar relationship and performance management approaches will be appropriate.

Unfortunately, when these underlying demand and supply characteristics do not exist, long-term relationship and performance management approaches are not appropriate and relationships must be managed differently. When demand is *ad hoc*, irregular or infrequent, and design requirements are non-standard, and the client is unlikely to return to the market in the future, then there are few incentives to encourage suppliers (either at the first-tier or through the supply chain) to make the necessary dedicated investments and relationship-specific adaptations to make collaboration work in the long-term.

On the contrary, in such demand and supply circumstances, buyers and suppliers can be expected to pursue their own short-term self-interests by playing the market for what it will bear. This means that opportunism and adversarial contracting strategies are not a sign of failure in construction (as some writers assume), rather they are a logical response by buyers and sellers to the inherent instability of demand and supply characteristics. Opportunism is a rational response for those involved in one-off games, in which there are no incentives for higher rewards from not maximising returns in the short-term. Obviously, collaboration is a better alternative if there are incentives that allow the parties to the exchange to envisage higher returns or rewards in the future. In such circumstances maximising short-term advantages is not a logical response to the superior commercial opportunities that may be feasible in the future from entering into bilateral dependency operationally.

This means that there must be circumstances in which the highly transparent and trusting collaborative relationships espoused by the *relational* school are appropriate. The point is, however, that this particular approach cannot be a generic solution to the problems of business relationship and performance management in construction. The reason for this is self-evident. Unless the demand and supply conditions support (provide incentives for) bilateral dependency, and unless the investments that are made in these ways of working lead to superior commercial outcomes to any of the more opportunistic alternatives available to either party in the short-term, then it is unlikely that this type of approach will be sensible for either a buyer or a supplier. When it is not, we can expect buyers and suppliers in construction (and for that matter in any other industry) to pursue short-term and highly opportunistic relationship and performance management approaches.

There is, however, an additional issue that is addressed in the power and leverage perspective. This perspective takes as its fundamental starting point the view that if the relationships between buyers and suppliers are essentially contested because of the non-commensurability of their objective interests then what may be desirable for one party in any exchange may not be equally desirable for another (Cox, 2004a). If this is the case then an arm's-length or a collaborative relationship approach may be more or less acceptable to one party than another. Furthermore, even if there is common agreement between exchange partners about the need for either an arm's-length or a collaborative relationship approach, and even if by working together in either of these ways 'the size of the pie' to be shared grows, it is still possible for one party to appropriate a larger share of 'the pie' than the other.

In the *power and leverage* perspective the determinant of who gets what, how and when (who wins and who loses, or who relatively wins more than the other) from all forms of exchange must be a reflection, therefore, of the power resources available to both parties when they interact. This perspective contends that there are a number of different ways in which buyers and suppliers can interact and these operational ways of working may be more or less commercially appropriate for either party under different circumstances. It is only by understanding, therefore, the full range of relationship and performance management approaches, and the commercial outcomes of these for both exchange parties in particular circumstances, that it is possible to provide guidance for managers about which relationship and performance management approaches are more or less appropriate.

Recommending collaboration as always the best way to manage relationships and performance outcomes is, from this perspective, clearly nonsensical.

In what follows, the basic approach that is used to provide guidance to managers when adopting this power and leverage perspective is outlined. The discussion focuses first on the range of sourcing approaches that can be adopted by buyers when they enter into relationships with suppliers. This is followed by a discussion of the ways in which power and leverage circumstances can be understood, and then by an analysis of the different relationship management styles that buyers and suppliers can use in exchange transactions. Finally, there is a discussion of how sourcing choices, relationship styles and power circumstances can be combined to allow managers (whether acting as buyers or suppliers) to understand which relationship management approaches are most appropriate to the optimisation of their own performance under particular circumstances.

2.3 Sourcing options available for managing buyer and supplier exchange

In what follows the basic sourcing options available to buyers, as they source external resources from suppliers, are discussed. The discussion is based on a theoretical distinction between buyer sourcing approaches that links together the level of involvement that buyers and suppliers can have with one another (reactive and arm's-length or proactive and collaborative), as well as the nature and degree of the buyer's involvement in developing the supplier and the supplier's suppliers own competencies (at the first-tier or throughout the supply chain(s) as a whole).

As Figure 2.1 demonstrates there are four basic sourcing approaches available to buyers (Cox et al., 2003).

Supplier selection

Sourcing for most buyers is normally based on relatively short-term and arm's-length contracting relationships, with the buyer selecting from among relatively competent suppliers in the market, which individually decide what their supply

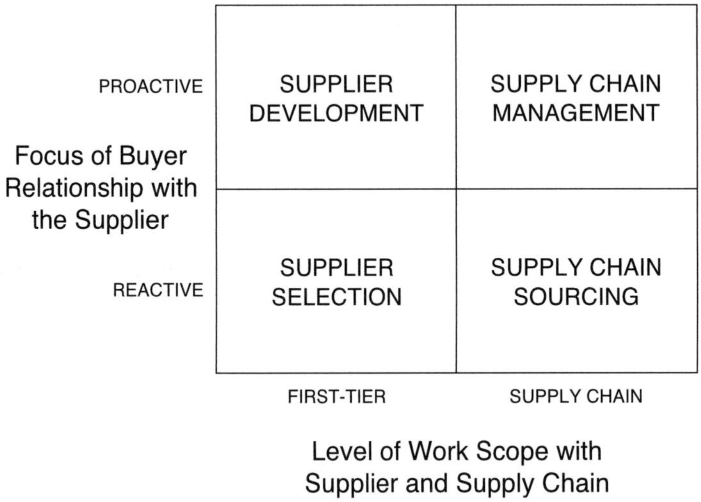

	FIRST-TIER	SUPPLY CHAIN
PROACTIVE	SUPPLIER DEVELOPMENT	SUPPLY CHAIN MANAGEMENT
REACTIVE	SUPPLIER SELECTION	SUPPLY CHAIN SOURCING

Focus of Buyer Relationship with the Supplier

Level of Work Scope with Supplier and Supply Chain

Figure 2.1 The four sourcing options for buyers (Source: Cox et al. (2003), p. 5)

offering will be. The essential role of the buyer is then to select from the available suppliers on the basis of the currently perceived best trade-off between functionality and the total costs of ownership. If the buyer does not have a long-term operational requirement the relationship will always operate in this manner. This is because there is no basis (the incentive structure does not warrant the necessary relationship investments) for the buyer or the supplier to collaborate. This is the normal approach adopted by construction clients who are entering the market infrequently or on a one-off basis.

On the other hand, if the buyer (construction client, architect, design house, main contractor etc.) requires continuous supply it is still possible for this non-collaborative approach to be appropriate. Those who espouse collaboration would always recommend that if a long-term demand requirement exists then collaboration is the most appropriate sourcing choice. This may not be the case because market competition can constantly generate innovation without extensive forms of buyer and supplier collaboration. In such circumstances, short-term and arm's-length relationship management approaches based on regular supplier selection techniques can be used continuously over time to test the market to assess whether the performance of suppliers has improved.

In this way of working the buyer operates in a commercially opportunistic, but operationally reactive (arm's-length) mode with suppliers. Buyers pass basic product or service specification, volume and timing information to suppliers while allowing the suppliers to develop their own operational and commercial competencies without significant buyer involvement in the process of supply innovation. In this way of working great emphasis will normally be placed by both the buyer and the supplier on comprehensive clause contracting, with terms and conditions rigorously delineated and enforced pre- and post-contractually. This is why construction is a claims-based industry, as each party fights to assign risk and uncertainty to the other party in order to maximise its short-term advantages in what is often a one-off rather than repeat game.

Supply chain sourcing

This reactive way of working can be extended by the buyer beyond the first-tier relationship with the supplier into the extended network of buyer and supplier relationships within the myriad of supply chains that service the end customer or client. The approach adopted by the buyer is the same as under supplier selection but it involves the buyer in much more extensive transaction costs. The buyer uses exactly the same reactive sourcing techniques as outlined above, except it now seeks to select from among suppliers, not just at the first-tier but from as many tiers as possible, from raw materials through to the final delivery of the end product or service by the first-tier supplier. Once again, at each tier in the supply chain, the buyer selects from currently relatively competent suppliers on the basis of the currently perceived best trade-offs between functionality and total cost of ownership.

The buyer's role is still essentially reactive and at arm's-length operationally, providing only basic and limited contractual information, and relying on suppliers in the chain to provide innovation through competition. This variant is, however, far more time and resource intensive for buyers. This is because buyers have to incur transaction costs for search, selection and negotiation with suppliers throughout the supply network rather than just at the first-tier.

In the construction environment this approach would normally not be used by an occasional or one-off client. This is because supply chain sourcing involves extensive search and negotiation costs throughout the supply chain, and these transaction costs (investments) would not make sense for a buyer that is not returning to the market on a fairly regular basis. For these reasons supply chain sourcing is normally only ever adopted by construction buyers that have a continuous requirement for supply inputs, and either lack the internal competence to develop their suppliers or their supply chain, or face severe risks of post-contractual lock-in and moral hazard if they create long-term collaborative relationships with suppliers (Cox, 2004a).

Supplier development

Rather than a buyer operating reactively by making selection decisions in response to the supply offerings made by suppliers in markets that may, or may not, be highly competitive, it is possible for it to adopt a far more operationally proactive (colla-borative) approach. When a buyer acts proactively it is normal that the relationship will shift operationally from one that is short-term and arm's-length with limited involvement by the buyer in the supplier's business, to one in which the relationship becomes more long-term and both parties collaborate extensively.

In this way of working the buyer and supplier jointly make dedicated investments in the relationship, create technical bonds, develop cultural norms to guide the way they work together and also make relationship-specific adaptations in order to create new products and service offerings (in terms of improved value for money offerings based on improvements in functionality and reductions in the total costs of owner-ship). In this approach the performance improvement that occurs is normally higher than would have been the case if market contestation had been utilised by the buyer and in the absence of the joint long-term working relationship. When a buyer and supplier work together in this way at the first-tier in the supply chain, and agree to work towards 'stretch' (improvement) targets beyond what is currently achievable in the market, this is known as supplier development.

The buyer, in this way of working, is offering a long-term relationship for a commitment by the supplier to provide greater transparency over its input costs, margins and production techniques (and vice versa) in order to create innovation beyond that which would be possible if the buyer simply allowed market competi-tion to occur. This approach is much more resource intensive for both the buyer and supplier than reactive approaches because it involves transaction costs for development work rather than just for search, selection and negotiation. It can also be buyer-led or buyer and supplier jointly managed.

Clearly, this approach is not feasible for all construction clients. This is because it requires both a regular and continuous demand requirement and sufficient volume of work to overcome the supplier's natural reticence to provide transparency over its operational and commercial ways of working and to make the necessary dedicated investments and relationship-specific adaptations. It is logical to assume, therefore, that supplier development is only really feasible for major construction clients with high volumes, or for major contractors (or their subcontractors) who have a regular and continuous demand for supply requirements from their first-tier suppliers.

Supply chain management

Supply chain management has many definitions. We define it here as a sourcing technique that involves the buyer undertaking proactive supplier development work, not only at the first-tier of the supply chain, but also at all stages in the supply chain from first-tier through to raw material supply. This definition is, therefore, similar to the concept of 'network sourcing' (Hines, 1994). It is obvious that, given this definition, this form of relationship and performance management will be the most resource intensive and time-consuming to adopt for both the buyers and the suppliers in a supply chain.

It is clear that if it is possible for the buyers and suppliers in a supply chain network to develop proactive long-term collaborative relationships, and if these relationships can be directed towards constant innovation in functionality and cost, then supply chain management must be the most advantageous proposition for a buyer at the end of the chain. There is also no empirical doubt that some car manufacturers have gone some considerable way to demonstrate that this is possible in the automotive supply chain. Furthermore, some major retailers and global manufacturers have also demonstrated a capability to drive this type of sourcing approach through their supply chain networks.

The problem is, however, that just because some buyers can achieve this does not mean that everyone else can. Research in construction and a wide number of other industries shows that very few companies are, or ever will be, in a position as buyers to be able to undertake supply chain management (i.e. extensive forms of joint operational collaboration throughout their extended network of supply chains) in practice (Cox *et al.*, 2004a, b; Ireland, 2004). There are two primary reasons for this.

First, supply chain management is the most resource intensive sourcing approach for both buyers and suppliers in the chain. It involves not only transaction costs for the buyer associated with search, selection and negotiation, but it also involves those costs linked to the creation of dedicated investments and relationship-specific adaptations for supplier development work. It is clear also that these costs are exponentially increased for buyers in this sourcing variant because these competencies must be developed, not just at the first-tier but also throughout the whole of the supply chain. This is a massive undertaking and one that is not really possible for very many companies, primarily because they lack the internal resources and capabilities to be able to undertake the work, or to make the required long-term commitments to their suppliers.

The second reason why this approach is unlikely to be successful relates to the problem of power and leverage. Research has demonstrated that supplier development and supply chain management tend to work best in circumstances when buyers have *dominance* over suppliers or, at the very least, there is an *interdependence* in the power relationships between them (Cox, 1997a, 1999; Cox *et al.*, 2000, 2002, 2003, 2004a). It is not surprising, therefore, that many of the companies that have been able to adopt these approaches normally have high levels of global volume, with regular and standardised demand requirements from suppliers that operate within highly contested markets, with relatively low switching costs between them.

This environment closely approximates to power and leverage situations of *buyer dominance* and/or *interdependence*, and this helps to explain why it is that some power circumstances are more conducive to the implementation of supplier development and supply chain management than others. The research reported here demonstrates that buyers rarely operate in supply chains characterised by extended power situations of *buyer dominance* or *interdependence*, and often have few opportunities to engineer them. This alone explains why, whatever some may argue, most practitioners will never be in a position to implement proactive approaches, whatever the internal competences and capabilities of the buyer.

In the construction industry there are very few, if any, public or private sector organisations that we are aware of who have both the internal competence and a sufficiently conducive external environment within which to develop supply chain management approaches. This is not to say that no one can adopt this approach, but that the number is likely to be very small indeed. This is because even when a sufficiently conducive external environment exists (regular standardised and high-volume demand with willing supplicant suppliers), there is often a lack of internal competence to develop the effective operational and commercial leverage to make this approach work effectively. This seems to be particularly true in the public sector, where many of the preconditions for effective proactive sourcing exist, but where current government thinking oscillates between market-testing and complete outsourcing, without a proper understanding of 'appropriateness' in reactive or proactive sourcing. There are, of course, private sector organisations – notably in the utilities, property management and house-building sectors – where similar problems can be found and where a more radical supply chain management approach may be feasible.

What this discussion shows is that there can be no single 'best practice' approach to relationship and performance management that buyers and suppliers ought to adopt in the future. This is because, whether buyers and suppliers enter into proactive or reactive relationship and performance management approaches together, the commercial outcome for both parties may or may not be the same. Thus, what may be the best option for a buyer may not be the best option for a supplier. Furthermore, even if both parties can agree that one approach is the best for both of them, there is still the issue of how the benefits from the exchange will be divided between the two exchange partners. Even if both parties agree to share the value created equally this may not represent a fair reflection of the relative risk that both parties may have to carry in order to make the relationship work. This means, paradoxically perhaps, that equity in exchange can be fair and unfair.

Given this, competence in relationship and performance management cannot be judged – as it appears to be by proponents of the *relational* school – on whether or not buyers and suppliers have adopted proactive approaches. On the contrary, competence requires that buyers know about all of the sourcing approaches available to them (including insourcing), and also understand which approach is the currently most beneficial option, as well as how it can be implemented effectively. 'Appropriateness' means, therefore, the ability to recognise under which circumstances any of the four approaches outlined here is the best option available for a buyer or supplier.

Whether or not proactive or reactive approaches can be adopted depends on a range of complex choices both internally within an organisation and externally in the supply chains to be managed (Cox *et al.*, 2003, 2004a). While many writers in the *relational* school argue the case for long-term collaborative approaches as 'best practice' sourcing it is rarely the case that buyers or suppliers have either the competence or resources to be able to successfully implement such approaches effectively. In these circumstances pursuing an alternative approach may be the most 'appropriate' and, in some cases, the only alternative available.

To develop 'appropriateness' in relationship and performance management it is not enough, however, to know the basic sourcing options available. One must also know what are the four basic styles that are available for managing relationships and optimising performance. Linked with this, one must also understand the four

power circumstances that create the power regimes within which buyers and
suppliers have to manage their relationships. These issues are discussed below.

2.4 Relationship management styles and power regimes

There is a growing consensus in the literature about the relationship management
outcomes that can exist between buyers and suppliers, but less agreement on which
relationship management styles are the most appropriate for optimising performance under particular power and leverage circumstances. The discussion that
follows cannot do justice to the complexity of this topic but the basic outlines of
the *power and leverage* approach to relationship alignment and misalignment is
presented here (Cox, 2004b, c, d; Cox *et al.*, 2004a, b).

Buyers and suppliers must select from among a range of sourcing options and
implement them. To do so effectively three elements must be in place. The first
is a specification of the sourcing approaches available (as described above). The
second is an understanding of the power and leverage environments within
which relationships must be managed. The third is an understanding of the
relationship management styles that can be used to manage particular sourcing
approaches effectively. Finally, all of these elements must be brought together in
order to align a particular sourcing approach with a specific power and leverage
circumstance using the appropriate relationship management style.

The only way in which a buyer or a supplier can understand whether or not it is
possible to undertake reactive or proactive sourcing (at the first-tier or within the
supply chain) is through strategic source planning. The first stage of strategic
source planning involves the mapping of the operational supply chain (with all
of its relevant tiers) for the product and/or service being sourced. The second
aspect requires an analysis of the commercial relationships in the supply chain to
understand the gross and net profit margins being earned by the actors at each
tier and for each dyadic relationship. Only in this way is it possible to understand
the current power and leverage situation for all buyers and suppliers in the chain.
This method for understanding the link between operational practice and commercial exchange is referred to as *power regime analysis* (Cox *et al.*, 2000, 2002, 2003).

Figures 2.2 and 2.3 show the basic building blocks, using the buyer and supplier
power matrix, to develop a comprehensive understanding of the power and
leverage situation within a supply chain power regime. If *supplier development* and
supply chain management sourcing approaches are only really effective in situations
of *buyer dominance* ($>$) and *interdependence* ($=$), it will be obvious from the hypothetical power regime presented on Figure 2.3 that *supply chain management* is not
really possible in this power regime as a whole. While *supplier development* activities
may be possible in certain tiers of the supply chain (those marked with the symbols
$>$ or $=$), for the bulk of the relationships presented proactive sourcing approaches
are currently not possible. This means that buyers will normally have to adopt
reactive sourcing approaches because they will be unable to provide the incentives
that would be necessary to induce suppliers to invest in the necessary dedicated
investments and relationship specific adaptations to make a proactive approach
possible.

Whichever power and leverage situations buyers and suppliers find themselves
in, all business relationships have to be managed with 'appropriate' relationship

BUYER DOMINANCE (>)	**INTERDEPENDENCE (=)**
Few buyers/many suppliers Buyer has high % share of total market for supplier Supplier is highly dependent on buyer for revenue with few alternatives Supplier's switching costs are high Buyer's switching costs are low Buyer's account is attractive to supplier Supplier's offering is a standardised commodity Buyer's search costs are low Supplier has no information asymmetry advantages over buyer	Few buyers/few suppliers Buyer has relatively high % share of total market for supplier Supplier is highly dependent on buyer for revenue with few alternatives Supplier's switching costs are high Buyer's switching costs are high Buyer's account is attractive to supplier Supplier's offering is relatively unique Buyer's search costs are relatively high Supplier has moderate information asymmetry advantages over buyer
INDEPENDENCE (0)	**SUPPLIER DOMINANCE (<)**
Many buyers/many suppliers Buyer has relatively low % share of total market for supplier Supplier has little dependence on buyer for revenue and has many alternatives Supplier's switching costs are low Buyer's switching costs are low Buyer's account is not particularly attractive to supplier Supplier's offering is a standardised commodity Buyer's search costs are relatively low Supplier has very limited information asymmetry advantages over buyer	Many buyers/few suppliers Buyer has low % share of total market for supplier Supplier has no dependence on buyer for revenue and has many alternatives Supplier's switching costs are low Buyer's switching costs are high Buyer's account is not particularly attractive to supplier Supplier's offering is relatively unique Buyer's search costs are very high Supplier has substantial information asymmetry advantages over buyer

Attributes of Buyer Power Relative to Supplier — HIGH (top rows), LOW (bottom rows)

Attributes of Supplier Power Relative to Buyer — LOW (left), HIGH (right)

Figure 2.2 The power matrix: attributes of buyer and supplier power (Source: Cox et al. (2003), p. 54)

management styles if they are to be effective. This means that there must be a correlation between particular ways of working between buyers and suppliers and successful performance outcomes. Successful performance outcomes for buyers and suppliers must imply that there is an alignment between the goals and aspirations of the buyer and those of the supplier that makes a relationship successful for both parties to an exchange (Cox *et al.*, 2004a). To understand how these can be aligned, it is first necessary to understand theoretically the way in which buyers and suppliers can conduct their relationships with one another. The basic theoretical choices are outlined in Figure 2.4.

Figure 2.4 demonstrates that when a buyer and supplier interact there are at least two fundamental aspects to the relationship. The first is the way of working, which refers to the level of operational linkage between the two parties. Operationally, buyers and suppliers can choose to make few dedicated investments in their relationship and operate on a fairly short-term contractual basis. This arm's-length way of working involves the buyer providing only basic specification, volume and timing information to the supplier, with the supplier providing the buyer with limited specification, timing and pricing information.

There is, of course, an alternative way of working known as collaboration. Under a collaborative relationship approach the buyer and supplier make extensive

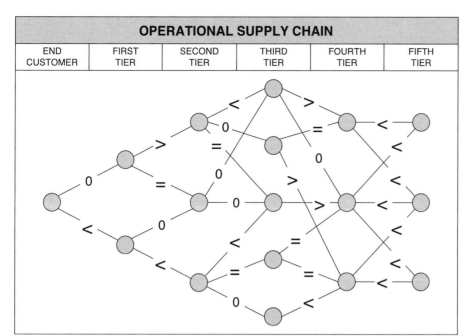

Figure 2.3 Hypothetical power regime (Adapted from: Cox (2001), p. 46)

dedicated investments in the relationship. On top of basic specification, timing, price and volume information, both parties will normally make relationship-specific adaptations to their operational processes and provide detailed information about future product and service road maps, as well as creating technical linkages in their respective operations (Cannon and Perreault, 1999). The aim of this way of working is normally to create a product or service offering at a total cost of ownership and/or functionality that is not currently available in the market, and could not be created by more arm's-length ways of working. Such relationships tend to be long-term in duration.

The second aspect of a relationship is the commercial intent of the two parties when they enter into a transaction. If the buyer or supplier is primarily interested

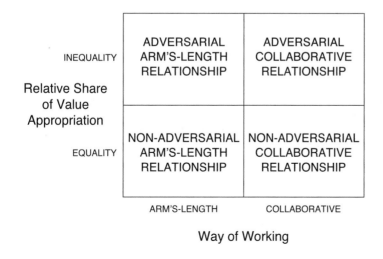

Figure 2.4 Relationship portfolio analysis (Source: Cox (1999), p. 23)

in maximising its share of value from the relationship at the expense of the other side, this is referred to as adversarial value appropriation. If, on the other hand, the intention of the buyer or supplier is to provide open and transparent commercial information about profit margins and the costs of operations, such that any improvements can be shared relatively equally, then this is referred to as a non-adversarial value appropriation.

By bringing these two aspects together it is clear that there are four basic relationship management styles that buyers and suppliers can choose from in order to manage relationships. These are:

(i) Adversarial arm's-length, where the exchange partner seeks to maximise the commercial share of value but normally uses short-term market-testing.
(ii) Non-adversarial arm's-length, where the exchange partner pays the current market price without recourse to aggressive bargaining, but tests the market actively.
(iii) Adversarial collaboration, where the exchange partner provides extensive operational linkages and relationship-specific adaptations, but seeks to maximise the appropriation of commercial value.
(iv) Non-adversarial collaboration, where the exchange partners operate in a transparent operational manner with long-term relationship commitments and share any resulting commercial value equally.

While it is clear that exchange partners have a choice of four broad options, which one of these approaches is the best for buyers or suppliers to adopt is not an easy matter to decide upon. This is because managers have to understand how each of the four relationship management styles have to be linked with particular sourcing approaches, under specific power and leverage circumstances, to create business relationships that optimise performance for themselves, first, and only secondly for their exchange partners. How this is achieved is explained below and in Chapter 3.

2.5 A way of thinking about 'appropriateness' in buyer and supplier exchange

The argument presented here has two major dimensions. First, one approach to relationship and performance management is not necessarily superior to all others and, as a result, buyers and suppliers have to select the most appropriate approach for themselves, given the power and leverage circumstances they are in. Second, even when buyers and suppliers understand which approach is the most appropriate for them to use it is not always possible for buyers or suppliers to implement that approach successfully.

The primary reasons for this failure of implementation are normally because of a lack of capability and competence internally and/or non-conducive power circumstances externally. This means that either managers do not understand what they should be doing, or they do but their exchange partners do not want to adopt the operational and commercial approach that the managers prefer. In practice, both of these obstacles are very difficult to overcome and many business relationships are, as a consequence, misaligned and sub-optimal for both parties.

There is, however, another reason for failure. Buyers and suppliers sometimes misperceive circumstances and pursue inappropriate relationship management styles, given the internal and external power circumstances they are operating in. These problems can sometimes be overcome if practitioners have an open mind and are prepared to change their behaviour to align relationship management styles appropriately with power circumstances and the sourcing approach being adopted. In order to align business relationships appropriately buyers and suppliers have to adopt the power and relationship linkages outlined in Figure 2.5 (Cox *et al.*, 2004a).

Figure 2.5 shows that sometimes there are power and leverage circumstances in which buyers are dominant in the relationship (*buyer dominance*) and sometimes the reverse is true and suppliers are dominant (*supplier dominance*). In such circumstances it is unlikely that relationship and performance outcomes for either the buyer or the supplier can be optimised unless they both have willing supplicant partners. This means that when a buyer is dominant it can adopt reactive or proactive sourcing approaches, but if performance is to be optimised for it then it will expect its suppliers to accept either market-testing (if a reactive approach is being used) or collaborative ways of working (if a proactive approach is being used) in which most of the commercial value from the exchange is passed to the buyer. Conversely, if the supplier is dominant it will expect the buyer to accept either arm's-length (if the favoured approach is reactive) or highly collaborative (if a proactive approach is preferred) relationships, in which most of the commercial value from the exchange is appropriated by the supplier.

On the other hand, there will be power and leverage circumstances in which neither party has the upper hand and an equivalence of power and leverage resources exists because both parties have countervailing power against each other. In such circumstances, when both parties have relatively high and reciprocal power and leverage resources relative to the other, a power situation of *inter-dependence* exists and this is likely to encourage non-adversarial ways of working commercially, with relative equity in the sharing of commercial value from the exchange. In such an environment of power balance, the pre-conditions for reciprocity in close and collaborative operational ways of working may also be high, and proactive sourcing is often appropriate for both parties.

When both parties have only low relative power and leverage resources against one another, however, a situation of *independence* exists, and in this circumstance an arm's-length reactive approach is likely to be sensible for both parties to adopt. Furthermore, since neither party can exert power and leverage against the other, a fairly reciprocal adversarial approach may be adopted commercially by both parties, although the buyer may gain most from this relationship because improvements in the performance of supply offerings are likely if the supplier is operating in a highly contested market.

What this discussion shows is that, rather than assuming that there is one sourcing and relationship management approach that is always 'best practice', in the real world both parties to an exchange have a range of options from which to choose that may be more or less appropriate under different power and leverage circumstances. It is ironic, therefore, that the construction management literature has recently been dominated by the faddish view that one approach to relationship and performance management, namely reciprocal collaboration or partnering, is always the most appropriate for all buyers and suppliers to adopt under all circumstances. This is particularly ironic because historically the construction industry, especially in the project environment, has always recognised the need for the development of tight comprehensive clause contracts to deal with short-term

Who Appropriates Value from the Relationship?

	BUYER DOMINANT ARM'S-LENGTH RELATIONSHIP	BUYER–SUPPLIER RECIPROCAL ARM'S-LENGTH RELATIONSHIP	SUPPLIER DOMINANT ARM'S-LENGTH RELATIONSHIP
ARM'S-LENGTH	Short-term operational relationship, with limited close working between buyer and supplier Buyer adversarially appropriates most of the commercial value created and sets price and quality trade-offs Supplier is non-adversarial commercially and a willing suppliant, accepting work rather than high margins/profitability from the relationship **Buyer Dominance power situation (>)**	Short-term operational relationship, with limited close working between buyer and supplier Buyer accepts current market price and quality trade-offs Supplier accepts normal (low) market returns Both buyer and supplier operate adversarially commercially whenever possible, but normally have few leverage opportunities **Independence power situation (0)**	Short-term operational relationship, with limited close working between buyer and supplier Supplier adversarially appropriates most of the commercial value created and sets price and quality trade-offs Buyer is non-adversarial commercially and a willing suppliant, paying whatever is required to receive given quality standards **Supplier Dominance power situation (<)**
COLLABORATIVE	BUYER DOMINANT COLLABORATIVE RELATIONSHIP Long-term operational relationship, with extensive and close working between buyer and supplier Buyer adversarially appropriates most of the commercial value created and sets price and quality trade-offs Supplier is a non-adversarial supplicant commercially, and accepts work rather than high margins/ profitability from the relationship **Buyer Dominance power situation (>)**	BUYER–SUPPLIER RECIPROCAL COLLABORATIVE RELATIONSHIP Long-term operational relationship, with extensive and close working between buyer and supplier Buyer and supplier share relatively equally the commercial value created Buyer and supplier agree price and quality trade-offs, with supplier making more than normal returns Both buyer and supplier operate non-adversarially commercially **Interdependence power situation (=)**	SUPPLIER DOMINANT COLLABORATIVE RELATIONSHIP Long-term operational relationship, with extensive and close working between buyer and supplier Supplier adversarially appropriates most of the commercial value created and sets price and quality trade-offs Buyer is a non-adversarial supplicant commercially, and pays whatever is required to receive given quality standards **Supplier Dominance power situation (<)**

Way of Working

BUYER DOMINANCE   BUYER–SUPPLIER RECIPROCITY   SUPPLIER DOMINANCE

Figure 2.5 Value appropriation, power and relationship management styles (Source: Cox et al. (2004a), p. 97)

opportunistic behaviour in the arm's-length relationships that have dominated (and will continue to dominate) exchange relationships in the industry.

To contend, therefore, that this adversarial and arm's-length approach is out-dated and inappropriate, and that it should be superseded in all circumstances by collaborative relationships based on trust and transparency, is clearly nonsensical. This is because, while it may be an appropriate thing to do in some circumstances for some actors, there are alternative relationship management approaches that may be more appropriate than reciprocal forms of collaboration under particular power and leverage circumstances. For example, a buyer or supplier wishing to enter into a proactive collaborative working relationship with an exchange partner would be foolish to prefer reciprocal forms of collaboration to either buyer dominant or supplier dominant collaboration. This is because in these two alternative approaches the buyer and supplier could maximise their share of value commercially, rather than having to share it with the other party. Clearly, if this type of relationship and performance management approach is sustainable with the other party in the exchange it is a preferable outcome to reciprocal collaboration.

What all of this means is that there appears to be a correlation between power and leverage circumstances and appropriate relationship management styles and sourcing options (Cox, 2004a, b). Thus, *supplier selection* and *supply chain sourcing* approaches, which focus on arm's-length rather than collaborative ways of working, are appropriate for buyers and suppliers to engage in under all power and leverage circumstances, if the necessary internal competence to manage these relationships effectively is available. But, for these relationships to be aligned and for performance to be optimised for the parties in the exchange, the buyer and supplier have to adopt the appropriate relationship management approaches as outlined in Figure 2.6. Thus, if the buyer is dominant and adversarial commercially, the relationship is only aligned if the supplier is non-adversarial. If the supplier is dominant then the reverse of this situation pertains. If the power structure is one of *interdependence* then both parties should be non-adversarial commercially, and if the power circumstance is of *independence* then both parties can be expected to be adversarial.

Similarly, if the buyer or supplier wishes to adopt a proactive approach of *supplier development* or *supply chain management*, then the necessary internal competencies have to be available in both collaborating organisations, and a conducive external power structure with aligned relationship management style has to be in place for performance to be optimised. In these circumstances only some relationship approaches are feasible and others are not. Thus, if a power situation of *independence* exists there is no basis for collaboration to occur, and any attempts to do so operationally are likely to be a waste of time and effort for both parties. If *buyer dominance* or *supplier dominance* occurs, however, the dominant party will have the opportunity to be commercially adversarial, and force the supplicant party to operate non-adversarially and pass the bulk of any value created in the exchange to it. If *interdependence* occurs then the exchange will be aligned if both parties operate non-adversarially and agree to share the value created equally.

This demonstrates, therefore, that relationships can be aligned or they can be misaligned under both reactive and proactive approaches (Cox *et al.*, 2004a). Furthermore, it is clear that reactive and/or proactive relationship management options will be more or less appropriate to the parties to any exchange – whether in construction or in any other industry – depending on whether the operational investments of time, resource and effort necessary to make a particular approach work are possible and provide for performance outcomes that are superior to all

SOURCING APPROACH	POWER AND LEVERAGE CIRCUMSTANCE	APPROPRIATE RELATIONSHIP MANAGEMENT STYLES
SUPPLIER SELECTION	BUYER DOMINANCE (>)	Buyer Adversarial Arm's-Length / Supplier Non-Adversarial Arm's Length
	INDEPENDENCE (0)	Buyer and Supplier Adversarial Arm's Length
	INTERDEPENDENCE (=)	Buyer and Supplier Non-Adversarial Arm's Length
	SUPPLIER DOMINANCE (<)	Buyer Non-Adversarial Arm's Length / Supplier Adversarial Arm's Length
SUPPLY CHAIN SOURCING	BUYER DOMINANCE (>)	Buyer Adversarial Arm's-Length / Supplier Non-Adversarial Arm's Length
	INDEPENDENCE (0)	Buyer and Supplier Adversarial Arm's Length
	INTERDEPENDENCE (=)	Buyer and Supplier Non-Adversarial Arm's Length
	SUPPLIER DOMINANCE (<)	Buyer Non-Adversarial Arm's Length / Supplier Adversarial Arm's Length
SUPPLIER DEVELOPMENT	BUYER DOMINANCE (>)	Buyer Adversarial Collaboration / Supplier Non-Adversarial Collaboration
	INDEPENDENCE (0)	Not Applicable
	INTERDEPENDENCE (=)	Buyer and Supplier Non-Adversarial Collaboration
	SUPPLIER DOMINANCE (<)	Buyer Non-Adversarial Collaboration / Supplier Adversarial Collaboration
SUPPLY CHAIN MANAGEMENT	BUYER DOMINANCE (>)	Buyer Adversarial Collaboration / Supplier Non-Adversarial Collaboration
	INDEPENDENCE (0)	Not Applicable
	INTERDEPENDENCE (=)	Buyer and Supplier Non-Adversarial Collaboration
	SUPPLIER DOMINANCE (<)	Buyer Non-Adversarial Collaboration / Supplier Adversarial Collaboration

Figure 2.6 Appropriateness in sourcing strategies, power circumstances and relationship management (Source: Cox (2004b), p. 355)

other of the feasible alternative options. This also means, of course, that there is always the possibility that what may be in the interests of one party may not always be in the interests of the other.

Furthermore, even when parties to an exchange recognise that they are in an *interdependence* power situation and that reciprocal collaboration works well for both of them, it can be argued, as we shall see in Chapter 3, that there may still be superior relationship and performance outcomes to reciprocal collaboration for both parties. If this is true, and if a complete win–win for both parties is not feasible in business relationships between buyers and suppliers, then it is inevitable that exchange between buyers and suppliers will be permanently contested. This issue is the subject matter of the next chapter.

References

Bain, J. S. (1956), *Barriers to New Competition*, Harvard University Press, Cambridge, MA.

Barlow, J. (1997), 'Institutional economics and partnering in the British construction industry', *AEA Conference on Construction Econometrics*, February, Neuchatel, Brazil.

Bennett, J. and Jayes, S. (1995), *Trusting the Team: The Best Practice Guide to Partnering in Construction*, Reading Construction Forum, Reading.

Bennett, J. and Jayes, S. (1998), *The Seven Pillars of Partnering*, Thomas Telford, London.

Bowles, S. and Gintis, H. (1988), 'Contested exchange; political economy and modern economic theory', *American Economic Review*, **78**(2), pp. 145–150.

Campbell, N. C. G. and Cunningham, M. T. (1983), 'Customer analysis for strategy development in industrial markets', *Strategic Management Journal*, **4**, pp. 369–380.

Cannon, J. P. and Perreault, W. D. (1999), 'Buyer and seller relationships in business markets', *Journal of Marketing Research*, **36**(4), pp. 439–460.

Carlisle, J. A. and Parker, R. C. (1989), *Beyond Negotiation*, John Wiley, Chichester.

Christopher, M. (2000), 'The agile supply chain: competing in volatile markets', *Industrial Marketing Management*, **29**(1), pp. 37–44.

Christopher, M., Payne, A. and Ballantyne, D. (1991), *Relationship Marketing*, Heinemann, London.

CII (1989), *Partnering: Meeting the Challenges of the Future*, Construction Industry Institute, Special Publications, Austin, TX, USA.

CII (1991), *In Search of Partnering Excellence*, Construction Industry Institute, Special Publications, Austin, TX, USA.

CII (1994), *Benchmarking Implementation Results, Teambuilding and Project Partnering*, Construction Industry Institute, Austin, TX, USA.

Cox, A. (1997a), *Business Success: A Way of Thinking about Strategy, Critical Supply Chain Assets and Operational Best Practice*, Earlsgate Press, Stratford-upon-Avon.

Cox, A. (1997b), 'On power, appropriateness and procurement competence', *Supply Management*, 2 October, pp. 24–27.

Cox, A. (1999), 'Power, value and supply chain management', *Supply Chain Management: An International Journal*, **4**(4), pp. 167–175.

Cox, A. (2001), 'Managing with power: strategies for improving value appropriation from supply relationships', *Journal of Supply Chain Management*, **37**(2), Spring, pp. 42–47.

Cox, A. (2004a), 'Strategic outsourcing: avoiding the loss of critical assets and the problems of adverse selection and moral hazard', *Business Briefing: Global Purchasing and Supply Chain Strategies*, Business Briefings Ltd., London.

Cox, A. (2004b), 'The art of the possible: relationship management in power regimes and supply chains', *Supply Chain Management: An International Journal*, **9**(5), pp. 346–356.

Cox, A. (2004c), 'Business relationship alignment: on the commensurability of value capture and mutuality in buyer and supplier exchange', *Supply Chain Management: An International Journal*, **9**(5), pp. 410–420.

Cox, A. (2004d), *Win–Win? The Paradox of Value and Interests in Business Relationships*, Earlsgate Press, Stratford-upon-Avon.

Cox, A. and Ireland, P. (2002), 'Managing construction supply chains: a common sense approach', *Engineering, Construction and Architectural Management*, **9**(5/6), pp. 409–418.

Cox, A., Ireland, P., Lonsdale, C., Sanderson, J. and Watson, G. (2002), *Supply Chains, Markets and Power: Mapping Buyer and Supplier Power Regimes*, Routledge, London.

Cox, A., Ireland, P., Lonsdale, C., Sanderson, J. and Watson, G. (2003), *Supply Chain Management: A Guide to Best Practice*, Financial Times-Prentice Hall, London.

Cox, A., Lonsdale, C., Sanderson, J. and Watson, G. (2004a), *Business Relationships for Competitive Advantage: Managing Alignment and Misalignment in Buyer and Supplier Transactions*, Palgrave Macmillan, Basingstoke.

Cox, A., Sanderson, J. and Watson, G. (2000), *Power Regimes: Mapping the DNA of Business and Supply Chain Relationships*, Earlsgate Press, Stratford-upon-Avon.

Cox, A. and Thompson, I. (1998), *Contracting for Business Success*, Thomas Telford, London.

Cox, A. and Townsend, M. (1998), *Strategic Procurement in Construction*, Thomas Telford, London.

Cox, A., Watson, G., Lonsdale, C., and Sanderson, J. (2004b) 'Managing appropriately in power regimes: relationship and performance management in 12 supply chain cases', *Supply Chain Management: An International Journal*, **9**(5), pp. 357–371.

DETR (1998), *Rethinking Construction*, DETR, London.

Emerson, R. E. (1962), 'Power-dependence relations', *American Sociological Review*, **27**(1), pp. 31–41.

Godfrey, K. A. (ed.) (1996), *Partnering in Design and Construction*, McGraw-Hill, New York, NY, USA.

Gummesson, E. (1987), 'The new marketing: developing long-term interactive relationships', *Long Range Planning*, **20**(4), pp. 10–20.

Gummesson, E. (1997), 'Relationship marketing as a paradigm shift: some conclusions from the 30R approach', *Management Decision*, **53**(4), pp. 267–272.

Gummesson, E. (1999), *Total Relationship Marketing*, Butterworth-Heinemann, Oxford.

Hellard, R. B. (1995), *Project Partnering: Principles and Practice*, Thomas Telford, London.

Hines, P. (1994), *Creating World Class Suppliers*, Pitman, London.

Hinks, A. J., Allen, S. and Cooper, R. D. (1996), 'Adversaries or partners? Developing best practice for construction industry relationships', in Langford, D. A. and Retik, A, (eds.), *The Organisation and Management of Construction Industry: Shaping Theory and Practice*, E & FN Spon, London.

Holti, R. and Standing, H. (1996), *Partnering as Inter-related Technical and Organisational Change*, Tavistock, London.

Ireland, P. (2004), 'Managing appropriately in construction power regimes: understanding the impact of regularity in the project environment', *Supply Chain Management: An International Journal*, **9**(5), pp. 372–382.

Koskela, L. (1997), 'Lean production in construction', in Alarcón, L. F. (ed.), *Lean Construction*, AA Balkema, Rotterdam, Netherlands.

Latham, M. (1994), *Constructing the Team*, HMSO, London.

Lamming, R. C. (1993), *Beyond Partnership*, Prentice Hall, New York, NY, USA.

Lamming R. C., Caldwell, N. D., Harrison, D. A. and Philips, W. (2001), 'Transparency in supplier relationships: concepts and practice', *Journal of Supply Chain Management*, **37**, Fall, pp. 4–10.

Macbeth, D. and Ferguson, N. (1994), *Partnership Sourcing*, Pitman, London.

Marx, K. (1967), *Capital, Vol. 1*, International Publishers, New York, NY, USA.

McGeorge, W. D. and Palmer, A. (1997), *Construction Management – New Directions*, Blackwell Science, London.

Ng, S., Rose, T. M., Mak, M. and Chen, S. E. (2002), 'Problematic issues associated with project partnering: the contractor perspective', *International Journal of Project Management*, **20**(6), pp. 437–449.

Pfeffer, J. and Salancik, G. R. (1978), *The External Control of Organizations: A Resource Dependency Perspective*, Harper & Row, New York, NY, USA.

Porter, M. E. (1990), *Competitive Strategy*, Free Press, New York, NY, USA.

Saad, M., Jones, M. and James, P. (2002), 'A review of the progress towards the adoption of supply chain management in construction', *European Journal of Purchasing and Supply Management*, **8**(3), pp. 173–183.

Sako, M. (1992), *Prices, Quality and Trust*, Cambridge University Press, Cambridge.

Smyth, H. J. (2005), 'Procurement push and marketing pull in supply chain management: the conceptual contribution of relationship marketing as a driver in project financial performance', *Journal of Financial Management of Property and Construction*, **10**(1), pp. 33–44.

Thompson, P. J. and Sanders, S. R. (1998), 'Partnering continuum', *Journal of Management in Engineering*, **14**(5), pp. 73–78.

Turner, J. R. and Müller, R. (2003), 'On the nature of the project as a temporary organisation', *International Journal of Project Management*, **21**(1), pp. 1–8.

Vrijhoef, R. and Koskela, L. (2000), 'The four roles of supply chain management in construction', *European Journal of Purchasing and Supply Management*, **6**(3/4), pp. 169–178.

Womack, J. P., Jones, D. T. and Roos, D. (1990), *The Machine that Changed the World*, Rawson Associates, New York, NY, USA.

Womack, J. P. and Jones, D. T. (1996), *Lean Thinking*, Simon Schuster, New York, NY, USA.

3

The problem of win–win in construction management: feasible relationship and performance outcomes

3.1 Introduction

Although all companies are involved in dyadic exchange relationships in markets, and also directly and indirectly in the multiple markets that exist in supply chain networks, this does not mean that they can all manage within them in the same ways. While some companies may be able to develop proactive relationship and performance management strategies that extend throughout the markets within their supply chain power regimes, other actors may only be able to develop reactive strategies that operate at the dyadic (buyer and supplier) market level. When this occurs the limits on action normally arise because of non-conducive internal and external power and leverage situations for the companies involved (Cox *et al.*, 2003, 2004). It seems clear, therefore, that although the proactive approaches associated with *supplier development* and *supply chain management* can make a significant contribution to relationship and performance practice, the idea that future business success in construction will be based primarily on the adoption of such approaches is misguided in the extreme.

This is because, as we saw earlier, the standard structures of demand and supply in construction supply chains and markets often limit the scope for buyers and/or suppliers to develop proactive and long-term collaborative ways of working together. This does not mean that it is impossible for construction buyers and suppliers, who have the power levers of *buyer dominance*, *supplier dominance* or *interdependence*, to develop such ways of working. Such approaches can be developed and may turn out to be highly effective mechanisms for performance improvement, but these approaches are not feasible unless a relatively high volume and regular, or frequent, demand and supply structure is in place. Only with this in place is it possible for buyers to provide suppliers with the necessary commercial incentives to encourage both the buyer and the supplier to make the necessary investments of time, resource and money to make a proactive approach work (Ireland, 2004).

Unfortunately, for the vast majority of actors in construction supply chains and markets this virtuous circle of regular high volume demand, with standard requirements and a relatively stable and secure supply market, does not exist and cannot be created, whatever the best intentions of those involved. This means that reactive relationship and performance management approaches are normally the best that will be achievable. This is because demand is normally infrequent or one-off and supply markets are often highly contested with limited scope for long-term supplier differentiation and stability.

In such circumstances it is very difficult for proactive approaches to be adopted, but there is a further problem in the effective management of relationships and performance in construction that impacts on both reactive and proactive approaches in equal measure. Most writers who have espoused the benefits of proactive partnering normally do so because they believe that these approaches achieve superior outcomes for both parties to the exchange when compared with more reactive and arm's-length ways of working. For most writers proactive and highly collaborative relationships based on trust and transparency are regarded as a win–win for both parties to the exchange. We take issue with this argument and contend that, despite the claims made by many writers, for buyers and suppliers win–win outcomes (in which both parties simultaneously fully achieve the maximisation of everything they objectively or ideally desire) are not feasible. This proposition is underpinned by a relatively simple argument.

There is a fundamental problem for buyers and sellers associated with the non-commensurability of their objective economic or commercial interests. The search for profits (*value capture*) is the basic rationale for all companies when they enter into dyadic exchange relationships as suppliers. In direct contrast, organisations, when they act as buyers, seek to minimise their total costs of ownership (and therefore the levels of profits that are achievable for the supplier) relative to a given level of functional performance from the supplier. This non-commensurability of interests ensures that all buyer and supplier exchange is, objectively speaking, essentially contested. It also demonstrates how the search for an 'ideal' form of mutuality (a win–win) is impossible, as the 'ideal' outcome possible for a buyer is not commensurable with the 'ideal' outcome possible for a supplier. This leads to the conclusion that, in business in general and construction in particular, the task of each party in an exchange must be to maximise their performance outcomes given the power and leverage circumstances they experience, and not to search for illusory win–win outcomes (Cox, 2004a, b).

Given this, as we shall see, if a win–win in which both parties achieve their 'ideal' performance outcomes is not feasible, then buyers and suppliers have to recognise, in an objective sense, that exchange will always be contested. This means that whatever performance outcome is arrived at in any relationship there will normally (unless one party has actually achieved their 'ideal' position) be a superior alternative outcome that one or both parties to the exchange would prefer. If this is the case, then all relationships (whether long-term and collaborative or short-term and arm's-length) can only ever be temporary accommodations between two actors whose interests are inherently in conflict. When a buyer and supplier interact in these circumstances the best that can be achieved will be either a win for one party and a partial win or lose for the other, or, what appears to be the case in the majority of business relationships, both parties achieve a partial win.

Mutuality in buyer and supplier relationships does not mean, therefore, that both parties simultaneously achieve their ideal performance outcomes (a *positive-sum* or a win–win outcome). It means instead that the outcome is *nonzero-sum*. This means that it can accommodate performance outcomes that involve win–partial win, partial win–partial win and partial win–win. In these mutuality outcomes, except in the case of partial win–partial win, one party clearly captures far more value than the other, ensuring that tension and conflict remain in the exchange relationship. As we shall see, however, even in partial win–partial win outcomes there is still scope for conflict and tension because one party can achieve more than the other in relation to their 'ideal' performance outcomes.

By adopting this way of thinking about relationship management approaches and performance outcomes, and assuming that any approach will be preferred by actors if it allows them to maximise their objective economic interests (i.e. their ideal performance goals), it allows us to understand why *zero-sum* (win–lose) outcomes can be perfectly acceptable (and in some circumstances preferable to *nonzero-sum* outcomes) for any party in a relationship. If the game that is being played operationally and commercially is one-off – which is often the case in the project environment that dominates construction – it is obvious that maximising one's own short-term interests will be a tempting prospect for both parties. Since much of construction relationship management is not based on repeat games (frequent demand and supply requirements involving high levels of bilateral dependency operationally over time) opportunism and the pursuit of win–lose outcomes can be seen as perfectly rational and logical relationship strategies in this industry. This is true, even though for some actors, who have relatively high levels of construction demand and on a relatively constant basis, there are sometimes preferable long-term *nonzero-sum* (win–partial win and partial win–partial win) outcomes.

3.2 Current thinking about win–win and mutuality in business and construction management

Part of the task in writing this book has been the desire to demystify the current thinking in construction about the superiority of highly collaborative proactive approaches, based on trust and transparency, when compared with more traditional ways of working based on reactive and highly opportunistic exchange. The recent fad in favour of partnering approaches to construction tends to assume that this is a superior approach because it creates win–win outcomes that provide higher levels of performance for both parties to those that can be achieved by the use of more traditional reactive approaches. In our view this may sometimes be true, but, in other circumstances, this may not be the case and more traditional and reactive approaches may provide superior performance outcomes for one or both parties than any proactive approach currently available.

Many business and construction management writers argue that mutuality (win–win rather than win–lose) is the only real basis for sustainable business relationships and performance optimisation between buyers and sellers. The quotes below demonstrate this orthodoxy.

'An intention on both sides to achieve an agreement on win–win terms so that both parties can see why it is in their own interest to ensure implementation of each component precisely as agreed.' (Carlisle and Parker, 1989, p. 36)

'... the principled negotiation method ... (focuses) ... on basic interests, mutually satisfying options, and fair standards.' (Fisher and Ury, 1991, p. 14)

'The relationship is based on trust, dedication to common goals, and an understanding of each other's individual expectations and values. Expected benefits include improved efficiency and cost effectiveness, increased opportunity for innovation, and the continuous improvement of quality products and services.' (CII, 1991, p. iv)

'A partnership will not succeed unless there is mutual trust and this is only achieved through the parties acting consistently with their joint objectives.'
(Harback et al., 1994, p. 24)

'Mutual commitment . . . creates opportunities; relationships are mutually demanding besides being mutually rewarding.' (Håkansson and Snehota, 1995, p. 25)

' . . . partnering . . . should involve a commitment between firms to cooperate . . . based on the premise that this will allow each organization to meet its own business objectives more effectively, at the same time as achieving the objectives of the project as a whole.'
(Bennett and Jayes, 1995, p. 2)

'The basic philosophy underlying relationship marketing is . . . the establishment of mutually beneficial partnerships with customers.' (Christopher, 1997, p. 29)

' . . . the need . . . [is] . . . to establish collaborative customer-supplier relationships founded on cooperation for mutual benefit.' (Hines et al., 2000, p. 274)

'Cooperative behaviour describes a series of [collaborative] moves . . . that generally leads to an integrative (win/win) conclusion. Cooperative behaviour is characterized by reciprocal collaborative moves.' (Lazar, 2000, p. 72)

There are two criticisms one can make about this view. First, there is a presumption that performance optimisation can only be achieved for buyers and sellers if their relationships are sustainable over time. This may not always be true because buyers and sellers often enter into relationships in which they have no desire for long-term sustainability and, in such circumstances, often have no qualms about win–lose outcomes. Second, even when buyers and sellers need long-term and sustainable relationships, to argue that both sides must gain something from the relationship does not tell us exactly what the win–win is in any relationship. It is perfectly conceivable that both sides can gain something from a relationship, even though one party gains a disproportionate share of the value compared with the other, and even though conflict remains.

The problem with current writing on business relationship and performance management is that either it suffers from a normative bias in favour of defining mutuality (win–win) in terms of equity (equal benefit) and order (conflict resolution), or it uses the concept in such a vague and poorly defined way that it can mean anything that the author or reader wishes. These two problems are discussed below. The first series of quotations demonstrate the equity/order bias; the second demonstrate the general vagueness of current conceptual definitions.

Equity/order biased interpretations

' . . . the states of war . . . (between suppliers and their customers) . . . can only be ended when all of the parties willingly negotiate a set of principles to guide their joint behaviour in the future and then devise a mechanism for mutual verification that everyone is abiding by the principles.' (Womack and Jones, 1996, p. 277)

'[Transaction Cost Economics] view(s) governance (of transactions) as the means by which to infuse order, thereby mitigate conflict and realize mutual gains.'
(Williamson, 2000, p. 12)

'Partnering involves two or more organizations working together to improve performance through agreeing mutual objectives, deriving a way of resolving any disputes and

committing themselves to continuous improvement, measuring progress and sharing the gains.' (DETR, 1998, p. 12)

The problem with these interpretations is threefold. First, they assume, incorrectly, that performance optimisation cannot be achieved if conflict exists in a relationship. Second, they do not specify how both sides in a transaction can win. It is just assumed that, since relationships cannot be sustained unless both sides gain from the relationship, long-term sustainability is only possible if both parties win. This is tautological reasoning. Third, why, if one party to an exchange is more equal than another, does it make commercial sense for them to adopt an equity-based approach? Surely relationships can be sustained even with inequity and conflict? Writers who provide only very vague definitions of the concept compound these problems of deductive logic.

Vague definitions

'Win–win . . . means . . . a situation in which each issue requiring resolution has been settled in a way which meets the needs of both parties, even though either, or both, may have been hoping for more.' (Carlisle and Parker, 1989, pp. 35–36)

'Credible contracting is very much an exercise in farsighted contracting, whereby the parties look ahead, recognize hazards, and devise hazard mitigating responses – thereby to realise mutual gain.' (Williamson, 1999, p. 1090)

'Mutuality is a measure of how much a company is prepared to give up their own goals or intentions in order to increase the positive outcomes of others and, through this, increase its own ultimate well-being.' (Ford et al., 2002, p. 82)

'The partnering . . . method aims to replace adversarial relationships between client and contractor with a situation where the two parties work closely together towards shared objectives and a win/win outcome.' (Watson, 1994, p. 32)

The major problem with these definitions is that they do not specify in a robust and rigorous way the terms of any exchange between a buyer and seller. To argue that the needs of both parties must be met (or that they must make mutual gains) tells us nothing about what these needs or gains are, or how much of them must be met for either party to find the exchange acceptable. To be able to understand whether or not a relationship can be sustained (or indeed whether or not it must be sustained) it is necessary to specify more clearly what it is that is exchanged by both parties in a relationship both operationally and commercially, and what level of performance must be achieved for either party for them to judge the relationship outcome a success.

3.3 The essentially contested nature of dyadic exchange

To understand what a business transaction involves requires a basic understanding of what the goals of buyers and suppliers are when they enter into exchange relationships. At its simplest, the buyer wishes to exchange money for goods and/or services, and the supplier wishes to receive money in return (Cox *et al.*, 2004). This describes the basic exchange relationship but it does not describe in detail the relative *value for money* that the buyer achieves, or the relative *value from supply* that the supplier receives. To understand this it is necessary to define what these two concepts mean in detail by providing a clear specification of what it is in practice that firms seek when they act as buyers and as suppliers.

The fundamental problem for the analysis of specific business transactions between buyers and suppliers is that they have dissimilar operational and commercial goals transactionally. The buyer is normally concerned operationally with the *functionality* (performance, quality, on-time delivery etc.) of the goods and/or services provided, and commercially with their *total costs of ownership*. The buyer is, therefore, always seeking to maximise the value for money it receives from the supplier by, ideally, increasing functionality and reducing the total costs of ownership. When buyers enter into exchange relationships with suppliers, if they cannot achieve their ideal, then they have to make decisions about potential trade-offs between these two operational and commercial ideals. These preference trade-offs are outlined in Figure 3.1.

The choices facing suppliers when they supply goods and/or services are not the same. The supplier is, in general, interested in making profits, but delivers goods and/or services to increase operationally the revenue received from a specific buyer. The supplier is also concerned commercially with maximising the price (or margins) that can be obtained from the delivery of a particular product and/or service functionality. The ideal for the supplier is, therefore, always to increase revenue and to increase returns. The trade-offs facing suppliers, if they cannot achieve this ideal performance outcome, from the delivery of a particular functionality to a buyer are presented in Figure 3.2.

The issue of how buyers and suppliers rank order their preferences in any exchange relationship is a complex issue and cannot be discussed here in detail (Cox, 2004b), but a moment's reflection will indicate that there must be an inevitable tension and conflict in business relationships. This arises because of the dissimilarity of operational and commercial drivers for buyers and

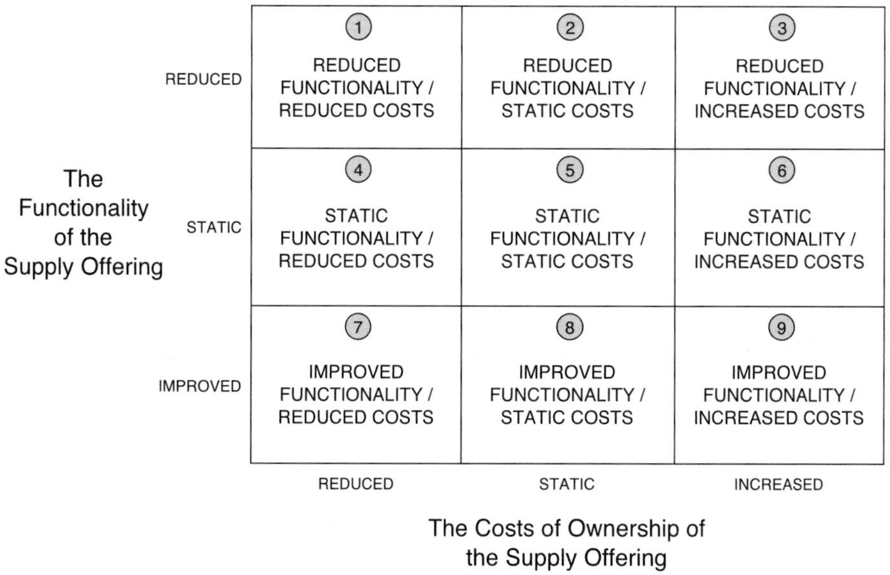

		REDUCED	STATIC	INCREASED
The Functionality of the Supply Offering	REDUCED	① REDUCED FUNCTIONALITY / REDUCED COSTS	② REDUCED FUNCTIONALITY / STATIC COSTS	③ REDUCED FUNCTIONALITY / INCREASED COSTS
	STATIC	④ STATIC FUNCTIONALITY / REDUCED COSTS	⑤ STATIC FUNCTIONALITY / STATIC COSTS	⑥ STATIC FUNCTIONALITY / INCREASED COSTS
	IMPROVED	⑦ IMPROVED FUNCTIONALITY / REDUCED COSTS	⑧ IMPROVED FUNCTIONALITY / STATIC COSTS	⑨ IMPROVED FUNCTIONALITY / INCREASED COSTS
		REDUCED	STATIC	INCREASED

The Costs of Ownership of the Supply Offering

Figure 3.1 Value for money options for the buyer (Source: Cox et al. (2004), p. 53)

53

	① REDUCED REVENUE / REDUCED RETURNS	② REDUCED REVENUE / STATIC RETURNS	③ REDUCED REVENUE / INCREASED RETURNS
REDUCED			
STATIC	④ STATIC REVENUE / REDUCED RETURNS	⑤ STATIC REVENUE / STATIC RETURNS	⑥ STATIC REVENUE / INCREASED RETURNS
IMPROVED	⑦ IMPROVED REVENUE / REDUCED RETURNS	⑧ IMPROVED REVENUE / STATIC RETURNS	⑨ IMPROVED REVENUE / INCREASED RETURNS
	REDUCED	**STATIC**	**INCREASED**

Share of
Buyer's
Revenue
Received by
Supplier

Returns Received from
Servicing Buyer's Account

*Figure 3.2 Value from
supply options for the
supplier (Source: Cox et al.
(2004), p. 62)*

suppliers when they enter into transactions. The problem is outlined in summary in
Figure 3.3.

The 'ideal' performance outcome for a buyer is to achieve increased functionality
and reduced total costs of ownership. For the buyer to receive this requires,
however, that the supplier does not achieve its 'ideal' performance outcome. For
the supplier this is a constantly increasing share of the revenue available from the
customer, with the ability to increase prices so that above normal returns are
earned for any given level of functionality provided. That these two ideal outcomes
are not fully commensurable should be clear because the pricing 'ideal' of the
supplier is a direct cost of ownership for the buyer. Some writers confuse this
issue by arguing that both parties should concentrate on growing 'the size of the
cake' rather than squabbling over how it should be divided (Carlisle and Parker,
1989). There are two problems with this argument. First, how 'the cake' should

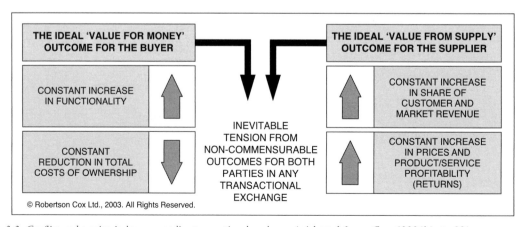

Figure 3.3 Conflict and tension in buyer–supplier transactional exchange (Adapted from: Cox (2004b), p. 92)

be divided is still an issue even if it grows. Second, the 'ideal' value outcomes for a buyer and supplier remain the same (not fully commensurable) irrespective of 'the size of the cake'.

Thus, if buyers are pursuing their 'ideal' performance outcome they should be ensuring that suppliers pass value to them in the form of increasing functionality and lower total costs of ownership – whatever 'the size of the cake' on offer. To achieve this they should ensure that suppliers operate in fully contested markets, where they can never achieve monopoly pricing or earn above normal returns (Smith, 1776). On the other hand, if suppliers are pursuing their 'ideal' outcome, they should close markets to their competitors and create sustainable isolating mechanisms that allow them to premium price and earn above normal returns (Rumelt, 1987). If a supplier can achieve this performance outcome the buyer will be unable to obtain reductions in the total costs of ownership, with suppliers only ever earning break-even or low normal returns. Given this, it is clear that there must, objectively speaking, be an irresolvable conflict in business relationships.

3.4 On the commensurability of value capture and mutuality

Given this conflict of objective commercial interests in transactions, it is clear that a win–win (ideal mutuality) in which both parties simultaneously achieve their ideal performance outcomes is not feasible. Despite this, more limited forms of *mutuality* based on *nonzero-sum* outcomes are feasible in buyer and supplier relationships. Figure 3.4 shows that when buyers and suppliers enter into exchange relationships they may, or they may not, fully achieve their goals of *value for money* (the buyer) and *value from supply* (the supplier). In other words, the buyer may, or may not, achieve the desired improvement in functionality and/or reductions in the total costs of ownership. The supplier may, or may not, achieve the desired increases in revenue or in pricing and profit levels.

As Figure 3.4 demonstrates, when buyers and suppliers interact who wins or loses from the exchange relationship must depend on the balance of power between both parties (Cox, 1997; Cox *et al.*, 2000, 2002, 2003, 2004). Thus, if *buyer dominance* occurs in a relationship, and if the parties to the exchange both understand the rules of the game, then it is likely that the buyer will win and the supplier will achieve either only a partial win or a lose outcome. On the other hand, if *supplier dominance* occurs, and the same understanding of the rules of the game pertains, then the outcome will favour the supplier. If *interdependence* occurs then both parties will achieve a partial win–partial win outcome. If *independence* occurs then a win–partial win favouring the buyer or partial win–partial win will be the outcome (Cox *et al.*, 2004). This shows that there may be some performance outcomes that provide the 'ideal' for one party but not for the other party. This immediately sensitises us to the fact that equivalence of outcomes is not a pre-requisite for either party to achieve their own 'ideal'.

Figure 3.4 shows that there are nine transactional outcomes that can occur in buyer and supplier exchange. Only one of these outcomes fully equates with the 'ideal' (mutually beneficial) concept of win–win in business relationships. This is the outcome, described in Cell C in the matrix, where both the buyer and supplier fully achieve their performance goals. This outcome can be termed an *ideal normative win–win outcome*. Objectively speaking it is not, however, a feasible performance

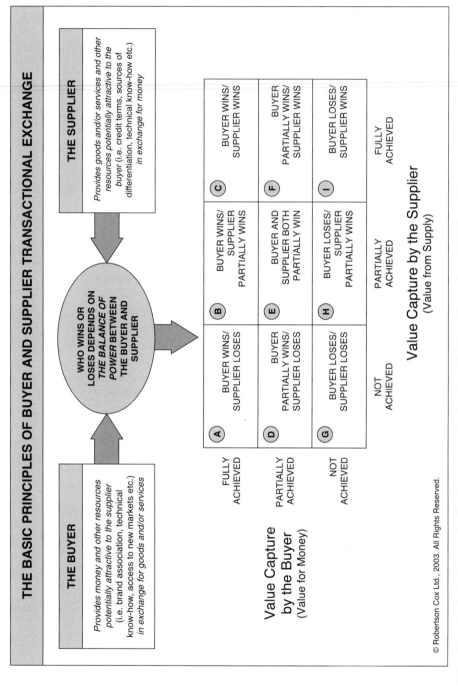

Figure 3.4 Possible outcomes for buyers and sellers from transactional exchange (Adapted from: Cox (2004b), p. 95)

outcome in exchange relationships due to the inevitable conflict between the buyer's search for cost reductions and the supplier's search for above normal returns.

Mutuality is, however, a feasible outcome, but not in ideal normative terms. Mutuality can still occur when one party achieves all of its ideal goals and the other party achieves some of its goals, or when neither party achieves its ideal but both parties achieve some of their goals. It is these *nonzero-sum* outcomes involving win–partial win, partial win–partial win and partial win–win (represented by Cells B, E and F in the matrix) rather than the *positive-sum* or win–win outcome (represented by Cell C) that encompass what is actually meant by mutuality in business relationships.

All three of these outcomes provide the basis for long-term sustainable business relationships, even though one party achieves their 'ideal' in two of them (win–partial win and partial win–win) and neither party achieves their 'ideal' in one of them (partial win–partial win). The problem is, however, that none of these three scenarios is simultaneously 'ideal' for both parties and conflict still exists objectively in the relationship, which cannot be avoided. This is because, even in Cell E, where both parties only partially achieve their performance goals, each has an alternative outcome that they can be expected to prefer if it is available to them (Cells B and F).

Buyers will, therefore, normally prefer Cell B, followed by Cell E and then Cell F. This is because in Cell B the buyer fully achieves its 'ideal' performance outcome, while the supplier does not. This normally means lower costs of ownership and/or higher levels of functionality for the buyer when compared with the outcome achieved by operating in Cell E, where the buyer's goals are only partially met. The worst mutuality outcome for a buyer is Cell F. This is because in this scenario the buyer only partially achieves its goals, while the supplier fully achieves its. This implies that the total costs of ownership for the buyer will normally be higher and the level of functionality received will tend to be lower in Cell F than in Cell E and, in particular, in Cell B – the most favoured outcome for the buyer.

The problem for those who argue that conflict can be eradicated from business transactions through trust (Sako, 1992), or by creating order-generating governance mechanisms (Williamson, 1996), is that the rank order preferences of the supplier for the three *mutuality* outcomes is the opposite of the buyer's preferences. The supplier's objective rank order preference is for Cell F first, as this outcome maximises the share of revenue and profits from the transaction. Suppliers will then normally prefer Cell E to Cell B because in the former the buyer does not fully achieve its desired functionality or cost reduction goals, which it is able to achieve in Cell B. For this reason, Cell B is the least desirable of the three *mutuality outcomes* for the supplier.

This also indicates that trust and order-generating governance mechanisms are unlikely to provide all of the beneficial outcomes suggested for the buyer and supplier. This is because, even if buyers and suppliers concentrate on growing 'the size of the cake' together, they will still have to decide how it is to be divided. Thus, it can be expected that, if there are superior choices for buyer and suppliers, they are likely to choose those outcomes that maximise their position relative to one another. In this situation a permanent war of manoeuvre, in which both parties seek to move relationships to their most advantageous position relative to one another, must be the underlying reality of business relationships and transactional exchange.

The fact that *mutuality* does not eradicate tension or conflict is an important conclusion, but there is a further insight about business relationships that has to be acknowledged. This relates to the fact that *zero-sum* (win–lose or partial win–lose) outcomes can be perfectly acceptable for buyers and suppliers in many types of transactional exchange. Thus, each of the four remaining *zero-sum outcomes* (in Cells A, D, H and I) is not an outdated practice that should be consigned to the dustbin of business practice. On the contrary, each one of these outcomes occurs regularly in business, and this must be a reflection of the appropriateness of these ways of managing transactions under specific power and leverage circumstances. Indeed, one can go so far as to argue that under certain circumstances for one party in an exchange some *zero-sum* outcomes may be preferable to *nonzero-sum* outcomes.

If we consider first the choices available to buyers, it is clear that in comparison with Cell B outcomes (the preferred *nonzero-sum* option for the buyer) Cell A outcomes may be preferable in some circumstances. This is because in Cell A the buyer fully achieves its ideal performance goals, but the supplier does not achieve any of its performance goals at all. This implies that the costs of ownership will be reduced because the supplier is making no profits, even though the supplier is also forced to improve functionality. One can argue that, if this situation were sustainable for the supplier, it would be a superior outcome for the buyer than would be Cell B (or any other of the cells available). The problem with this outcome for the buyer is, of course, that it is unlikely to be achievable on a sustainable basis unless the supplier is prepared to undertake a 'loss leadership' approach. This does not detract, however, from the argument that there must be circumstances under which Cell A (win–lose) is the most desirable option for the buyer when compared with all other possible options.

The same logic applies to Cell D, where the buyer partially achieves its performance goals but the supplier does not. Clearly this approach may also be preferable to the options available to the buyer in Cells E and F. Once again, however, the problem for the buyer is the sustainability of the relationship if the supplier is not capable of sustaining a 'loss leadership' approach over time.

The supplier faces similar choices when considering these options. The supplier might realistically find the *zero-sum* option in Cell I a better leverage position than the first choice (Cell F) under some *nonzero-sum* options. In Cell I the supplier is normally dominant in power terms and able to impose quality and price trade-offs in the market. In this situation the buyer will be a price and quality receiver, and the supplier can be expected to make above normal profits. The major problem for the supplier is also whether this is sustainable. If the supplier believes that it has sufficiently robust isolating mechanisms to sustain its power in the relationship, then this may be a preferable option to Cell F, where the supplier normally has to increase functionality and/or reduce pricing and profitability demands on the buyer. Similarly, the supplier might be expected to prefer Cell H to Cells E and B, because the buyer in both these options is able to reduce the leverage of the supplier. The same issues arise here for the supplier about sustainability.

One can conclude, therefore, that some *zero-sum* outcomes (especially those in Cell A for the buyer and Cell I for the supplier) may be preferable to each of three *nonzero-sum* (*mutuality*) outcomes in Cells B, E and F. The only major problem for the *nonzero-sum* options is that, other things being equal, they may be less sustainable transactions over time than the three *mutuality* outcomes. The major reason for this is because one side loses while the other either partially or fully wins. This does not mean, however, that *zero-sum* outcomes (Cells A, D, H and I) cannot be sustained for a considerable period of time.

Despite what some writers believe about the need for *mutuality* in exchange, buyers have no great difficulty operating in Cell A or D if a supplier is willing to operate with them in this situation. This might occur when a supplier wishes to provide a 'loss leader' to drive other competitors out of the market; or wishes to develop brand association with a major customer and attempt to recoup profits from premium pricing with other buyers in the market. It can also be possible for buyers to transact with suppliers, operating in highly competitive markets, which must 'loss lead' to win the business, but then have to withdraw. However, the contested nature of the supply market means that there are sufficient suppliers available to allow the buyer to continuously behave opportunistically against them individually. Similarly, suppliers do not have a problem operating in Cell I or H if they can impose prices and functionality standards without fear that buyers can source elsewhere.

If this is true then the best that a buyer or a supplier can achieve may in fact be to find exchange partners who are willing to operate in *zero-sum* rather than in *nonzero-sum* outcomes. It all depends on what the risks are to the buyer or supplier of the power circumstances moving against it if it continues to operate in this fashion. For the buyer this could eventually mean that the supplier goes out of business and it finds itself with a very restricted supply market to source from. The supplier, on the other hand, might drive away customers or force them to seek substitutes, consider insourcing, or the direct development of competitors. Despite these risks from the excessive use of buyer and supplier power, it can be argued that a great deal of business activity occurs in these circumstances and that, if the down-side risks can be avoided, these may be highly desirable strategies for buyers and suppliers to pursue.

3.5 Appropriateness in construction relationship management and performance optimisation

Williamson (2000) has argued that all transactions must involve the 'Commons triple': 'The ultimate unit of activity ... (transaction) ... must contain in itself the three principles of conflict, mutuality and order.' (Commons, 1932, p. 4)

The analysis presented here takes issue with this view and argues instead that, while transactions always involve conflict, they do not necessarily contain *mutuality* and order. If the 'ideal' goals of the buyer and the supplier are non-commensurable, this means that win–win outcomes are an illusion and that *ideal normative mutuality* in business relationships can never be achieved. This realisation means that it is unlikely that 'order' can ever be achieved in transactional exchange, if we mean by it the avoidance of conflict and the development of *ideal normative mutuality*. The best that can be said for 'order' in business transactions is that both parties accept the terms of the exchange entered into and agree to abide by the legal (contractual) framework that governs the relationship. Beyond this it is clear that, if *positive-sum* or win–win outcomes that are simultaneously 'ideal' for both parties are not achievable, transactions must always be the site of a continuous war of manoeuvre, with each party striving to achieve their 'ideal' goals in constantly changing circumstances.

Despite this, *mutuality* or *nonzero-sum* performance outcomes are clearly appropriate relationship management choices, but this does not mean that they are always present in transactions – nor should one argue that they should be. The problem is that *mutuality* outcomes need not occur in transactions for exchange relationships to function. It is perfectly possible for buyers and suppliers to view *zero-sum* outcomes equally as desirable as *mutuality* outcomes, if not more so in some cases. The real issue is the sustainability of the relationship with the other party in the transaction. If the buyer and supplier can find exchange partners who are happy to operate in *zero-sum* scenarios in the short-term, and there is no difficulty in finding similar volunteers in the future, then *zero-sum* can be a highly appropriate way of operating.

This allows us to question the current view that win–win or *mutuality* is a superior relationship management approach to *zero-sum* options. *Nonzero-sum* and *zero-sum* outcomes are nothing more than choices for parties to an exchange. Which of these options is the most appropriate depends on the circumstances in which buyers and suppliers operate. If one party believes that there are more congenial *nonzero-sum* or *zero-sum* relationship management outcomes available to it then there is the likelihood that it will move to those relationship approaches that allow it to get as close as possible to its 'ideal' performance outcomes. If it does not do so then it is incompetent from a business and performance optimisation point of view – it is forgoing an advantage that it could have achieved with another party.

This insight fundamentally challenges transaction cost economising approaches to relationship management. These approaches hold that exchange partners should seek ways to provide mutually beneficial credible contractual commitments against opportunism in the interest of economising on the cost of transactions (Williamson, 1985). It would appear that this is a fundamental misunderstanding of what actually occurs in transactional exchange in the real world. While reducing the costs of transactions may be one driver for a buyer, it is not the only one. Buyers are sometimes more interested in increasing functionality than they are in reducing the costs of ownership. Furthermore, it is debatable whether suppliers are primarily interested in reducing transaction costs. Indeed, there may well be many circumstances in which suppliers are just as interested in increasing the costs of transactions in order to maximise price, revenue and profitability. It seems clear that Williamson may have fundamentally misunderstood the basic principles of transactional exchange – transaction cost economising may work for buyers in some circumstances, but it is not clear how this approach assists suppliers in the achievement of their 'ideal' performance outcomes.

The analysis presented here assumes, therefore, that conflict between the parties to a transaction is inevitable and unavoidable (as is opportunism). This implies that buyers and suppliers must have resources that provide them with the ability to achieve their *value for money* or *value from supply* goals. In so far as one party to an exchange can achieve the realisation of its 'ideal' goals (in the non-commensurable conflict between these two potential outcomes), we can describe the players as powerful, relative to one another (Cox, 2004b). This means that buyer–supplier relationships do not require *mutuality* in order to function. On the contrary, they can operate in circumstances of conflict and manoeuvre, where both parties accept the current terms of any exchange, while constantly striving to achieve their 'ideal' performance outcomes in the future. This implies that neither *nonzero-sum* (*mutuality*) nor *zero-sum* outcomes are preferable optimisation choices.

This is because either type of outcome may be the most appropriate way of managing a relationship, depending on the prevailing balance of power between the buyer and supplier now, and in the future.

The discussion that follows in the sixteen chapters in Parts B1 and B2 demonstrates that, in the real world of business and construction management, not only are there cases in which buyers and suppliers operate reactively and proactively, but there is also evidence that each of these broad relationship management types can result in *nonzero-sum*, *zero-sum* and *negative-sum* (lose–lose) outcomes. This means that it is not so much the choice of relationship management approach that is crucial (i.e. whether it is reactive or proactive), but rather the type of performance outcome that results from its implementation. Thus, it is perfectly possible for buyers and suppliers in construction supply chains and markets to achieve their 'ideal' performance outcomes using reactive or proactive relationship management approaches.

The cases discussed in Parts B1 and B2 provide an overview of the range of relationship management approaches (means) and performance outcomes (ends) that can occur in construction supply chains and markets. The sixteen cases have been derived by linking together the eight feasible performance outcomes (ends), outlined in Figure 3.5, and the two basic relationship management approaches (means), reactive (*supplier selection* or *supply chain sourcing*) and proactive (*supplier development* or *supply chain management*), as discussed in Figure 2.1 in the previous chapter. The sixteen cases are outlined in Figure 3.6.

The cases show that all eight of the performance outcomes outlined in Figure 3.5 are feasible when either reactive or proactive relationship management approaches are implemented. What follows from this is a realisation that the current view that proactive approaches are superior in all cases to reactive approaches may be misguided. This is because, although proactive approaches do provide superior performance outcomes for some actors in construction supply chains and markets in particular circumstances, in other circumstances reactive approaches may be just as, if not more, successful in achieving desired performance outcomes.

In any case, the fact that many participants in construction supply chains and markets lack the necessary internal and external power levers will mean that they are only in a position to implement reactive approaches. This implies that it is not so much the type of approach that is selected that is important, but whether or not the approach that is selected is the most appropriate for the exchange party given the power and leverage situation in which it finds itself externally, and whether or not a company has the necessary internal competence and capability to deliver the appropriate reactive or proactive relationship management approach successfully.

What should also be transparent from a study of these sixteen construction case studies is that relationship management (whether reactive or proactive) may result in both parties only achieving something of what they value, but this is not always the case. Indeed, as the cases here show, sometimes one party can achieve all that it desires ideally and still sustain relationships with others that do not achieve everything they would prefer. Furthermore, there are many circumstances in construction when one party gains and the other does not, as well as circumstances in which both parties fail to achieve any of their desired goals. This means that the desire to pursue relationship management approaches that provide for equal performance benefits for the other exchange partner may, in some circumstances,

Value Capture by the Supplier (Value from Supply)

Value Capture by the Buyer (Value for Money)	NOT ACHIEVED	PARTIALLY ACHIEVED	FULLY ACHIEVED
FULLY ACHIEVED	**(A) BUYER WINS/ SUPPLIER LOSES** **Buyer** receives the maximum feasible increase in functionality and the maximum feasible reduction in total costs of ownership. **Supplier** makes a commercial loss or breaks even with a declining share of revenue	**(B) BUYER WINS/ SUPPLIER PARTIALLY WINS** **Buyer** receives the maximum feasible increase in functionality and the maximum feasible reduction in total costs of ownership **Supplier** earns rents (but not the maximum feasible) or normal returns, whether revenue is maximised or not	**(C) BUYER WINS/ SUPPLIER WINS** **Not Feasible** *This is because, irrespective of any increases in functionality, the maximum feasible reduction in total costs of ownership for the buyer must be at the expense of the ability of suppliers to earn the maximum feasible rents*
PARTIALLY ACHIEVED	**(D) BUYER PARTIALLY WINS/ SUPPLIER LOSES** **Buyer** can receive all feasible functionality and total cost of ownership trade-offs, except the maximum feasible increase in functionality with the maximum feasible reduction in total costs of ownership at the same time, or a decrease in functionality with an increase in the total cost of ownership at the same time **Supplier** makes a commercial loss or breaks even, with a declining share of revenue	**(E) BUYER AND SUPPLIER BOTH PARTIALLY WIN** **Buyer** can receive all feasible functionality and total cost of ownership trade-offs, except the maximum feasible increase in functionality with the maximum feasible reduction in total costs of ownership at the same time, or a decrease in functionality with an increase in the total costs of ownership at the same time **Supplier** earns rents (but not the maximum feasible) or normal returns, whether revenue is maximised or not	**(F) BUYER PARTIALLY WINS/ SUPPLIER WINS** **Buyer** can receive all feasible functionality and total cost of ownership trade-offs, except the maximum feasible increase in functionality with the maximum feasible reduction in total costs of ownership at the same time, or a decrease in functionality with an increase in the total costs of ownership at the same time **Supplier** earns the maximum feasible rents with the maximum feasible share of revenue through full market closure
NOT ACHIEVED	**(G) BUYER LOSES/ SUPPLIER LOSES** **Buyer** receives no, or a reduced, functionality and increased total costs of ownership **Supplier** makes a commercial loss or breaks even with a declining share of revenue	**(H) BUYER LOSES/ SUPPLIER PARTIALLY WINS** **Buyer** receives no, or a reduced, functionality and increased total costs of ownership **Supplier** earns rents (but not the maximum feasible) or normal returns, whether revenue is maximised or not	**(I) BUYER LOSES/ SUPPLIER WINS** **Buyer** receives no, or a reduced functionality and increased total costs of ownership **Supplier** earns the maximum feasible rents with the maximum feasible share of revenue through full market closure

Figure 3.5 Performance outcomes for buyers and suppliers (Source: Cox (2004b), p. 118)

Relationship Management Approach

Performance Outcome	REACTIVE (Supplier Section) (Supply Chain Sourcing)	PROACTIVE (Supplier Development) (Supply Chain Management)
Buyer wins Supplier wins	**Not Feasible**	**Not Feasible**
Buyer wins Supplier partially wins	Case 1	Case 9
Buyer wins Supplier loses	Case 2	Case 10
Buyer partially wins Supplier wins	Case 3	Case 11
Buyer partially wins Supplier partially wins	Case 4	Case 12
Buyer partially wins Supplier loses	Case 5	Case 13
Buyer loses Supplier wins	Case 6	Case 14
Buyer loses Supplier partially wins	Case 7	Case 15
Buyer loses Supplier loses	Case 8	Case 16

Figure 3.6 Sixteen construction relationship and performance management case studies

be misguided in the extreme. These issues are discussed in more detail in the concluding chapter in Part C.

References

Bennett, J. and Jayes, S. (1995), *Trusting the Team: The Best Practice Guide to Partnering in Construction*, Reading Construction Forum, Reading.

Carlisle, J. A. and Parker, R. C. (1989), *Beyond Negotiation*, John Wiley, Chichester.

Christopher, M. (1997), *Marketing Logistics,* Butterworth-Heinemann, Oxford.

CII (1991), *In Search of Partnering Excellence*, Construction Industry Institute, Special Publications, Austin, TX, USA.

Commons, J. R. (1932), 'The problem of correlating law, economics and ethics', *Wisconsin Law Review*, **8**(1), pp. 3–26.

Cox, A. (1997), *Business Success: A Way of Thinking About Strategy, Critical Supply Chain Assets and Operational Best Practice*, Earlsgate Press, Stratford-upon-Avon.

Cox, A. (2004a), 'Business relationship alignment: on the commensurability of value capture and mutuality in buyer and supplier exchange', *Supply Chain Management: An International Journal*, **9**(5), pp. 410–420.

Cox, A. (2004b), *Win–Win? The Paradox of Value and Interests in Business Relationships*, Earlsgate Press, Stratford-upon-Avon.

Cox, A., Ireland, P., Lonsdale, C., Sanderson, J. and Watson, G. (2002), *Supply Chains, Markets and Power: Mapping Buyer and Supplier Power Regimes*, Routledge, London.

Cox, A., Ireland, P., Lonsdale, C., Sanderson, J. and Watson, G. (2003), *Supply Chain Management: A Guide to Best Practice*, Financial Times–Prentice Hall, London.

Cox, A., Lonsdale, C., Sanderson, J. and Watson, G. (2004), *Business Relationships for Competitive Advantage: Managing Alignment and Misalignment in Buyer and Supplier Transactions*, Palgrave Macmillan, London.

Cox, A., Sanderson, J. and Watson, G. (2000), *Power Regimes: Mapping the DNA of Business and Supply Chain Relationships*, Earlsgate Press, Stratford-upon-Avon.

DETR (1998), *Rethinking Construction*, DETR, London.

Fisher, R. and Ury, W. (1991), *Getting to Yes*, Random Century, London.

Ford, D., Håkansson, H. and Johanson, J. (2002),'How do companies interact?', in Ford, D. (ed.), *Understanding Business Markets and Purchasing*, Thomson Learning, London.

Håkansson, H. and Snehota, I. (eds.) (1995), *Developing Relationships in Business Networks*, Routledge, London.

Harback, H. F., Basham, D. L. and Buhts, R. E. (1994), 'Partnering paradigm', *Journal of Management in Engineering*, **10**(1), pp. 23–27.

Hines, P., Lamming, P., Jones, D., Cousins, P. and Rich, N. (2000), *Value Stream Management: Strategy and Excellence in the Supply Chain*, Financial Times-Prentice Hall, London.

Ireland, P. (2004), 'Managing appropriately in construction power regimes: understanding the impact of regularity in the project environment', *Supply Chain Management: An International Journal*, **9**(5), pp. 372–382.

Lazar, F. D. (2000), 'Project partnering: improving the likelihood of win/win outcomes', *Journal of Management in Engineering*, **16**(2), pp. 71–83.

Rumelt, R. P. (1987), 'Theory, strategy and entrepreneurship', in Teece, D. (ed.), *The Competitive Challenge*, Harper & Row, New York, NY, USA.

Sako, M. (1992), *Prices, Quality and Trust*, Cambridge University Press, Cambridge.

Smith, A. (1776), *The Wealth of Nations*, Penguin Edition, 1985, Harmondsworth.

Watson, G. H. (1994), *Business Systems Engineering: Managing Breakthrough Changes From Productivity and Profit*, Wiley, New York, NY, USA.

Williamson, O. E. (1985), *The Economic Institutions of Capitalism*, Free Press, New York, NY, USA.

Williamson, O. E. (1996), *The Mechanisms of Governance*, Oxford University Press, Oxford.

Williamson, O. E. (1999), 'Strategy research: governance and competence perspectives', *Strategic Management Journal*, **20**(12), pp. 1087–1108.

Williamson, O. E. (2000), *Empirical Microeconomics: Another Perspective*, Unpublished Paper, University of California, Berkeley, CA, USA.

Womack, J. P. and Jones, D. T. (1996), *Lean Thinking*, Simon Schuster, New York, NY, USA.

Forthcoming title

Cox, A. (forthcoming), *The Rules of the Game: How to Capture Value in Business*, Earlsgate Press, Stratford-upon-Avon.

Part B1

Cases in construction relationship management and performance outcomes: reactive sourcing approaches

In Parts B1 and B2 the theoretical issues about relationship management choices and outcomes are taken up in some detail. Each of the chapters describes a specific construction relationship management approach and charts the outcomes that occurred within these relationships for the parties involved. The sixteen cases show that under both reactive (*supplier selection* or *supply chain sourcing*) and proactive (*supplier development* or *supply chain management*) relationship management approaches that all of the nonzero-sum, zero-sum and negative-sum performance outcomes discussed earlier are feasible, but that win–win (positive-sum) outcomes are never feasible in buyer and supplier exchange. The discussion focuses in Part B1 on eight reactive and then in Part B2 on eight proactive relationship management cases. To protect commercial sensitivities the actual names of the buyers and suppliers involved in the cases are not provided and certain financial information has been altered.

The logistics warehouse case: reactive supply chain sourcing with a buyer win and supplier partial win outcome

4.1 Introduction

This first reactive case focuses on the procurement and supply management of a major warehouse facility by a large UK logistics company. The case focuses on the buyer–supplier relationship between the client, a major provider of logistics services, and a large construction firm. Although this was the first time they had been in a contractual relationship with each other, both of these firms have had extensive experience of the construction of similar warehouse projects through design and build arrangements.

With a requirement for the construction of new warehouse facilities only every other year, the client does not have a continuous need to source from the construction supply market for these facilities. As a result, it has not invested significant internal resources in the development of a proactive competence in construction procurement and supply management. It was content, therefore, to rely on a short-term reactive relationship management approach.

Despite this, the client felt that by undertaking reactive sourcing in a professional manner, using external third-party professional services when necessary, it would not adversely impact its ability to achieve its ideal performance outcome of significantly improved functionality and reduced total costs of ownership, with the supplier only earning low or normal returns from the relationship (i.e. a Cell B outcome in Figure 3.5). The findings from this case study show that a reactive approach, if undertaken professionally, can provide a buyer with its ideal even if a supplier fails to achieve its own, and that there are circumstances in which there are few incentives for either party to engage in a more proactive approach.

In this case, even though the client lacked the level or frequency of demand that is normally highly attractive to the supply market, and even though it was not in a position to implement any form of long-term collaborative or proactive relationship management, by working with third-party professional services providers the client was able to lower the total costs of ownership significantly and maximise the functionality of the solution. This performance outcome was made possible by the client understanding the complexities of construction supply chains and markets and developing strategies to reduce the level of information asymmetry and the construction firm's scope for opportunism. As a result, the construction firm was only able to make acceptable, but not maximised, returns from this relationship – a buyer win/supplier partial win outcome.

4.2 Background to the case: the construction of a logistics warehouse

The design and construction of a large warehouse and distribution facility for a major logistics provider, Efficient Logistics Service Provider (ELSP), requires the integration of a large number of supply chains, as illustrated in Figure 4.1. The diagram suggests that the configuration of supply chains is simple, but given their limited understanding of construction supply markets, the high value of the project, the significant risks involved and the project's strategic importance to the business, those responsible for construction procurement and supply management within the client organisation relied on professional advice from external third parties.

This advice included expert guidance on outline project design, specification of key elements, preparation of tender documents, tender submission analysis, supplier selection and negotiation, and all aspects of cost, commercial, project and contract management. This facilitated the appointment of the design and build contractor, Warehouse Construction Projects (WCP), who was responsible for the management and integration of the wide number of upstream supply chains under a JCT standard form of contract (with contractor's design). This *ad hoc* appointment was made as part of a reactive relationship management approach.

The project involved the design and construction of a large warehouse and distribution facility. Part of the client's network of highly automated distribution centres, this $50\,000\,\text{m}^2$ facility was to operate seven days a week and be staffed with a total contingent of 500 people working a variety of shift patterns. The building was to comprise a large open warehouse area with 15-metre-clear internal height, and a steel-framed internal mezzanine floor allowing amenities/offices on two floors. Loading and despatch was to comprise 40 bays incorporating electro-hydraulic dock levellers, manual sectional doors and dock shelters. The entire dock face was to be protected by a 5-metre-deep canopy. Externally, the project was to include car and lorry parking areas, gatehouse, vehicle wash and refuelling facilities.

At the outset of the relationship, the client (ELSP) had to provide an outline design and specification (within the tender documentation) upon which the construction firm (WCP) could develop its proposal. This contained a requirement to use mass concrete pad footings, pre-cast reinforced concrete ground beams and upper floor planks, retaining wall panels, external wall cladding, and a carbon-steel-fibre-reinforced concrete slab that encompassed pre-cast concrete dock leveller pits. However, the precise specification for these elements was left to the discretion of the design and build contractors, who were able to draw on their own knowledge and experience to develop a solution to meet the client's commercial and operational objectives – lowest feasible total cost of ownership and highest feasible level of functionality.

The selected construction firm provided a solution that contained a number of distinct and innovative elements. First, the design included a curved roof structure that created a series of unsupported canopies along the south elevation. This

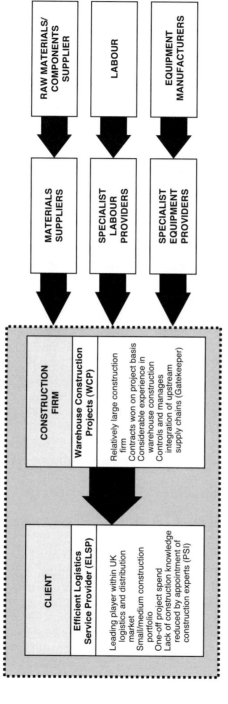

Figure 4.1 Construction supply chains for the construction of a logistics warehouse

provided a distinctive and strong motif to the loading dock face. Second, to over-come poor ground conditions, increase the bearing capacity of the ground material and avoid differential settlement of the warehouse slab the construction firm proposed a groundworks solution based on cement/lime stabilisation. Third, the overall design of the facility was very closely integrated with the landscape design to ensure compatibility with the local countryside. Finally, the construction firm installed an innovative drainage solution below the car park and landscaping areas based on buried steel-tube culverts. This ensured that localised flooding was avoided and the water table was not adversely affected.

With the creation of extensive new hard-paved areas for lorry aprons and parking ground, water run-off into the existing watercourse was a major area of concern. The osier beds to the south of the site were to be protected from flooding and various settlement ponds around the site were vulnerable to silt build-up. To control site discharge into watercourses, stormwater storage was provided by burying over 220 metres of helically wound steel tube culverts below the car park and landscaping areas. Therefore, to deliver the solution to the client's require-ments, the construction firm had to translate the innovative design into reality and use its knowledge and experience to overcome any difficulties that arose.

The buyer – Efficient Logistics Service Provider (ELSP)

In this particular case, ELSP identified a need to add to its network of existing facil-ities with the construction of a new logistics and distribution warehouse to meet the evolving needs of its business. The client lacked internal competence in construc-tion procurement and supply management and was unwilling, given the infrequent nature of its demand, to invest in the development of such competence as its primary 'business' is the provision of logistics services, and construction is only perceived to be a support activity to this primary business.

The client (ELSP) chose, therefore, to rely heavily on external professional service providers to make an informed sourcing decision relating to outline project scope, design and specification, contract strategy, preparation of tender documents, tender submission analysis, supplier selection and negotiation, and all aspects of commercial contract award and post-contractual performance measure-ment and management. With this advice the client was in a position to go to the construction supply market and appoint the contractor best placed to deliver its commercial and operational objectives.

At the outset of the project, the total cost for the project was initially estimated to be just under £6 million. However, after putting the design and construction project out to tender, ELSP received prices ranging from £5.5 to £6.25 million. Using a wide array of supplier and tender assessment criteria, developed in conjunction with professional services, a design and build contractor was selected that submitted an initial price of £5.5 million, which was then reduced through negotiation of alter-native technical solutions and products/services to £5.1 million. Despite having submitted the lowest price, WCP was appointed under a JCT standard form of contract (with contractor's design) due to its significant experience with delivering similar projects in the logistics environment to a very high quality, within timescales, incorporating the latest technology, and in a non-adversarial manner.

The client's use of a third party professional service provider (Professional Services Inc – PSI) enabled it to develop an informed knowledge of construction supply chains and markets. While this understanding was predominantly focused on the first-tier, it also encompassed knowledge of the value for money of the key products/services required for the warehouse facilities from many of the upstream supply markets in the chain and many of the key construction products/services required for the warehouse facilities. This allowed the client to challenge many of the cost elements within the initial tender bid from WCP and the other unsuccessful bidders. It also allowed ELSP to challenge some of the solutions proffered by WCP, to find acceptable technical solutions at a lower price, to achieve a high level of visibility of the returns (profit margins) being made by WCP on the tender bid and to limit these to normal returns for the industry of 2%. The client's inability to offer an attractive level of demand to WCP and any of the other potential construction firms meant that the development of a long-term proactive sourcing approach was not possible. This meant that WCP had to rely on a reactive relationship management approach at the level of the supply chain (i.e. *supply chain sourcing*).

The supplier – Warehouse Construction Projects (WCP)

The supplier (WCP) had an annual turnover of £275 million and a net operating profit of £25 million (9% return) in 2004. It can, therefore, be considered to be a major player in the UK construction market. However, faced with a highly competitive and uncertain market environment, WCP has attempted to create a reputation for the delivery of high quality and cost-effective warehouse solutions that allow major industrial clients to attain their commercial and operational objectives. As part of this market differentiation strategy, WCP has identified major construction clients that require warehouse facilities and focused its efforts in a coordinated manner to aggressively target work from these firms. By focusing on this one sector, and striving to become the best provider within it, WCP hopes to enjoy success in the long-term.

The supplier (WCP) has recognised that its ability to develop long-term and proactive collaborative solutions for its customers is often seriously challenged by the *ad hoc* and infrequent nature of demand from most clients. Given this, it has been possible for it to earn a very reasonable return of 9% for the industry. This has been achieved by developing proactive sourcing relationships with its own preferred suppliers, but only passing on to the client the benefits that it is forced to through aggressive commercial negotiations by the customer.

4.3 The buyer–supplier relationship management approach

In analysing this case it is first necessary to understand the dimensions of buyer and supplier power. This provides a way of understanding which relationship management approaches are feasible and also whether the client is in a position to maximise value for money (an increase in functionality and a reduction in the total cost of ownership), or whether the construction firm is in a position to maximise value from supply (an increase in the share of customer and market revenue, and an increase in profitability leading to above-normal returns) at the expense of the client.

The client (ELSP) – construction firm (WCP) dyad

The relationship between the client and construction firm is the key dyad within many construction supply chains, as it often has a major influence on the appropriation of value and profit margins of those upstream players providing products and services to the project. If clients have insufficient information about their current and future construction requirements and a limited understanding of construction supply markets, they are likely to face opportunistic construction firms who will attempt to use information asymmetries to earn higher revenues and returns. However, it will be shown that the client, by working with professional services (PSI), acquired a robust understanding of what was required for the development of an appropriate reactive construction supply management approach to deliver its desired value proposition.

For this particular project, the initial contract value for the design and construction of the warehouse solution was budgeted eventually at £5.1 million. With a programmed duration of 12 months, this project accounted for approximately 2% of the construction firm's annual turnover. This level of expenditure does not provide the client with a key power resource because the project accounts for a relatively low share of the construction firm's turnover. However, although this expenditure may seem insignificant and not provide the client with any form of power and leverage advantage, it should be considered in conjunction with the attractiveness of the customer's account for the supplier.

A regular need to source from the construction supply market can turn a relatively low value single project into a high value portfolio of projects and provide a client with a key power resource. The client (ELSP) did not possess this lever. Nevertheless, it did return to the market on a biannual basis and this provided an incentive for the supplier to win the business because this was not a purely one-off arrangement – there was the possibility of some work in the future. Perhaps the greatest lever available to the buyer in this case was, however, its own significant reputation as a major blue chip company, which any successful supplier could use to win work from other potential customers, who might be less well informed. When clients source construction on a one-off basis, it may be possible for a construction firm to act in an opportunistic manner due to its use of information asymmetries, or the client's inability to monitor the contractor. In this case, however, ELSP successfully minimised the level of information asymmetries and scope for supplier opportunism through the use of an expert third party professional service provider (PSI).

Given the relative infrequency of its demand profile, ELSP had no desire to invest time, financial and management resources in the development of a long-term proactive construction sourcing approach. Despite spending £2–8 million on construction on an annual basis, it could not envisage a return on the required dedicated investments and relationship-specific adaptations. As a result, ELSP had no alternative but to adopt a short-term and reactive relationship management approach in the pursuit of its commercial and operational objectives. In working with PSI to acquire an understanding of the structure of the supply chain through which products and services are created, the client adopted a wholly appropriate reactive *supply chain sourcing* approach.

On the supply-side of this buyer–supplier relationship, two of the critical power resources for the construction firm that dictate whether it is able to obtain value from supply are *scarcity* (related to the number of alternative suppliers perceived to be capable of delivering the client's requirements) and *utility* (related to the value/importance of the transaction to the client). The majority of construction firms operate within highly contested markets and are unable to restrict the level of competition (and create a high degree of supplier scarcity) through the ownership of key external supply chain resources.

When considering utility and scarcity, the role of information, critical in the construction industry, impacts the level of supplier power resources. The construction firm (WCP)'s strategy was based on offering a differentiated supply competence, by delivering very high quality and cost-effective solutions that are customised to the specific requirements and working environment of the client, and distinct from the competition to maintain a strong brand image within the marketplace. Behind this was WCP's own ability to develop a proactive sourcing approach that provided it with lower cost and better quality supply inputs that it could leverage to its own advantage and not be passed on in full to the customer. It was hoped by WCP that this would increase ELSP's perception of value (enhance the utility of the transaction for ELSP) and decrease the perceived level of contestation (create an impression of supply market scarcity), while also providing it with above normal returns (9% on average).

Where there are a large number of construction firms offering similar solutions to a fragmented but relatively well-informed client base, neither party has a significant power advantage over the other. Under such circumstances, a construction firm cannot be opportunistic before the award of the contract (*ex ante*) and usually passes value (in the form of lower tendered prices or higher levels of functionality) to the client, which has an advantage during the supplier selection process, as it is relatively easy to compare alternative solutions. The client (ELSP) was able to achieve this by using a highly competent professional services provider, PSI, which was also able to negate supplier opportunism after the award of the contract (*ex post*). The overall performance outcome of the relationship for both ELSP and WCP is discussed in the next section.

4.4 Performance outcome from the buyer–supplier relationship

At the outset of the project, the client and construction firm had conflicting ideal operational and commercial goals and objectives. The client (ELSP) was attempting operationally to maximise the functionality of the warehouse solution at the same time as attempting commercially to minimise the total costs of ownership for this solution so that it could maximise the value for money received. In direct contrast, the ideal objective of the construction firm (WCP) was to maximise the revenues and returns received from this specific client.

The client was unable to engineer a position of *buyer dominance* over the construction firm, but at the same time avoided a position of dependence (*supplier dominance*). Although ELSP lacked a regular level of demand characterised by high volume, its expenditure was deemed to be attractive by the construction firm given the biannual nature of demand and the reputational benefits that might arise from being associated with this blue chip company. Despite the relatively high buyer search costs, the client attempted to minimise the potential for supplier opportunism by employing construction experts (PSI) to provide a greater understanding of the supply chain and the supply chain's markets, better inform its sourcing decision, monitor the supplier, and reduce the levels of complexity and uncertainty associated with this project. These supply chain and market circumstances, summarised in the top half of the following diagram, resulted in a scenario where neither party was in a position of dominance, but one party was still able to fully achieve its commercial and operational goals and objectives. As a result, the client and construction firm both gained from the relationship, but to varying degrees. Figure 4.2 contains a summary of the dyad between ELSP and WCP, and the performance outcome from the relationship.

In terms of final cost, the client demonstrated a high level of competence in the sourcing of this construction project. In conjunction with professional services (PSI), ELSP acquired a robust understanding of the construction supply chains and markets that facilitated the development of a detailed design and specification for the warehouse facility and the subsequent selection of the construction firm best

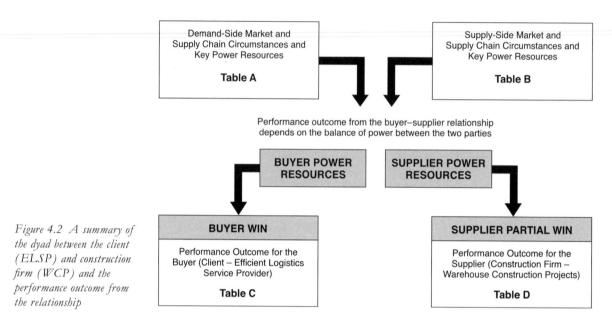

Figure 4.2 A summary of the dyad between the client (ELSP) and construction firm (WCP) and the performance outcome from the relationship

Table A Demand-Side Market and Supply Chain Circumstances and Key Power Resources

There are many buyers in the total construction market but fewer buyers for major warehouse solutions with specialist requirements

The client (ELSP) has a relatively low share of total construction market but a slightly **higher share of the infrastructure sector** with an average annual construction expenditure of £6.5 million (this figure fluctuates from £2 million to £8 million). Therefore, the construction firm has a very low dependency on the buyer for revenue

ELSP has an **infrequent need** to go to the construction market typically requiring one new warehouse and the refurbishment of two others biannually

The requirements of ELSP are **relatively simple** (because of the clear design and specification), but there is **low/medium complexity** associated with certain elements that require considerable supplier knowledge and expertise to integrate into the project

ELSP has **medium switching costs** with a relatively large number of competent suppliers able to provide a high quality offering

ELSP, after working in conjunction with professional services, has a **relatively clear value proposition** – a high quality product delivered on time and at an acceptable cost

ELSP has only a limited awareness of the potential scope for **standardisation** of design and specification and **prefabrication** of key components common for this project and future warehouse projects

ELSP has **relatively high search costs**, but through working with professional services and investment in internal resources has reduced the level of **information asymmetries** and scope for **opportunism** and acquired a relatively robust knowledge and understanding of construction products and services and the strategies of the industry players

Table B Supply-Side Market and Supply Chain Circumstances and Key Power Resources

There are many suppliers in the total construction market but fewer suppliers capable of providing relatively complex warehouse solutions to ELSP's specific requirements

In this case, the contract value for the construction element of the project was approximately £5.1 million. This project accounts for a **low/medium share of the annual turnover** of WCP (approximately 2%)

WCP is **not as highly dependent** on ELSP (as other suppliers may be) for revenue as, through the use of a segmented approach to targeting work in profitable segments, it is able to be selective with the projects it undertakes

WCP considers ELSP's business to be **relatively attractive**, as it has attained considerable knowledge and expertise related to delivering similar projects and as a result it is easy to service

WCP has relatively **high switching costs**

WCP's offerings are not commoditised and standardised but **highly customised** to the specific requirements and working environment of ELSP

WCP has a **solid brand image** and **reputation**. This reputation has been strengthened by constantly delivering high quality projects on time, within financial budgets to prestige clients within the manufacturing and logistics environments

Unlike relationships with some other clients, WCP has **limited information asymmetry** advantages over the client due to ELSP's investment in obtaining the required information for robust construction sourcing

---

Table C Performance Outcome for the Client (ELSP) – Buyer Win

The client, Efficient Logistics Service Provider (ELSP), was faced with costs lower than initial budget by £900 000 and £400 000 lower than initial lowest cost tender bid

These figures were based on internal cost information and verified by independent cost consultants

At the same time as maximising cost reductions, ELSP ensured that the construction firm (WCP) only made low returns

Transfer of learning from previous similar projects meant that:

    Functional expectations fully met (and innovation in certain areas meant that it actually exceeded functionality)

    Delivery of project one week early

    Subsequent maintenance costs lower than expected

Table D Performance Outcome for the Construction Firm (WCP) – Supplier Partial Win

Warehouse Construction Projects (WCP) calculated that it made a profit of £100 000 (a 2% return)

WCP enhanced its reputation within the industry for delivering quality products, within cost and time constraints

WCP believed that this might lead to other work with the client, ELSP, and within the logistics market and other industrial sectors

---

placed to meet its requirements. This enabled the client to achieve a reduction in total construction costs from the initial estimate of just under £6 million (based on previous similar projects) to exactly £5.1 million without compromising quality and functionality, or adversely impacting project duration.

An independent cost consultant, employed by the client, monitored and benchmarked supplier performance. This firm confirmed that the client, by achieving costs savings against an initial budget of almost £900 000, and of £400 000 against WCP's initial offer of £5.5 million, had reduced the total costs of ownership to their lowest feasible figure. The achievement of this commercial objective was facilitated by the client's development of a robust sourcing methodology that involved the necessary reactive supply management activities to support its strategy of understanding key construction supply chains and leveraging the extensive knowledge of the cost consultant and other professional services. The reactive supply management activities undertaken by ELSP included the development of a clear concept design, the specification of a number of common elements contained within its other facilities, a high level of cost transparency of supply inputs, the implementation of a rigorous tendering process, in-depth source planning, robust supplier selection and negotiation, and effective contract, financial, risk and project management.

In addition to fully attaining its commercial objectives in relation to reducing construction cost to its absolute minimum, the client's sourcing approach also meant that it was able to fully achieve its operational objectives in relation to maximising the functionality of the warehouse solution. This was also made possible by the construction firm's considerable experience in the design and build of similar warehouse facilities for other major logistics providers.

In the development of the detailed design, WCP identified a major issue with the client's outline design in relation to the drainage of the site. With the creation of extensive new concrete-paved areas for lorry aprons and parking, groundwater run-off into the existing watercourse was a major area of concern. After commissioning a hydrological survey, it was able to design a drainage solution to avoid changes to the water-table, flooding of nearby osier beds, and a build-up of silt in adjacent settlement beds. To control site discharge into local watercourses, WCP was able to draw on its experience of similar projects to suggest a solution where storm-water storage was provided by burying steel-tube culverts below the car park and landscaping areas.

As a result of WCP transferring learning from previous projects to provide an innovative solution, the client avoided major problems, such as localised flooding, and achieved a level of functionality that exceeded that contained within its original outline design and specification. In addition, despite the changes to the original design and the development of a more sophisticated solution, it was found to have significantly lower maintenance costs and ELSP still received the final solution one week early. This early delivery of the project also enabled the client to overcome a problem that threatened the operational sustainability of its business. A major fire in one of its nearby warehouses had created significant difficulties for the client as it struggled to maintain a high quality and efficient logistics service in the local area. Although obviously not planned to alleviate these problems, the delivery of this project one week early ensured that the disruption to its operations were minimised.

The previous discussion has shown how the client fully achieved its ideal performance outcome – lowering total costs of ownership to their minimum and maximising the functionality of the solution. This 'win' performance outcome was made possible by the client's robust reactive relationship management approach that allowed it to understand how to develop strategies to leverage construction service providers. At the same the construction firm (WCP) achieved a win of sorts, that is a partial rather than a full win. The partial win from this project came from the fact that, although it only made close to a 2% return (below its strategic average and only a low or normal return for the industry), it was able to develop a relationship with a major blue chip company, position itself successfully for future work, develop its own competence in delivering technically complex projects and use the brand association with the customer to win more work with other potential customers.

As a result, in addition to the solution being acknowledged by industry experts as innovative in terms of design, WCP was able to further enhance its reputation within the marketplace for the delivery of projects that exceed the expectations of major clients. The construction firm (WCP) stated that this enhanced reputation definitely allowed it to partially close the market, as it led to the award of even more profitable work with other major logistics providers and firms reliant on large warehouse and storage facilities for their operations. Therefore, while WCP was unable to maximise its returns from this particular relationship, and only partially achieved full value from supply, it was definitely in a position to do so in other business relationships.

4.5 Summary

In summary, see Table 4.1, the major finding from this case is that neither ELSP nor WCP had any incentive to develop a proactive sourcing approach and were therefore content to rely on reactive sourcing. The fact that ELSP chose to develop a reactive *supply chain sourcing* approach with PSI's assistance demonstrates their

Table 4.1 Summary of the relationship management approach and performance outcome

Nature of Relationship Management Approach	Given its infrequent demand profile the client had no real incentive to invest time, financial and management resources in the development of a long-term proactive construction relationship management approach. The client could not envisage a return on the investment
	The client's failure to possess a level of demand characterised by high volume and high frequency meant that the client was not in a position to do so anyway
	As a result, the client had no alternative but to adopt a short-term and reactive relationship management approach (*supply chain sourcing*) in the pursuit of its commercial and operational objectives
Nature of Buyer 'Win'	Costs lower than initial budget by £900 000 and on initial tender bid by £400 000
	Transfer of learning from previous similar projects meant that functional expectations fully met (and innovation in certain areas meant that it actually exceeded functionality)
	The project was delivered one week early
	Subsequent maintenance costs for the warehouse facility lower than for the client's other facilities
Nature of Supplier 'Partial Win'	WCP calculated that it made a low or normal profit of approximately 2% rather than the above normal returns of 9% or more that it normally achieves
	WCP enhanced its reputation within the industry for delivering quality products, within cost and time constraints
	WCP believed that this may lead to other work with ELSP and with other clients within the logistics market and other industrial sectors
Conclusions	In this case, reactive *supply chain sourcing* was a highly appropriate approach for ELSP to adopt
	It is unlikely that it would have achieved a significantly improved outcome from the adoption of a more proactive approach
	WCP could have achieved even more if ELSP had been less competent in its reactive sourcing approach
	A win–win is not feasible in this case because above normal returns for WCP can only occur at the expense of higher total costs of ownership for ELSP

competence in reactive approaches to relationship management. It was the third party professional advice from PSI that allowed ELSP to reduce the profits that WCP had hoped to make from 9% to approximately 2% in this relationship. This ensured that the buyer achieved its ideal – increased functionality at the lowest total costs feasible (i.e. with the lowest cost provider available being unable to make above normal returns) – even though the supplier did not. This was a win–partial win outcome in Cell B in Figure 3.5.

The supplier was still relatively satisfied, however, because of the attractiveness of the customer, whose brand association it could use in the future to earn higher returns from other customers, which were less powerful, competent and/or professionally well advised than ELSP. The buyer in this case, therefore, achieved a full win but the supplier only achieved a partial win from the reactive *supply chain sourcing* approach adopted. If ELSP had been less competent it is likely that it would have had to pay far more for the same technical outcome and allow the supplier to achieve higher returns and a partial win–win outcome in the supplier's favour (a Cell F rather than the Cell B outcome that actually occurred).

The sports stadium case: reactive supply chain sourcing with a buyer win and supplier lose outcome

5.1 Introduction

This second reactive sourcing case focuses on the procurement and supply management of structural steelwork for a prestigious one-off project. The project involved the construction of a major sports stadium with a highly innovative and iconic design. Though designed primarily for major sporting events the new 85 000-seat stadium was also designed to be the country's leading venue for music concerts.

The case focuses on the buyer–supplier relationship between the construction firm, Showcase Stadium Solutions (SSS), and supplier of structural steelwork, Innovative Steelwork (IS), for the highly complex retractable roof structure and supporting arch. The construction of such a revolutionary structure, designed to be a major landmark, involved considerable strategic, operational and financial risks for those involved. For this reason, the client selected a construction firm that had considerable experience of working on similar prestigious stadium projects across the world. To minimise its exposure to the potential risks, the construction firm only selected suppliers of critical components, such as the structural steelwork, that had a track record of successfully working on other major high-risk projects.

When a construction firm has a level of demand that is highly attractive to the supply market it is normal for it to be in a position to effectively leverage upstream suppliers to maximise its own value for money. When a buyer only has uncertainty or irregularity of demand, and its requirements are highly complex and non-standardised, and information asymmetries are present, it is normal for the supplier to be able to maximise value from supply at the expense of the buyer. Given that these latter circumstances existed in this case, combined with the inability of the construction firm to engineer any form of long-term collaborative or proactive relationship management approach with the specialist material supplier, one would normally expect upstream suppliers to be opportunistic and pursue higher levels of profitability at the expense of the buyer. However, this does not occur in this case and it was the buyer who fully achieved its commercial and operational objectives (a win), while the supplier failed to achieve any of its operational or commercial objectives (a lose).

5.2 Background to the case: the construction of a major sports stadium

The construction of a major sports stadium requires the integration of many supply chains. Figure 5.1 suggests that the configuration of supply chains is simple, with only one specialist material supplier, but the reality is obviously very different. With considerable complexities and uncertainties involved with certain elements of the construction activity, such as the retractable roof and removable lower-tier seating, the construction firm decided to appoint specialist subcontractors to deliver these items.

The client's brief for the project was to create a flagship multi-purpose venue for major sports, cultural and music events. The ability to host all these events meant that the completed stadium is expected to operate at a profit. Therefore, not wishing to compromise on design, it was the client's wish to include, where budgets permitted, the very latest in technology to provide state-of-the-art features. In addition, the client wished to 'future proof' (build-in flexibility) the stadium to facilitate the retro-fitting of advanced experience-enhancing technologies in the future to avoid it becoming a 'white elephant'.

To create a world-class stadium, built to the highest specifications and using the latest technology, involves considerable costs. The purchase of the land and early design fees alone cost £150 million. The client considered the initial design to be critical and employed internationally renowned architects and structural engineers with considerable experience of designing the world's greatest buildings and structures. The basic cost of building the stadium was £300 million. This included the sourcing of over 200 000 tonnes of ready-mixed concrete and 35 000 tonnes of structural steel. The cost of fitting-out the stadium accounted for an additional £100 million. The client employed an independent cost consultant to review all the construction costs to ensure that value for money was obtained.

To create a visually striking and highly functional stadium, the innovative design had a number of key features. First, although designed primarily for football, rugby and music events, a revolutionary solution has been developed to ensure that the stadium can also host athletic events. A temporary prefabricated athletics platform can be installed, covering some of the lower-tier seats but creating the increased surface needed to fit an athletics track. The platform, supported by pillars, takes just a few weeks to install and remove, making the stadium a versatile, multi-sport venue.

The second key design feature of the new stadium was its partly retractable roof. When retracted it ensures that the turf obtains sufficient daylight and ventilation to maintain a perfect playing surface. For this very simple reason, a sliding roof remained an integral part of the design for the new stadium and was preferable to a palletised pitch (a patchwork pitch that could be moved in and out of the stadium) or the regular re-laying of the pitch. Furthermore, in poor weather the retractable roof can be closed within ten minutes to cover all seats. As well as contributing to the aesthetics of the stadium, two 100-metre-high steel arches that span 200 m across the stadium bowl are an integral part of the stadium's sliding roof support structure.

These two arches effectively form the third main design feature of the stadium and provide an iconic and dramatic landmark across the city skyline. The arches both consist of 400 steel tubes, forming 20 modules and two tapered end sections,

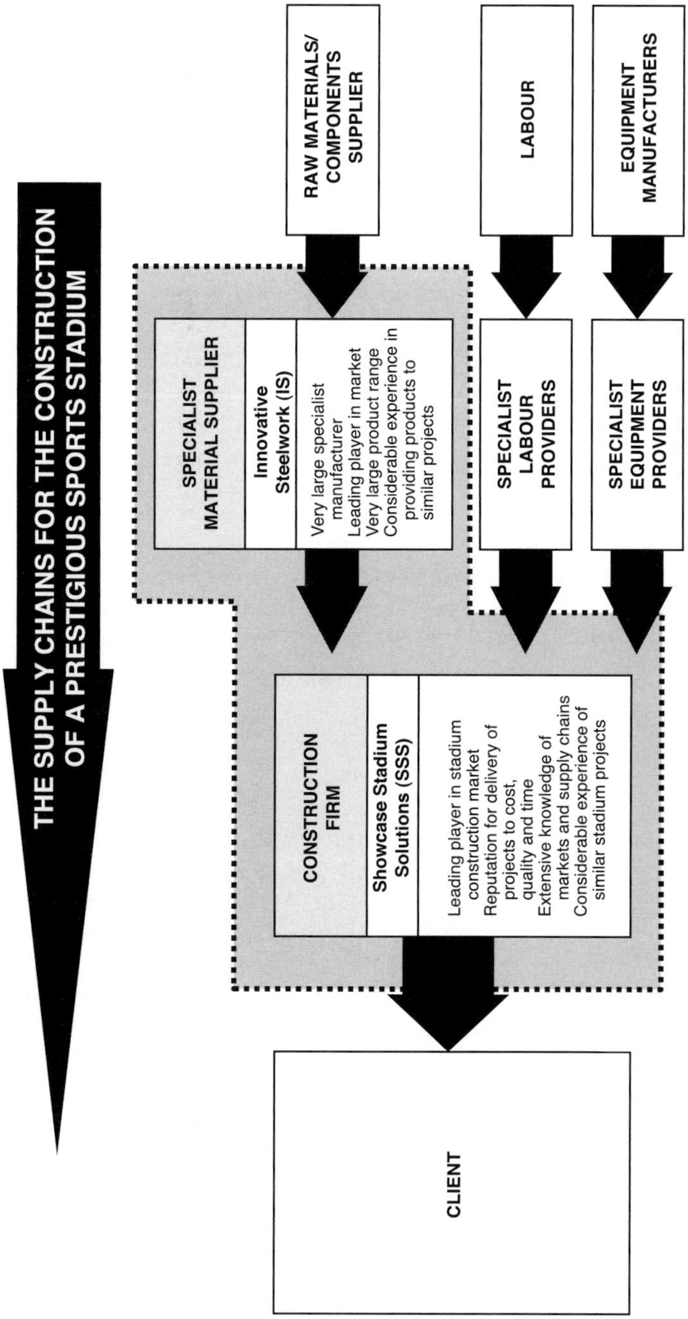

Figure 5.1 Construction supply chains for the construction of a major sports stadium

which are attached to giant hinges, embedded in concrete bases which are founded on piles 25 metres deep. The arches were fabricated gradually on-site over a twelve-month period. The design and build contractor, SSS, had responsibility for the construction of the concrete bases, while the specialist supplier, IS, had the responsibility for the supply of the steel and subsequent manufacture and lifting of the two arch structures.

The lifting process of the two 1250-tonne arches involved considerable complexity and uncertainty, not least the changeable weather. The full lifting process was undertaken incrementally in a series of precise stages, altogether lasting eight weeks, with movement taking place at times when the site was cleared. Constant checks were made throughout the lifting process until the arches reached their final positions.

The discussion here focuses on the relationship between SSS and IS within this one-off construction project. The relationship involved the supply and manufacture of the structural steel for the roof structure and two supporting arches, and the lifting of the arches into position. This required the buyer to develop a highly 'specialised' design and specification for the steelwork involving products of very high quality and reliability. To deliver the solution to the buyer's requirements, the supplier had to translate the innovative design into reality and use its knowledge and experience to overcome any difficulties that arose.

The buyer – Showcase Stadium Solutions (SSS)

In early 1997, the design and build contract for the new stadium, valued at £300 million, was awarded to SSS. The client had considered the initial concept design to be critical and had previously employed internationally renowned architects and structural engineers to complete this task. The buyer (SSS) developed a detailed engineering design for all elements of the project including the steelwork roof structure. From this design, a detailed specification was produced to accompany the design when seeking tenders from suppliers. During this process, it was hoped that all potential risks could be predicted and managed as, with the contract being fixed-price, SSS would bear the full cost of any overruns.

The buyer (SSS) maintains a record for innovation and quality, delivering stadium projects within contract time and to budget. This is underlined by the fact that SSS has constructed over 20 major sport stadiums around the world and is highly acclaimed for its work. Now recognised by a global audience, SSS delivered the 100 000-seat Stadium Europe. This state-of-the-art, world-class stadium was delivered three months ahead of schedule and has won over 15 major international engineering and construction awards. In expanding its business, the company has maintained a corporate philosophy of flair, enthusiasm and innovation to whatever it builds.

Following a robust reactive supply chain sourcing procurement route, because of the high value and risks involved with the steelwork for the project, SSS identified that although price was considered to be the single most important factor, the selection of the supplier should be based on an array of criteria. In addition to the specialist material supplier's knowledge and experience of working on similar innovative stadium projects, the main selection criteria included: cost, quality, duration, an ability to manufacture and supply the required steelwork to programme, and an implicit understanding of how to overcome potential problems that might arise on such a project.

At the outset of the project, the total cost of the structural steelwork element was initially estimated to be £75 million. However, after developing the initial concept design into a more detailed structural design and producing a specification for the innovative roof structure, SSS put the package of work out to tender and received prices ranging from £72 to £80 million. Using the robust selection criteria mentioned previously, a preferred supplier, Innovative Steelwork (IS), was identified who submitted a price of £72.5 million. Although not the lowest price, this contractor was selected due to its significant experience with delivering similar high-risk projects to a very high quality, within timescales and incorporating the latest technology. Therefore, in analysing the different value propositions and attempting to maximise value for money from the supply market, the construction firm decided to pay a slightly higher price to guarantee quality and delivery.

The construction firm's extensive knowledge of the players within the upstream supply market for steel also provided another justification for the selection of IS. With a very tight programme that could not be extended, the issue of security of supply was critical. Structural steelwork is frequently subject to very long lead-times as steel suppliers act opportunistically and prioritise production to service more profitable contracts or those customers with a regular demand. These problems would not arise with the selection of IS as it has a 'preferred partnering framework' with its major supplier – Major Steel (MS) – which, as one of the world's largest suppliers of steel, is able to offer certainty of supply and considerable project and materials management expertise.

In this regard, the construction firm demonstrated considerable expertise and knowledge of the supply market for structural steelwork, but also extended this understanding upstream of this particular dyadic relationship. The construction firm's inability to offer certainty and regularity of demand to the supplier of the structural steelwork meant that a proactive relationship management approach was out of the question in this case and the only alternative was a reactive approach at the level of the supply chain – *supply chain sourcing*.

The supplier – Innovative Steelwork (IS)

One of the most significant early decisions for any client sourcing commercial, industrial or residential construction is whether to incorporate a steel or concrete structural frame. This fundamental choice has a wide-ranging affect on many subsequent aspects of the building design, programme and performance. These, in turn, all have an impact on the cost and value of the project and are fundamental to its overall success.

Steel has, for many years, been the dominant form of construction for commercial buildings in the UK. The reasons for this are numerous and well reported. Off-site fabrication of structural steel frames can substantially increase the quality, speed, safety, flexibility and sustainability of construction. The quality of a steel building frame may be superior to a concrete frame cast in-situ, as the majority of the work can be carried out under closely controlled factory conditions. This prefabrication means that on-site trades or the weather does not affect the erection of the steelwork, and the 'right-first-time' build may also minimise time and disruption on site. Furthermore, steel does not suffer from creep or shrinkage and, when properly protected, does not rot or decay. In terms of speed, easier on-site erection can lead to significant savings in time and lead to fewer accidents.

The predictability of cost and programme may also be improved. Time related savings when specifying a structural steelwork frame compared with reinforced concrete may equate to 2 to 3% of overall building costs.

In terms of flexibility and adaptability, the construction of long, spanning, structural steelwork systems reduces the number of vertical columns in a building, or supports in a structure, and offers complete flexibility of internal layout. Also, if requirements change in the future, steel frames are easier to alter than the concrete alternative. Steel also offers a clean, efficient and rapid construction method, which reduces the impact of building activities on the environment. The small amount of waste produced is generally recycled, and the steel itself is 100% recyclable without any loss of quality.

Turning to cost, the recent increase in global demand for steel has led to significant price increases for all steel products including reinforcement bar and structural steel sections. The impact of these increases on building costs is a critical consideration for clients in the context of the decision between a steel or concrete frame. However, it is useful to place the recent steel price increases into context over a longer time frame. Over the last decade, based on Department of Trade and Industry construction material cost indices, the price of steel sections reduced by 8 per cent, ready mixed concrete prices went up by 44 per cent and reinforcement bar prices increased by 15 per cent. These changes in raw material costs are part explanation for the increasing competitive advantage for structural steelwork against reinforced concrete. Cost effectiveness is of course only one of the many advantages provided by structural steelwork building frames, but it is clearly an important one that is widely recognised by the majority of construction industry decision makers.

The ultimate client for the stadium in this case selected a structural steel framework for the roof structure. The specialist supplier, IS, was selected and given the responsibility for the supply of the steel and subsequent manufacture and lifting of the roof and two arch structures. The supplier (IS) directly employs designers, draughtsmen, fabricators and erectors to maintain total control over the delivery of complete steelwork solutions. Its unrivalled experience in stadium construction for a variety of sporting clients, combined with its design and build expertise, provides the company with ongoing business in the industry.

In 2002, IS had a very solid financial base with an annual turnover of approximately £400 million, an operating profit of £30 million and a net asset value of £100 million. The company was in a position to undertake and finance projects of up to £350 million in value with appropriate insurances and guarantees. For this particular project, the contract value for the design and subsequent supply, fabrication and erection of the steelwork solution was approximately £72.5 million. This figure accounted for approximately 24% of total project costs. The contract duration was three years.

Specialist material suppliers facing uncertain project-by-project revenues and intense competition are faced with a fight for survival. While they would ideally prefer long-term preferred supplier relationships with construction firms to ensure revenue predictability and profitability, they typically have to settle for the short-term adversarial pursuit of projects. In such an environment, the supplier may attempt to differentiate its offerings through reputation and recognition within the marketplace. The supplier (IS) certainly attempted to create a reputation for the delivery of high quality and cost effective solutions that exceed client's expectations. One aspect of this is the collaborative framework that it has developed with Major Steel (MS), one of the world's largest suppliers of steel, so that it can offer certainty of supply.

5.3 The buyer–supplier relationship management approach

By describing the key buyer and supplier power resources and the market and supply chain circumstances operating it is possible to analyse what the appropriate relationship management approach was for both parties in this case, and also to provide an understanding of whether the buyer was in a position to maximise value for money, or whether the supplier was in a position to maximise value from supply.

The construction firm (SSS) – specialist material supplier (IS) dyad

The construction firm's ability to control the specialist material supplier and maximise value for money is dependent on its capacity to attain the power resources within the relationship and at the same time effectively monitor the supplier to reduce the scope for opportunism. The external power resources of the construction firm, Showcase Stadium Solutions (SSS), in relation to the material supplier, Innovative Steelwork (IS), are determined by the following demand and supply characteristics.

Firms operating within the major stadiums sector are faced with a level of demand characterised by very high levels of uncertainty. This irregularity of demand also makes it very difficult for the construction firms to engineer a regular demand for key raw materials, such as the structural steelwork and ready-mixed concrete required for the construction of modern stadiums. Without this regular demand, construction firms find it very difficult to develop long-term relationships with the suppliers of these materials.

The problems with the low frequency of demand and unpredictability of future revenues are exacerbated by the uncertainty surrounding the actual location of future projects. In a similar manner to location impacting on the supply of ready-mixed concrete (as discussed in Chapter 8), guaranteed availability is a critical factor in the supply of structural steelwork. As a result, the construction firm selects the steelwork designer and fabricator on a project-by-project basis according to the location of the site, product specification, quality, price and (most importantly) the ability to meet the required demand levels in a timely manner.

For this particular project, the contract value for the structural steelwork was approximately £72.5 million over a three-year period. This figure equated to approximately 9% of the material supplier's total turnover. This expenditure level provides the construction firm with a key power resource for a number of reasons. First, given its value, the single project accounts for a far higher share of the supplier's turnover than any other project. Second, the costs associated with servicing a single contract of this size are significantly lower than if multiple contracts to the same value had to be serviced. Finally, and arguably most importantly, the contract has a high prestige attached to it. Successful delivery of an iconic and leading edge structure would significantly enhance the reputation of the supplier in the marketplace.

However, although this expenditure may appear attractive to the supplier and contribute to a position of relative power for the construction firm, it should be considered in conjunction with the frequency with which the parties transact. In this relationship with IS, any advantages obtained by SSS from being able to offer a relatively high volume of demand are somewhat diminished because it is unable to offer a level of demand characterised by high frequency.

In addition to volume and frequency, the complexity of the product and service offering is a further factor that influences the level of power in the relationship. With a very unique, innovative and leading-edge roof structure there are very high levels of complexity with regard to its integration into the entire project. However, this complexity was relatively well understood by the construction firm, which has had extensive experience of integrating complicated steelwork solutions into similar stadium projects. The purchasers in the construction firm, therefore, understood the complexities of the product and supply market and had full knowledge of all of the potential suppliers capable of meeting the detailed functional requirements of the client. Given this, SSS found it relatively easy and inexpensive to monitor the supplier and prevent opportunistic behaviour based on information asymmetries. Furthermore, the reputation of the supplier did not significantly increase the contractor's perception of value or decrease the perceived level of contestation in the market.

It has been argued in Part A that when demand is *ad hoc* and irregular, and design requirements are non-standard and highly complex, there are few incentives to encourage suppliers (either at the first-tier or through the supply chain) to undertake the necessary dedicated investments and relationship-specific adaptations to make collaboration and proactive relationship management work in the long-term. This contention was supported by the circumstances surrounding the power resources on the demand-side within this relationship. Despite the attractiveness of the construction firm's expenditure to the upstream construction supply market, it was not sensible for SSS to seek a proactive and collaborative relationship management approach with IS. Instead, SSS implemented a short-term and reactive sourcing approach (*supply chain sourcing*) and pursued their own self-interests (maximising value for money).

On the supply-side of this dyadic relationship, the specialist material supplier was operating within a market with relatively low levels of contestation and a low degree of fragmentation. This is attributable to the fact that although there are many suppliers in the structural steelwork market, there are significantly fewer competent and experienced suppliers perceived to be capable of supplying a very high quality product at the rate and specific time demanded by the construction firm's programme of works. In this case, the ability of the supplier (IS) to develop a close collaborative relationship with a major upstream steel supplier had a direct bearing on the extent to which the supplier of the structural steelwork faced direct competition. The framework agreement between IS and Major Steel (MS) enabled the supplier to offer security of supply, while other suppliers faced difficulties with long lead-times and late delivery of raw materials. This provided a relationship-specific advantage that effectively reduced the level of competition and provided the supplier with an opportunity to premium price and appropriate higher margins.

Therefore, the relationship between SSS and IS may be characterised as *structurally interdependent*. This may arise *ex ante* due to the high levels of innovation and expertise required on the part of the supplier that precludes entrants to the market. The buyer is faced with a restricted number of suitable and interchangeable solutions and the supplier is faced with a situation in which there are a limited number of available customers. Unlike suppliers of commoditised and standardised solutions, the appropriate relationship management approach for providers of complex solutions in an interdependent relationship is to use their dominance over their customers and to use an arm's-length and reactive approach that attempts to premium price above the prevailing market rate so as to make above normal returns and not pass value to the construction firm.

The discussion below shows how the inability of SSS to offer IS a regular level of demand for its structural steelwork solutions, combined with high buyer switching costs, weakened its negotiating position and opened up the possibility of supplier opportunism. This led to a number of major difficulties during the construction of the roof structure that impacted on the performance outcome of the buyer–supplier relationship but, ultimately, to the detriment of the supplier.

5.4 Performance outcome from the buyer–supplier relationship

At the outset of the project SSS and IS had conflicting operational and commercial goals and objectives. In this particular relationship, SSS was attempting operationally to maximise the functionality of the roof structure and commercially to minimise the total costs of its construction. In other words, the construction firm was attempting to maximise the value for money from the supplier's offering. In direct contrast, the initial aim of IS was to create a commercial position of power and leverage over SSS. This position, it was hoped, would enable the supplier to earn above normal returns.

The discussion above also highlighted that, although SSS lacked a level of demand characterised by high regularity and volume, it was attractive to IS given the lack of alternative contracts of an equivalent size in the local area and the fact that it was a highly prestigious contract. Other factors including the inability of SSS to lock the supplier into a long-term relationship, the absence of any information asymmetries, high switching costs for both parties, and the fact that the requirements were highly complex and non-standardised should have led to a situation where neither party could leverage the other to fully achieve its goals and objectives. This implies that, even though a proactive sourcing approach was not really appropriate, both parties might expect a partial win–partial win outcome (Cell E in Figure 3.5) to be the best that could be achieved from a reactive sourcing approach.

Despite this, the case demonstrates that, although there was interdependence in the dyadic interaction between SSS and IS, see Figure 5.2, a number of unexpected events led to a situation where only SSS gained from the relationship and achieved its objective of maximising value for money. In maximising value for money, SSS achieved its commercial goal of maximising the reduction in total costs of ownership and its operational goal of maximising the functionality of product offering. Unfortunately, unforeseen events meant that, despite the expectation of a partial win–partial win outcome for both parties in this interdependent relationship, IS failed to achieve any of its commercial and operational objectives and it experienced a win–lose outcome (Cell A in Figure 3.5).

In terms of final cost, SSS demonstrated considerable competence in the sourcing of structural steelwork for this project. The construction firm (SSS) developed a very detailed programme of works that was largely planned around the construction of the steelwork solution for the roof structure within a two-year window. This included a twelve-month period for the gradual on-site fabrication of the two arches and a further year for the lifting of these arches into place and the construction of the suspended retractable roof structure. The completion of the project on time was highly dependent on the timely supply, fabrication and construction of the steelwork solution for the roof and arches.

At the same time as attempting to guarantee the supply of the steelwork to programme, SSS developed a robust sourcing framework that eliminated the potential for the material supplier (IS) to be opportunistic and facilitated the reduction of costs to their absolute minimum. To be awarded the contract, SSS

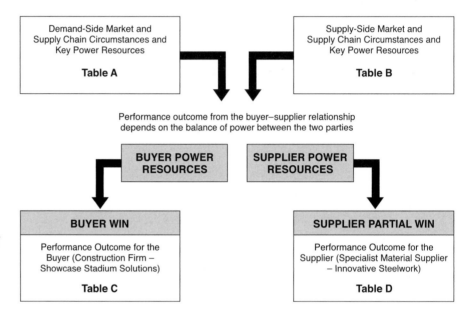

Figure 5.2 A summary of the dyad between the construction firm (SSS) and specialist material supplier (IS) and the performance outcome from the relationship

Table A Demand-Side Market and Supply Chain Circumstances and Key Power Resources

There are many construction firms acting as buyers in the structural steelwork market but significantly fewer buyers for steelwork for such a prestige contract

Showcase Stadium Solutions (SSS) has a relatively low share of total construction market but a **very high share of global stadium construction market** with a project value of £300 million (construction costs only – contract fixed price). Therefore, the supplier has a relatively high dependency on the client for revenue

SSS has a regular need to source from the structural steelwork market but there is **no current certainty/regularity** about requirements and volumes for specific steelwork

The requirements of the client (and SSS) are **highly complex** (in terms of product and the project environment), **non-standardised** and require considerable supplier expertise for their integration into the project

SSS has **high switching costs**, as although there are a large number of structural steelwork suppliers there are few suppliers with the reputation and capability of providing very high quality and reliable products

The client has a **relatively clear value proposition** – a high quality and globally prestigious stadium delivered on time and at an acceptable and predictable cost

SSS is aware of the potential scope for **standardisation** and **prefabrication** of specific component elements but any proactive sourcing is hindered by the client's highly one-off and unique demand specification

SSS has **relatively low search costs**, as it has extensive knowledge and understanding about structural steelwork products and services and the strategies of the industry players

Table B Supply-Side Market and Supply Chain Circumstances and Power Resources

Steelwork is a major material within construction projects, as almost every construction project requires it for the main structural elements

There are many suppliers in the structural steelwork market but significantly fewer suppliers capable of delivering the required amount of steelwork to the required quality levels to tight timescales

The total value of the structural steelwork, approximately £75 million, accounts for a relatively **high share of the annual turnover** (15%) of Innovative Steelwork (IS)

IS is **relatively dependent** on SSS for revenue, as there is a high degree of uncertainty surrounding alternative contracts (of equivalent size) in the stadium market

IS considers the business from SSS to be **highly attractive** as it has considerable knowledge and expertise related to similar projects (with complex design and specification and a need to adhere to strict health and safety requirements)

IS has **relatively high switching costs**

Supplier's offerings tend to be relatively commoditised and standardised. However, for this project there is **extensive customisation** to the specific requirements of the client associated with the requirements being very unique

Before the start of this project, IS had a **very strong brand image** and **reputation** for delivering innovative products of a very high quality

IS has **very limited information asymmetry advantages** over SSS

Table C Performance Outcome for the Construction Firm (SSS) – Buyer Win

Steelwork costs lower than original budget by £2.5 million. The original estimate for the steelwork element was £75 million and final cost of steelwork was £72.5 million

Functional expectations of client (and Showcase Stadium Solutions – SSS) fully met (i.e. the successful delivery of a high quality 'prestige design') after remedial action by SSS to replace a critical section of the steelwork. This section contained incorrectly-sized steelwork

Further modifications allowed the retractable roof to be opened further and faster than originally designed

Problems with buildability were also effectively overcome through effective contract management

SSS covered the expense of this rework and knock-on expenses through claims against the material supplier, Innovative Steelwork (IS)

Delivery of project on time, despite the problems experienced

---

Table D Performance Outcome for the Specialist Material Supplier (IS) – Supplier Loss

Innovative Steelwork (IS) calculated that it made a loss of £1.5 million on this project. This was largely due to:

    Claims made against it in relation to the supply of incorrectly-sized and poorly fabricated steelwork

      The requirement to pay additional sums to the steel fabricators to avoid extensive liquidated damages and overcome the problems with buildability

IS seriously damaged its reputation within the industry for delivering quality projects within time and cost constraints

Major industry players recognised that the problems were solely the fault of IS so they were expected to have a significant impact on future revenues

---

had to develop a detailed structural design and specification for the innovative roof structure and demonstrate that it fully understood the client's vision and functional requirements. The client wanted an iconic and innovative roof structure, but also had an understanding of the true costs of construction. The initial estimate for the cost of the steelwork for the roof structure, contained within the price provided to the client by SSS, was £75 million.

However, in having a very clear value proposition, SSS was able to understand the cost implications of over-specifying certain elements of the steelwork. Before work got underway, further development of the structural design and specification demonstrated that the cost of the structure could be reduced to £72.5 million (the lowest feasible figure for total cost of ownership) through a simple redesign of the 400 steel tubes that formed the basis of the two arches. With a fixed price contract this represented a cost saving of £2.5 million for SSS. This redesign also facilitated modifications to the roof closing mechanism allowing the retractable roof to be opened further and faster than originally designed, providing the client with a maximised level of functionality.

The fact that the construction firm fully achieved its commercial and operational objectives was attributable to its sophisticated approach to reactive sourcing from construction supply markets. In a highly competitive marketplace where investment in robust construction procurement and supply management is not commonplace, SSS had recognised its operational and commercial importance and dedicated appropriate financial and technical resources to reactive sourcing activities at a supply chain level. This enabled the construction firm, SSS, to obtain the cost saving and functionality improvements despite having to overcome a series of problems with IS.

A minor problem occurred when poor fabrication had to be corrected on the two tapered end sections that attached one of the arches to its giant hinges. The joints on these end sections required further strengthening and minor repair work had to be carried out on the concrete bases into which the giant hinges were embedded. The major problem occurred during the fabrication of the two arches, when the material supplier discovered a problem with the alignment of the two 10-metre-long central steel sections on both arches. In error, IS had produced incorrectly-sized sections based on the original design and had over-looked the modification. This mistake stopped the fabrication of the arches for two weeks while replacements were produced, but any delay to the end of the project was avoided through effective contract management and the threat of significant liquidated damages. The construction firm (SSS) also covered the knock-on expenses associated with the two-week delay through claims against IS.

The supplier (IS) calculated that it made an overall loss of £1.5 million by supplying and erecting the structural steelwork roof solution for this particular project. To correct the poor fabrication of the two tapered end sections on one of the arches and avoid delays to the programme that would have led to significant liquidated damages, IS employed additional steel fabricators and agreed to pay overtimes rates. This additional and unanticipated labour requirement meant that IS had to pay an extra £400 000 to its workforce to ensure the orderly continuation of steel and related work on site. The need to undertake repairs to the concrete bases into which one of the arches was to be anchored also resulted in a claim for £0.5 million being agreed between SSS and IS on completion of the project.

The need to replace the two incorrectly-sized sections of steelwork also had significant cost implications for IS. The cost of manufacturing replacement sections of the correct diameter was estimated to be in the region of £1.5 million. An additional claim for £100 000 was demanded by SSS to cover their costs associated with the two-week delay. Although vigorously contested by IS in a highly adversarial manner, this claim was awarded after the end of the project, as it was IS's obligation to cover those costs incurred by other parties as a consequence of its inability to meet deadlines within the programme. The costs of replacing the two sections of steelwork and the two claims made against it in relation to the supply of incorrectly-sized and poorly fabricated steelwork effectively turned the anticipated profit of £1 million for the project into a loss of £1.5 million. This loss accounted for approximately 2% of the original total contract value.

As a result of the problems experienced on this project, IS damaged its reputation for delivering very high quality structural steelwork, on time, and to the exact functional requirements of the client. With reputation being a major consideration for many practitioners responsible for sourcing highly complex construction products and services, IS was unable to 'leverage' the supply of materials to this high profile project to close the market to competition on future projects. In addition to having a major impact on the profitability of this project, IS therefore expected the problems experienced on this project to have a significant adverse impact on its future revenues.

5.5 Summary

In summary, see Table 5.1, the first major finding from this case is that even though a *buyer–supplier interdependent* power situation can exist it does not follow that a proactive approach to sourcing involving close collaboration is feasible.

Table 5.1 A summary of the relationship management approach and performance outcome

Nature of Relationship Management Approach	Despite the attractiveness of its expenditure, SSS's inability to offer certainty and regularity of demand to the supplier of the structural steelwork (IS) meant that IS was unwilling to undertake the necessary dedicated investments and relationship-specific adaptations to make collaboration and proactive relationship management work in the long-term
The only alternative open to the construction firm, SSS, was a highly leveraged short-term and reactive sourcing approach at the level of the supply chain – *supply chain sourcing*
Nature of Buyer 'Win'	Costs lower than expected by £2.5 million (according to comparison with historical rates provided by external cost consultant)
Functional expectations exceeded. The improved functionality of the roof structure was achieved despite the problems with the initial design and prefabrication of one section of steelwork
Despite the many problems, the on-time delivery of the project to the client was possible and the supplier was forced to bear all of the costs of its own operational failures
Nature of Supplier 'Loss'	Failure to make any profit on the project (IS had to pay two claims and additional sums to the fabricators that effectively eliminated surplus revenue)
The extra payments to steel fabricator supplier avoided liquidated damages, which would have exceeded these additional payments
Problem with availability of steelwork fabricators (had to pay higher rates to ensure product delivered on time and not faced with liquidated damages)
Failure to turn one-off contract into regular workload because of reported difficulties, with potential damage to reputation for operational excellence
Conclusions	The need for a prestige 'design' led to the development of an initial steelwork design that encountered problems with poor prefabrication
Problem with access to competent steelwork erectors
Reactive sourcing approaches are perfectly acceptable and sometimes may be preferable to proactive sourcing approaches
Win–lose or zero-sum outcomes are perfectly acceptable for those that win in one-off games, and that do not have to indulge in repeat games, where nonzero-sum outcomes are always necessary

In the absence of the regular and frequent high levels of demand that incentivise buyers and suppliers to work together closely, power interdependencies do not ensure that a proactive approach will be appropriate. On the contrary, in this case a reactive *supply chain sourcing* approach was the most appropriate sourcing option for SSS and IS, and one might expect that both parties would recognise this and negotiate a partial win–partial win outcome as the most realistic performance outcome.

Despite this, the case also demonstrates that, if one party is not capable of delivering operationally what was contracted, it is perfectly possible for the other party, assuming it understands the rules of the game of exchange, to ensure that it achieves all that it ideally desires while the other party fails to achieve anything at all. In this case SSS, through robust reactive *supply chain sourcing* and negotiation, was able to reduce its initial budgeted costs by £2.5 million from £75 million to £72.5 million and ensure that its supplier bore all of the costs associated with failing to deliver to the time and cost schedules agreed. In doing so the buyer achieved everything that it ideally desired, but the supplier experienced a lose outcome – IS potentially damaged its reputation for operational performance and lost money at the same time.

This was not a problem for the buyer because there are other suppliers in the market with similar competencies and SSS was not in regular need of these supply items. In this case a reactive and fairly leveraged *supply chain sourcing* approach worked to the buyer's, but not to the supplier's, advantage. Any other outcome would have been sub-optimal for the buyer even though it would have been preferable for the supplier if the buyer had shared the consequences of failure with it. This indicates that win–win outcomes are not feasible in buyer and supplier exchange and that nonzero-sum outcomes may be less desirable for buyers or suppliers than zero-sum outcomes when the other party has to pay the price of failure and there is no direct impact on their own performance if the other party fails. In other words, nonzero-sum outcomes may only be necessary when both parties need one another in repeat games – in one-off games, such as the case analysed here, zero-sum outcomes are perfectly acceptable for the winning party.

The corporate office and manufacturing facility case: reactive supplier selection with a buyer partial win and supplier win outcome

6.1 Introduction

This third case focuses on the construction of a corporate office and manufacturing facility for a major chemical company. The case analyses the buyer–supplier relationship between a large construction firm, High Quality Design and Build (HQDB), and a specialist supplier of mechanical and electrical (M&E) products, Specialist M&E Services (SMES). To deliver the client's expectations, the construction firm had to rely on a short-term reactive *supplier selection* relationship management approach in its integration of the upstream M&E supply chain required for the project. This was due to HQDB's high levels of uncertainty regarding its future requirements, which meant that it was not in a position to offer prospective specialist M&E suppliers any promise of future work to encourage them to enter into a long-term collaborative relationship.

The discussion highlights how, in the context of the specific power and leverage situation that arose in this case, this short-term and largely arm's-length approach tended to favour SMES rather than HQDB. This was primarily because, while HQDB could offer SMES a volume of demand that was highly attractive, it was not in a position to fully dictate the terms of the relationship. Given the absence of certainty about the regularity of demand, combined with the fact that HQDB's requirements were highly complex and non-standardised, there was potential for SMES to be opportunistic and pursue above normal returns at the expense of HQDB.

Despite the possibility for opportunism, both parties gained something from the transaction. While HQDB only partially attained its value for money objectives, SMES was able to fully attain its commercial and operational objectives. This means that, from the perspective of SMES, this was a partial win–win favouring its interests. The adoption of a proactive and highly collaborative approach was not feasible for HQDB. For SMES a proactive approach was neither feasible nor desirable because all of its objectives in this one-off game could be achieved by reactive means.

6.2 Background to the case: the construction of a corporate office and manufacturing facility

The construction of a corporate office and manufacturing facility for a chemical company requires an understanding both of highly complex construction products and services, as well as the structure of the supply markets from which they are sourced. To achieve its business objectives, the client requires an understanding of the relevant construction products and services so that it can develop a clear design and specification. To turn the client's requirements into reality and deliver the required value proposition, the construction firm has to understand, successfully manage and integrate a number of upstream supply chains, as shown in Figure 6.1.

Figure 6.1 presents the four stages within this particular supply chain for mechanical and electrical (M&E) products and services. The diagram suggests that the supply chain is relatively simple, but this is not the case in reality. Mechanical and electrical products and services form a key element of a typical construction project and may encompass all heating, ventilation, air conditioning, refrigeration, lighting, other electrical, sanitary, water and waste services. As a major category of construction expenditure their combined value, although varying significantly across projects, can account for anything up to 50% of a project's total cost and a considerable proportion of the total construction risk.

The case analysed discusses a 'typical' M&E package within a one-off construction project. The project involved the construction of a major new chemical processing facility and adjoining corporate office. The M&E element within this project required the installation of heating, ventilation, air conditioning, refrigeration, cooling, lighting, electrical products, lifts, drainage, and key elements of the fire protection system. However, the nature of the requirements varied considerably within the project. While the small office facilities only required a 'standard' M&E design and specification based on common components, the risks involved with processing highly corrosive and flammable chemicals meant that a 'highly specialised' design and specification was required for the M&E element within the hazardous manufacturing facility.

The client, Chemicals Plc, identified a need to upgrade its manufacturing facilities so that it could introduce leading-edge manufacturing processes and techniques in the processing of high quality chemicals. It was anticipated that such an investment would lead to a significant return and maintain its position as a major player in the global market. However, the company also had a problem with its current facilities for the processing of acetic acid, as they were proving highly inefficient when compared to overseas competitors and required significant investment to meet future EU legislation. Chemicals Plc was faced with a major strategic decision: whether to cease the processing of this chemical or redevelop its facilities. As acetic acid is one of the world's most important chemicals and a key raw material for the production of many other chemicals, as shown in Table 6.1, the second option was selected.

With its existing facilities deemed unsuitable for expansion and redevelopment, Chemicals Plc decided to construct a new facility for the processing of acetic acid. The location of this new facility was a critical decision for the client given the difficulties that it had historically experienced in obtaining planning permission for chemical processing facilities. To get planning approval for brownfield sites near residential properties is an extremely lengthy and uncertain process – the

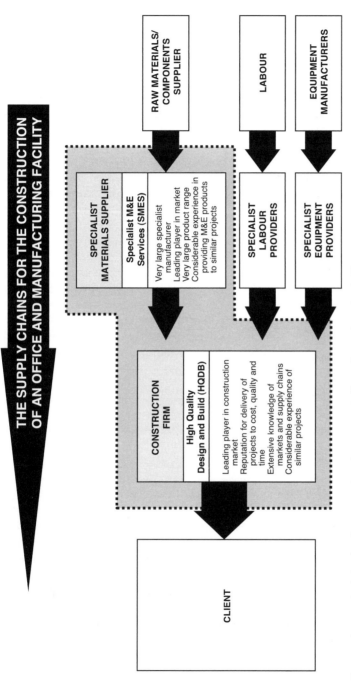

Figure 6.1 Construction supply chains for the construction of a corporate office and manufacturing facility

issue of waste from toxic chemicals is always one that generates opposition from local residents.

Given the need to have the facility up and running as soon as possible, Chemicals Plc decided to locate the new development on land it had recently purchased. The land had been acquired with the intention of constructing a major new headquarters to replace a number of smaller disparate offices. However, the fact that the site already had outline planning approval in place for a general industrial facility (use class B20) meant that it was the most appropriate decision, financially and economically, to use this land for the new manufacturing plant. A small corporate office was also required next to the facility to house the necessary management, engineering and administrative resources to ensure the plant's smooth operation.

Traditionally, in the construction industry, clients sourcing construction on an irregular basis are not in a position to undertake proactive construction sourcing and require external third party professional advice on the development of the design and specification for the project, and the subsequent selection and appointment of construction suppliers to deliver these requirements. Given the high value of the project, the significant risks involved, and its strategic importance to the organisation Chemicals Plc decided to act in a risk-adverse manner and seek external third party advice in this case.

Using internal and external construction experts, the client developed a relatively detailed design and specification for its construction requirements. However, this was less detailed with regard to the specific components to be integrated

Table 6.1 The hazardous chemicals processed within Chemicals Plc's facility

Chemical produced from acetic acid	Common use of chemical
Vinyl acetate monomer	Used in the manufacture of polyvinyl acetyls that find a wide range of applications including paints, adhesives, textile treatments, pharmaceutical packaging, automotive fuel tanks and as an inter-layer for laminated safety glass
Acetic anhydride	Used in the manufacture of cellulose acetate that has a diverse range of applications such as photographic and cinematographic film, X-ray film, biotechnology devices, and protective coatings for various substrates such as paper, glass, metal, leather and wood. Cellulose acetate plastics have excellent properties and can be moulded and extruded into various consumer products such as toothbrush handles and steering wheels
Acetate esters (ethyl acetate, n-butyl acetate and iso-propyl acetate)	An important industrial solvent that is used primarily in the manufacture of coatings, printing inks, resin coatings, varnishes, adhesives and cosmetics. Also used in the pharmaceutical industry as a process and purification solvent and in the food industry as a flavouring substance
Purified teraphthalic acid (PTA)	Used in the manufacture of polyethylene terephthalate (PET) that finds applications in the photographic film and magnetic tape sectors, polyester fibres (for polyester/cotton clothing blends) and plastic bottles (for drinks and foodstuffs)
Monochloroacetic acid (MCA)	Used in the manufacture of herbicides for the agrochemicals sector and materials for the pharmaceuticals, cosmetics and speciality chemicals sector. Also used in carboxymethyl cellulose that has a wide variety of applications including wallpaper adhesives and thickeners for drilling muds, foods, pharmaceuticals, cosmetics and textiles

within the M&E element of the project. The client only precisely specified a small number of components related to the heating, ventilation, air conditioning and fire protection systems to be installed within the chemical processing and storage area. These components were critical to the health and safety of the facility and were based on similar M&E solutions within the client's other chemical processing facilities.

The project was awarded to High Quality Design and Build (HQDB) and this case explores the relationship management and performance outcome from the M&E exchange transaction between HQDB and Specialist M&E Services (SMES). This required HQDB to develop a 'standard' design and specification for the office complex and a highly 'specialised' design and specification for the manufacturing facility.

The buyer – High Quality Design and Build (HQDB)

It is widely argued that the construction industry is highly competitive with many interchangeable players. Nevertheless, the need to integrate a highly specialised M&E product into a very complex and high-risk project effectively reduces the number of firms able to undertake this type of work. Firms with the required level of competence and expertise are largely confined to the major construction players, with considerable experience of working on similar projects.

In early 2003, Chemicals Plc awarded the contract for the construction of its new facility to HQDB. At the outset of the project, the total cost of the construction element was initially estimated to be £20.25 million. However, after detailed design work and development of the specification, the client put the work out to tender and received prices ranging from £20 to £21.5 million. Using robust supplier selection criteria, a preferred contractor was identified that had submitted the lowest price bid of £20 million. Although it provided the lowest price, this contractor was actually selected largely due to its significant experience with delivering similar projects in a high-risk chemical processing environment to a very high quality, within timescales and incorporating the latest technology.

The buyer (HQDB) was established in 1950, since when it has become one of the leading construction and support services groups with an annual turnover of nearly £750 million and more than 5000 employees. The company offers a comprehensive range of construction options to the public and private sectors, from major building and infrastructure projects through to smaller building and civil engineering works. The company maintains a strong track record for innovation and meeting client's precise needs, delivering projects on time and to the highest standards of quality and value.

Despite this track record, HQDB faces uncertain project-by-project revenues and intense competition in its fight for survival. However, in order to differentiate and to avoid the need to pursue projects on a short-term adversarial basis, the long-term strategy of HQDB is to develop long-term preferred supplier relationships with a number of major clients to ensure revenue predictability and enhanced profitability. Before it could implement such a collaborative approach, HQDB recognised that it needed to identify sectors where it was perceived to have a high quality differentiated offering and then use this reputation to insert itself onto the preferred supplier list of its potential clients that had a regular spend. In the meantime, HQDB acknowledged that it could only adopt a reactive relationship management approach with clients.

Before we consider HQDB's external supply relationship with SMES, it is important to consider the internal capability of HQDB so that we know to what extent it had to subcontract elements of the project. If there are no complexities or uncertainties involved in an M&E 'package', and a construction firm has the in-house expertise in the area, it may decide to integrate the element itself. However, the fact that M&E packages normally involve a high degree of complexity, non-standardised requirements, and/or a very difficult working environment means that the majority of construction firms do not maintain an internal M&E capability and subcontract the works to a specialist M&E firm to undertake the integration[1]. In this case HQDB could have selected from a number of firms to integrate the different M&E elements within the project, but it decided instead to source from a single major player within the market capable of delivering all of its M&E requirements.

At the outset of the project, the total cost of the M&E element was estimated to be approximately £7 million. This figure was confirmed when HQDB put the package of work out to tender and received prices ranging from £6.75 to £7.2 million. After consideration of the tenders, the construction firm selected SMES who submitted the second lowest price of exactly £6.9 million. Given the risks involved, this subcontractor was selected due to its considerable experience of working on similar hazardous projects and delivering an M&E solution to a very high quality and within timescales.

The supplier – Specialist M&E Services (SMES)

In 2002, the value of M&E contracting output was valued at £12.1 billion, or approximately 20 per cent of the total UK construction market. While the market for M&E products and services mirrors that of many construction products or services, the complexity associated with part of this solution effectively reduces the level of competition within the M&E supply market. When drawing up the tender list of potential suppliers with the required level of competence and expertise, HQDB only included those major players with considerable experience of similar projects.

For this particular project, SMES was selected to undertake the design and installation of mechanical and electrical engineering services. The key selection criteria were cost, quality and the firm's knowledge and understanding of the special planning and operating procedures required for a high-risk chemical processing environment where flammable liquids are stored. The M&E element within this project involved the installation of heating, ventilation, air conditioning, refrigeration, cooling, lighting, electrical products, lifts, drainage, and key elements of the fire protection system. The company also used innovative installation methods (including prefabrication and pre-assembly) to deliver work to very high quality standards and strict health and safety regulations to ensure future maintenance costs were minimised.

Although mechanical and electrical products are a major category of expenditure for all construction and civil engineering companies, the percentage of total cost

---

[1] A complicating factor is the fact that a number of the large M&E contractors are actually owned and controlled by the largest construction companies. This may militate against the construction firm making the most appropriate sourcing decision if there are secondary objectives, such as reciprocity, in play.

attributable to M&E varies significantly across projects[2]. For similar projects in the chemical processing industry, the M&E element can range from 20% to 40% depending on the client's requirements. In this project, the £6.9 million cost of the M&E element accounted for 34.5% of total construction costs (£20 million).

The supplier (SMES) had a turnover of £175 million in 2001. As a major player in the market it offers an integrated range of services including design, installation, commissioning and maintenance of M&E solutions. The firm's in-house design expertise gives it a considerable advantage in being able to promote early involvement in projects either to undertake the complete design or to support the design consultant in achieving a well-engineered solution. This is particularly important in achieving predictability of output in respect of cost, time, quality and safety. This capability enabled HQBD to deliver a higher level of functionality to the client, as a potential major problem with the operation of the facility was identified and addressed.

6.3 The buyer–supplier relationship management approach

In analysing the appropriateness of the relationship management approach adopted between HQDB and SMES the key buyer and supplier power resources in the market and supply chain are discussed. The analysis focuses on to what extent either HQDB was in a position to maximise value for money, or SMES was in a position to maximise value from supply.

The construction firm (HQDB) – specialist material supplier (SMES) dyad

Construction firms are frequently faced with opportunistic behaviour from upstream construction suppliers due to high levels of information asymmetry, but this was not the case in this relationship. The construction firm (HQDB) had extensive information, knowledge and understanding regarding the nature of its external spend, the construction supply markets from which it sources, and the appropriateness of available technologies from upstream suppliers. However, its inherent uncertainty and irregularity of demand, combined with the relatively high degree of competition within the supply market, means that HQDB has to select its M&E suppliers on a project-by-project basis according to the technical specification, quality and price of the product and service offering.

The construction firm (HQDB)'s ability to control and leverage M&E suppliers is dependent on market and supply chain circumstances and its possession of key power resources within the relationship. In this case, the contract value for the M&E package was £6.9 million. The fact that it was one of the largest projects that SMES was undertaking at the time, and accounted for approximately 5% of SMES's turnover, provided HQDB with a considerable power resource in the relationship. However, despite the lack of alternative exchange relationships of

---

[2] The analysis of the total costs of 172 projects undertaken by a number of leading UK construction and civil engineering firms highlighted that while variances in M&E expenditure exist across the key sectors, there are also obvious differences between 'types' of project. In general, the average M&E content of a warehouse (8%) is significantly lower than the average for health facilities (30%) while the input for offices varies between 4% and 23%.

the same attractiveness, the power derived from this resource was effectively diminished because of the uncertainty surrounding the ability of HQDB to offer SMES a guarantee of future regular demand.

Mechanical and electrical products also tend to be relatively complex because they are not always fully understood by those involved in specifying and procuring them. However, while this is the case for clients, one can assume that purchasers within construction firms would have full knowledge of potential suppliers of components to meet the functional requirements of the solution. As a result, it is relatively easy and inexpensive to monitor the vendor and reduce the potential of opportunistic behaviour based on information asymmetries. In addition, although there are a multitude of M&E firms offering potentially similar products and services, this particular case involved a highly complex solution that only a large M&E firm with considerable resources and expertise in the area could undertake.

Given the lack of long-term power and leverage resources for the buyer, it is not surprising that HQDB was left with no alternative but to adopt a short-term and reactive relationship management approach (*supplier selection*) in the pursuit of its commercial and operational objectives. Despite the attractiveness of this particular project to SMES, the failure of HQDB to engineer certainty and regularity of demand for M&E components across other on-going projects prevented it from developing a long-term collaborative and proactive relationship with the specific upstream supplier. This supplier was unwilling to undertake any significant dedicated investments and relationship-specific adaptations without the promise of continuity and an acceptable return on that investment.

On the supply-side, M&E contractors operate within highly contested markets. This is illustrated by the fact that there is no single dominant player within the M&E contracting market; the largest firm has a market share of below five per cent and the top ten companies only account for a fifth of the total market. However, as stated previously, one factor that impacts upon the level of contestation in this supply market is that there are a limited number of suppliers who could actually undertake large and highly complex projects. These tend to be the major players, such as SMES, with considerable experience of similar projects. While physical size reduces the number of potential bidders, the level of supplier scarcity is also increased by the presence of another isolating mechanism: the relative superior competence of firms like SMES. The understanding of the need to constantly innovate enables SMES to offer solutions that are functionally superior to those offered by many of its competitors. This in turn allows it also to achieve operational and commercial efficiencies that are superior to its competitors and which allows it to earn higher returns than its customers might initially assume. This was the outcome in this particular case.

Where there are large numbers of suppliers selling to a fragmented but well-informed customer base, neither party has power over the other and the buyer–supplier relationship is usually one of independence. However, given that both parties are in possession of key power resources, this relationship may be characterised as *buyer–supplier interdependent*. This interdependence arises *ex ante* due to the limited number of potential suppliers selling to a concentrated number of buyers who have low costs of search and an attractive level of demand.

Suppliers of M&E products and services under such circumstances are usually able to appropriate higher levels of value from the supply chain compared to suppliers within fragmented and contested marketplaces. They are not forced to pass all the value to the construction firm and are able to premium price above the prevailing market rate. In the HQDB and SMES relationship, the power situation of interdependence, which ought to have resulted in a partial win–partial win outcome, was overturned by unforeseen factors that arose during the course of the contract. These unforeseen factors changed the power circumstance and allowed SMES to achieve a full win for itself while forcing HQDB to accept only a partial win performance outcome.

6.4 Performance outcome from the buyer–supplier relationship

At the outset of the project, the construction firm and specialist material supplier had conflicting operational and commercial goals and objectives. The construction firm (HQDB) was attempting operationally to maximise the functionality of the M&E element within the chemical processing facility at the same time as attempting commercially to minimise the total costs of this element so that it could maximise the value for money it received from SMES. In direct contrast, the initial objective of SMES was to increase the revenues and returns received.

The construction firm was unable to engineer a position of dominance over the supplier, but at the same time avoided a position of dependence on it. Although HQDB lacked a regular level of demand, the contract was deemed to be attractive by SMES given its value and the lack of alternative contracts of an equivalent size. Other factors including the inability to lock the supplier into a long-term relationship, the absence of key information asymmetries, and the fact that the contract was relatively simple for SMES to service led initially to a position of interdependence. As neither party was in a position of dominance it was somewhat surprising that while HQDB could not leverage SMES to fully achieve its goals and objectives, SMES was able to maximise value from supply and achieve above normal returns. This arose in this case because the buyer suffered from a major information asymmetry because HQDB did not fully understand the returns that were possible for the supplier due to its superior commercial and operational competence compared to others operating in this supply market.

A summary of the dyad between HQDB and SMES and the performance outcome from the relationship is shown in Figure 6.2.

In terms of final cost, HQDB created a robust framework that facilitated the reduction of total construction costs from an initial estimate of £20.25 million to £20 million without compromising quality or adversely impacting project duration. Within this £250 000 reduction in total costs, the construction firm achieved a £100 000 reduction in M&E costs. These cost figures were verified and controlled by an independent cost consultant that monitored and benchmarked supplier performance. However, while there was a reduction of £0.25 million in the final project cost and £0.1 million for the M&E element, HQDB did not have a mechanism in place to leverage the extensive knowledge of the cost consultant and understand the full opportunity in relation to minimising the total costs of ownership.

In addition to failing to attain its commercial objectives in relation to minimising cost to its absolute minimum, HQDB was also unable to achieve its operational objectives in relation to maximising the functionality of the M&E solution. The construction firm (HQDB) only achieved levels of functionality as defined in the design and specification and received the final solution on time. Despite this beneficial outcome for HQDB, SMES calculated that it made an overall profit of £750 000 on the supply and integration of all the M&E elements to this particular project. This equated to an 11% return on the £6.9 million contract value. This demonstrates a 'full win' for the supplier in commercial terms, but only a 'partial win' for the buyer given the level of competition in this marketplace, its possession of key power resources related to an attractive level of demand and its own profit margin of 2.3% from the overall project in which it was shouldering the highest levels of risk.

The construction firm (HQDB)'s willingness to allow SMES to earn a high level of return was a reward for the non-adversarial manner in which it reactively

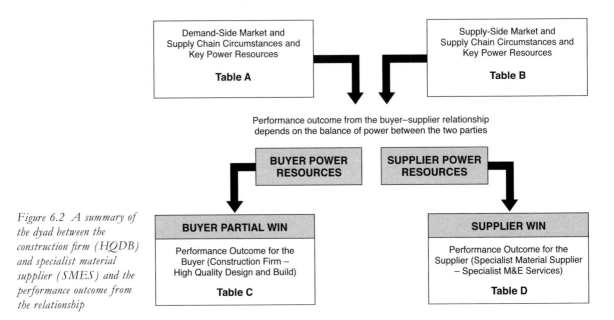

Figure 6.2 A summary of the dyad between the construction firm (HQDB) and specialist material supplier (SMES) and the performance outcome from the relationship

Table A Demand-Side Market and Supply Chain Circumstances and Key Power Resources

There are many construction firms acting as buyers in the M&E market but fewer buyers for specialist M&E products and services in chemical manufacturing sector

High Quality Design and Build (HQDB) has a relatively low share of total construction market and a **low/medium share of the chemical processing sector** with a project value of £20 million. Therefore, the supplier has a relatively low dependency on the buyer for revenue

HQDB has a **regular need** to source from the M&E market but there is no certainty/regularity about specific requirements and volumes

The requirements of the client (and HQDB) are **highly complex** (in terms of product and service and the project environment), **non-standardised** and require considerable supplier expertise for their integration into the project

HQDB has **relatively low switching costs**

HQDB, in translating the requirements of the client, has a **relatively clear value proposition** for the entire project and its sub-elements. For the M&E element, a critical element of the works, this was a high quality product delivered on time and within budget

HQDB is aware of the potential scope for **standardisation** of design and specification and **prefabrication** of specific components but constrained by the client's specification

HQDB has **low search costs** and is not faced with a high level of information asymmetries or supplier opportunism because it has an extensive knowledge and understanding of construction products and services and the actions and strategies of specialist material suppliers

Table B Supply-Side Market and Supply Chain Circumstances and Key Power Resources

There are many suppliers in the total M&E market but fewer suppliers able to undertake projects of this scale and with the necessary expertise to operate within a highly specialised and controlled environment (chemical processing)

The total value of the M&E element of the project (12 month contract), £6.9 million, accounts for a relatively **high share of the annual turnover** (5%) of Specialist M&E Services (SMES)

SMES is relatively **highly dependent** in the short-term on HQDB for revenue because of the uncertainty surrounding alternative contracts

SMES considers HQDB's business to be **relatively attractive**, as it has considerable knowledge and expertise related to similar projects

SMES has relatively **low switching costs**

The offerings of SMES are not commoditised and standardised but **highly customised** to the specific requirements of the client and working in a chemical processing environment

SMES has a **very strong brand image** and reputation. This reputation has been strengthened by constantly delivering high quality projects on time and within financial budgets

SMES has relatively superior operational and commercial competence compared with its competitors and this provides for a **significant information asymmetry** over HQDB, despite HQDB having extensive knowledge of construction supply markets. Additional information asymmetries exist in relation to the highly specialist M&E equipment related to chemical processing to be housed within the manufacturing facility

---

Table C Performance Outcome for the Construction Firm (HQDB) – Buyer Partial Win

The construction firm, High Quality Design and Build (HQDB), was faced with total construction costs lower than original budget by £250 000. The original estimate was £20.25 million and final construction cost was £20 million

M&E costs lower than original budget by £100 000. The original estimate was £7 million and final cost was £6.9 million

Functional expectations of the client (and HQDB) fully met. To achieve this a change had to be made to the original design and specification to overcome a problem that may have arisen during the operation of the chemical facility

Delivery of project to client on time

Low or normal return of 2.3% earned by HQDB

Table D Performance Outcome for the Specialist Material Supplier (SMES) – Supplier Win

Specialist M&E Services (SMES) calculated that it made an above normal return of £0.75 million or 11% on this project

SMES significantly enhanced its reputation for delivering very high quality M&E solutions within time and cost constraints

This enabled the firm to effectively close the market to competition and obtain additional work with the client in this supply chain, other chemical companies and within other industrial sectors

---

identified and addressed the issue of operational practice and commercial returns. In addition to the M&E solution being acknowledged by industry experts to be very innovative in terms of design and its integration into the construction process, SMES was also able to further enhance its reputation within the marketplace (and effectively close the market to further competition) by successfully delivering a very high quality solution, in a very flexible manner, within very strict time deadlines. Therefore, at the same time as earning a maximum level of return from this relationship, SMES enhanced its reputation within the marketplace. This definitely led to other contracts, where SMES could also earn rents, from other major construction firms that were delivering projects to clients across all industrial sectors.

6.5 Summary

In summary, see Table 6.2, the major finding from this case is that while reactive arm's-length sourcing can result in a partial win–partial win performance outcome it can also result in one side achieving a partial win while the other achieves a full win. This can occur when a buyer (HQDB in this case) fails to develop an understanding of the true operational and commercial competence of the supplier and the supplier can use current supplier market pricing as standard behind which it can mask its own ability to make above normal returns. In this case, HQDB was able to deliver a product and service on time and to the quality desired by its client but it was only able to earn a return of 2.3%, while its supplier, unbeknown to HQDB, was making a return of 11%. If buyers do not have the competence to understand the operational and commercial returns being made by their suppliers then it is unlikely, using a *supplier selection* approach to management, that they will ever be able to exert maximum feasible operational and commercial leverage on their suppliers. In this case it was the short-term and one-off nature of demand and its ignorance of operational practice and commercial returns that stopped the buyer from leveraging its supplier effectively.

Table 6.2 A summary of the relationship management approach and performance outcome

Nature of Relationship Management Approach	The construction firm's failure to possess a guaranteed and regular demand meant that it was not in a position to incentivise suppliers to make a long-term investment in a proactive relationship management approach
	Despite the attractiveness of this single contract (due to its high value and limited complexity), the inability of the construction firm to consolidate demand for M&E components across other projects meant that a reactive supplier selection relationship management approach was the only realistic option available to it
Nature of Buyer 'Partial Win'	M&E costs lower than original budget by £100 000
	Functional expectations fully met
	Delivery of project to client on time
	HQDB only achieved a low or normal return of 2.3% on the overall project
Nature of Supplier 'Win'	SMES calculated that it made a profit of £0.75 million on this project, which equated to an 11% above normal return
	SMES significantly enhanced its reputation for delivering very high quality M&E solutions within time and cost constraints. This enabled it to close the market to competition and obtain additional work
Conclusions	There is a fundamental question regarding whether a construction firm should have an internal M&E capability. This 'make or buy' decision is one facing a number of the larger contractors, as they consider their most appropriate procurement and supply strategies
	This may be essential when relatively superior competent suppliers of specialist M&E offerings can make above normal returns when the contractor is taking most of the contractual risk and earning only low or normal returns

The healthcare facility case: reactive supplier selection with a buyer partial win and supplier partial win outcome

7.1 Introduction

This case focuses on the sourcing of a major healthcare facility by a large NHS Trust, Major City Hospital NHS Trust (MCHT), and its relationship with a major construction firm, Specialist Construction Projects (SCP). The project was the NHS Trust's first experience of this type of sourcing, but the construction firm had considerable experience of delivering similar healthcare projects.

Given that MCHT required this type of major facility on a very infrequent basis, it was not in a position to offer prospective construction firms any promise of future work to encourage them to enter into a long-term collaborative relationship. A proactive approach to sourcing was, therefore, not feasible for MCHT or SCP. The NHS Trust (MCHT) hoped, however, that it would be able to maximise its sourcing leverage and achieve value for money by undertaking reactive sourcing in a robust and professional manner.

The eventual performance outcome in this case highlights a common dilemma facing buyers and suppliers in the construction industry. When there is considerable evidence of buyer ignorance and information asymmetry between the construction firm and its client, it is feasible for the construction firm to use this power resource to satisfice[1] rather than to maximise the value that the client receives. The construction firm can exploit the client's lack of knowledge and experience opportunistically to increase its level of revenue or profitability through variations and claims. In such a situation, the construction firm is likely to achieve its commercial and operational objectives at the expense of the client, which, at best, will only partially attain its objectives.

On the other hand, if the client understands the characteristics of its own construction expenditure, is able to augment its knowledge of the supply market by working with a highly competent professional services supplier, and also invests in internal resources to manage the project effectively so that it acquires a robust knowledge and understanding of construction products and services and

---

[1] To satisfice is to seek solutions and designs that are 'good or satisfactory solutions instead of optimal ones' (Petroski, 2003, p. 8).

the strategies of the firms providing them, then it is possible for the client to create countervailing power against the opportunism of the construction firm. This case shows that this understanding enabled MCHT to reduce the level of information asymmetry and the scope for opportunism by SCP. This resulted in a situation where the client and construction firm achieved a partial win–partial win outcome.

7.2 Background to the case: the construction of a major healthcare facility

The construction of a major healthcare facility requires the integration of a number of supply chains, as illustrated in Figure 7.1. The diagram suggests that the supply chain is linear and simple but the reality may be quite different. If there are complexities or uncertainties involved with certain elements of the construction activity and/or the construction firm does not possess the required expertise, the construction firm may decide to appoint specialist subcontractors to deliver 'packages' of work, for example, specialist structural steelwork M&E, and cladding solutions (as discussed in Chapters 5, 6 and 13 respectively).

The discussion focuses on a 'typical' relationship between client and construction firm within a one-off construction project. The project involved the construction of a major new facility for MCHT. The facility required the design and construction of a 250-bed acute block comprising five major treatment departments (including accident and emergency (A&E) and radiology), four operating theatres, ten 24-bed wards, a mental health unit, teaching facilities, office accommodation and associated plant rooms. The project also included all the associated external works including new access roads, car parks and associated infrastructure services.

While a 'standard' specification existed for the offices, toilets and other non-clinical rooms, the need for a highly sterile environment led to highly 'specialised' design and specifications for key elements of construction requirements. With a number of these elements located within the major clinical areas (four operating theatres, three sterile treatment rooms and three large areas for consultation and treatment), it was imperative that products of very high quality and reliability were specified and that highly competent suppliers integrated these products into the solution.

The buyer – Major City Hospital NHS Trust (MCHT)

At the simplest level, the end customer can be considered as the sponsor of the building process: the organisation that initiates the construction process and appoints the project team. In this particular case, MCHT identified a need to upgrade its existing facilities with the construction of a new acute block to meet the needs of the local population. Obviously, the Trust's primary 'business' is the provision of healthcare services, and construction is only a support activity to this primary business. For this reason, MCHT was dependent on construction expertise from outside the organisation.

Traditionally, in the construction industry, small and occasional clients appoint an architect to develop their brief, and advise on the appointment of other professional services, construction firms and subcontractors. In this case, MCHT appointed an architect to assist with these activities and subsequently play an active role in the management of the project to eliminate potential opportunism by the contractor. Despite MCHT's relative inexperience in the construction

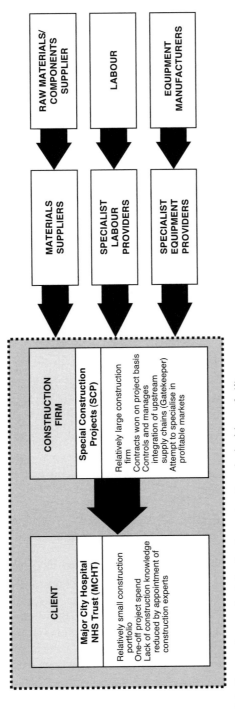

Figure 7.1 Construction supply chains for the construction of a healthcare facility

marketplace and with the assistance of external professional services, MCHT also recognised the importance of selecting a competent construction firm using a robust methodology with an array of clear supplier selection criteria.

Following the Official Journal of the European Communities (OJEC) procurement route because of the value of the project, MCHT identified that although price was considered to be the single most important factor, the selection of the construction firm should be based on an array of criteria. These criteria included: excellence in implementation (project cost, project quality, project duration, expertise in innovation and an ability to provide full service) business support (knowledge of industry and follow-up service) and construction approach (use of best practices and methodological approach). From these criteria, the most important were deemed to be project cost, quality of offering and the company's knowledge and experience of providing healthcare solutions.

The buyer (MCHT) eventually selected Special Construction Projects (SCP) to undertake the design and construction for the new healthcare facility. At the outset of the project, the total cost of the construction element was initially estimated to be £75 million. However, after detailed design work and development of the specification, MCHT put the work out to tender and received prices ranging from £70 to £80 million. Using robust selection criteria, a preferred contractor was identified that submitted a price of £72.5 million. Although not the lowest price, this contractor was selected due to its significant experience with delivering similar projects in the healthcare environment to a very high quality, within timescales and incorporating the latest technology.

The buyer (MCHT), like all construction clients, required value for money, but without clear objectives assessment of what is value for money is impossible. In such circumstances, the client's role in the procurement process is confined to strategic oversight: in conjunction with professional services it sets the objectives and the construction industry turns these objectives into reality. As such, the strategic decisions made at the very outset of a project are the most crucial because they form the basis for the overall procurement and contract strategy. It is, therefore, critical for the client to understand the marketplace and the strategies and approaches of the construction firms so that it can develop an appropriately structured value proposition and avoid the problems from inappropriate sourcing and relationship management. In this regard, MCHT demonstrated considerable expertise but this understanding was confined to the first-tier and did not extend upstream of this particular dyadic relationship.

The supplier – Special Construction Projects Plc (SCP)

Low technical and financial barriers to entry have led to the highly fragmented and contested nature of the construction industry. Despite this, the supply chain for a healthcare facility requires a construction firm to integrate a multitude of highly specialised products and services into a complex project and this reduces the number of firms able to undertake this role. Construction firms with the required level of competence and expertise are largely confined to those major players that have had considerable experience with similar projects.

The company selected to undertake the design and construction element of the project was SCP, with an annual turnover of £240 million. This turnover makes it one of a small number of large organisations within the construction industry (only one per cent of construction firms has a turnover of more than £5 million).

Table 7.1 *The top ten UK construction groups by turnover,
2004 (Source: Annual reports and various online databases)*

	Construction Group	Turnover: £m
1	AMEC Plc	4816
2	Balfour Beatty Plc	4171
3	Taylor Woodrow Plc	3361
4	Bovis Lend Lease	3155
5	George Wimpey Plc	3006
6	Barratt Developments Plc	2434
7	Persimmon Plc	2131
8	Mowlem Plc	2094
9	Carillion Plc	1992
10	Laing O'Rourke	1541

Table 7.1 shows the top ten firms operating in the UK construction sector (SCP's revenue of £240 million would have positioned them at number 6 in the list). These ten firms account for less than ten per cent of UK construction revenues.

Construction firms facing uncertain project-by-project revenues and intense competition experience a continuous fight for survival. While they would ideally prefer long-term preferred relationships with clients to ensure revenue predictability and profitability, they typically have to settle for the short-term adversarial pursuit of projects. In such an environment construction firms attempt to differentiate their offerings through reputation and recognition within the marketplace. The supplier (SCP) has attempted to create a reputation for the delivery of high quality and cost-effective solutions that exceed client's expectations within the healthcare sector.

Regardless of how functionally superior or cost-effective a construction firm's product or service offering may be in the marketplace, if it is not on tender lists in the first place a firm's ability to capture market share will be reduced. When major construction clients consider sourcing construction, then certain well-known companies are the most often recognised within the marketplace. This is perhaps not surprising given that these companies are the major established players, with large turnovers and significant marketing expenditures.

It should be recognised, however, that the majority of contractors do not have a segmented strategic approach for the possible markets in which they could operate. However, unlike the majority of construction firms, SCP does focus its efforts on those industries where it is perceived to provide a differentiated product/service offering from competitors. By focusing on certain sectors, such as healthcare, and striving to become the best provider within that sector it has been able to enjoy continuous success over time.

7.3 The buyer–supplier relationship management approach

This section provides a background to the dyadic relationship between MCHT and SCP. In analysing the key buyer and supplier power resources and the market and supply chain circumstances, it provides an understanding of buyer and supplier power and whether MCHT was in a position to maximise value for money (an increase in functionality and a reduction in the total cost of ownership), or whether SCP was in a position to maximise value from supply (increases in share of customer and market revenue, and increases in prices and product/service profitability leading to above-normal returns).

The client (MCHT) – construction firm (SCP) dyad

The relationship between the client and the construction firm is the key dyad that determines the appropriation of value and profit margins within any entire construction supply chain. It has been argued previously that if clients have limited understanding and insufficient information about the supply base they are unlikely to have direct control over what they are sourcing. This may result in the potential for the construction firm to use information asymmetries to earn higher margins, or influence the client in the use of specific suppliers so that it has a position of relative power in the particular transaction to further increase returns. In this case, MCHT's ability to control SCP was dependent on its capacity to obtain key power resources within the relationship and, at the same time, effectively monitor SCP in order to reduce the scope for opportunism. Conversely, SCP's ability to earn above normal returns was dependent on its ability to obtain the power to use information asymmetry opportunistically both pre- and post-contractually.

Construction projects are typically of high value and very important for the long-term success of the client and construction firm. In this case, the contract value for the construction works of £72.5 million over three years accounted for approximately 10% of the supplier's annual turnover. This expenditure may be adjudged to provide the client with a key power resource because the single project accounts for a relatively high share of the construction firm's turnover. However, although this expenditure may seem relatively significant, and contribute to a position of relative power for the client, it should be considered in conjunction with the frequency with which the parties transact.

In this dyadic relationship the construction activity is a one-off project for both MCHT and SCP and, as a result, neither party has any need (or incentive) to develop a long-term relationship with the other. The advantage obtained by MCHT from the possession of a relatively high volume of demand is effectively diminished, therefore, because it is unable to offer a high level of frequency. Furthermore, the one-off nature of construction procurement, combined with the complexity of projects, typically results in situations where clients do not possess sufficient knowledge and information with regard to supply to stop suppliers from using opportunism – especially post-contractually – to earn above normal returns even though they operate in what are contested markets pre-contractually.

Given that MCHT had no planned construction expenditure in the future, it had no realistic alternative but to adopt a short-term and reactive *supplier selection* relationship management approach with SCP. The buyer (MCHT) attempted, however, to minimise the self-evident asymmetries in the possession of key operational and commercial information through the use of an expert professional services provider. This resulted in a number of significant benefits including: a robust understanding of the utility and scarcity of the construction firm's power resources pre-contractually, and a reduction in the scope for opportunism by the construction firm post-contractually (eliminating the potential for superfluous variations to the original project and subsequent claims).

On the supply-side of this relationship, the critical power resources for SCP that dictated whether or not it would be able to obtain value from supply were scarcity (real or maintained through the deliberate use of misinformation) and utility. The majority of construction firms operate within highly competitive markets and are unable to close the market to competition through the monopoly ownership of key external supply chain resources. As a result, there is limited scope for these construction firms to use isolating mechanisms to create a high degree of supplier scarcity. However, in the case of commoditised markets, information in the form of brand building can be used to create an impression of supply market scarcity.

When considering utility, the role of information, critical in the construction industry, also impacts on the level of supplier power resources. Pre-contractually, SCP tried to offer a tailored and differentiated offering that was distinct from the competition to maintain a strong brand image within the marketplace. The use of branding and reputation was seen by SCP as a mechanism to increase MCHT's perception of value and decrease the perceived level of contestation from other potential suppliers. However, this is probably the most ineffective isolating mechanism as it is difficult and costly to maintain and only offers a short lived barrier. Post-contractually, information asymmetry can be used by opportunistic suppliers to achieve higher returns due to ignorance by the client of the commercial consequences of operational practices (claims).

7.4 Performance outcome from the buyer–supplier relationship

At the outset of the project the client and construction firm had conflicting operational and commercial objectives. Operationally, MCHT was attempting to maximise the functionality and, commercially, to minimise the total costs of ownership of the final construction asset. This attempt to maximise the value for money it received from the supplier was only partially achieved. In direct contrast, SCP sought to maximise the value it received from supplying the healthcare facility by using post-contractual opportunism to achieve above normal returns. The supplier (SCP) was only partially successful in achieving this goal.

The buyer (MCHT) avoided this post-contractual leverage by SCP, despite its inexperience in construction sourcing, by employing construction experts to provide a sophisticated understanding of the supply market and to inform its sourcing decision pre-contractually. It also used this expert advice to monitor the supplier and also to reduce the levels of complexity and uncertainty normally associated with projects of this type post-contractually. This ensured that it could not be taken advantage of as fully as SCP would have liked post-contractually.

Despite this, in the relationship there were a number of factors that provided SCP with power levers pre- and post-contractually. The supplier (SCP) had targeted specific (and normally highly profitable) markets to focus on and in which it could provide tailored and differentiated offerings. This brand image provided SCP with a form of market closure pre-contractually, despite the high level of actual contestation in the market and, therefore, with an opportunity (once it had won the contract) to attempt to use opportunism post-contractually. This opportunity was effectively denied to larger construction suppliers who did not have a sufficiently differentiated supply offering in the market.

Figure 7.2 contains a summary of the dyad between MCHT and SCP and the performance outcome from the relationship.

The buyer (MCHT) was reasonably happy with what it received. This was because it received its facility on time and to specification. In terms of final cost, MCHT demonstrated competence in developing a robust framework that facilitated the reduction of construction costs from the initial estimate of £75 million to £72.5 million, without compromising quality or adversely impacting project duration. Cost figures during the construction phase of the project were verified and controlled by an independent cost consultant who monitored and benchmarked supplier performance, and helped MCHT to undertake robust contract and project management. Despite this reduction of £2.5 million in the final project cost, MCHT and its professional advisers (architect and cost consultant) did not

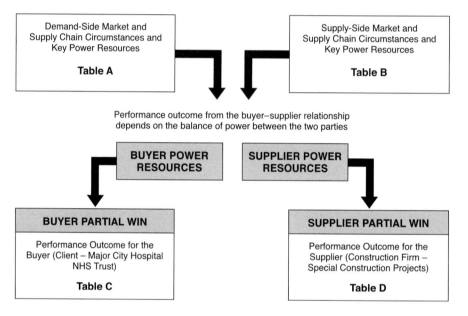

Figure 7.2 A summary of the dyad between the client (MCHT) and construction firm (SCP) and the performance outcome from the relationship

Table A Demand-Side Market and Supply Chain Circumstances and Key Power Resources

There are many buyers in the total construction market but fewer buyers in the healthcare sector (mainly public sector organisations)

Major City NHS Trust (MCHT) has a relatively low share of the total construction market but relatively **high share of the healthcare sector** with a project value of £72.5 million. Therefore, the supplier (SCP) has a relatively **high dependency** on the buyer (MCHT) for revenue

MCHT has an **infrequent one-off need** to go to the construction market and no future plans for further capital investment

The requirements of MCHT are **highly complex** (in terms of product and service and the project environment), **non-standardised** and require considerable supplier expertise for their integration into the project

MCHT has **high switching costs**

MCHT, after working in conjunction with professional services, has a **relatively clear value proposition** – a high quality product delivered on time and at an acceptable cost

MCHT is relatively unaware of the potential scope for **standardisation** of design and specification and **prefabrication** of key components common across the project

MCHT has **high search costs**, but through working with professional services and investment in internal resources, has reduced (without completely eradicating) the level of **information asymmetries** and **scope for opportunism** and acquired a relatively robust knowledge and understanding of construction products and services and the strategies of the industry players

Table B Supply-Side Market and Supply Chain Circumstances and Key Power Resources

There are many suppliers in the total construction market but fewer suppliers operating in the healthcare sector with the required level of expertise for this particular project

The value of the project, £72.5 million over three years, accounts for a relatively **high share of the annual turnover (10%)** of Special Construction Projects (SCP)

SCP is **not as highly dependent** on the NHS Trust (as other suppliers would be) for revenue as through the use of a segmented approach to targeting work in profitable segments, it is able to be selective with the projects it undertakes

SCP considers the MCHT's business to be **relatively attractive** as it has considerable knowledge and expertise related to similar projects

SCP has relatively **high switching costs**

Supplier's offerings are not commoditised and standardised but **highly customised** to the specific requirements of MCHT and working in a healthcare environment

SCP has a **very strong brand image** and reputation. This reputation has been strengthened by constantly delivering high quality projects on time and within financial budgets

SCP has **some information asymmetry** advantages over MCHT (especially post-contractually) despite MCHT's investment in expert knowledge

---

Table C Performance Outcome for the Client (MCHT) – Buyer Partial Win

The client, Major City Hospital NHS Trust (MCHT), was faced with total construction costs lower than original budget by £2.5 million. The original estimate was £75 million and final construction cost was £72.5 million

The functional expectations of MCHT were met but not exceeded

Delivery of project was on time

Table D Performance Outcome for the Construction Firm (SCP) – Supplier Partial Win

Special Construction Projects (SCP) made a profit of £5.5 million (7.5%) rather than the expected £2.175 million (3%) on this project

SCP enhanced its reputation within the industry for delivering quality projects within time and cost constraints

This led to other work with other clients

---

have a mechanism in place to fully understand the cost minimising opportunity in this one-off project, although it was able to stop SCP making post-contractual claims by ensuring that it had included sufficient clauses in the contract documentation that covered post-contractual opportunism of this type.

The supplier (SCP) calculated that it made an overall profit of £5.5 million on this particular project, equal to a 7.5% return. These returns were somewhat higher than the 3% (or £2.175 million) assumption that had been built into its initial tender submission. These benefits were achieved because post-contractually SCP had superior knowledge of its own supply chains than that available to the cost consultants employed by MCHT. This superior information arose as a result of the cost consultants being unaware of the true 'cash in hand' payments being made to many sub-contract staff (which in some cases were 20% lower than the agreed contracted rates). Furthermore, the cost consultant was not aware of the fact that much of the equipment used on the project was fully depreciated and the overhead elements in the initial bid had suggested that it was not.

These provide just two examples of the types of post-contractual opportunism that were available to SCP that MCHT, despite having recourse to expert advisers, could not eradicate. By such methods SCP was able to inflate its returns and to raise them above the low or normal returns that had been expected by MCHT. Despite this, the game was not all one-sided. This was because the cost consultants were able to spot a number of double counting and erroneous costing and invoicing claims made by SCP throughout the duration of the contract.

As a result, SCP was unable to achieve post-contractually its ideal of above normal double-digit returns. This was because, due to a robust *supplier selection* approach that factored in contractual clauses to stop post-contractual claims and opportunism, SCP was forced to deliver within the budget figure of £72.5 million. The supplier (SCP) was, however, still able to make higher returns post-contractually than the 3% expected because it was able to reduce its operating costs without having to pass these gains on to MCHT. It also attained a number of other benefits. In addition to the project being acknowledged by industry experts to be highly innovative in terms of design, SCP was able to further enhance its reputation within the marketplace by successfully delivering a very high quality facility, on time and within budget. This enhanced its reputation and led to the award of other more profitable work with other public sector organisations.

7.5 Summary

A summary of the relationship management approach and performance outcome for this case is given in Table 7.2.

Table 7.2 A summary of the relationship management approach and performance outcome

Nature of Relationship Management Approach	The client, with no planned construction expenditure in the future, saw no need to develop a long-term collaborative and proactive relationship with the construction firm
	The only option considered by the client was the implementation of a short-term and reactive *supplier selection* relationship management approach
	The client hoped that if this reactive approach was undertaken in a robust and professional manner then its commercial and operational objectives of maximising functionality and minimising total costs of ownership could still be achieved
	This necessitated the use of expert advisers by the buyer in the form of an architect and cost consultant
Nature of Buyer 'Partial Win'	Estimated costs were reduced by £2.5 million
	Functional expectations met but not exceeded
	Delivery of project on time
	Further cost savings may have been possible as the supplier made a higher return than expected of 7.5% rather than 3%
Nature of Supplier 'Partial Win'	£5.5 million profit on project, with a reasonable return of 7.5%
	No double-digit returns because of limits on post-contractual leverage
	Enhanced reputation in the marketplace by delivering a high quality and critically acclaimed project that fully met the buyer's expectations
	This recognition led to other work that was even more profitable
Conclusions	Transparency over both sides of the buyer and supplier relationship is essential to understand the true nature of what is happening in any exchange
	In this case both parties achieved a very acceptable outcome, but both could have achieved more with different partners
	The buyer could have received a lower overall cost of construction
	The supplier could have made higher returns
	Despite this, both parties achieved a partial win

The major finding from this case is that reactive sourcing approaches based on *supplier selection* can create performance outcomes in which both parties partially achieve their goals but do not fully do so. In this case, MCHT received a fully functional healthcare facility to design and on time, and within a budget figure that was £2.5 million less than originally estimated. This may at first appear to be a full win for the buyer but it was in fact only a partial win because there were significant savings that could have been made in the form of the £3.325 million that SCP was able to retain by using superior knowledge post-contractually to attain a 7.5% (£5.5 million) rather than 3% (£2.175 million) return from the overall project cost of £72.5 million. This case demonstrates the truth for buyers that ignorance can be bliss.

Reference

Petroski, H. (2003), *Small Things Considered: Why There Is No Perfect Design*, Knopf, New York, NY, USA.

The motorway case: reactive supplier selection with a buyer partial win and supplier lose outcome

8.1 Introduction

This case analyses a buyer and supplier relationship in the construction of a new 40-mile-long, dual three-lane (plus hard shoulder) motorway. Prestige Construction (PC) was awarded the £495 million design and construction contract by the responsible government agency (the Department of Roads – DoR), with PC having almost four years to complete the project. The case focuses specifically on the sourcing of a key quarry product within this project – ready-mixed concrete. The supplies of ready-mixed concrete and other quarry products are considered to be critical to road construction, because these products form the 'base' for the road structure and are directly linked to its strength, quality and durability. Furthermore, they also constitute a significant proportion of total construction costs.

The discussion focuses primarily on the relationship between the construction firm, Prestige Construction (PC) and the sole supplier of ready-mixed concrete to the project, ABC Ready Mix (ABC). The case shows that PC was able to partially achieve its value for money goals but that ABC was unable to achieve any positive performance outcomes at all. In this case it is also necessary to understand how the supply chain and relationship management strategies of the client can have a significant impact upon the ability of the upstream players to implement particular relationship management approaches. The analysis shows how DoR's short-term and reactive approach prevented PC from implementing a collaborative and proactive sourcing approach with ABC to the ultimate detriment of the effectiveness and efficiency of the DoR's road building programme.

8.2 Background to the case: the construction of a major motorway

The construction of a motorway is extremely costly. In this case the estimated cost for the project was £500 million and value for money was politically very important for the DoR. It was essential, therefore, that a competent contractor (in this case PC) should be selected to deliver the motorway on time and within budget. The contractor (PC) had the overall responsibility for the project's design and construction including the selection of upstream suppliers.

For the construction of any road or motorway, quarry products[1] (including ready-mixed concrete) are key because they represent a high proportion of total project costs and they have a direct impact on build quality. For a motorway of this type PC was, therefore, faced with the challenge of ensuring that the quality and durability of the road surface was maximised so that future maintenance and disruption to travellers is minimised, while minimising the costs of construction materials. This is not a straightforward task. In many construction cases the ultimate client develops the design and specification internally and/or in conjunction with professional services. In this case, however, the design and build (D&B) arrangement meant that PC controlled this aspect of the work. The contractor (PC) was contracted to deliver the road to National Motorway Standards, but how this was to be achieved precisely was left to it.

The construction of a new motorway requires the integration of many supply chains as shown in Figure 8.1. In addition to the client, construction firm and supplier of the ready-mixed concrete, it also includes the supplier of the cement required for the production of concrete. In this case, the cement supplier (ABC Quality Cement) was also part of the same corporate group as the ready-mixed concrete supplier (i.e. ABC Quality Construction Materials Group).

When completed the motorway is designed to appear the same throughout with a black asphalt surface, white lines and reflecting road studs. While the road surface consists of a modern, low-noise surfacing known as stone mastic asphalt, underneath there are several layers of material to provide the strength to carry the traffic loads and provide a high quality road with a very long life.

Figure 8.2 shows the structure of the new motorway. The first layer of material laid onto the carefully excavated earth is a layer of cement bound material (CBM) that provides a sub-base layer. Used along the entire length of the road, it comprises sand and gravel that has been quarried from sites within the motorway boundary, mixed with a small percentage of cement to bind the sand and gravel together. The thickness of this sub-base depends upon the ground conditions underneath. While this layer uses similar quarry products, this case examines the sourcing of the ready-mixed concrete that forms the core of the road. This layer of concrete, positioned between the sub-base and the final surface, is a 200-mm-thick layer of continuously reinforced concrete pavement (CRCP) and is made with high-strength pavement quality (PQ) concrete with a layer of high-tensile steel-reinforcement positioned midway in the depth of the slab. The construction firm utilised a number of innovative methods to support a faster and more efficient construction process to ensure that the project was delivered on time.

These methods related to the placing and tying together of the reinforcement bars and the pouring of the concrete. The concrete is laid around the reinforcement using a machine known as a slip-form paver. The wet concrete is mixed in a

---

[1] Quarry products encompass a range of materials including aggregates (crushed rock, sand and gravel), cement, ready-mixed concrete and asphalt. These materials are considered to be critical to road construction because they effectively form the 'base' for the actual road and are directly linked to the strength, quality and durability of the entire road structure, and they also constitute a significant proportion of total construction costs.

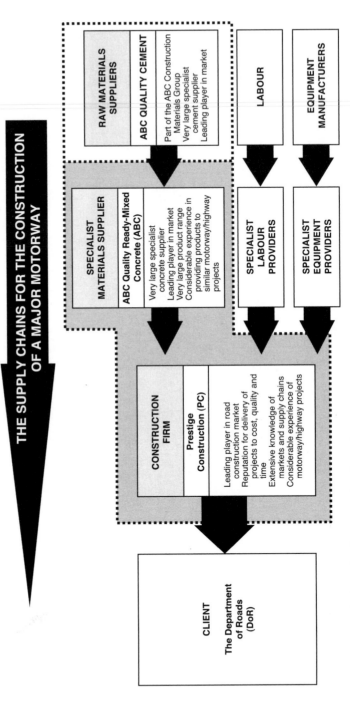

Figure 8.1 Construction supply chains for the construction of a major motorway

Types of Road Construction on New Motorway

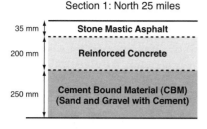

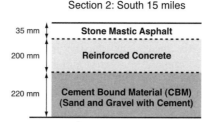

Figure 8.2 The structure of the new motorway

batching plant situated in an on-site quarry and transported to the paving machine to match the required concrete delivery rate of 2500 to 3000 tonnes a day. This delivery rate guaranteed the laying of approximately 400 linear metres of full width carriageway (three lanes and hard-shoulder) each working day. Once the concrete layer is complete the final surface can be laid, the white lines painted, road studs fixed, safety barriers erected, signs put up and all the other finishing touches completed for the road to be opened to traffic. This suggests that the physical construction process is straightforward. However, the sheer scale and scope of the project introduced considerable complexities into the supply chain relationships beyond the programming of the work and critical logistical management of materials, heavy plant and equipment.

The buyer – Prestige Construction (PC)

The Department of Roads (DoR) awarded the design and build contract for the new motorway, valued at £495 million, to PC. Although PC's knowledge and experience of providing similar road projects was a critical selection criterion, in this case price was actually considered to be the single most important factor. Other selection criteria included: excellence in implementation (quality of offering, project duration and expertise in innovation) and construction approach (use of industry best practices). While the DoR anticipated that many firms would bid, the size and scale of the project meant that only the largest contractors were willing to undertake the project and accept the associated risks.

The buyer (PC) serves the international markets for rail, road and power systems, buildings and complex structures. The different groups within PC have historically been successful through the adoption of a strong focus on delivering increases in profit, not turnover, and through working closely with clients. The company is an industry leader in large design and construct, DBFO (design, build, finance and operate) and ECI (early contractor involvement) schemes, and aims to deliver engineering excellence through cost efficient, value for money, customer focused solutions for all road infrastructure projects. In 2001, PC had a turnover of around £4 billion of which just over £2 billion was related to civil and other specialist engineering, design and management services, principally in transport.

At the outset of the project, the total cost of the construction element was estimated to be £495 million. Despite knowing the likely costs of construction, the DoR did not know whether or not it was maximising value for money. The DoR's role in the project procurement process is that of strategic overview: it sets the broad functional objectives and the construction industry turns these objectives into reality. In turn, the construction firm (PC in this case) attempts to maximise the value that it receives from the supply markets from which it sources. It is, therefore, critical for PC to understand the marketplace and the strategies and approaches of its material suppliers so that it can develop an appropriately structured value proposition and avoid any unforeseen problems from inappropriate sourcing.

In this regard, PC demonstrated considerable expertise and knowledge of the supply market for ready-mixed concrete, but this understanding did not extend upstream of this particular dyadic relationship. Furthermore, PC's inability to consolidate demand for ready-mixed concrete across its portfolio of projects meant that it could not offer certainty and regularity of demand to its upstream supplier – ABC Quality Ready-Mixed Concrete (ABC). Without a promise of a long-term commitment from PC, ABC was unwilling to undertake extensive dedicated investments and relationship-specific adaptations and a proactive relationship management approach was, therefore, not possible. The only alternative available to PC was to manage the relationship using a reactive *supplier selection* approach at the first-tier of the supply chain.

The supplier – ABC Quality Ready-Mixed Concrete (ABC)

The building materials sector encompasses a wide range of materials and components including concrete, aggregates, cement, bricks, tiles, glass and timber, but in the aggregate sector five major companies account for over 70% of the UK market, with three players dominating the cement sector. The supplier of ready-mixed concrete in this case, ABC Quality Ready-Mixed Concrete (ABC), is part of the ABC Quality Construction Materials Group. The ABC Group is a leading international producer and supplier of materials, products and services used essentially in the construction industry. The Group is substantial in its commercial size and geographic spread, with over 25 000 employees operating in 40 countries. It has a turnover close to £4 billion. The manufacture and supply of concrete and aggregates accounts for around two-thirds of this figure (£2.6 billion), with the manufacture and supply of cement accounting for approximately 23% (£0.9 billion). Almost a quarter of revenues were from the UK market. For this particular project, the contract value for the ready-mixed concrete was approximately £10 million.

In pursuing an aggressive strategy of growth, chiefly around its core products of aggregates, ready-mixed concrete and cement, the company has become the world's fifth largest building materials group. In addition to this pursuit of growth around its core products, the company has also developed a number of other strategies: to be vertically integrated in aggregates, concrete and cement; to generate improved returns by achieving the full synergies of integration; to make customer focus an overriding business principle; to be the lowest cost producer for its core products; to operate in mature and selected growth markets; and to ensure the sharing of best practice across the organisation. These strategies have resulted in the company operating over 400 quarries and 20 cement plants across the world to meet the continuing demand for construction materials.

By output volume, ABC is the largest supplier of ready-mixed concrete in the UK. A leader in the development of concrete technology, the company's geographical coverage is unrivalled. This is an important differentiating factor because of the nature of the supplier's products, that is they are not usually transported over long distances because of very high delivery costs. Indeed, to minimise overall construction costs, ready-mixed concrete is typically only transported between 5–10 miles (8–16 km) from batching plant to customer site. This, combined with the significant volumes required for this project, means that the supplier ideally has to have nearby quarries and the ability to set up a batching plant-on site (at one of its quarries).

The decision to appoint ABC to supply the ready-mixed concrete was, therefore, a relatively simple one because of the combination of the two main selection criteria – security of supply and the reduction of environmental impact (minimisation of transportation). The need to have a supply of 2500 to 3000 tonnes (approx. 1000 cubic metres or 150 truck loads) a day meant that there were few alternatives to the localised supply from ABC, as no other suppliers operated quarries in the area.

8.3 The buyer–supplier relationship management approach

The analysis of PC's relationship management approach with ABC in the following discussion explains the power resources available to both parties to achieve the maximisation of their value for money and value from supply objectives.

The construction firm (PC) – specialist material supplier (ABC) dyad

The construction firm (PC)'s ability to control ABC and maximise value for money is dependent on its ability to obtain key power resources and at the same time effectively monitor ABC to reduce the scope for opportunism pre- and post-contractually. For this particular sector of the construction industry, demand is characterised by very high levels of uncertainty surrounding the DoR's spending on road construction. With frequent policy changes (related to funding and whether new roads should be built at all), expenditure tends to be highly irregular and unpredictable. This irregularity of demand makes it very difficult for construction companies to engineer a regular demand for the key raw materials required for the construction of roads. Construction firms, therefore, find it very difficult to develop long-term relationships with the suppliers of materials.

This problem with the low frequency of demand and the unpredictability of future revenues is exacerbated by the uncertainty surrounding the actual location of future projects. Location is a critical factor in the supply of quarry products and ready-mixed concrete, as transportation of these materials accounts for a significant proportion of costs (40–70%) and timely supply is critical. To minimise these costs concrete batching plants and aggregate quarries should ideally be as close to the site as possible. Competition occurs, therefore, at the local level and the high degree of general contestation in the 'wider' raw material supply markets is effectively eliminated. As a result, construction firms normally select ready-mixed concrete manufacturers on a project-by-project basis, according to the location of the site, the product specification and their quality, price and ability to meet the required demand levels.

For this particular project, the contract value for the ready-mixed concrete was approximately £10 million. This figure equates to approximately 1% of ABC's total UK turnover and 2.5% of total UK revenues from the manufacture and supply of ready-mixed concrete. With around 23 million cubic metres of ready-mixed concrete produced annually in the UK this contract represents less than 1% of total production. Despite the apparent insignificance of these figures, this expenditure may be adjudged to provide PC with a key power resource because the single project accounts for a far higher share of ABC's turnover than any other project and the costs of servicing a single contract of this size is significantly lower than if multiple contracts to the same value had to be serviced.

Although this expenditure may seem significant and contribute to a position of relative power for PC, it should be considered in conjunction with the frequency with which the parties transact. In this relationship with ABC the advantage obtained by PC from the possession of a relatively high volume of demand (when compared to other single projects) is effectively diminished because it is unable to offer a high level of frequency.

In addition to volume and frequency, the complexity of the product and service offering are additional factors that determine the level of relative power in the relationship. Although ready-mixed concrete is highly commoditised and standardised, there are relatively high levels of complexity and innovation with regard to its integration into the road structure. This complexity was, however, well known by PC, which has extensive experience in the use of this concrete placement technology in similar projects. It can be assumed, therefore, that PC would have full knowledge of any potential suppliers in the required local area capable of meeting the functional requirements of its design solution. As a result, it was relatively easy and inexpensive for it to monitor ABC and prevent opportunistic behaviour based on information asymmetries.

On the supply-side ABC was operating within a market with low contestation because there were only a small number of manufacturers in the local geographical area capable of supplying a high quality product at the rate and specific time demanded by PC's programme of works. In this situation the ownership of a site-specific asset (the quarry and batching plant) normally has a direct bearing on the extent to which the supplier of the ready-mixed concrete faces direct competition. With only ABC owning a quarry in close proximity to the project (actually on-site) there was no competition from other material suppliers. The property rights associated with the ownership of the quarry normally provides a site-specific advantage that effectively creates a localised monopoly and, thereby, gives a supplier (such as ABC) an opportunity to premium price and appropriate above normal returns.

It is also frequently argued that the level of supplier scarcity in the ready-mixed concrete market is further increased by the presence of another isolating mechanism. Although the operation of an informal collusive cartel is strongly denied by the leading companies it is widely believed that true competition does not take place because the market for ready-mixed concrete consists of a series of localised markets that are controlled and coordinated by the major players. Under such an oligopolistic market structure it is possible (although we do not have direct evidence that this does in fact occur) for firms to co-operate on sourcing, pricing and output decisions to earn above normal profits. If this does ever occur such an outcome radically changes the balance of power in favour of the supplier rather than the buyer.

The structural shift in the balance of power towards ABC in this case is largely attributable to this high level of supplier scarcity at the local level. In this case, however, this potential position of *supplier dominance* was eroded by the fact that the PC's expenditure was highly attractive and constituted a very high percentage of the local market demand for the duration of the project. This created a situation of interdependence between the buyer and supplier. This meant that ABC would not be able to premium price its offering to PC as much as it would have been able to do when it could act as a truly dominant supplier to many small buyers all of whom were locally dependent upon them.

8.4 Performance outcome from the buyer–supplier relationship

At the outset of the project, PC and ABC had conflicting operational and commercial goals and objectives. The construction firm (PC) wanted to achieve value for money in the form, operationally, of maximising the functionality of the road

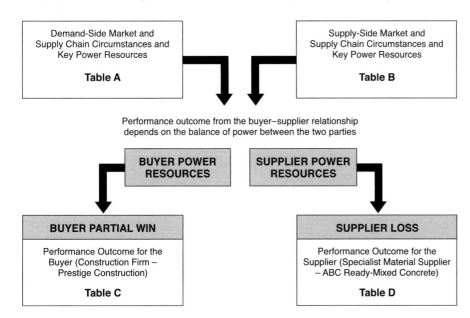

Figure 8.3 A summary of the dyad between the construction firm (PC) and specialist material supplier (ABC) and the performance outcome from the relationship

Table A Demand-Side Market and Supply Chain Circumstances and Key Power Resources

There are many construction firms acting as buyers in the road construction market but significantly fewer buyers for ready-mixed concrete (RMC) in the local market (especially buyers for road contracts)

Prestige Construction (PC) has a relatively low share of the total construction market but a **higher share of the local RMC and aggregate market** for integration into road construction projects with a project value of £595 million. Therefore, ABC (the supplier in this case) has a relatively low/medium dependency on PC for revenue

PC has a regular need to source from the RMC market but there is **no current certainty/regularity** about requirements and volumes for specific concrete types in the locality

The requirements of PC are **relatively straightforward** (in terms of the project environment and to a lesser extent the products themselves) and are easily integrated into the project

PC has **high switching costs**, as although there are a large number of suppliers there are few local suppliers with the reputation and capability of providing very high quality and reliable products

The client (and PC) has a **relatively clear value proposition** – a high quality motorway delivered on time and at an acceptable and predictable cost

PC is aware of the potential scope for **standardisation** and **prefabrication** of specific component elements but any proactive sourcing is hindered by the client's demand specification

PC has **relatively low search costs**, as it has extensive knowledge and understanding about RMC products and services and the strategies of the industry players (including the potential for cartelistic behaviour)

Table B Supply-Side Market and Supply Chain Circumstances and Key Power Resources

Ready-mixed concrete (RMC) is a major raw material as almost every construction project requires concrete for the sub-structure (foundations) or structure (walls or floors)

There are a small number of large suppliers in the RMC market but fewer suppliers operating in the region capable of delivering products to the required quality levels to tight timescales

The total value of the RMC, approximately £9.75 million, accounts for a relatively **low share of the annual turnover** of ABC (<1%). However, the attractiveness of this business increases if only UK ABC revenues are considered (the contract accounts for about 4% of these revenues)

ABC is **relatively dependent** on PC for revenue, as there is a high degree of uncertainty surrounding alternative contracts (of equivalent size) in the local area

ABC considers PC's business to be **relatively attractive** as there are low costs associated with servicing the contract. ABC has a local quarry and batching plant and sufficient transport to deliver the required amounts of RMC to site

ABC has relatively **low switching costs**

Supplier's offerings (taken as a whole) are relatively **commoditised** and **standardised** but there is **limited customisation** to the specific requirements of the client and working in a road construction environment

ABC has a **very strong brand image** and **reputation** for delivering innovative products of a very high quality

ABC has very **limited information asymmetry** advantages over PC

Table C Performance Outcome for the Construction Firm (PC) – Buyer Partial Win

In this transaction Prestige Construction (PC) was faced with costs lower than original budget by £0.25 million. The original estimate for the RMC element was £10 million and final cost of RMC was £9.75 million

PC did not know whether further costs savings could have been obtained

Functional expectations of client only met after remedial action by PC to replace a section of the highway. This section contained sub-standard RMC that was evident because of large cracks

PC covered the expense of this rework through claims against the supplier (ABC)

Delivery of project on time, despite the problems experienced

---

Table D Performance Outcome for the Specialist Material Supplier (ABC) – Supplier Loss

ABC Quality Ready-Mixed Concrete (ABC) calculated that it made a loss of £0.5 million on this project. This was largely due to:

  Claims made against it in relation to the supply of sub-standard ready-mixed concrete (RMC)

  The requirement to supply additional RMC to the project

ABC damaged its reputation within the industry for delivering quality projects within time and cost constraints

Major industry players recognised that it was ABC's fault so it was expected to impact on future revenues

---

and, commercially, by minimising the total costs of construction relative to the bid price it had submitted to DoR. This objective was only partially achieved. The material supplier (ABC) hoped to win the contract for all of the work and also to earn above normal returns. It was not successful in either of these goals.

The construction firm (PC) developed a programme of works that required a guaranteed supply of 2500 to 3000 tonnes of ready-mixed concrete on a daily basis. While meeting this demand, PC also developed a sourcing arrangement that eliminated the potential for ABC to be opportunistic and facilitated the reduction of costs from the initial estimate of £10 million to £9.75 million without compromising quality or adversely impacting timely supply. While there was a reduction of £0.25 million in the cost of the ready-mixed concrete, the construction firm did not, however, have a mechanism in place to fully understand the opportunity available to minimise the total costs of ownership for this category of spend throughout the duration of the project. The maximum feasible reduction in total cost of ownership may have been significantly greater than the £0.25 million achieved.

The construction firm (PC) obtained the cost saving despite having to undertake extensive remedial work to a section of the concrete roadway to meet the required quality standards. Several days after a short section of the concrete core had been laid a number of large cracks appeared. Although at first it was not clear whether the construction technique was at fault, the subsequent testing of the concrete showed that ABC had delivered an incorrect mix to a 200-metre section of the motorway. This section had to be totally replaced, the cost of which was covered by subsequent claims against the material supplier. Despite these problems, the project was still delivered to the client on time and provided a level of (static) functionality as defined within the specification.

The fact that PC achieved these outcomes was attributable to its approach to sourcing from construction supply markets. Prestige Construction recognised the operational and commercial importance of professional procurement and supply management and assigned sufficient financial and technical resources to the activity. However, the focus was solely on reactive supply management activities including: research of the supply market; the development of a clear design and specification; implementation of a robust tendering process; robust supplier selection and negotiation; and effective contract, risk and project management.

Despite this reasonable outcome for PC, ABC calculated that it made an overall loss of £0.5 million on the project. This loss, accounting for approximately 5% of the total contract value, was attributed to the supply of sub-standard ready-mixed concrete to a section of the motorway. The need to replace this section resulted in a claim for £1 million being agreed between PC and ABC on completion of the project. This claim effectively turned the anticipated profit of £0.5 million into a loss of the same amount.

With such bad news quickly transmitted within the industry, ABC damaged their reputation for delivering very high quality ready-mixed concrete to the exact requirements of the client. As a result, it was unable to use the efficient supply of materials to this major project as a mechanism to reduce the effective level of competition within the local supply market in the future. In fact the total opposite, an increase in the level of competition, was expected. Therefore, in addition to having a major impact on the profitability of this particular project, with reputation and brand image being a major consideration for many practitioners responsible for sourcing construction products and services, ABC expected the problems experienced on this project to have a negative impact on future revenues and returns.

8.5 Summary

In summary (see Table 8.1), the major finding from this case is that reactive sourcing approaches can lead to situations in which the buyer (PC) achieves a partial win but the supplier (ABC) experiences a lose outcome. In this case, the buyer could have achieved more if it had been able to manage its demand across all of its local projects in such a way that the local supplier could work more collaboratively with it because it had guaranteed future workloads. However, because the ultimate client (the DoR) does not provide regular or consistent levels of demand for roadworks it was impossible for PC in this case to develop

Table 8.1 A summary of the relationship management approach and performance outcome

Nature of Relationship Management Approach	PC's failure to possess key power resources related to certainty and frequency of demand meant that it was not in a position to offer ABC the key demand-side 'incentives' required for ABC to make a long-term investment in a proactive relationship management approach This difficult situation facing PC was largely attributable to the highly reactive approach of the ultimate client (DoR) – the largest sponsor of road construction projects in the country Despite the attractiveness of this single contract (due to its high value and limited complexity), the inability of PC to consolidate demand for ready-mixed concrete across other road construction projects in the same location meant that a reactive *supplier selection* relationship management approach was the only option available to it
Nature of Buyer 'Partial Win'	Costs lower than original estimate expected by £250 000 Functional expectations fully met. This was the case despite initial problems with the adversarial and opportunistic supplier 'trying it on' and subsequent problems with poor quality ready-mixed concrete The delivery of product (ready-mixed concrete) was made on time according to PC's programme of works
Nature of Supplier 'Loss'	Failure to make any profit on project. The loss of £500 000 was largely attributable to claims made against it in relation to sub-standard ready-mixed concrete Failure to turn one-off contract into regular workload ABC gained a reputation for delivering poor quality product and being adversarial and opportunistic in the pursuit of increased revenue. It was felt that this would adversely impact future revenue and returns
Conclusions	The supplier was either incompetent or attempted to be opportunistic (or both) but the buyer was able to counter this through effective negotiation and through legal recourse The power situation of interdependence ought to have provided a partial win–partial win outcome, but the supplier's behaviour led to a loss for it while the buyer only achieved a partial win This was because the buyer lacked the ability, due to its own and its ultimate customer's inability to manage demand over the long-term on a regular basis

a more proactive approach with ABC and vice versa. In such circumstances buyers and suppliers are forced to adopt short-term and often highly opportunistic sourcing arrangements.

It can be seen from this case that when this occurs opportunism or incompetence (or a combination of both) can backfire. In this case, ABC (either through opportunism or incompetence) provided a poor batch of concrete and suffered such a heavy financial penalty that it made a loss from the project. It is possible that a more proactive and collaborative approach might have eradicated this problem, but this could only have been achieved if the level and frequency of demand from PC provided sufficient incentives for ABC to make the necessary dedicated investments in the relationship and vice versa. In this circumstance, PC might have discovered that it could have sourced its ready-mixed concrete at a much lower cost as well as providing opportunities for ABC to avoid a loss. Since the level of demand was not regular in this case, opportunism and short-termism was rife and a partial win–lose outcome favouring PC occurred.

The heavy engineering plant case: reactive supply chain sourcing with a buyer lose and supplier win outcome

9.1 Introduction

This case focuses on the procurement and supply management of a heavy engineering plant by a Major Electricity Generator (MEG). In response to the Government's low emissions policy, and as part of the company's moves to ensure an efficient supply of power to its customers, MEG required the construction of a new gas-fired 900 MW power plant. After providing a background of the supply chains required for the project, the case focuses on the relationship between MEG and a large construction firm – Heavy Engineering Contractors (HEC).

The electricity generator (MEG) only acquires major capital expenditure projects on a very infrequent basis and, as a result, was not in a position to offer first-tier construction firms a regular revenue stream. Without this regular level of demand there was no incentive for HEC to enter into a long-term proactive and collaborative relationship with the client. As a result, both parties were content to rely on a short-term reactive relationship management approach.

Unfortunately, as we shall see, this approach provided considerable opportunities for HEC to take advantage of MEG and its professional advisers pre- and post-contractually. In this case, MEG could not avoid supplier opportunism and subsequently failed to achieve any of its commercial and operational objectives. The electricity generator (MEG) experienced a lose outcome from the relationship however, this was not the case for HEC who experienced a win outcome of above normal returns.

9.2 Background to the case: the construction of a heavy engineering plant

The construction of a large heavy engineering and power plant for a major electricity generator requires the integration of a number of construction supply chains. Figure 9.1 suggests that the configuration of supply chains is simple, but given the client's inexperience of sourcing from construction supply markets, the high value of the project, the significant risks involved, its risk-averse corporate culture, and

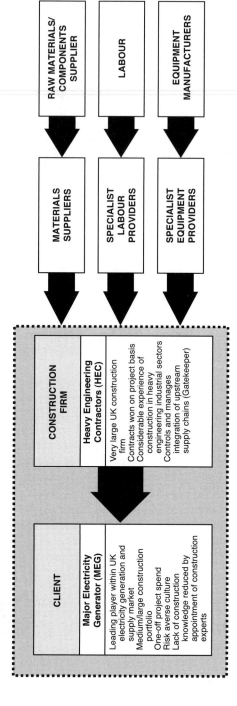

Figure 9.1 Construction supply chains for the construction of a heavy engineering plant

the project's importance to the sustainability of MEG's business, those responsible for construction procurement and supply management relied heavily on professional advice from external third parties.

These professional service firms provided guidance on feasibility study, preliminary design, detailed engineering design and specification, preparation of tender documents, tender submission analysis, supplier selection and negotiation, and all aspects of cost, procurement, project and contract management. This advice allowed the client, MEG, to appoint HEC, which was responsible for the management and integration of the wide number of upstream supply chains.

The need to replace its ageing and inefficient generation plant while managing emissions of noxious substances and greenhouse gases was a key challenge for MEG on this project. Having recognised the need to reconfigure its asset portfolio and replace one under-performing facility, MEG had to address two major issues before it could go to the construction market. The first involved which type of energy source to use for the power generation process. Once this question had been addressed, the client could then focus on the second issue – the location for the facility.

The decision regarding which energy source to use within the power plant was not straightforward, as it involved a complex calculation of return on investment. This calculation was complicated because it was based on predictions and estimates for future consumer demand, fuel prices, operating and maintenance costs, decommissioning costs, government legislation (e.g. emission targets, or a climate change levy) and other indirect costs.

Nuclear generation was not a feasible option for MEG, which wanted a speedier solution to its problems. Although commercially nuclear is an attractive option, having relatively high capital costs but low marginal operating costs, the environmental and safety concerns surrounding nuclear plants meant that MEG would be faced with a lengthy consultation period that would lead to a significant delay in bringing the facility into operation. The electricity generator (MEG) then considered generation from renewable sources (wind, wave, tide, solar, fuel cells) generated at small to micro plants. Renewable energy projects enjoy a favourable regulatory regime; however, MEG decided that these technologies have challenges of their own. With limited experience of such facilities and having uncertainties over capital costs, capacity, reliability, environmental impact, distribution costs and regulation, MEG decided that a fossil fuel energy source, either coal or gas, was the best option.

While the construction costs of a coal plant approach the high capital costs of a nuclear facility, a coal plant's higher operating costs are comparable to a gas-fired plant. A coal-fired facility is very attractive if fuel prices are low, but financial risks are very high as coal has a higher exposure than gas to changes in the fuel price. The client did not totally discount coal as the fuel source. This was because coal gasification offers the possibility of carbon dioxide capture and sequestration, and the sale of by-products such as hydrogen gas and carbon.

To be competitive, natural gas-fired turbine plants depend on a low gas price. With a significantly lower capital cost (25% of a nuclear plant and 40% of a coal-fired plant) and a shorter construction period, power generation companies tend to prefer them as they start up more quickly and pay-back capital much earlier than their alternatives. There is also greater private sector confidence in building gas-fired plants, as the technology is well understood and they create less regulatory controversy. With an existing portfolio consisting largely of gas-fired power plants it was not too surprising that MEG eventually opted for another power plant containing 'combined cycle' gas turbines (CCGT).

The electricity generator (MEG) made the decision based on common-sense economic considerations. The CCGT systems have relatively low capital costs, high reliability and lower emissions of sulphur dioxide, and they provide cycle thermal efficiencies of over 50%, which are significantly higher than the 33% figure at an average coal-fired plant. Within CCGT systems, gas turbines generate rotational energy that drives AC generators with extra power being taken from waste heat coming from the gas turbine exhaust. Each turbine has a Heat Recovery Steam Generator (HRSG) from which steam is fed to a separate steam turbine, which drives another AC generator.

Once MEG had decided to construct another gas-fired power plant it had to identify a suitable location for the facility. This decision was based on a number of considerations. First, the station had to be sited as close as possible to a gas supply in the form of a pipeline taken from a large town, gas rig or a gas terminal built at a deep-water harbour. A modern gas-fired power station uses about 400 tonnes of natural gas per hour. Second, the facility has to be sited as close as possible to a centre of demand to link onto the National Grid. The electricity is generated at 15 kV and 18 kV and is stepped up for transmission. With distribution power cables costing between £600 000 (for overhead distribution) and £7.5 million (for underground distribution) per kilometre it is important that the client minimises this distribution cost.

The third consideration was the availability of adequate land, and whether it had sufficient capacity for a second power station to be built on it in the future if needed. The site also had to have good access to roads or to a railway line. Gas is normally delivered through gas pipelines, but in an emergency diesel fuel can be used instead and can be delivered by road or rail. The power station also required an adequate amount of cooling water. This can be provided from the sea or, if cooling towers are used, rivers of a suitable size. Finally, if the site is close to areas of high population or areas of natural beauty, it is also necessary to take into consideration environmental impacts such as noise, safety, emissions and visual appearance.

After considering all of these factors, MEG decided to locate a 900 MW gas-fired plant on a 20-hectare brownfield site near to a city with a population of 300 000 and on the banks of a major river. Given the location, MEG decided to supply the facility with natural gas via a 30-mile-long underground pipeline and two pressure reducing stations. There was also considerable local resistance to the construction of the facility. To reduce the visual impact of the site, 40 000 plants, shrubs and trees were planted and the site was landscaped in a natural manner to encourage the development of a habitat attractive to local wildlife.

The original design and specification for the 900 MW combined cycle gas turbine (CCGT) power plant was based around two generating modules each incorporating two 144 MW gas turbines, two waste heat recovery boilers and one 168 MW steam turbine, with an auxiliary back-up boiler. However, in the pursuit of a higher cost efficiency, increased reliability, and lower environmental emissions, MEG made a late change so that the solution included two 156 MW gas turbines and one 144 MW steam turbine. Despite the design change, the total Generator Registered Capacity (GRC) remained at 900 MW.

At the outset of the project, the total construction cost (excluding the M&E cost) of the facility was estimated to be £32 million. The solution involved the construction of the main buildings for the power station such as the turbine and generator hall, control room, administrative offices and amenities. It was estimated that the new facility would require a three-year programme of work for construction, field testing and commissioning.

Using external construction experts, MEG developed a relatively detailed design and specification for its construction requirements, but made a number of late changes to the design, including the types of gas and steam turbines to be used in the facility. This created a number of difficulties for MEG in its management of HEC and this adversely affected the performance outcome.

The buyer – Major Electricity Generator (MEG)

Since privatisation the utilities sector now encompasses many generation companies, utility owners and operators across electricity, gas and water. These organisations operate either within a normal commercial market or as national/regional monopolies. Many of these businesses operate in more than one sector and some have global operations. In the electricity sector there are now 42 companies regarded as major power producers (compared to just seven in 1990). The reduction in horizontal market concentration has resulted in greater competition in the market and has led to a significant reduction in the market shares of the largest generators.

The client, Major Electricity Generator (MEG), has an asset portfolio dominated by gas-fired power generation plants. This is not characteristic of the electricity sector. The expansion of gas-fired capacity since privatisation has brought about a more balanced generating capacity mix with coal stations accounting for 34% of the total, gas for 38%, nuclear for 20%, and others (including oil, pumped storage and renewables) for the remaining 8%.

The client (MEG) selected HEC to undertake the construction of the new power facility. At the outset of the project, the total cost of the construction element was initially estimated to be in the region of £35 million. After detailed development of the design and specification for the required solution, the client put the work out to tender through the OJEC procurement route and received prices ranging from £30 to £38 million. Using robust assessment criteria, HEC was selected with a bid of £32 million. The contractor (HEC) was chosen because it had significant experience of delivering similar projects in a high-risk heavy engineering environment to a very high quality, within timescales and incorporating the latest technology.

The client (MEG), like all construction clients, required value for money, but had a risk averse corporate culture where over-specification was commonplace. As a result, MEG pursued a value proposition that prioritised functionality and it did not pursue the lowest price for the construction solution. The client (MEG) did not, therefore, understand the full range of possible value propositions available to it, and its use of professional services compounded this because its experts only had a limited understanding of construction supply markets. This ensured that MEG would adopt a sub-optimal *supplier selection* approach to the relationship.

The supplier – Heavy Engineering Contractors (HEC)

Heavy Engineering Contractors (HEC) was selected to construct the £32 million power generation facility. It is a major player in the UK construction industry with an annual turnover of approximately £350 million. The company offers a comprehensive range of construction options to the public and private sectors, with considerable experience of major building, engineering and infrastructure projects. The firm maintains a very strong track record of delivering high quality and innovative solutions to clients within high-risk industrial environments. This reputation is also built on consistently meeting a client's precise functional needs, and delivering projects on time and within costs constraints. Although not provided on this project, the company can also assist clients with the feasibility study, preliminary design, detailed engineering design and procurement.

Construction firms, such as HEC, typically face a very uncertain future. They are not in a position to develop long-term preferred supplier relationships with clients to ensure revenue predictability and profitability, as the majority of clients in the heavy engineering sector only require major construction projects on a very infrequent basis. As a result, these clients are unable to consolidate their major construction requirements into a 'package' and have to source from the supply market on a one-off basis. To overcome this problem and in an attempt to avoid the short-term pursuit of projects, HEC has attempted to identify those heavy engineering sectors where it is perceived to deliver value for money and use this reputation to become preferred supplier to the minority of clients with large, regular construction portfolios.

9.3 The buyer–supplier relationship management approach

The following discussion of the relationship management approach used by MEG and HEC highlights the power and leverage resources available to both parties and the extent to which either party was able to utilise these to achieve the maximisation of its respective value for money or value from supply objectives. As we shall see, MEG was unable to achieve any of its value for money goals, while HEC was able to maximise its value from supply goals.

The client (MEG) – construction firm (HEC) dyad

If clients are unsure about their current and future construction requirements and have a limited understanding of construction supply markets they are unlikely to have direct control over what they are sourcing. As a result, they will almost certainly face opportunistic construction firms that leverage asymmetries of information in the pursuit of higher revenues and above normal returns. A client's ability to control a construction firm is dependent on its capacity to obtain power resources within the relationship and at the same time effectively monitor the supplier to reduce its scope for pre- and post-contractual opportunism. While the ability of the client to monitor the supplier can be improved by working with professional services, the external power resources of the client in this case, MEG, in relation to the construction firm, HEG, were not assisted by the limited competence of the professional services providers utilised.

For this particular project, the contract value for the construction of the new gas-fired power plant was £32 million. With a programmed duration of 36 months, this project accounted for approximately 3% of HEC's annual turnover (£350 million). This level of expenditure did not provide MEG with a key power resource because the project accounted for a relatively low share of HEC's turnover. Although this expenditure may appear insignificant, unattractive and not to provide MEG with any form of power lever, a competent professional services adviser should consider it in conjunction with the frequency with which the buyer and supplier transact.

A regular need to source from the construction supply market can turn a single low-value project into a high-value portfolio of projects and provide a client with a key power lever. Despite having a constant need to repair and maintain its power generation facilities to ensure continuity of service, in this case MEG sourced major capital expenditure projects as one-off projects without consideration of the potential leverage that could arise from linking construction with repair and maintenance. As a result, MEG was unable to offer HEC a level of demand characterised by high volume **and** high frequency.

In addition to volume and frequency, the complexity of the required solution impacts directly on the balance of power in the relationship. This is because, given the infrequency with which clients enter the market and their relative technical incompetence compared with their potential suppliers, it is possible for suppliers to behave opportunistically pre- and post-contractually. While the appointment of competent expert professional service providers can reduce the risk of supplier opportunism, in this case it did not do so. This was because the professional service provider did not seek to reduce the complexity, rather it was increased at the design and specification stage. The provider gave an unclear design and specification that was confusing due to late amendments and over-specified key components. As a result, the risk of supplier opportunism was not totally eliminated and HEC was able to identify opportunities to pursue increased revenues and returns at MEG's expense.

To fully understand the power and leverage situation it is also necessary to consider the scarcity of MEG's business and the availability of equivalent contracts for HEC. In the wider construction industry there are a large number of clients with an equivalent level of construction expenditure, but there are far fewer 'prestigious' clients operating within heavy engineering industries requiring major construction solutions. Despite the scarcity of clients in this marketplace, HEC was able to use its considerable reputation for delivering high quality and cost-effective solutions to differentiate itself vis-à-vis its competitors and engineer a greater certainty of demand. This augmented the power position of HEC relative to MEG and allowed both parties to develop a robust *supply chain sourcing* relationship management approach.

On the supply-side of this transaction, therefore, HEC attempted to control key power and leverage resources that could provide it with opportunities to achieve its own commercial and operational objectives. The majority of construction firms operate within highly contested markets and are unable to restrict the level of competition. By having a strong reputation for delivering solutions to very high quality levels within difficult conditions, HEC was able to increase MEG's perception of value (enhance the utility of the transaction for the client) and decrease the perceived level of contestation (create an impression of supply market scarcity). Despite this, the key power resource available to HEC was the relative incompetence of MEG and its advisers. If the advisers had done their job properly then it would have been difficult, notwithstanding HEC's reputation, for it to use opportunism pre- and post-contractually. As we shall see, MEG and its advisers were not competent in sourcing and this provided an opportunity for HEC to make above normal returns while failing to provide MEG with any of the key commercial and operational outcomes that it desired.

9.4 Performance outcome from the buyer–supplier relationship

From the very beginning of the project MEG and HEC had conflicting operational and commercial objectives. The client (MEG) was attempting operationally to maximise the functionality of the power generation facility and, commercially, to minimise the total costs of ownership for this solution so that it could maximise value for money. In direct contrast the objective of HEC was to maximise the revenues and returns that it received from MEG.

The client (MEG) was unable to engineer a position of dominance over HEC because it lacked (or did not see the opportunities to provide) a regular level of demand characterised by high volume that would be attractive to HEC. The client (MEG)'s relative power was also low because of the complexity of the project, its risk averse culture internally, its tendency to allow expert advisers to engineer over-specified requirements and the dependency this engendered for it with HEC's detailed technical solution. The client (MEG), therefore, had relatively high switching costs once the contract was signed but, despite a degree of uncertainty surrounding future contracts, HEC had relatively low switching costs because it was not locked into a long-term relationship and not dependent on MEG for future revenue.

Given its inexperience in construction sourcing, MEG attempted to minimise the potential for supplier pre- and post-contractual opportunism by employing professional engineering experts to provide a greater understanding of the supply market, as well as of construction technologies and supplier behaviours and costings. Despite this, the external advisers demonstrated little understanding of supplier opportunism and contributed to the problem pre-contractually by providing much greater scope for opportunism by over-specifying requirements and demonstrating an ignorance of how costs could be inflated post-contractually. This contributed to a relative 'lose' outcome for MEG and a 'win' outcome for HEC.

Figure 9.2 shows a summary of the dyad between MEG and HEC and the performance outcome from the relationship.

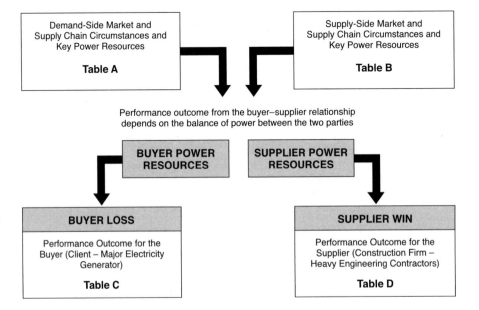

Figure 9.2 A summary of the dyad between the client (MEG) and construction firm (HEC) and the performance outcome from the relationship

Table A Demand-Side Market and Supply Chain Circumstances and Key Power Resources

There are many buyers in the total construction market but significantly fewer buyers for specialist heavy engineering facilities in a highly regulated market

Major Electricity Generator (MEG) has a **low share of the total construction market** with a single project value of £32 million. Therefore, the construction firm (HEC) has a low dependency on MEG for revenue

MEG has an **infrequent one-off need** to source from the construction market and has no future plans for further capital investment related to the construction of new heavy engineering plant

The requirements of MEG are **highly complex** (in terms of the project environment and to a lesser extent the design and specification itself) and require considerable supplier expertise for their integration into the project. The complexity is further increased by the unclear design and specification

MEG has **medium/high switching costs** because, although there are a large number of suppliers, it perceived there to be a limited number of suppliers capable of delivering very high quality projects in a timely manner within the complex environment

MEG has a **relatively clear value proposition** – a high quality product delivered on time and at an acceptable cost. However, MEG lacked a coherent construction sourcing strategy to achieve this and the desired value proposition was further complicated by an over-emphasis on quality and over-specification by engineers within a risk averse culture

MEG is unaware of the potential scope for **standardisation** of design and specification and **prefabrication** of key components common across the project

MEG has **relatively high search costs** but, by using limited professional services, has attempted (unsuccessfully) to reduce the level of **information asymmetries** and scope for **supplier opportunism**

Table B Supply-Side Market and Supply Chain Circumstances and Key Power Resources

There are many suppliers in the total construction market but fewer suppliers capable of providing relatively complex construction solutions to MEG's specific requirements and with the necessary expertise and experience to operate within a highly specialised, regulated and controlled environment

The total value of the project, approximately £32 million, accounts for a **low/medium share of the annual turnover** of Heavy Engineering Contractors (HEC) (approximately 3%)

HEC is **not dependent** on MEG for revenue. There is, however, a high degree of uncertainty surrounding future alternative contracts in the heavy engineering sector

HEC considers MEG's business to be **relatively attractive** as there are low costs associated with servicing the contract

HEC has relatively **low switching costs**

HEC's offerings are not commoditised and standardised but **highly customised** to the specific requirements of MEG and working in a regulated environment

HEC has a **very strong brand image** and **reputation** for delivering innovative products of a very high quality within regulated environments where safety is critical

HEC has **extensive information asymmetry advantages** over MEG with the client lacking a robust understanding of construction products and services and the typical opportunistic strategies of the industry players

---

Table C Performance Outcome for the Client (MEG) – Buyer Loss

The client, Major Electricity Generator (MEG), was faced with construction costs higher than original budget by 7.5% (£2.4 million). The original estimate was £32 million and final construction cost was £34.4 million

The extra cost was attributable to the numerous changes to the original design and specification that had to be made to overcome problems

Delivery of project late because of delays associated with:

    HEC's misinterpretation of MEG's unclear requirements

    Very late changes to the design and specification

    Lead-time on a number of key components, e.g. steelwork

Lateness of project had knock-on impact on continuity of service and additional costs of £2.5 million

The late changes to the design and specification meant that the final solution did not meet the functional expectations of the engineers

Despite these changes there was still evidence of 'gold-plating' and over-specification in the final solution

Table D Performance Outcome for the Construction Firm (HEC) – Supplier Win

Heavy Engineering Contractors (HEC) made a profit of £3.25 million on this project or close to a 10% return
This figure included extra revenues from MEG in relation to numerous changes to the original design and specification.
  These were made during the construction phase
HEC significantly enhanced its reputation for delivering quality solutions in a flexible manner within a difficult working
  environment. The late delivery of the project was acknowledged within the industry as MEG's fault and typical of
  high-risk and uncertain projects
This enhanced reputation led to other work with other utility companies and within other industrial sectors characterised
  by heavy engineering

In terms of the final construction cost, MEG was faced with an unanticipated additional level of expenditure to complete the project that significantly exceeded its original estimate. At the outset of the project it was estimated that the total construction cost would be £32 million. This figure rose by 7.5% (£2.4 million) to £34.4 million after the client made numerous changes to the original design and specification of the power generation facility at the start of the construction phase.

The changes to the design and specification were made as a direct result of initial energy efficiency calculation errors on the part of MEG and its professional advisers. The original design and specification for the 900 MW combined cycle gas turbine (CCGT) power plant was based around two generating modules each incorporating two 144 MW gas turbines, two heat recovery boilers and one 168 MW steam turbine. In the pursuit of a higher cost efficiency (to exceed future government targets), increased reliability, lower environmental emissions and improved future flexibility this configuration was changed to include two 156 MW gas turbines and one 144 MW steam turbine. While there was no change to the costs of the turbines and associated M&E element, this late change increased the construction costs.

The gas turbines used within the facility are very large (12 m long and 5 m in diameter) and very heavy (350 tonnes). When installed the turbines have to be housed within a high-strength steelwork framework and positioned on a reinforced concrete base. The late change to the specification of the turbine meant that the framework and base had to be redesigned and their components sourced again. The procurement of the additional ready-mixed concrete required for the new bases did not cause too many difficulties, as there was a high degree of competition within the local market. However, as the change was made very late HEC, having already poured the first layer of the base, was faced with the inconvenience (and extra costs) of breaking up a section of this sub-base and re-positioning the form-work into which the remainder of the concrete was to be poured. These additional costs were relatively insignificant compared to those linked with the specification of different steelwork.

The procurement of the high-strength steelwork for the frame to house the new turbines created a number of major difficulties for both MEG and HEC because the steel components for the original frame had to be replaced. With a very tight programme that could not be extended (to ensure continuity of service for MEG), the timely supply of the steelwork was critical. Structural steelwork is frequently subject to very long lead-times as steel suppliers act opportunistically and prioritise production to service more profitable contracts or those customers with a regular demand. As this contract was unattractive to the steel supplier, HEC was left with no alternative but to pay far in excess of market prices to guarantee supply within acceptable timescales knowing that it would recover these costs from MEG.

Despite paying these higher prices, HEC faced a delay to the programme that it knew it would find very difficult to overcome. The steelwork was on site within eight weeks, but over the remainder of the project HEC was only able to recover half of this delay and delivered the project four weeks late. However, with the blame for this delay entirely at the door of the client, HEC received the extra revenues that it had claimed in connection with this issue and avoided the liquidated damages clause of £250 000 per week. Furthermore, given MEG's actions at the outset of the project, HEC knew that the sanction of the liquidated damages clause was not enforceable. As a result, HEC protected its interests and ensured that MEG carried all of the downside risks in the relationship.

The late delivery of the project had a significant knock-on impact on the continuity of service for the client. This new gas-fired power generation facility, built as part of the client's strategy to lower its emissions in line with the Government's policy, was intended to replace an old coal-fired facility that was technologically out-of-date, had very high levels of noxious substances and greenhouse gases and was commercially under-performing. The four-week delay in testing and commissioning the new power plant meant that the client had to maintain the operation of this inefficient facility at an additional approximate cost of £2.5 million.

The client's failure to fully, or even partially, attain value for money was further demonstrated by its inability to achieve other operational objectives. Given the late changes to the design and specification, the functionality of the final solution failed to meet the expectations of the advisory engineers responsible for the operation of the facility. These engineers were extremely disappointed with the performance outcome. Although they recognised that they had over-specified the original solution, the anticipated cost reductions, used as justification for the design changes and reduction in the safety margin, had not materialised. The professional advisers to MEG had effectively reduced the level of functionality at the same time as increasing the total construction costs of the solution.

Furthermore, although MEG was never aware of the fact, HEC acted in an adversarial and opportunistic manner whenever possible to further increase its own revenues and returns post-contractually. On the construction of this particular project HEC made an overall profit of £3.25 million. This figure included extra revenues from the client in relation to the numerous changes to the client's original design and specification that were made during the construction phase of the project. This level of profit equated to a return of close to 10% on the overall cost of £34.4 million for the project. This increased profitability, above the £1 million (or 3% anticipated in the original contract negotiations), was achieved by HEC finding ways post-contractually of reducing the original bid costs through effective sourcing and internal efficiencies, which were not passed on to MEG.

9.5 Summary

The major finding from this case is that if a buyer over-specifies its requirements and also fails to control opportunism then it is likely that, not only will its costs increase post-contractually, but also that opportunistic suppliers will earn above normal returns. More worrying in this case was the fact that MEG, due to its inappropriate reactive sourcing approach, failed to obtain the minimum functionality that it had required and was forced to pay £2.4 million in additional direct costs and £2.5 million in additional indirect costs. This was clearly a lose outcome for the client since it did not receive the operational efficiencies that had been expected and had to pay additional amounts to receive a sub-standard facility relative to its original functional specification. This implies its control and monitoring of the supplier was sub-optimal both pre- and post-contractually.

On the other hand, the outcome, see Table 9.1, was clearly a win for the supplier. In addition to maximising its return from this project to a level that is above normal for the industry (at close to 10%), HEC achieved a number of additional benefits that increased its revenues and returns in the future. The

Table 9.1 A summary of the relationship management approach and performance outcome

Nature of Relationship Management Approach	Despite having a considerable capital expenditure budget, MEG's failure to possess a regular demand for construction projects meant that it could only develop a reactive sourcing approach
	Given the one-off nature of its demand MEG was not expert in managing construction supply chains and markets
	MEG employed professional services to acquire a better understanding of construction products, services and supply markets in order to minimise the potential for supplier opportunism
Nature of Buyer 'Loss'	The final construction costs were higher than the original budget by 7.5% (£2.4 million). The original estimate was £32 million and final construction cost was £34.4 million. There was also an additional indirect cost of £2.5 million due to the delay in delivery
	The extra cost was attributable to the numerous changes to the original design and specification that had to be made to overcome problems during the construction phase
	Delivery of project four weeks late because of delays associated with the client's unclear requirements, late changes to the design, and long lead-time on a number of key components. The lateness of project had a knock-on impact on continuity of service
	The late changes to the design meant that the final solution did not meet the functional expectations of the engineers responsible for operating the facility. There was also still evidence of 'gold-plating'
Nature of Supplier 'Win'	HEC made a profit of £3.25 million. This figure included extra revenues from the client in relation to numerous changes to the original design and specification and cost reductions achieved by HEC but not passed on to MEG after the deal had been struck
	HEC significantly enhanced its reputation for delivering quality solutions within a difficult working environment. The late delivery of the project was acknowledged as totally the client's fault
	This enhanced reputation led to other work that enabled HEC to increase future revenues and returns
Conclusions	Employing incompetent professional services providers that over-specify requirements and do not understand how suppliers can inflate initial bid prices in order to reduce them post-contractually is a recipe for opportunism post-contractually by suppliers
	Suppliers who find that they have incompetent clients and professional advisers working for the client are bound to take advantage of the situation post-contractually
	Even in reactive buying it is necessary to have fully competent client and advisory staffs to deal with commercially and operationally astute suppliers

solution was acknowledged to be innovative in terms of design, further enhancing its reputation in the market. This reputation was not affected by the delivery of the project one month late and over original budget, as the market recognised that such outcomes were commonplace within a risk averse industry. The contractor (HEC) enhanced its reputation and this led to the award of highly profitable work with other clients in the heavy engineering construction market.

The water pipeline case: reactive supply chain sourcing with a buyer lose and supplier partial win outcome

10.1 Introduction

This case focuses on the procurement of ductile iron and plastic pipes within a major water pipeline project for a Water Authority, Innovating Utilities (IU), by a large construction firm, Superior Utility Contractors (SUC). The contractor (SUC) sourced all the pipes from a leading pipe manufacturer, Universal Pipelines (UP). The contractor (SUC) and UP had considerable experience of delivering similar major pipeline projects within the water industry.

In this case, in contrast to the evidence of buyer ignorance that was a major factor in other cases discussed herein, the client in this supply chain attempted to use its extensive knowledge of construction to develop a proactive rather than a reactive strategy to leverage its upstream suppliers to achieve better value for money. Unfortunately, the client in this case (IU) did not fully understand what was necessary to deliver a proactive approach and ended up adopting a reactive approach with SUC. Relatedly, SUC, the first-tier construction firm in this case, was not able to deliver what IU wanted because it had doubts about the commitment of the client to this more collaborative approach. As a result, SUC was caught in the middle and failed to achieve any of its desired goals while its primary pipeline supplier, UP, was able to partially achieve its.

The actions of the pipe supplier, UP, also impacted directly on the ability of SUC to achieve any form of positive performance outcome. The supplier (UP), while operating within a relatively contested market, was able to use brand reputation and information asymmetry to create grounds for opportunism in the pursuit of higher levels of profitability for itself. As a result, the pipe supplier was able to partially achieve its operational and commercial objectives at the expense of both IU and SUC.

10.2 Background to the case: the construction of a major water pipeline

The construction of a new water transmission pipeline requires the integration of a number of supply chains. The supply chain for the pipes required for the pipeline, as shown in Figure 10.1, mirrors that of many construction products and services. In

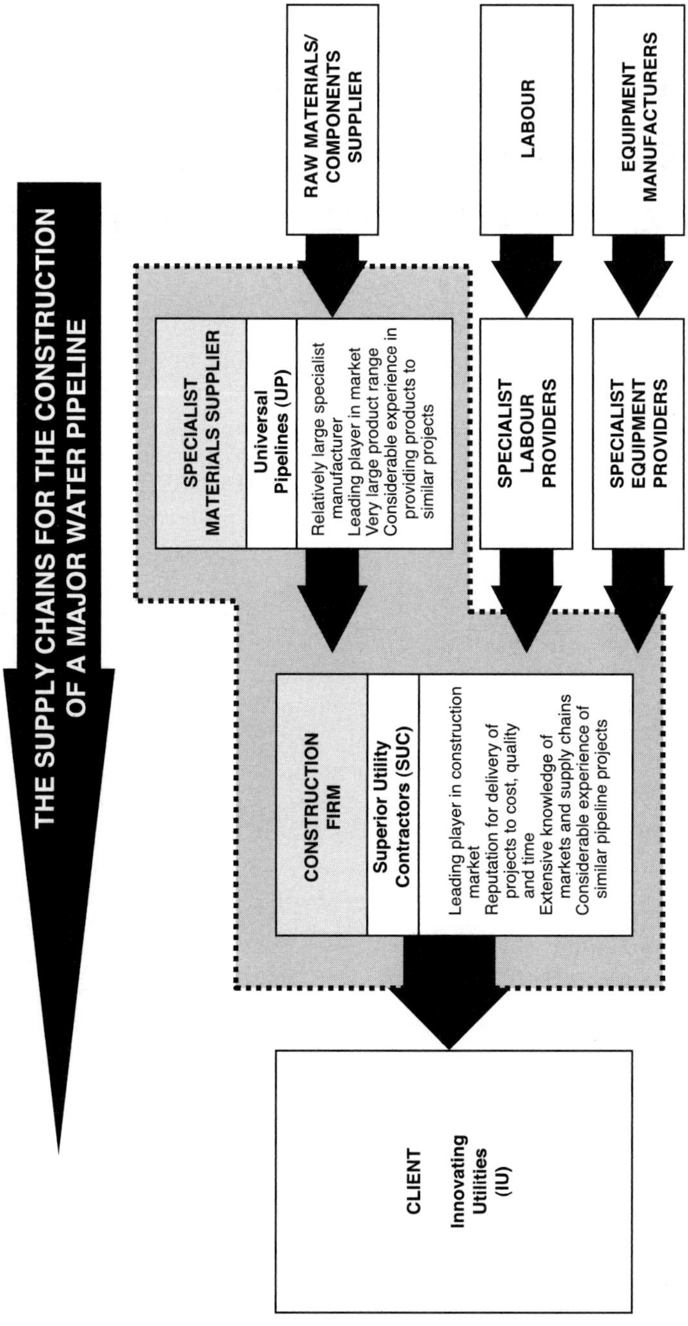

THE SUPPLY CHAINS FOR THE CONSTRUCTION
OF A MAJOR WATER PIPELINE

**RAW MATERIALS/
COMPONENTS
SUPPLIER**

LABOUR

**EQUIPMENT
MANUFACTURERS**

**SPECIALIST
MATERIALS SUPPLIER**

Universal
Pipelines (UP)

Relatively large specialist
manufacturer
Leading player in market
Very large product range
Considerable experience in
providing products to
similar projects

**SPECIALIST
LABOUR
PROVIDERS**

**SPECIALIST
EQUIPMENT
PROVIDERS**

**CONSTRUCTION
FIRM**

Superior Utility
Contractors (SUC)

Leading player in construction
market
Reputation for delivery of
projects to cost, quality
and time
Extensive knowledge of
markets and supply chains
Considerable experience of
similar pipeline projects

CLIENT

Innovating
Utilities
(IU)

Figure 10.1 Construction supply chains for the construction of a major water pipeline

conjunction with professional services (in-house and external), the client develops a detailed design and specification, which forms the basis of the tender documents upon which the construction firm is selected. The construction firm, like the pipe manufacturer and raw material suppliers at upstream stages, normally operates within a highly competitive and adversarial supply market. The diagram also suggests that the supply chain is linear and simple, but complexity increases in upstream stages where the project may involve considerable intricacy and uncertain ground conditions.

In this case, despite the development of a very detailed design and specification based on extensive ground and site investigation, the occurrence of unexpected events, uncovered when the excavations began, forced IU to revise the original design and specification. This had cost and profit implications for both IU and SUC on completion of the project.

The project involved the construction of a five-kilometre length of new clean water mains pipeline. This involved the combined use of different diameters and lengths of ductile iron and high-density polyethylene pipes. The specific choice of type and diameter of pipe was made according to technical and functional requirements and cost was only a secondary factor. This was because engineers and not procurement professionals effectively specified the products and made the sourcing decision. In addition to the physical laying of the pipeline, the project also involved additional construction and civil engineering work in relation to two bored road crossings, two crossings of a motorway, two rail crossings and the construction of three clean water pumping stations. Despite the fact that the pipeline was laid underground for its entire length several different techniques were used in its construction. Total contract value was estimated to be £8 million at the outset of the project.

Within this case, a single construction firm (SUC) operating at the first-tier integrated the entire construction package and delivered it to IU, with no sub-contracting of the works. The pipes (ductile iron and plastic) were sourced from one company, UP, a leading supplier of both types of pipe. In addition, although contractually a one-off project, it should be noted that IU constructs over 50 kilometres of new pipeline, and rehabilitates over 750 kilometres of iron mains in a typical year through a small list of preferred contractors.

The construction firm – Superior Utility Contractors (SUC)

The highly contested nature of the traditional construction industry does not operate in this supply chain and market. This is because, while pipeline installation is relatively simple, there is considerable complexity associated with dredging, rock blasting, hydrographic surveying, piling, heavy rigging and other related civil and mechanical engineering works in uncertain environmental conditions. This reduces the number of firms able to undertake the work. Firms with the required level of competence and expertise are largely confined to major players with considerable experience on similar projects. This means that a restricted supply market exists for project delivery.

The selected company to undertake the construction of the new water mains project was SUC. Its capabilities cover every aspect of utility provision from gas, water and electricity networks to comprehensive, multi-function telecommunications systems, plus all of the associated building and civil engineering work required to create and maintain efficient national, regional and industrial infrastructures. With experience gained in the UK and overseas, SUC was perceived to be at the forefront of developing, constructing, testing, commissioning and maintaining water distribution infrastructures to operate at any pressure in any location. The contractor (SUC) had an annual turnover of £400 million. However, this turnover was smaller than that of other leading industry players and pipeline contractors, but still made it one of a small number of larger organisations (only one per cent of construction firms has a turnover of more than £5 million) in the market.

Despite the market being somewhat restricted, the majority of construction firms face uncertain project-by-project revenues and intense competition occurs for major projects. To overcome this competition SUC had attempted to develop long-term preferred supplier relationships with clients to ensure revenue predictability and profitability instead of the short-term adversarial pursuit of projects. It had focused its efforts in a segmented and coordinated manner in certain sectors (e.g. water, gas and electricity) where it was perceived to offer a high quality differentiated offering.

Despite this embryonic proactive approach by SUC, the client in this supply chain, IU, had initially overlooked SUC when selecting the preferred suppliers for its long-term framework agreement. As a result, although IU wanted to work with SUC to achieve better value for money, its initial signal to SUC was that SUC were not considered suitable for a proactive sourcing approach. Without offering certainty and regularity of demand to SUC, which could not then offer it to the pipe supplier (UP) operating at the second-tier, a proactive approach could not be implemented and a sub-optimal reactive *supply chain sourcing* approach was the best that could be achieved by both IU and SUC.

The specialist material supplier – Universal Pipelines (UP)

There were two different types of pipes used in the project, both supplied by UP. The first type was high-density polyethylene. While not protected by a specific patent, polyethylene is now an established pipeline material for water, gas and industrial uses and provides a cost-effective, reliable pipe system that is easily installed, with excellent properties such as corrosion resistance, chemical resistance and flexibility. The second type of water mains pipe used in the project was made from ductile iron (an iron/carbon/silicon alloy) (according to BS EN 545). Ductile iron pipeline systems provide durable and reliable long-term service due to the material properties of ductile iron and the advanced lining and coating systems that are available.

The supplier (UP) provides products to the water and sewerage, telecommunications, highways, civil engineering, construction and housing markets. It is a leading worldwide supplier of a range of ductile iron and polyethylene pipes, fittings and valves and provides over 2000 kilometres of pipes per annum. It is perceived to be at the forefront of materials and manufacturing technology and is able to offer complete solutions for customers, backed by a dedicated sales force with full marketing, technical, sales and operational infrastructure. The company has, therefore, been able to create a strong brand reputation and become a leading supplier to the water industry. The company offers a comprehensive range of 17 500 different water pipeline products of which over 550 are protected by patents.

The pipeline supplier (UP) is a part of the Universal Building Products Group (UBPG), which is one of the world's largest industrial groups providing glass, high-performance materials, housing and building products with an annual turn-over of £10 billion, 10% of which is attributable to the pipeline division. Total annual sales normally exceed £1 billion of which £150 million is related to the manufacture and supply of pipeline systems for the transportation of water and sewage. For this particular project, the contract value for the polyethylene pipes, valves and fittings was approximately £375 000, while the ductile iron pipe, valves and fittings accounted for £500 000. This figure equated to less than 1% of the supplier's turnover.

While there are a number of suppliers who can provide different types of pipes, valves and fittings, the decision to select one supplier for the different types of pipes was made primarily on the very high quality of UP's offerings, and its knowledge and understanding of the special planning and operating procedures required for a regulated clean water transmission environment. The decision to use a single supplier was also made possible because the two types of pipe did not use pro-prietary technology and could be fitted together easily. The supplier (UP)'s products were also available to be installed through innovative methods (including elements of prefabrication and pre-assembly) to ensure that future maintenance costs were minimised.

For IU, expenditure on the physical pipes (through first-tier construction firms) accounted for a relatively insignificant proportion of total capital expenditure. However, the percentage of total capital cost attributable to the pipes varies significantly across projects and depends upon the associated installation costs (equipment and labour). These costs are higher where ground conditions are difficult and uncertain, or where major roads, rivers or canals have to be crossed. For this project, the costs of pipes accounted for approximately 11% of total project cost.

Despite the reputation of UP, there is no single dominant player within the market, with the largest firm having a market share of below 10%. The relative power of the larger pipe manufacturers vis-à-vis the first-tier construction firms was also affected by a number of other factors. In the pursuit of lower costs, construction firms have recently considered the potential to consolidate the demand specification for their pipeline expenditure and to explore the feasibility of standardisation and prefabrication of certain components. However, there are a number of potential barriers to the implementation of such a sophisticated approach to supply management. These include uncertainty regarding future demand levels from specific clients for particular types of pipeline.

10.3 The buyer–supplier relationship management approach

In this section the dyadic relationship between SUC and UP is discussed in more detail. This discussion includes an analysis of the key buyer and supplier power resources available to both parties and whether there is scope for these parties to maximise respectively their value for money and value from supply objectives. As we shall see, the failure of IU to develop a robust proactive sourcing approach with SUC forced SUC into a difficult position where it failed to achieve its operational and commercial objectives, while UP was partially able to achieve its.

The construction firm (SUC) – specialist material supplier (UP) dyad

This dyadic exchange is characteristic of many upstream relationships within the construction industry. Given that SUC was not a preferred supplier within IU's forthcoming partnering framework, it was faced with considerable uncertainty regarding future workload and was not in a position to engineer a regular demand for specific types of pipes. This typically ensures that construction firms are only able to select manufacturers on a project-by-project basis according to the technical specification, quality, price and ease of installation of the product and service offering. With proactive sourcing strategies very difficult to implement in these circumstances, a construction firm may also be faced with adversarial and opportunistic behaviour from suppliers.

At this point it is worth stressing the potential impact that IU's sourcing strategy had on the commercial leverage position of SUC. While this single contract may be considered to be of low relative volume and importance for UP, this would not have been the case if this one-off expenditure formed part of a regular programme of capital investment projects. If IU's annual capital expenditure was consolidated and shared equally between five preferred contractors, each firm might expect over £60 million of work – equivalent to approximately eight projects of this type. The pipeline supplier (UP) would certainly value the level of regular expenditure flowing from these eight projects (channelled through SUC), as this would guarantee a regular stream of revenue and would constitute relatively high volume and frequency of demand.

A construction firm's ability to control and/or leverage a manufacturer of pipes is, therefore, dependent on the possession of key power resources within the relationship. In this case, the contract value for the polythelene pipes, valves and fittings was approximately £375 000, while the ductile iron pipe, valves and fittings accounted for a further £500 000. This figure equates to less than 1% of UP's UK turnover and may be considered to be of low relative volume and importance to its business.

Turning to the complexity of the product and service offering, although the pipes required were relatively commoditised and standardised, there were relatively high levels of complexity in relation to their integration in uncertain ground conditions. However, at the start of this project it was felt that this complexity was relatively well understood by SUC, which possessed the requisite information from the pre-tender ground investigation undertaken by IU. One can assume, therefore, that purchasers within SUC believed that they had full knowledge of all potential suppliers of appropriate components to meet the functional requirements of the solution. As a result, SUC considered it relatively easy and inexpensive to monitor the supplier and prevent opportunistic behaviour based on information asymmetries. It will be shown later that this belief was misplaced.

Furthermore, as contended earlier, the failure of SUC to turn this one-off project into a regular programme of capital investment projects from IU, combined with a lack of work with other water authorities, prevented it from developing long-term proactive relationships with any of its upstream suppliers of key components. The inability of SUC to offer these suppliers the key incentives related to frequency and volume of demand meant that at the time of the project key material suppliers (such as UP) were unwilling to undertake the required dedicated investments and relationship-specific adaptations for a collaborative and proactive relationship management approach. As a result, SUC had to adopt a short-term and reactive *supply chain sourcing* approach in the pursuit of its own self-interest (maximising value for money).

On the supply-side, UP was actually operating within a relatively highly contested market due to a high degree of competition and product inter-change-ability. Despite this, brand building can generate reputation effects that create supply market closure in favour of preferred suppliers. As a result, the level of contestation decreases because buyers assume (often mistakenly) that there are only a small number of manufacturers capable of supplying products to the very high quality levels required. This supply market scarcity can also be exacerbated by government regulations that place a significant emphasis on adherence to 'gold-plated' quality standards. It can also be made worse by the relative superior competence of particular pipe manufacturers, who build into their standard operating practices an understanding of the need to constantly innovate, rather than to rely on the copying or adaptation of what others are doing.

On the basis of this understanding, UP was able to manufacture products either that are objectively superior, in terms of their functional performance, than those offered by its competitors, or that are perceived to be better as a result of the firm's reputation. This situation enabled UP to gain and sustain, at least temporarily, a higher share of the market than would otherwise have been possible. This created a major negotiation problem for SUC, as it effectively meant that there were no longer a large number of suppliers offering commoditised products to a well-informed but highly fragmented customer base, with neither party having power over the other. Under these circumstances, the supplier usually passes value (in the form of lower prices or constant innovation) to the buyer, which has an advantage during negotiations because it is relatively easy to undertake robust comparisons between alternative products.

The discussion that follows shows how SUC's inability to offer UP a regular demand for its pipes weakened this negotiating position and opened up the possibility of supplier opportunism. This situation arose because SUC was not part of the client's partnering framework for the delivery of its forthcoming capital investment programme and SUC did not know how to monitor supplier opportunism effectively.

10.4 Performance outcome from the buyer–supplier relationship

At the outset of the project, SUC and UP had conflicting operational and commercial objectives. The construction firm (SUC) was attempting operationally to maximise the functionality and commercially to minimise the total costs of ownership of the final water pipeline. This objective was not achieved. In contrast, the objective of UP was to increase operationally the revenues and commercially the returns from working with SUC.

The construction firm (SUC) was not in a position of dominance over UP because it lacked the regular level of high volume demand that would have been extremely attractive to UP. Its relative power was also low because UP was not locked into a long-term relationship and its switching costs with IU and SUC were low. Despite SUC's experience in construction sourcing, understanding of the available technologies and knowledge of the supply market, the lack of a favourable position of relative power also meant that SUC could not monitor UP effectively to stop post-contractual opportunism. This led to a tension in the relationship between SUC and UP. As both parties possessed insignificant power resources, neither party was in a position to fully achieve its business objectives. As we shall see, SUC did not benefit at all commercially from the project (due to its inability to resolve the problems that arose in relation to a misinterpretation of the ground investigation and inappropriate pipe installation techniques) and UP was only partially able to achieve its commercial objectives.

Figure 10.2 contains a summary of the dyad between SUC and UP, and the performance outcome from the relationship. In terms of final cost, because of technical problems during installation, SUC was faced with an increased and unanticipated level of expenditure on pipes, valves and fittings that significantly exceeded its original estimate and could not be reimbursed from IU. At the outset of the project, it was estimated that the total costs of pipes, valves and fittings was £875 000. This figure rose to £985 000 after SUC had to change the design and specification of the water pipeline and procure replacement pipework during the construction phase.

The changes to the design and specification were made as a direct result of errors on the part of SUC. Installation of a critical section of pipeline using heavy lifting equipment into an inadequately supported trench resulted in a collapse of the trench walls, fracture of the pipe and damage to key plant and equipment. Construction work had to stop for two weeks while the cause of the accident was investigated. After the investigation, a much shallower trench had to be dug and the original ductile iron pipes were replaced with polyethylene pipes. The new pipes, valves and fittings were specifically designed to cope with the high loads to be exerted on the pipeline by a planned dual carriageway running above it.

The project was further delayed by the limited availability of the new polyethylene pipes. The pipeline supplier (UP) only manufactured the newly specified pipes to order and stated a lead-time of four weeks. To acquire the pipes within

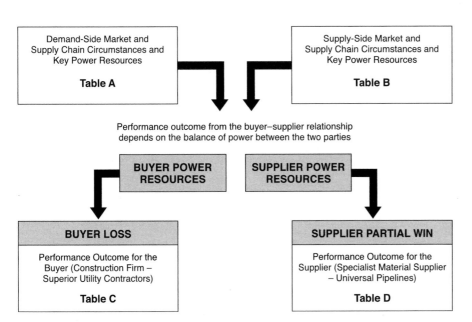

Figure 10.2 A summary of the dyad between the construction firm (SUC) and pipe manufacturer (UP) and the performance outcome from the relationship

Table A Demand-Side Market and Supply Chain Circumstances and Key Power Resources

There are many construction firms acting as buyers in the construction pipeline market but fewer buyers for specialist plastic and ductile iron water and wastewater pipeline products and services in a highly regulated market

Superior Utility Contractors (SUC) has a relatively low share of the total construction market but a **higher share of the pipeline market** with a project value of £8 million. Therefore, the supplier (UP) has a low dependency on SUC for revenue

SUC has a **regular need** to source from the pipeline market but there is **no current certainty/regularity** about requirements and volumes for specific products

The requirements of the client (and SUC) are **highly complex** (in terms of the project environment and to a lesser extent the products themselves) and require considerable supplier expertise for their integration into the project

SUC has **medium switching costs** as although there are a large number of suppliers few have the same reputation for providing very high quality products

The client (and SUC) has a **relatively clear value proposition** – a high quality product delivered on time and at an acceptable cost. However, there are problems with this value proposition as there is an over-emphasis on quality and over-specification and gold-plating is evident

SUC is aware of the potential scope for **standardisation** and **prefabrication** of specific component elements

SUC has **relatively low search costs**, as it has extensive knowledge and understanding about water pipeline products and services and the strategies of the industry players

Table B Supply-Side Market and Supply Chain Circumstances and Key Power Resources

There are many suppliers in the total pipe manufacturing (plastic and ductile iron) market but fewer suppliers able to deliver products of this high quality and with the necessary expertise and experience to operate within a highly specialised and controlled environment

The initial total value of the pipes, approximately £875 000, accounts for a relatively **low share of the annual turnover** of Universal Pipelines (UP) (<1%). However, this figure would increase if the construction firm (SUC) was guaranteed a regular workload from the client in this supply chain for similar projects and continues to source from UP

UP is **not dependent** on SUC for revenue. There is, however, a high degree of uncertainty surrounding alternative contracts for the specific plastic pipes used in this project

UP considers the client's business (through SUC) to be **relatively attractive** as there are low costs associated with servicing the contract

UP has relatively **low switching costs**

UP's offerings (taken as a whole) are commoditised and standardised but there is **very limited customisation** to the specific requirements of the client (and SUC) and working in a regulated environment

UP has a **very strong brand image** and **reputation** for delivering innovative products of a very high quality

UP has **few information asymmetry advantages** over SUC

Table C Performance Outcome for the Construction Firm (SUC) – Buyer Loss

The construction firm, Superior Utility Contractors (SUC), was faced with pipe costs higher than original budget by £110 000. The original estimate was £875 000 and final cost was £985 000. A premium had to be paid for delivery of other pipes to very short timescales

Delivery of project late because of delays associated with:
    SUC's misinterpretation of pre-tender ground investigation
    Inappropriate pipe installation techniques for ground
    Lead-time on 'new products'

Functional expectations of client only met after remedial action by SUC

SUC did not make any profit on the project

Table D Performance Outcome for the Pipe Manufacturer (UP) – Supplier Partial Win

---

Universal Pipelines (UP) made a profit of £80 000 or an 8% return on this project. This was largely due to the
  changes in the design and specification and the requirement for extra pipes when the contractor (SUC) was faced
  with a trench collapse caused by inappropriate installation techniques and unforeseen ground conditions
UP did not damage its reputation within the industry for delivering quality projects within time and cost constraints
Major industry players recognised that it was not UP's fault so it did not impact on future revenues

---

this timescale and minimise the financial impact of the liquidated damages clause
set out in the contractual documents with IU if they did not deliver on
time, SUC agreed to pay the full market price for the pipes without their usual
discount. Despite the additional cost implications of £110 000, SUC identified
this as the best option because this payment ensured that the pipes were on site
within one week effectively reducing the potential delay to the client by three
weeks. However, the project was still delivered two weeks late to the client,
which meant that SUC was faced with liquidated damages of £180 000 (lower
than the £450 000 if the project had been delivered five weeks late). This cost
effectively ended the prospect of any profit being made by SUC from this
£8 million project.

   On the other hand UP, which had used opportunism because of the arm's-length
and reactive sourcing approach being adopted with it by both IU and SUC, made an
overall profit of £80 000 from supplying the pipes for this particular project. This
represented an 8% return on an overall contract value with SUC of £985 000. This
return, while clearly not above normal in general terms, was perfectly acceptable,
and higher than that normally received in other similar water pipeline projects.
This meant that UP was able to leverage a partial win outcome from the situation
at least in commercial terms – it made a normal profit and did not damage its own
reputation. The construction firm (SUC), on the other hand, made no profit and
damaged its reputation for being able to deliver projects on time.

10.5 Summary

The major finding from this case is that a client who does not understand the
leverage that it possesses from having a large regular volume that could be
managed in a more frequent and standardised fashion, and then forces a construction firm to manage a project on a short-term and *ad hoc* basis, is likely to
significantly weaken its own and the construction firm's leverage over input
suppliers. Furthermore, if the client also ensures that the contractor is unable to
properly contest the market, due to a risk averse culture and gold plating of
specifications, then this will further compound the leverage problem.

   In this case, the misguided approach by the client, IU, exacerbated the leverage
problems faced by SUC at the first-tier. By failing to provide SUC with a regular
and relatively high-volume demand for pipes, when a crisis occurred for SUC operationally, its primary pipe supplier (UP) simply chose to behave opportunistically in
order to increase its own returns at the expense of SUC. The consequence was that
SUC experienced a lose outcome with no profits from the project and its reputation
damaged due to the delay in project completion. The pipe supplier (UP), while not
achieving everything it would desire ideally, achieved a partial win outcome of 8%
returns with no damage to its own reputation.

The irony in this case is that IU did not suffer directly as a consequence of its sourcing actions because the damage was experienced by SUC. The client (IU) could have engineered a much more proactive approach to supply chain management in this case by allowing SUC to have a longer-term relationship, with a guaranteed share of its annual demand. By doing this, IU would have empowered SUC in its relationship with UP and the overall costs of this and subsequent projects might have been lower with better functional delivery.

Table 10.1 is a summary of the relationship management approach and performance outcome for this case.

Table 10.1 A summary of the relationship management approach and performance outcome

Nature of Relationship Management Approach	The failure of SUC to turn this one-off project into a regular programme of capital investment projects for IU, combined with a lack of work with other Water Authorities, ensured that only a reactive approach to sourcing could be adopted by SUC with UP
	The inability of SUC to offer its suppliers the key incentives related to frequency and volume of demand meant that it was unwilling to make the required dedicated investments and relationship-specific adaptations for a collaborative and proactive relationship management approach
	This was avoidable but only if IU and/or other Water Authorities provided more commitment to SUC so as to empower it in its relationship with its own suppliers
Nature of Buyer 'Loss'	Costs were higher than contained in the original forecast by £110 000 due to unforeseen changes to the design and specification of the pipes, valves and fittings for a section of the pipeline
	No profit was made by SUC on the project as a result
	The project did not meet functional requirements (attributable to unclear ground investigation, design and specification and supplier opportunism)
	The project was delivered late because of delays associated with claims and variations to original contract documents, e.g. design and specification (due to unclear design, problems with ground conditions and problems with integration into project). The late delivery meant that SUC had to pay liquidated damages of £180 000 to the client (IU)
	This damaged SUC's reputation
Nature of Supplier 'Partial Win'	An 8% return was made on the project (mainly through additional costs for new pipes associated with changes to original design and specification stemming from unforeseen ground conditions)
	Reputation intact because SUC was blamed not UP, who used opportunism with impunity
Conclusions	Clients should be better informed about how their short-term approaches to project management can significantly weaken the leverage position of their construction suppliers at the first-tier
	A more proactive approach is nearly always appropriate for clients that have a constant and/or frequent demand for serial projects
	Thinking about how demand flows through the supply chain, and how it can be used to empower buyers at all stages, is a critical lesson to learn from misguided reactive sourcing approaches
	SUC may have made technical errors but its problems of leverage arose from the misguided sourcing approach adopted by the client

The manufacturing facility extension case: reactive supplier selection with a buyer lose and supplier lose outcome

11.1 Introduction

This case focuses on the procurement of an extension to a small manufacturing facility by an automotive component manufacturer – Automotive Component Manufacturer (ACM). The project was the client's first contact with the industry since the construction of its only manufacturing facility 15 years earlier. The small construction firm, Small Town Design and Build (STDB), had a high level of experience of delivering similar-sized projects. With a one-off construction requirement the client displayed little understanding of construction supply chains and markets and the adversarial and opportunistic attitudes of many firms operating within them. This meant that a proactive sourcing approach was out of the question and a reactive *supplier selection* approach had to be utilised.

The analysis demonstrates how ACM's lack of a robust approach to construction sourcing created major problems for both parties. Adopting a short-term view of value for money, ACM selected the supplier providing the lowest tender price. Unfortunately, lacking a full understanding of the true costs of construction, ACM did not question why this price was substantially lower than all others. During the construction phase of the project it soon became apparent that the decision had been misguided because the supplier could not complete the project at the price quoted.

After realising that it had miscalculated the likely cost of the extension, STDB had to take action to ensure that it did not encounter significant cash-flow problems that could, potentially, threaten its survival. Faced with very low rates, STDB decided to cut corners and use poorer quality materials. This enabled it to lower the material cost but it had a detrimental impact on the functionality of the solution. After the collapse of a retaining wall, ACM was faced with a major dilemma. It could retain the agreed rates and either receive a poor quality solution or place the supplier at risk of going out of business, or it could negotiate a higher price for the project raising the total costs of ownership but ensuring a high quality facility. By opting for the latter solution ACM created a situation in which neither it, nor STDB, could attain any of its commercial and operational objectives.

11.2 Background to the case: the construction of an extension to a manufacturing facility

The project involved the design and construction of an extension to a small automotive component supplier's only manufacturing facility. The $275\,m^2$ extension was to comprise an open manufacturing area with 10-metre-clear internal height allowing for the subsequent installation and operation of the latest production equipment in a modern 'clean' working environment. This equipment, including innovative power presses and laser cutting equipment, was required to meet the evolving needs of a customer-base that constantly demands lower defect rates and higher functionality levels. Externally, the project was to include a covered loading bay, block-paved car parking areas, concrete service yards and a landscaped area.

The design and construction of an extension to a manufacturing facility for a small automotive component manufacturer requires the integration of a number of supply chains, as illustrated in Figure 11.1. While an experienced client with a regular portfolio of projects might have the necessary resources to manage this task internally, this is not the case for the majority of clients, which normally have to seek external assistance.

This project was ACM's first interaction with the construction industry since the design and construction of its manufacturing facility fifteen years earlier. This inexperience, combined with its limited understanding of construction supply markets, the uncertainties involved with the project and the project's strategic importance to the business, forced ACM to seek professional advice from external third parties at all stages of the project. This included expert guidance on outline design, specification of key elements, preparation of tender documents, tender submission analysis, appointment of the design and build contractor (under a JCT standard form of contract) and specific aspects of cost, project and contract management.

The client's outline design and specification for the extension to the manufacturing facility included a requirement to use concrete foundations to column positions, pre-cast concrete ground beams to perimeter, a carbon-steel-fibre reinforced concrete slab with power float finish, a structural steelwork portal frame, external wall cladding and retaining wall panels. The precise specification for these elements was left open to the design and build contractor, who was able to draw on its own knowledge and experience to develop a solution that it hoped would meet ACM's commercial and operational objectives, lowest total cost of ownership and highest level of functionality.

The buyer – Automotive Component Manufacturer (ACM)

In the late 1990s, ACM decided that it needed to improve its manufacturing facilities to remain competitive because its customers – the major automotive manufacturers – were considering sourcing body and chassis parts from low-cost overseas markets. The buyer (ACM) also identified a need to reduce its dependency on these customers for revenue because the automotive market was becoming increasingly unpredictable and margins were being aggressively reduced. As part of a strategy to reduce costs, improve operational efficiency and diversify into other markets ACM decided to extend its current manufacturing facilities. This was to allow it to house innovative equipment, such as laser cutters, that offered significant advantages in productivity, precision, part quality, material utilisation and flexibility. This also provided an opportunity to diversify its customer-base and reduce its dependency on the uncertain automotive market.

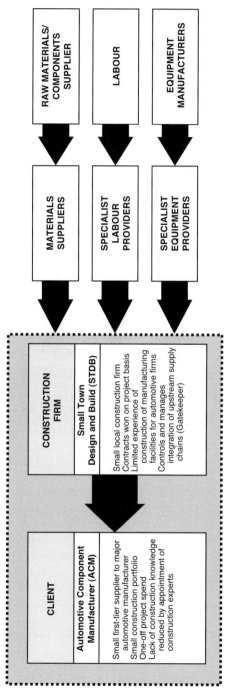

Figure 11.1 *Construction supply chains for the construction of a manufacturing facility extension*

Laser cutting, carried out on state-of-the-art laser machines, is one of the fastest growing processes in industrial manufacturing equipment and is used by metal fabricators and component manufacturers in place of older equipment like turret punches. The buyer (ACM) hoped that the inclusion of laser cutting equipment within the new factory extension would enable it to meet the evolving functional demands of its automotive customers at the same time as improving cost competitiveness. To house the new equipment the facility extension had to be built to very high levels of quality. The base for the laser system had to be precisely formed and levelled so that the resonator, beam delivery mechanism, machine frame, workstation control and drive system could be positioned accurately.

The buyer (ACM) recognised that it did not have the necessary internal construction supply management expertise to achieve value for money from construction procurement on its own. To minimise the risks relating to construction sourcing and the subsequent management of the contract, ACM employed construction experts to provide advice on outline project scope, design and specification, contract strategy, preparation of tender documents, tender submission analysis, supplier selection and key aspects of cost, project and contract management.

At the outset of the project, the total cost for the project was initially estimated to be £375 000. However, after putting the design and construction project out to tender, ACM received prices ranging from £310 000 to £420 000. Despite the advice of construction experts and the availability of a wide array of supplier and tender assessment criteria, ACM selected STDB, a design and build contractor, who had submitted the lowest bid price. Without a full understanding of the true costs of construction ACM did not question that the price submitted by STDB was £60 000 lower than any other price, and that all others were between £370 000 and £420 000. The implications of the decision to appoint STDB under a JCT standard form of contract (with contractor's design) soon became evident.

The supplier – Small Town Design and Build (STDB)

Since its formation in 1980, STDB had developed a relatively strong position in the local supply market with an annual turnover of approximately £1.3 million. The company offered a complete design and build service, but given its limited financial and management resources, it had concentrated on low value projects (£50 000 to £300 000). These projects tended to be for small private sector clients sourcing from the construction industry on a one-off basis. The firm had attempted to create a strong reputation within the local market for delivering high quality solutions on time and within costs constraints to these inexperienced clients. In the local supply market this reputation was critical to STDB as access to tender lists is largely through word of mouth and client recommendations. With no certainty surrounding future projects small construction firms, such as STDB, faced a very unpredictable future. They were not in a position to develop long-term preferred supplier relationships with clients because the majority of small clients do not require design and build solutions on a regular basis.

11.3 The buyer–supplier relationship management approach

In analysing this case the discussion focuses on whether ACM or STDB has the scope to leverage the other party to achieve the maximisation of its respective commercial and operational objectives. As we shall see, the incompetence of ACM created a situation in which both parties failed to achieve their objectives and a lose–lose or *negative-sum* outcome occurred.

The client (ACM) – construction firm (STDB) dyad

It has been argued in a number of the previous cases that if clients have a limited understanding of construction supply chains and markets, and are unsure about their current and future construction requirements, they are unlikely to have direct control over what they are sourcing and will almost certainly face opportunistic supplier behaviour. The client's ability to control a construction firm is dependent, therefore, on its capacity to obtain power resources within the relationship, and at the same time effectively monitor the firm to reduce this scope for supplier opportunism. While the ability of the client to monitor the supplier can be improved by working with professional services, the external power resources of the client (ACM) in relation to the construction firm (STDB) are determined by a number of key demand and supply characteristics.

For this particular project the contract value for the design and construction of the extension to the client's existing manufacturing facility was £310 000. With a programmed duration of six months this project accounted for approximately 24% of STDB's annual turnover. Although this project was insignificant in size compared to those in the other cases, this level of expenditure potentially provided ACM with a key power resource because the project accounted for a very high share of STDB's turnover. The project was the largest project being undertaken by STDB but, with no further plans for sourcing from the construction market, ACM was unable to offer STDB a level of demand characterised by high volume **and** high frequency. One might expect, therefore, that ACM would achieve some of its commercial and operational objectives but not necessarily achieve its ideal value for money objectives. This is typical for the majority of clients that source construction on a one-off basis[1].

In addition to volume and frequency, the complexity of the required solution is another demand-side factor that determines relative power in a relationship. For the majority of clients, inexperience in construction procurement, combined with the complexity of the required project, typically results in situations where they do not understand the supply market and how to maximise value for money when sourcing from it. Furthermore, when a client sources construction on a one-off basis, it may be possible for the construction firm to act in an opportunistic manner through the use of information asymmetries and/or the client's inability to monitor the contractor. In this case, however, ACM attempted to reduce its ignorance as a buyer by employing an architect to provide the necessary professional services. It hoped, ultimately mistakenly, that this would minimise the level of information asymmetry and the scope for supplier opportunism.

While the previous discussion has focused on the utility of ACM's demand to STDM, it is also necessary to consider the scarcity of ACM's business (i.e. the

---

[1] The nature of demand for construction can be segmented in a number of ways. Cox and Townsend (1998) differentiate between clients who have a regular requirement for construction work of similar value and content (process spenders), and infrequent purchase clients (commodity spenders). Cox and Thompson (1998) contend that clients that possess regular process spends are unlikely to constitute more than 25% of the total UK market, while Blismas (2001) contends that multi-projects accounted for 10% of the entire industry's output and as much as 30% of contractors' output in 1999.

availability of equivalent alternative contracts for STDM). In the construction industry, the majority of construction firms have to operate within a highly competitive and adversarial environment with no guarantee of alternative contracts because they are faced with irregular client demand. This was the case for STDB, which was not in a position to develop long-term relationships with clients and engineer a greater certainty of demand.

Given the previous discussion of demand-side power resources, it is not surprising that ACM, with no planned construction expenditure in the future, had no desire to invest time and financial resources in the development of a long-term collaborative and proactive relationship with STDB. As a result, ACM was left with no alternative but to adopt a short-term and reactive *supplier selection* relationship management approach. Despite this, ACM still thought that, if it was undertaken in a robust and professional manner, value for money could be achieved.

On the supply-side of this relationship, the critical power resources for STDB that dictate whether it is able to obtain value from supply are scarcity (related to the number of equivalent suppliers available to ACM) and utility (related to the value/importance of the transaction to ACM). The majority of construction firms operate within highly contested markets and are unable to restrict the level of competition (and create a high degree of supplier scarcity) through the ownership of key external supply chain resources. In this relationship, STDB was also unable to use information (in the form of brand or reputation) to increase ACM's perception of value (utility) and decrease the perceived level of contestation (scarcity).

When many construction firms offer similar solutions to a fragmented but relatively well-informed client base neither party has a significant power advantage over the other. Under such circumstances, the construction firm cannot be opportunistic before the award of the contract and usually passes value (in the form of lower prices or higher functionality) to the client which is able to compare suppliers during the supplier selection process. However, despite ACM using professional services to compensate for its lack of construction supply management expertise, STDB was able to bid opportunistically. The construction firm (STDB) decided to bid low to win the work in anticipation of being able to make claims later from an uninformed client experiencing high switching costs, in order to achieve the profits initially intended. This caused severe problems for both parties post-contractually.

11.4 Performance outcome from the buyer–supplier relationship

From the outset of the project, ACM was attempting operationally to maximise the functionality of the factory extension and commercially to minimise the total costs of ownership of the solution so that it could maximise value for money. In direct contrast, the objective of STDB was to maximise the revenues and returns received from this specific client but by opportunistic means. It was aided in this objective initially by the fact that, although ACM employed construction experts and professional advisers to reduce the levels of complexity and uncertainty normally associated with sourcing projects of this type, ACM did not always act upon their advice and decided to source from a significantly lower priced bidder. As a result, the advantage gained by ACM from having a high share of STDB's turn-over was effectively eliminated by its failure to take on board the advice of its professional advisers. An additional error occurred for ACM when it failed to adequately monitor the opportunistic behaviour of STDB and identify problems with poor workmanship.

Figure 11.2 gives a summary of the dyad between ACM and STDB and the performance outcome from the relationship. In the pursuit of the lowest bid price ACM accepted STDB's extremely low offer of £310 000, despite professional advice not to do so because the price was clearly well below the estimated £375 000 that what was deemed to be necessary to deliver the project satisfactorily. During

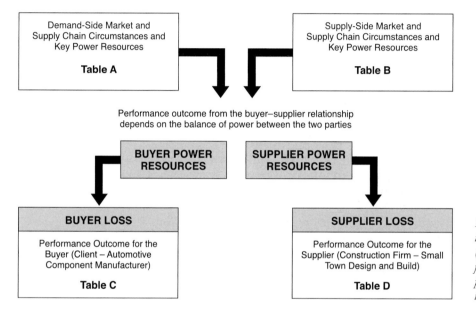

Figure 11.2 A summary of the dyad between the client (ACM) and construction firm (STDB) and the performance outcome from the relationship

Table A Demand-Side Market and Supply Chain Circumstances and Key Power Resources

There are a large number of buyers in the total construction market for similar projects. Simple manufacturing facilities form a large proportion of the industrial market

Automotive Component Manufacturer (ACM) has a **very low share of total construction market** with an estimated single project value of £375 000. However, with a low annual turnover the construction firm (STDB) has a relatively high dependency on ACM for revenue

ACM has a **very infrequent need** to source from the construction market. It has no current plans for further capital investment and sourcing from the construction market

The requirements of ACM are **relatively simple** and require limited supplier expertise for their integration into the project

ACM has **medium switching costs**, as although there are a large number of suppliers it would find it difficult to easily and quickly appoint an alternative supplier to provide a high quality solution

ACM has a **relatively clear value proposition** – a high quality product delivered on time and at an acceptable cost. However, ACM lacks a robust construction sourcing strategy to maximise value for money, as problems arise that impact on the trade-off between cost and quality

ACM is totally unaware of the potential scope for **standardisation** of design and specification and **prefabrication** of key components common across the project

ACM has **relatively high search costs**, as it has limited knowledge and understanding of construction products and services and the typical adversarial and opportunistic approaches of the industry players

Table B Supply-Side Market and Supply Chain Circumstances and Key Power Resources

There are a large number of similar construction firms in the supply market with the necessary expertise and experience to deliver this relatively simple project to the client (ACM)

The total value of the six-month project, £310 000, accounts for a relatively **high share of the annual turnover** (£1.3 million) of Small Town Design and Build (STDB) (approximately 24%). The project is actually the largest project undertaken by STDB

STDB has a **high level of dependency** on ACM for revenue, as it is the largest of the five projects that it is currently involved in, and there is a high degree of uncertainty surrounding future contracts

STDB considers ACM's business to be **relatively attractive**, as the proposed solution does not contain any complexities and there are low costs associated with servicing the contract

STDB has **medium switching costs**

STDB's offerings are not commoditised and standardised but **highly customised** to the specific requirements of ACM

STDB has a **good reputation** in the local area in which it undertakes projects for delivering projects that meet client's expectations within financial budget

STDB has **information asymmetry advantages** with ACM lacking a robust understanding of construction products and services and the typical opportunistic strategies of the industry players

---

Table C Performance Outcome for the Client (ACM) – Buyer Loss

Construction costs higher than original estimated budget by £20 000. The final construction cost was £395 000

The client, Automotive Component Manufacturer (ACM), had selected the lowest tender (£310 000) which was £60 000 lower than all the other tendered prices without fully understanding the true building costs

ACM thought it had a sophisticated sourcing strategy and sought to minimise construction costs by blindly selecting the lowest tender (against the expert advice provided)

After open-book audit it was evident that if the agreed contract sum was retained the supplier would go out of business and create significant problems for ACM. This was renegotiated to avoid this situation arising

Delivery of project four weeks late because of delays associated with poor workmanship and the renegotiation of original contract

Functional expectations of ACM only partially met after remedial action by the construction firm (STDB)

Table D Performance Outcome for the Construction Firm (STDB) – Supplier Loss

Despite receiving the extra payment from the client (ACM), the construction firm (STDB) still made a loss of £40 000 on this project

The extra expense was necessary to overcome problems with the cutting of corners and poor workmanship at the outset of the project. The most significant work involved rebuilding a retaining wall following a collapse

At the outset of the project, STDB was faced with very low rates that were discovered to be insufficient to ensure survival. The cash-flow problems led to the cutting of corners and the use of poorer quality materials

STDB damaged its reputation within the local supply market for delivering quality projects within time and cost constraints. With small contractors relying on word-of-mouth, the performance of this project adversely impacted future revenues and eventually it went out of business

---

the construction phase of the project it became evident that STDB had mis-calculated the cost of the extension to the manufacturing facility. This was because STDB had provided its bid price without seeking detailed prices from key material suppliers (structural steelwork and cladding), basing its submission on a similar project that it had recently completed.

This strategy was induced by STDB's current lack of forward work and by its desire to win sufficient revenue to keep its key staff within the company. The construction firm (STDB) assumed that the project was similar and that, if it bid low, it could always make the costs up from claims later. Unfortunately, this strategy was seriously mistaken because STDB soon discovered that its under-estimates were far more extreme than it had anticipated and that any claims would have to be very high indeed. This was because not only was the cost of claims to rectify the under-estimates significantly higher than STDB had antici-pated, but the short-lead time required for this project meant that it would have to pay a premium to receive the components on time. To avoid significant cash flow problems, STDB knew that it had to have claims accepted that would raise the price and/or act opportunistically and reduce costs where possible.

Initially, STDB attempted to claim that the price of inputs had unexpectedly risen, but acting on the advice of its professional advisers ACM refused to accept the claims being made. This put STDB in a very difficult financial position. If it could not claim more from ACM it would be faced with a loss on the project and potential bankruptcy. Recognising that the client and its advisers were not actively moni-toring or measuring its performance STDB decided, therefore, to cut corners by using poorer quality materials and employing a cheaper inexperienced labour force. Unfortunately, while this enabled STDB to immediately lower material and labour costs, it had a detrimental impact on the functionality of the solution.

The solution required the construction of relatively simple gravity retaining wall (1.5 metres in height and 25 metres in length) along part of the boundary of the site. As the new facility was to be built on sloping ground this wall was designed to prevent the soil from slipping into the adjoining car park area. Structural engineers had developed this wall design after consideration of the soil conditions, water drainage and pressures, slopes, wall location and dimensions, location of underground utilities and external surcharges. When constructing the wall STDB's workforce simply had to follow this design paying particular attention to the foundation soil preparation, dimensions of the base footing, size of the base course, location of the drainpipe, method and soils for backfilling, level and alignment of each course of blocks and wall batter (or setback) as the wall stacks up. The inexperienced workforce did not, however, appreciate the need to follow the design precisely and failed to properly compact and consolidate the fill material behind the wall.

After the completion of the retaining wall it appeared to be structurally sound. Two weeks later a number of cracks appeared in the wall and the central section 'tipped over' and was fatally compromised. The client (ACM)'s architect immedi-ately identified that this was an indication of faulty construction and impending failure. The gradual yielding and movement of the defective wall over the following two weeks finally led to the collapse of the central section. It was agreed by all parties that what remained of the existing wall had to be completely demolished and removed before it could be replaced.

At this point, it became evident to ACM that STDB was in commercial difficulty as a consequence of trying to deliver the solution for the agreed sum of £310 000 and had been attempting to cut costs whenever possible. The client (ACM) also recognised that this was adversely affecting the quality of the solution as a whole and that the collapse of the wall was likely to be the first of many problems. Therefore, ACM was faced with a decision over whether to stay with the agreed contracted price of £310 000 or renegotiate the contract.

The client (ACM) realised that if it stayed with the original contracted price it would receive a poor quality solution and that STDB would go out of business, which would lead to a major delay to the completion of the project and significantly higher costs overall. It had to accept that these costs would exceed those associated with the renegotiation of the original contract. By undertaking an open-book audit of the project finances and agreeing a higher price for the project (£395 000) ACM had to accept that the total costs of ownership would have to increase by £85 000, but the overall functionality required might still be achieved.

Unfortunately, despite the renegotiation of the original contract, the time taken to rebuild the retaining wall and the lead-time for certain components meant that the project was still delivered four weeks late. This caused a minor disruption to ACM's business and a one-week delay to the fulfilment of a large contract to a major player within the automotive market. Finally, despite the increased cost of the remedial work undertaken to correct poor workmanship, the functionality of the final solution failed to meet the expectations of the client. It received a completed facility that was sub-optimal, that affected its own reputation with its own customers, and at a higher cost than it should have done. This was a lose outcome for the buyer.

The construction firm (STDB) were able to renegotiate the contract to cover some of the costs of remedial work but overall it made a loss of £40 000 on the project. This loss would have been even more significant if the client had not agreed to pay the construction firm an additional £85 000 after the contract was renegotiated. This extra payment ensured the short-term survival of STDB but, with bad news quickly transmitted within the local construction market, it seriously damaged STDB's reputation for delivering very high quality and cost-effective solutions, on time, and to the exact functional requirements of the client. As a result, STDB was unable to win sufficient work in the future to cover operating costs and eventually went bankrupt. This was definitely a lose outcome for the supplier and a result of its misguided opportunistic approach to the bidding process and to the project management and construction phase of the relationship.

11.5 Summary

The major finding from this case is that a *negative-sum* outcome, in which both parties lose and fail to achieve any of the commercial and operational goals that they desired, is perfectly feasible in reactive sourcing. Although ACM eventually received a completed facility it did not provide the functionality that was specified; it was late and at a higher cost than had been originally estimated. The failure of STDB to provide the project on time also had a detrimental impact on the reputation of ACM due to a failure on its part to supply its own customers on time.

This was clearly a lose outcome for the buyer, ACM. It was, however, a much more severe lose outcome for the supplier in this case. Initially, STDB was able to mitigate its potential financial losses from under-bidding by renegotiating the contract and by forcing ACM to pay over the original estimated cost to allow ACM to rectify STDB's poor workmanship. Despite this, STDB still lost money on the project that it could not really afford. Eventually its reputation was destroyed in the local marketplace because of its opportunistic and incompetent behaviour and the company eventually went out of business.

This demonstrates that both parties can lose if they behave in an opportunistic and incompetent fashion. It also shows that it is essential for construction buyers to listen carefully to their professional advisers if they have no real knowledge of the supply chains and markets from which they source. On the other hand, opportunism can be a successful approach for suppliers when they are involved in one-off games with buyers, but sometimes the gamble of bidding low to win the business, and then being unable to deliver what the client requires, can backfire, as it did so dramatically to the supplier in this case.

Table 11.1 is a summary of the relationship management approach and performance outcome in this case.

Table 11.1 A summary of the relationship management approach and performance outcome

Nature of Relationship Management Approach	ACM, with no planned construction expenditure in the future, saw no return on investment in the development of a long-term collaborative and proactive relationship with the construction firm
	The only option considered was the implementation of a short-term and reactive *supplier selection* relationship management approach
	The client thought that if this reactive approach was undertaken in a robust manner then it could still attain value for money from construction procurement
Nature of Buyer 'Loss'	ACM blindly selected the lowest tender, which was £60 000 lower than all the other tendered prices, without fully understanding the true construction costs
	The problems that arose from this decision meant that the final construction cost was £395 000 rather than the originally estimated cost of £375 000
	The project was delivered four weeks late because of lead-times of key components and delays associated with the renegotiation of the original contract
	Functional expectations of ACM only met after remedial action by STDB
	The delay had a deleterious impact on ACM's ability to supply its own customers and affected its reputation with its customers generally
Nature of Supplier 'Loss'	At the outset of the project, STDB had agreed to a price that was insufficient to ensure that the project could be completed, with profitability and long-term survival threatened
	A loss of £40 000 was made on the project overall
	The extra expense was necessary to overcome problems with the cutting of corners and poor workmanship at the outset of the project. The most significant work involved rebuilding a retaining wall following a collapse
	STDB damaged its reputation within the local supply market. With small contractors relying on word-of-mouth, the performance of this project adversely impacted future work and eventually the company went bankrupt
Conclusions	Ignoring professional advice when the client has no real knowledge of construction supply chains and markets is normally a recipe for disaster
	Buyers who select suppliers on the basis of price alone are normally the prey of opportunistic and unscrupulous suppliers
	Suppliers playing the game of opportunism in one-off games have to ensure that the risks they are running are manageable and will not result in the eventual loss of their own reputation and financial ruin
	Because one supplier fails to use this approach successfully does not mean that suppliers will not use this approach in the future because the highly contested nature of many supply markets forces suppliers to consider this type of behaviour in order to survive
	Sensible buyers remember that lowest price does not always mean lowest total cost of ownership

References

Blismas, N. G. (2001), *Multi-project Environments of Construction Clients*, Unpublished PhD Thesis, Loughborough University, Loughborough.

Cox, A. and Thompson, I. (1998), *Contracting for Business Success*, Thomas Telford, London.

Cox, A. and Townsend, M. (1997), 'Latham as a half-way house: a relational competence approach to better practice in construction practice', *Engineering Construction and Architectural Management*, **4**(2), pp. 143–158.

Part B2

Cases in construction relationship management and performance outcomes: proactive sourcing approaches

In Parts B1 and B2 the theoretical issues about relationship management choices and outcomes are taken up in some detail. Each of the chapters describes a specific construction relationship management approach and charts the outcomes that occurred within these relationships for the parties involved. The sixteen cases show that under both reactive (*supplier selection* or *supply chain sourcing*) and proactive (*supplier development* or *supply chain management*) relationship management approaches that all of the nonzero-sum, zero-sum and negative-sum performance outcomes discussed earlier are feasible, but that win–win (positive-sum) outcomes are never feasible in buyer and supplier exchange. The discussion focuses in Part B1 on eight reactive and then in Part B2 on eight proactive relationship management cases. To protect commercial sensitivities the actual names of the buyers and suppliers involved in the cases are not provided and certain financial information has been altered.

The restaurant construction case: proactive supply chain management with a buyer win and supplier partial win outcome

12.1 Introduction

This case focuses on the procurement of a critical sub-component – the pre-fabricated internal sub-elements – for the construction of a new restaurant. The case focuses on the relationship between a fast-food restaurant chain, Fast Food Retailer (FFR), and a specialist manufacturer of prefabricated units, High-Tech Prefabricated Units (HPU). Fast Food Retailer and HPU both have considerable knowledge of the supply chains and markets in the construction industry and extensive experience of working together to deliver similar projects.

The case highlights key supply chain and business management issues that arise for those adopting long-term collaborative (proactive sourcing) relationships within the industry. In this case the client, FFR, had a continuous need for similar types of projects and was, therefore, in a position to develop a proactive supply chain management approach with key first- and second-tier construction suppliers. Fundamental to this approach has been the use of standardisation of design and specification and prefabrication of critical components.

By successfully implementing this approach FFR has achieved significant cost savings, increased the functionality of projects and, most significantly for its business model, reduced time to market for the construction of its new restaurants. In addition to fully achieving its own objectives and achieving a win outcome, FFR has been able to provide preferred suppliers (like HPU) with a guaranteed revenue stream and controlled, but reasonable, profit levels. This has enabled preferred suppliers to achieve a partial win outcome in relation to their own commercial and operational objectives.

12.2 Background to the case: the construction of a prefabricated restaurant facility

The construction of a new build prefabricated restaurant requires the integration of a number of supply chains, as illustrated in Figure 12.1. To create a new facility FFR, in conjunction with in-house and external professional services, develops a design and specification for their requirements. Instead of using a reactive and

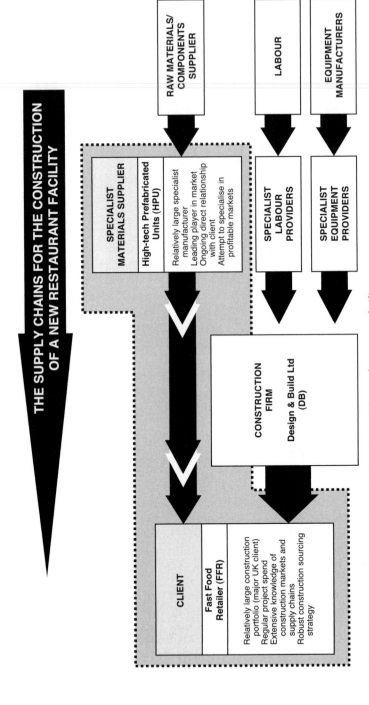

Figure 12.1 *Construction supply chains for the construction of a prefabricated restaurant facility*

arm's-length approach FFR has developed a more sophisticated approach to construction procurement. After setting a broad functional specification it selects one of its preferred contractors and works with that contractor to develop the detailed specification. At this stage FFR also involves not only the contractor but also a number of preferred specialist suppliers such as the prefabricated unit manufacturer (HPU).

The analysis here focuses primarily on the relationship between FFR and HPU and not on the client–contractor relationship involving the first-tier construction firm, Design & Build Ltd (DB). This particular project, the construction of a drive-through restaurant, forms part of FFR's ongoing construction programme. At the outset of the project the anticipated value (target cost) of the works was approximately £750 000. Once the site was acquired, conceptual design was undertaken internally so that control over brand image (absolutely critical to the company) could be maintained.

A single construction firm, DB, was selected from a preferred list of contractors (without a written contract) to undertake the detailed design, integrate the entire construction package and deliver it to the client. To achieve this DB had to work with a number of other preferred contractors. The specialist supplier (HPU) supplied and assembled the factory-built modular building onto the prepared foundations. The restaurant chain (FFR) procured the internal components for the modular buildings centrally so that quality and availability could be guaranteed and suppliers effectively leveraged.

The buyer – Fast Food Retailer (FFR)

In 2004, FFR had a total capital expenditure budget of around £75 million in the UK. In the same year the average development costs (including land, construction and equipment) for a new restaurant was estimated to be approximately £1 million. This level of regular expenditure in the UK enables it to construct 50 new restaurants and undertake major refurbishments in 60 outlets per year. The size and regularity of its expenditure means that it can be considered a major client in the UK construction industry.

For FFR the construction of new restaurants is a key activity that supports its primary business of selling food. Interestingly enough, FFR had not always recognised the critical importance of its construction activity to its strategic goals. Previously, FFR's approach to construction procurement was based largely on a traditional and rigid separation of design and construction. Eventually, FFR realised that the lack of integration and business focus which this created, linked with poor communication throughout the supply chain, created significant problems for timely delivery of, and quality within, projects.

With all design work carried out by external consultants there was often inefficient space planning, over-design and specification and a failure to fully understand what the customer really needed and wanted. Furthermore, FFR recognised that it was not receiving optimal value for money from its high volume and regular demand for similar types of projects. Individual projects were frequently not delivered on time and there was considerable uncertainty over final costs. There were also problems with defects and unfinished work on handover, and the quality of the final product was often unacceptable. Subsequent claims took a long time to be settled leading FFR to recognise that this primarily reactive approach was very inefficient and that a radical change was necessary.

As a result, FFR recognised that, because it had a relatively high volume and regular demand to offer firms within the construction industry, it could fundamentally improve the efficiency and effectiveness of its management of its construction supply chains if it adopted a more proactive approach (based on the lean principles first adopted in the car industry). The first stage of this change process involved an appraisal of its project management, design, engineering and procurement capabilities. The restaurant chain (FFR) recognised that it needed to fundamentally re-engineer the project process so that construction time and 'speed to market' could be minimised, and revenues earned as soon as possible. This was because speed to market to earn revenue from selling food was critical to the strategic goals of the company. At the same time, it also needed to minimise construction costs so that more outlets could be built for the same level of capital expenditure.

With speed to market critical, the company also recognised the need to improve the efficiency of the project process through standardisation of design and specification for key inputs and through the use of prefabricated modular components. It also became apparent that, for this product innovation to be implemented successfully, it had to be accompanied by innovation in supply and the complete re-engineering of its construction supply chains. To achieve this, FFR was forced to understand the criticality of construction to its own strategic goals, understand the significance of its demand portfolio relative to its potential supplier's business models, and acquire a much more detailed internal knowledge of construction markets and supply chains.

In analysing the criticality of particular construction activities and processes, FFR decided that internal control had to be retained over concept design, functional specification and the actual management of the development process. The restaurant chain (FFR) recognised that all other aspects of each project – including detailed design, site preparation, prefabricated unit assembly, other construction works and the supply of internal services/fittings – could be outsourced to external suppliers. In order to incentivise suppliers FFR decided to move to a long-term relationship by providing preferred suppliers with a long-term commitment to work, with guaranteed margins, but only if they were prepared to work with it on construction efficiencies in a transparent manner, using open-book costing and independent cost consultants for detailed target costing models. As we shall see, this promise of a regular workload and guaranteed margins incentivised these preferred suppliers to make dedicated investments in long-term relationships, which provided the basis for both parties to achieve most, but for the supplier not all, of that which they ideally desired.

In sourcing its prefabricated modules, despite the criticality of this to its re-engineering strategy, FFR recognised that it had neither the expertise nor the resources to undertake development, manufacture and supply internally. It decided, therefore, to develop very close collaborative relationships with two specialist suppliers. Two suppliers were selected to avoid the risks associated with single sourcing and to ensure the required number of units for its new-build programme could be delivered on time, and FFR guarded against supplier dependency and opportunism by procuring for itself the components required for integration into the prefabricated units internally. These items are normally issued directly by FFR to the prefabricated manufacturer's factories so that they can be installed before delivery to site. Since the actual erection of the prefabricated modules does not require specialist expertise, FFR normally allows the contractor undertaking the ground and infrastructure work, or the module supplier itself, to undertake the work. The restaurant chain (FFR) allocates its workload to its preferred contractors and specialist suppliers on a fairly equitable basis according to their supply capabilities.

In this case FFR used its considerable knowledge of the construction marketplace to select a highly competent construction firm (DB) using clear supplier selection criteria, with particular attention being paid to DB's use of best practices and speed to market. The construction firm (DB), having provided a target price of £700 000, was selected due to its experience in delivering projects to a very high quality and within tight timescales when faced with difficult site conditions. The specific project was its thirteenth for the client, all of which had been managed without a written contract.

The restaurant chain (FFR) adopted a similar approach to the allocation of its expenditure to specialist upstream suppliers. It initially developed its prefabrication approach with HPU, and only introduced Modular Solutions Ltd (MS) when the approach had proven beneficial and extra capacity was required. The restaurant chain (FFR) was not interested in creating single source dependency on HPU, even though a more proactive approach had been adopted. The two preferred suppliers were selected on the basis of cost, experience, recent track record, cultural attitude and flexibility and, most critically of all, on quality and ability to supply required quantities on time. The two suppliers' willingness to make the necessary dedicated investments in the relationship to support FFR's proactive supply chain management approach was also an important consideration in the supplier selection process.

The supplier – High-Tech Prefabricated Units (HPU)

Over the years standardisation and pre-assembly have been used on construction projects in an attempt to improve value for money. The approach is hardly new and, in most senses, not innovative. Standardisation is, in fact, nothing more than the extensive use of components, methods and/or processes in which there is regularity, repetition and a background of successful practice and predictability. Many different terms have been used to describe the process of prefabrication and pre-assembly and there is often confusion and misunderstanding related to their meaning. Table 12.1 summarises the four different levels of pre-assembly that are used within the industry.

Both HPU and MS manufacture and supply prefabricated units as part of FFR's modular construction approach. They manufacture these restaurant modules complete with catering equipment, signage, glazing, heating, plumbing, ventilation, ceramic finishes, joinery and internal walls in a controlled factory environment while the foundations are progressed on site. The modules are transported to site by road where they are then craned into position to form a complete building. Using this 'modular' approach, the client has effectively reduced the construction time for its restaurants on two levels.

First, the amount of standardisation in design and specification allows a greater degree of overlap of the design and construction phases, as only site and restaurant specific factors require bespoke design details. Second, the repeated use of standardised modules provides for efficient production, with minimum time required for on-site construction activities. As a result, this switch from traditional build to modular construction has reduced the construction programme of a typical restaurant from 16 to 4 weeks.

The prefabricated buildings market is very fragmented with many suppliers, all of which hold relatively low market shares. There is/are no single dominant

Table 12.1 *The different forms of prefabrication and pre-assembly*

Type of Pre-assembly	Definition
Component Manufacture and Sub-assembly	A number of components brought together to form a sub-assembly, but not assembled on-site. Examples include door furniture or light fittings
Non-volumetric Pre-assembly	Items that are assembled in a factory and may include several sub-assemblies and constitute a significant part of the building or structure. Examples may include wall panels, structural sections, electrical installations or pipework assemblies
Volumetric Pre-assembly	Items that are also assembled in a factory, but in contrast to non-volumetric assembly, they enclose usable space and are usually installed on-site within an independent structural frame. Examples may include toilet pods and modular lift shafts. This category accounts for approximately 75% of the prefabrication market
Modular Building	Items that are similar to volumetric units, but the units themselves form the building. They may be clad externally on-site. Examples may include out-of-town retail and restaurant outlets, office blocks, hotels and concrete multi-storey modular residential units

player/players in the market. Nevertheless, HPU is one of the major players in the market with a share of around 15%. It is a leading manufacturer of steel-framed modular buildings across a diverse range of industrial sectors. The firm has a turnover of £200 million and this strong financial base allows it to invest heavily in the latest production technology and manufacturing techniques, which ensures that it will remain at the forefront of design and innovation.

The market is also fragmented on the demand-side with a large number of potential end users or clients, with very different needs and requirements in terms of size and appearance. The majority of clients for prefabricated buildings are within the commercial, hotel and catering, educational, residential and healthcare sectors. Despite this fragmentation of demand, HPU has worked with FFR for many years. The arrangement between the two firms is one of mutual trust and there have never been any formal contractual arrangements between them. New restaurants' modules are now completed at a rate of one every 12 days in a production facility dedicated to meeting FFR's annual requirement of 25 units. In addition to investment in the production facility, HPU has developed a dedicated project management team and workforce for all of FFR's work, and there is a continued focus on efficiency of manufacturing and cost effectiveness through value engineering. The supplier (HPU) is willing to make these relationship-specific investments purely on the promise of a regular workload from FFR.

12.3 The buyer–supplier relationship management approach

This section analyses the key power resources available to FFR and HPU, and the specific market and supply chain circumstances at play, to provide both an understanding of the proactive relationship management approach being adopted and the performance outcome for both parties. As we shall see, the evidence indicates that FFR is able to achieve a win outcome, while HPU, although still very satisfied with the outcome, is nevertheless only able to achieve a partial win.

The restaurant
construction case

The client (FFR) – specialist manufacturer (HPU) dyad

The relationship with HPU allows FFR to obtain important product innovation and significant reductions in project delivery time. Despite achieving this, FFR has also engineered a relationship approach that minimises supplier opportunism. The client (FFR) has extensive knowledge and understanding of construction supply chains and markets and the appropriateness of available technologies from upstream suppliers. This understanding enables FFR to develop supply chain strategies that allow the selection (and subsequent control and leverage) of competent and congruent upstream suppliers to maximise the value for money that it obtains from construction procurement.

The client (FFR)'s ability to leverage HPU is based on its possession of key power resources. In this case the contract value for the project was approximately £750 000, of which £350 000 was attributable to the fitted-out prefabricated sub-units. While this single contract equates to a low share of HPU's total annual turnover (less than 1%), when one considers the frequency of the transaction and resulting annual workload (25 similar units), this expenditure accounts for a much higher proportion of its turnover and is highly attractive to it. In terms of revenue and investment in internal processes FRR is HPU's number one customer.

The client (FFR)'s power and leverage over HPU is clearly a function of its possession of a relatively high volume and frequent demand. The possession of key operational and commercial information that flows from the adoption of an open-book and target costing approach to sourcing also augments this leverage because it minimises the information asymmetry between HPU and FFR. The standardised nature of design and specification has also significantly reduced the level of complexity for both FFR and HPU. As a result, FFR fully understands the product offering and the supply market, and HPU considers FFR's business to be highly attractive because it is relatively simple to service. In addition, the fact that there are a relatively limited number of equivalent clients also effectively limits the availability of alternative contracts and increases the difficulty for HPU to switch. These switching costs are further increased by the dedicated investments (dedicated manufacturing process and IT system) that HPU has been required to make at its manufacturing plant by FFR as part of its proactive *supply chain management* relationship management approach.

On the supply-side of this dyad it is also important to recognise that the pre-fabricated unit manufacturers are operating within a fragmented market that has relatively high levels of contestation, because there are many suppliers all of which have a relatively low market share. In such highly competitive markets firms are usually unable to close the market to competitors. Nevertheless, in this case, because there are only a small number of manufacturers capable of supplying, or willing to supply, the required number of units in a collaborative manner (using open-book costing, fixed margins and without a formal written contract), to the very strict deadlines and high quality levels demanded by the client, there are only a limited number of competent and congruent suppliers available to FFR.

This clearly provides a countervailing power resource for HPU against FFR. It does not, however, provide an equivalence of power resources because FFR could switch to MS if HPU behaved opportunistically, or it could develop the capabilities of alternative suppliers over time. In this context it is clear that the buyer, FFR, is still relatively dominant and this implies that it will control the performance outcome in the relationship. Nevertheless, because there is a close operational dependency and medium switching costs between FFR and HPU it is likely that FFR will have to allow HPU to achieve a partial win in what is a nonzero-sum game for both parties. The buyer (FFR) is still, however, in control of the relationship and can be expected to achieve a full win.

12.4 Performance outcome from the buyer–supplier relationship

At the outset of the project, FFR and HPU had conflicting operational and commercial goals. The buyer (FFR) was attempting operationally to maximise the functionality of the final construction asset while ensuring that brand image was maintained. It was also attempting commercially to minimise the total costs of ownership and project duration so that it could maximise the value for money it received from the supplier. In direct contrast, the initial aim of HPU was to increase operationally its revenues and its commercial returns from FFR.

The buyer (FFR) was, however, able to fully achieve its commercial and operational goals because it had a regular level of demand characterised by high volume that was very attractive to potential suppliers. Its relative power was also enhanced because HPU was effectively locked into a long-term relationship due to the relatively high switching costs created for HPU by the dedicated investments FFR required it to make operationally and because FFR's understanding of the available technologies and the nature of the supply market meant that buyer search costs were relatively low.

Faced with these circumstances, HPU was deterred from acting opportunistically *ex ante* because of the promise of a regular demand, and *ex post* because of the threat of exit and relatively high switching costs created by the contract award and the establishment of a dedicated manufacturing facility. The buyer (FFR) further minimised the potential for opportunistic behaviour at all stages of the supply chain by employing independent costs consultants to examine the open books of suppliers and monitor supplier performance against target costs, with guaranteed margins.

In this relationship there were a number of factors that provided HPU with a degree of relative power and ensured that it was not completely at the mercy of FFR commercially and operationally. First, at least in the short-term, the number of potential suppliers was restricted because there were only a small number of manufacturers with the financial and technical capability to supply the number of units required, which were also willing to adopt a 'partnering' ethos and rely on trust without a formal written contract. Second, HPU had developed a very strong brand reputation by successfully delivering high quality products and services. Fundamental to this reputation is HPU's ability to invest heavily in leading-edge manufacturing technology, which ensures that it remains at the forefront of design and innovation. Furthermore, HPU was not totally dependent on FFR because it had a number of other customers across a diverse range of industries. The supplier (HPU) had developed a segmented approach for the targeting of other profitable markets in which it was able to leverage its differentiated high quality offering for higher returns than possible with FFR.

The dyadic interaction between FFR and HPU (see Figure 12.2) can be categorised, therefore, as one of *buyer dominance* with a win for the buyer and partial win for the supplier. In terms of total cost of ownership, FFR developed a sophisticated sourcing framework that drove continuous reduction of construction whole-life costs to their minimum feasible level. It was estimated that cost savings in the region of £100 000 were achieved on all projects due to the re-engineered sourcing approach focused on standardisation of design and specification and prefabrication of key elements. Cost figures during the project in this case were verified and controlled by an independent cost consultant which monitored and benchmarked supplier performance. This enabled FFR to undertake robust contract and project management and fully understand the financial impact of pursuing different value proposition trade-offs (i.e. the impact of reducing time to market vis-à-vis

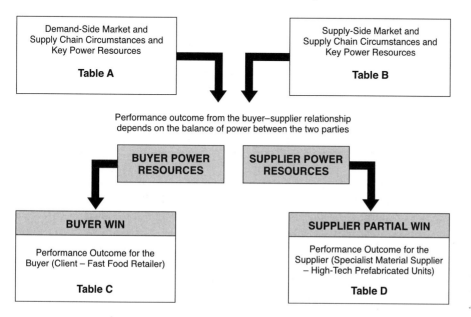

Figure 12.2 A summary of the dyad between the client (FFR) and specialist manufacturer (HPU) and the performance outcome from the relationship

Table A Demand-Side Market and Supply Chain Circumstances and Key Power Resources

There are many buyers in the total construction market but fewer buyers for prefabricated solutions (especially clients with a regular spend)

Fast Food Retailer (FFR) has a relatively low share of total construction market but relatively **high share of the prefabrication sector** with an annual construction expenditure of £100 million. Therefore, the specialist manufacturer (HPU) has a relatively high dependency on FFR for revenue

FFR has a **very frequent need** to go to the prefabricated construction market for new-build restaurants requiring approximately 50 units per year

The requirements of FFR are **relatively simple** (because of the standardisation of design and specification), but require supplier knowledge and expertise to manufacture

FFR has **medium switching costs** with only a small number of competent suppliers

FFR, through the development of a robust sourcing strategy, has a **very clear value proposition** – a high quality product delivered on time, at an acceptable cost and capable of easy installation. Time to market is also critical

FFR is fully aware of the potential scope for **standardisation** of design and specification and **prefabrication** of key components common across the project

FFR has **very low search costs**, because of its robust knowledge and understanding of construction products and services and the strategies of the industry players. This eliminates the scope for supplier opportunism

There are many suppliers in the total construction market but fewer suppliers capable of providing prefabricated solutions to the client's requirements and within their collaborative 'partnering' approach

In this case, the contract value for the project was approximately £750 000 of which £350 000 was attributable to the fitted-out prefabricated sub-units

While this single project accounts for a **relatively low share of the annual turnover** of High-Tech Prefabricated Units (HPU) (<1%), when one considers the frequency of the transaction and resulting annual workload (25 similar units) this expenditure accounts for a relatively **high share of HPU's annual turnover**. HPU is relatively **highly dependent** on FFR for this revenue

In addition to the guaranteed revenue, HPU considers FFR's business to be **very attractive**, as it has received significant dedicated investment from the client and attained considerable knowledge and expertise related to delivering the required products

HPU has relatively **high switching costs**

HPU's offerings are relatively **standardised** to the specific requirements of FFR and delivered to strict imposed time deadlines

HPU has a **very strong brand image** and reputation. This reputation has been strengthened by constantly delivering high quality projects on time, within financial budgets to a prestige client (FFR)

Unlike relationships with other clients, HPU has very limited **information asymmetry** advantages over FFR due to the open-book costing approach

---

Table C Performance Outcome for the Client (FFR) – Buyer Win

The client, Fast Food Retailer (FFR), was faced with costs lower on each project by approx. £100 000. This figure was verified by independent cost consultants

FFR's functional expectations fully met. These expectations are constantly evolving as proactive relationships with key suppliers facilitate supply innovation

Robust demand planning enabled delivery of project within the very strict time deadlines. These deadlines have reduced from 12 to 4 weeks

---

Table D Performance Outcome for the Specialist Manufacturer (HPU) – Supplier Partial Win

High-Tech Prefabricated Units (HPU) made a profit of £25 000 on the prefabricated units for this project

This equates to a 7% or normal return for the supplier

HPU enhanced its reputation within the industry for delivering quality products within very strict time deadlines and an ongoing cost reduction programme. This led to other work within other industrial sectors at much higher profit levels

---

reducing total cost of ownership), as well as controlling the returns earned by HPU to 7% on visible costs of ownership after value engineering and target costing.

In addition to maximising its functional expectations as defined in the re-engineered design and specification and achieving substantial cost savings, this proactive approach allowed FFR to obtain a number of other benefits. These included: reduced programme time from 16 to 4 weeks, significantly reduced disruption on site, improved quality of building components, reduced future maintenance, a high level of design flexibility that allows buildings to be expanded, adapted or relocated, and early store opening leading to an increase in sales revenue.

The fact that FFR fully achieved its operational and commercial goals is attributable to its sophisticated proactive (*supply chain management*) approach to construction sourcing. It possessed extensive construction procurement resources internally and received a high level of senior management support. This support provided the necessary upfront financial and technical resources for FFR to undertake the necessary long-term collaborative supply management activities. This investment was largely associated with the activities (e.g. research of the supply market and rigorous and robust source planning) necessary to develop a clear design and specification, implement a robust tendering process, facilitate effective supplier selection and negotiation, and undertake effective contract, risk and project management. Drawing on this considerable knowledge and understanding internally FFR was able to fully achieve all of its operational and commercial goals.

On the other hand, HPU may have received a regular demand for 25 units from FFR and assistance in developing FFR's own technical and product competence, but it was not allowed to make an above normal return from the relationship. In 2004, HPU made a profit of £625 000 from the 25 prefabricated units provided for FFR. This equates to a £25 000 profit for each unit produced, or a 7% return. Given the open-book approach, this level of profit (normal returns) was acceptable to FFR and was verified and benchmarked by the independent cost consultancy. While HPU was satisfied with this return, because of the regularity and certainty of demand from FFR it is normally able to make double-digit returns from providing one-off prefabricated units to less well-informed and demanding clients. This was, therefore, only a partial win commercially for HPU.

12.5 Summary

The major finding from this case is that when a buyer has a high volume and regular demand for similar types of projects it is sub-optimal to manage these as if each project was a one-off game. Assuming, as was the case here, that there is a strategic and commercial value from standardising project design and specification, then this regular demand and high volume relative to the marketplace can significantly augment the power and leverage of the buyer with the supply market. The case demonstrates, however, that this improved leverage can only occur if the buyer develops the internal competence to undertake a proactive sourcing approach.

Assuming that these competencies can be created then a proactive client is in a position to leverage its volumes throughout the supply chain, as demonstrated in this case. When specialist knowledge, such as comparative costs of ownership information, is not available in-house it can be sourced from competent cost consultants, as may specialist design skills. The project management and continuous supplier interfaces must be retained in-house. If this is achieved it is possible to develop the capability of suppliers and to enter into long-term collaborative relationships. This case shows, however, that when doing so, and even when trust may play an important role in relationship management, attention must always be paid to ensuring that the buyer's switching costs are relatively lower than those imposed on the supplier, and that effective competition is retained post-contractually. These protections against opportunism by the supplier are also reinforced if an open-book approach is adopted with guaranteed margins.

For the supplier in this case it is clear that this is, as a result, only a partial win outcome, but one with which it is very satisfied. The supplier can be seen as a willing partner because, while there is a better outcome available to it in theory, in practice the proactive buyer in this case is highly attractive. This is due to the guaranteed regular and high volume demand from the buyer that allows the supplier to differentiate itself in the market and, even though it is only allowed to make a reasonable and not excessive return, the fact that it is able to use the relationship to make higher returns from other, less powerful and competent, clients.

This means that proactive sourcing can be sustained, as this case clearly demonstrates, even in the absence of a win–win outcome. This is a win–partial win (or nonzero-sum) outcome that favours the buyer, but in which the supplier is more than happy to participate on a long-term basis. The buyer in this case is extremely competent at proactive sourcing (or partnering/alliancing) because it controls the relationship and avoids post-contractual dependency and supplier opportunism, while still fully achieving its own operational and commercial goals.

Table 12.2 contains a summary of the relationship management approach and performance outcome.

Table 12.2 A summary of the relationship management approach and performance outcome

Nature of Relationship Management Approach	FFR, with a large ongoing portfolio of projects, was in a position to use its extensive knowledge and understanding of its construction expenditure to develop a proactive sourcing approach with the objective of effectively leveraging upstream construction suppliers
	This strategy focused on the development of a proactive *supply chain management* relationship management approach with key first- and second-tier construction suppliers
Nature of Buyer 'Win'	A continuous cost reduction programme that has delivered significant cost savings (c. £100 000 according to detailed in-house cost information benchmarked by external cost consultant)
	Functional expectations exceeded (largely attributable to standardised design and specification)
	Construction time for a typical project has reduced from 12 weeks to 4 weeks over the duration of the ongoing relationship
	Robust demand planning facilitates guaranteed delivery of product on time
Nature of Supplier 'Partial Win'	£25 000 profit on project (negotiated through an open-book costing approach and agreed on an annual basis)
	This equates to a 7% return on annual turnover with the buyer
	Enhanced reputation for delivering quality projects that meet prestige buyer's expectations. This led to acquisition of more profitable work in other industrial sectors
	Buyer willing to invest in supplier's IT and manufacturing infrastructure. This also positively impacted on reputation for innovative design and production leading to further work in other sectors
Conclusions	Effective partnering/alliancing is often misunderstood by consultants and academics in construction
	This case demonstrates that effective partnering actually means different things for buyers and suppliers. In this case it is the buyer who has achieved its ideal outcome of a win–partial win because a win–win outcome is not feasible
	The case shows that nonzero-sum outcomes are perfectly sustainable between buyers and suppliers over the long-term
	The case also shows that the buyer must always guard against post-contractual supplier opportunism and dependency if it wants to protect its long-term power and leverage in collaborative relationships
	This case also shows that suppliers can be expected to accept a partial win if they have no better alternative options available and also if it assists them with effective leverage over other less powerful and competent buyers

The multi-storey car park case: proactive supply chain management with a buyer win and supplier lose outcome

13.1 Introduction

This case describes the sourcing of a multi-storey car park by a private sector car park operator, Free Space Unlimited (FSU), from a construction firm, Aldersbery Specialist Construction (ASC). In an attempt to reduce delivery time and improve the quality of the solution, FSU had specified the use of pre-cast structural concrete products for the main structure's external walls and floors. The contractor (ASC) had to source, therefore, a pre-cast structural concrete component that was a significant proportion of the total project cost from a second-tier supplier, Specialist Pre-Cast Products (SPP). The case shows that ASC, because of its continuous portfolio of projects from a number of different car park operators, was able to develop a proactive relationship management approach with key upstream suppliers.

The contractor ASC's proactive and highly collaborative approach was based on the standardisation of design and specification and the prefabrication of critical components. Working closely with FSU and SPP, ASC was able to specify a detailed design for the solution that specified the use of standardised pre-cast concrete elements. The successful implementation of this approach was key to ASC fully achieving its own commercial and operational objectives – maximum feasible reduction in total costs of ownership, maximum feasible increase in functionality and maximum reduction in time to market for the construction of the car park.

Although this approach provided SPP with a guaranteed revenue stream and a potential partial win outcome, a series of problems during the project, related to the supply of sub-standard and incorrectly-sized elements, meant it failed to achieve any positive performance outcome in this particular relationship. This win–lose outcome demonstrates that buyer–supplier relationships based on proactive collaboration do not always allow both parties to gain from the relationship.

13.2 Background to the case: the construction of a multi-storey car park

The supply chain for the pre-cast structural concrete products required for the car park, as shown in Figure 13.1, requires the management of a number of supply chains.

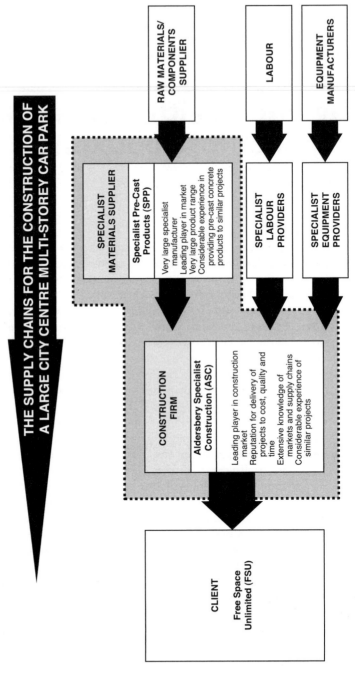

THE SUPPLY CHAINS FOR THE CONSTRUCTION OF A LARGE CITY CENTRE MULTI-STOREY CAR PARK

RAW MATERIALS/ COMPONENTS SUPPLIER

LABOUR

EQUIPMENT MANUFACTURERS

SPECIALIST MATERIALS SUPPLIER

Specialist Pre-Cast Products (SPP)

Very large specialist manufacturer
Leading player in market
Very large product range
Considerable experience in providing pre-cast concrete products to similar projects

SPECIALIST LABOUR PROVIDERS

SPECIALIST EQUIPMENT PROVIDERS

CONSTRUCTION FIRM

Aldersbery Specialist Construction (ASC)

Leading player in construction market
Reputation for delivery of projects to cost, quality and time
Extensive knowledge of markets and supply chains
Considerable experience of similar projects

CLIENT

Free Space Unlimited (FSU)

Figure 13.1 Construction supply chains for the construction of a multi-storey car park

A large private sector car park operator, FSU, had considerable experience of sourcing from construction supply markets. In conjunction with external construction professionals, FSU either developed a concept design and specification for its construction requirements, or a detailed version if it was very clear on its requirements and was not faced with any potential project uncertainty. For this particular project, FSU developed an outline design and specification. Instead of using this as the basis on which ASC (a design and build contractor) was to be selected in an adversarial arm's-length manner, FSU had developed a proactive approach to construction procurement.

As part of its proactive sourcing framework FSU had identified three competent construction firms, including ASC, capable of providing its construction requirements (approximately 12 new facilities per year). The car park operator (FSU) awarded its annual spend equitably between the three preferred suppliers and then leveraged them to maximise value for money (i.e. provide the highest level of functionality at the lowest total costs of ownership feasible). On this project, the design and construction of a high specification 900-space multi-storey car park in a city centre, FSU selected ASC to work with it in a collaborative manner to develop a detailed design and to deliver the entire construction package. The contractor (ASC) was responsible, therefore, for turning FSU's commercial and operational requirements into reality. A key decision in the development of the project's design and specification and determining the project's commercial viability related to the choice between a structural steelwork frame and one comprising pre-cast structural concrete elements.

Located on a city centre brownfield site, the final design for the four-storey car park solution involved extensive earthworks and ground stabilisation, in-situ concrete foundations and bases, a structural steel frame, pre-cast structural concrete slab sections, external brick cladding, pre-cast concrete ramps and stair towers, screening, waterproofing, fireproofing, M&E services (lifts and lighting) and finishes (barriers and painting). The total contract value for the project was estimated initially at £5.5 million, with the D&B contractor having 40 weeks to complete.

This case focuses on the relationship between the construction firm (ASC) and specialist supplier of pre-cast products (SPP). The construction firm (ASC) developed a design for a pre-stressed pre-cast concrete slab and reinforced topping supported by steel beams. The design incorporated two different pre-cast slab thicknesses (100 mm and 125 mm) that were required to span between beams 7.5 metres apart. To maximise the potential loading of the structural system, as shown in Figure 13.2, the composite construction included shear connectors welded to the top flange of the steel beam and transverse reinforcement. This also ensured that the individual pre-cast sections behaved like a monolithic slab. Within the pre-cast slab, high tensile steel wire was used for the pre-stressing tendons in various configurations to suit the particular spans and design loadings.

The quality and functionality of the solution can be measured in terms of its durability. The concrete elements within a car park are particularly susceptible to deterioration if they are not properly specified. It is recognised that pre-cast units are generally more durable than in-situ concrete due to factory controlled production conditions. The construction of a solid composite slab utilises the advantages of a pre-stressed pre-cast element acting compositely with an in-situ structural topping, thus combining the benefits of pre-cast and in-situ construction. These benefits include reduced construction depths, speed of erection, elimination of

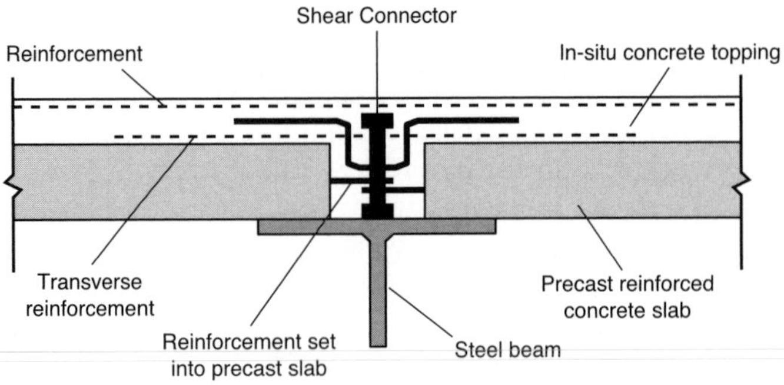

Figure 13.2 A cross-section of the composite floor structure

shuttering, minimal propping, very high levels of fire resistance, corrosion resistance, salt and freeze–thaw resistance, and the flexibility of architectural and engineering design.

The design of the car park incorporated a 'split level layout' for the ramp arrangement to combine a dynamic vehicular flow rate and excellent structural efficiency. This is probably the most popular layout as entry and exit traffic are separated and the flow pattern is simple and uncomplicated. When built around a structural steel frame, with column free spans, this layout provides the best combination of economy and operating efficiency. Furthermore, the design of the structure and foundations allowed for an additional two storeys of car parking in the future.

The appearance of the car park was also very important for FSU who had received criticism in the past for its 'concrete monstrosities'. The design for the external façade incorporated specially developed bricks on prefabricated cladding panels that not only reduced costs and fixing times but also produced a result that blended in well with existing buildings and the city's overall regeneration plan. Although pre-cast cladding panels were offered by SPP in this case, ASC decided to source from an alternative supplier whose products matched adjoining properties.

The buyer – Aldersbery Specialist Construction (ASC)

In developing the structural design for the solution ASC (and FSU) was faced with a key decision surrounding whether to use a structural frame consisting of pre-cast concrete elements or structural steelwork. The decision was not a straightforward one as it involved more than an assessment and comparison of the advantages and disadvantages of both options. The buyer (ASC) also recognised that the decision had a significant commercial impact on other elements of the solution. For example, the loading on foundations is greatly influenced by the material chosen for the frame. Steel is the lightest practical construction material and will often allow the use of simple foundations, whereas heavier materials (such as concrete) may require extensive and costly sub-structures that are not commercially viable. For this reason, steel is often the only feasible construction material for multi-storey car park structures. In this case, concrete was also a feasible option.

Pre-cast concrete frames can involve an entire structure being fabricated off-site, but it can also involve structural components that are supplied for incorporation into a structure on-site. The major benefits of pre-cast concrete frames include: faster programme times that are not affected by weather or labour shortages; a consistently very high standard of workmanship; improved buildability; and, a high quality finish that can be left exposed. By way of contrast the benefits of structural steel frames include: an ability to provide longer spans without a need for supporting columns; a lightweight solution; the solution can be designed around the car parking and not the car parking designed around the solution as with concrete frames; a high level of fire resistance; and low-cost maintenance. Furthermore, the cost of a steel frame in real terms has decreased through greater efficiency in both the steel manufacturing and fabrication industries and this has led to an earlier return on investment.

The structural design of a car park also determines its quality as a user-friendly structure. As this is directly linked to the revenue-generating potential of the car park operator, the structural form should provide its users with: rapid entry and exit without the risk of damage to vehicle or person; few obstructions to movement (e.g. columns in the drive path and badly parked cars caused by inefficient design or layout); a light and airy facility; and a safe and secure environment. A steel structure with pre-cast concrete slab is ideally placed to provide this type of environment because of its lightweight nature, long-span capabilities and minimal internal structure.

One major disadvantage of the use of a steel frame is the depth of the resulting floor. As the composite concrete slabs are quite thick (275 to 300 mm), and they sit on top of fairly large steel beams, the floor ends up deep, a distinct disadvantage on multi-storey car parks where ramps are needed. Construction depth can be saved using shelf or ledge angles but these are costly and time consuming. Despite this disadvantage FSU selected a solution based on a composite concrete floor slab, with a pre-stressed pre-cast element acting compositely with an in-situ structural topping, on top of steel beams.

From the development of the concept design it was evident that this project was to be the largest project within FSU's £45 million annual collaborative construction framework. The car park operator (FSU), therefore, awarded the design and build contract for the project (valued at £5.5 million) to ASC because of its extensive experience of providing similar large high quality and cost-effective solutions on time. This reputation was gained from providing solutions to all of the major private sector car park operators in the country. With collaborative relationships in place with all of these major downstream players (accounting for approximately £80 million or 66% of revenue), ASC recognised the potential to improve the efficiency of the project process through standardisation of design and specification for key inputs and the use of prefabricated components. The promise of a regular workload from its major clients provided ASC with a major power resource with its own suppliers and facilitated the development and implementation of a proactive supply chain management approach.

The construction firm (ASC) had, historically, recognised the inefficiencies from sourcing from the supply market on a project-by-project basis and had developed collaborative relationships with preferred suppliers to maximise value for money. This was ensured through the development of a robust methodology aimed at rationalising the supply base and identifying a number of preferred suppliers for the manufacture and/or supply of key construction products and services. The construction firm (ASC) also adopted an open-book costing approach with target costs and guaranteed profit margins for its key suppliers.

Using these techniques, ASC estimated that the total cost of the pre-cast structural concrete element would be £1.1 million. This figure, based on cost models from similar projects, was confirmed when ASC received prices back from its preferred pre-cast concrete suppliers ranging from £1.1 to £1.125 million. As all of these suppliers had a strong track record for delivering products on time and to a very high quality, ASC selected SPP who submitted the lowest price of exactly £1.1 million. The construction firm (ASC) did not expect any difficulties to arise from this decision. Unfortunately, as will be shown later, it was mistaken.

The supplier – Specialist Pre-Cast Products (SPP)

The supplier (SPP) is a leading manufacturer of high quality pre-cast concrete products. It offers a comprehensive service involving design, manufacture, delivery and installation. It manufactures a wide range of high quality pre-stressed and pre-cast concrete units under strictly controlled and highly efficient factory conditions. To ensure very high quality units the components are manufactured on steel beds to a standard width using a slip-forming process, and an air-entraining agent and water-reducing admixture are used to achieve the correct workability. The components are sawn to the required length on the manufacturing bed and if holes are required they can be formed during manufacture, the size and position depending upon the design criteria. All of SPP's pre-cast concrete units are designed to the requirements of BS 8110. High tensile steel wire or strand is used for the pre-stressing tendons, in various configurations to suit particular spans and design loadings. The supplier (SPP) also has a transport fleet providing fast, safe and efficient delivery of products to site.

In order to achieve competitive advantage, SPP recognised that it must constantly innovate by researching ways to improve and refine production processes and its products and services. The company has attempted to remain a market-leader within the pre-cast flooring market by reducing manufacturing lead-times, reducing costs, offering a fully comprehensive service and improving quality. The company also provides a number of value-adding services. For example, SPP provides layout drawings for the floor units prior to manufacture. These drawings show the structure supporting the pre-cast units, the position of service entries, typical sections and the loads for which the floor is designed.

The installation of the pre-cast concrete floor components is relatively straight-forward. The units are hoisted into position on the supporting structure by crane and a structural concrete topping can be laid together with the joint infill to form a composite concrete floor to increase the strength of the flooring system and form a monolithic floor. The completed floor provides an immediate working platform for the following trades. With over 80% of its contracts on a supply and fix basis SPP directly employs teams of fully trained experienced site fixing personnel (erectors, welders, general operatives, site managers and site engineers) to provide customers with a reliable and cost-effective solution. By having a policy of employing and developing its own direct labour force, the company has also been able to identify intricate installation problems at the earliest opportunity and ensure continuity of approach from contract to contract.

13.3 The buyer–supplier relationship management approach

In analysing the market and supply chain circumstances, and the power and leverage resources available to both parties in this exchange relationship, it is evident that the goals of ASC were fully achieved in this case. In contrast, despite possessing the power resources to leverage a partial win from the relationship, SPP's poor performance ensured that it achieved a lose outcome. This demonstrates that even under proactive sourcing arrangements supplier incompetence can lead to zero-sum rather than nonzero-sum outcomes.

The construction firm (ASC) – specialist material supplier (SPP) dyad

In this case the nature of ASC's relationship with SPP enabled it to avoid opportunistic supplier behaviour and deliver a low cost, high quality and innovative solution with significant reductions in project time to its customer (FSU). A key factor within this relationship is ASC's possession of extensive information and understanding of its own project portfolio, key construction supply markets and the appropriateness of available technologies. This understanding has enabled it to develop a robust proactive supply chain and relationship management approach.

The construction firm (ASC)'s ability to leverage SPP is dependent on its possession of key power resources within the relationship. In this case the contract value for the project was approximately £5.5 million of which £1.1 million was attributable to the pre-cast structural concrete products. While this single contract accounted for a low share of SPP's total annual turnover (less than 1%) and might, at first, be considered to be of low importance, when one considers the frequency of the transaction and the potential annual workload (15–20 similar car parks), this expenditure accounts for a much higher proportion of SPP's turnover (7.5%) making it much more attractive. In terms of revenue ASC becomes SPP's single most important customer. Despite ASC's ongoing relationship with FSU, however, SPP is not totally dependent on FSU for revenue because it has a large number of other customers in a wide range of industries.

The construction firm (ASC)'s position of relative dominance arising from a high volume and frequent demand was further strengthened by its ability to standardise the design and specification for pre-cast structural concrete products across its portfolio of projects, which enabled it to significantly reduce the level of complexity for SPP. As a result, SPP considered ASC's business to be highly attractive because it was relatively simple to service. This favourable power position was also strengthened by the scarcity of equivalent contracts for SPP. The fact that ASC was their major customer (by revenue) for pre-cast concrete components, and assuming that all performance measures were achieved, this revenue was guaranteed to make it difficult for SPP to exit from the relationship. This difficulty was increased by the high switching costs that were created by ASC's investment in a highly specialised and dedicated manufacturing process at SPP's manufacturing plant.

The construction firm (ASC)'s possession of these power resources enabled it to incentivise its key upstream suppliers to undertake the necessary dedicated investments and relationship-specific adaptations required for a long-term collaborative relationship management approach (*supply chain management*). This proactive and collaborative approach was at the 'supply chain level' because the possession of a guaranteed regular demand from ASC enabled SPP to cascade it upstream with its preferred supplier of the pre-stressed steel reinforcement that was required for the pre-cast concrete components.

On the supply-side of the relationship, the critical power resources for SPP in this transaction were related to scarcity and utility. The utility of SPP's components for

ASC was high because only a limited number of preferred suppliers were deemed by ASC to have the competence to deliver the quality required. The supplier (SPP) also benefited from the fact that its capability to deliver the quantity required by ASC annually was not matched by many other potential suppliers. This meant that, in practice, contestation was relatively low in this particular market. This was because there were only a limited number of competent suppliers capable of supplying the number of components in the required collaborative manner (using open-book costing) to the very strict deadlines and high quality levels demanded by ASC.

In such circumstances, a power position of *buyer–supplier interdependence* normally occurs and firms (suppliers) are usually able to price above the prevailing market rate and earn above normal returns. This implies that ASC's proactive approach might have been expected to result in a partial win outcome for both parties in this relationship. As we shall see, however, due to incompetence on the part of SPP this partial win–partial win outcome was replaced by a win–lose outcome.

13.4 Performance outcome from the buyer–supplier relationship

The two firms ASC and SPP had different operational and commercial objectives. The buyer (ASC) was attempting operationally to maximise the functionality of the pre-cast concrete elements and commercially to minimise the total cost of owner-ship. The supplier (SPP) was attempting to increase operationally the revenue it received, while also maximising the returns it earned commercially.

The buyer (ASC) was in a position to fully achieve its goals because it had a regular and high volume demand that was very attractive to SPP due to the lack of alternative contracts of an equivalent size. The supplier (SPP) was also effectively locked into a long-term relationship because of the relatively high switching costs created by the dedicated investments required to service ASC. These circumstances meant that SPP was deterred from acting opportunistically pre-contractually because of the promise of a regular demand, and post-contractually because of relatively high switching costs.

The power resources in the relationship did not, however, completely favour ASC. The supplier (SPP) had a very solid reputation for successfully delivering high quality cost-effective solutions within programme due to its heavy investment in innovative manufacturing processes. The number of alternative suppliers was also restricted because there were only a small number of manufacturers capable of supplying the number of pre-cast components demanded by ASC. Unfortunately for SPP, although there was interdependence in the dyadic relationship, a number of problems and unexpected events led to a situation in which ASC gained from the relationship and achieved its ideal performance outcome while SPP received a lose outcome.

Figure 13.3 shows a summary of the dyad between ASC and SPP and the performance outcome from the relationship.

In this case, FSU wanted an innovative solution but it also understood the true costs of construction. The buyer (ASC) had, therefore, the difficult task of trying to lower the cost and increase the functionality of the solution (to deliver value for money to FSU) while also attempting to maximise revenues and returns. The buyer (ASC) realised that since it was working with an informed client it could not be opportunistic in this downstream relationship and that it would have to increase its own revenues and returns by being more sophisticated in its upstream relationships with suppliers. One way to achieve this was to drive cost out of the supply chain but not to pass all of the benefits to the client.

The ability of ASC to deliver a high quality and cost-effective solution on time to FSU was highly dependent on the design and timely manufacture, supply, installation and finishing of the pre-cast structural concrete elements. To achieve this, and also to reduce costs to maximise its own returns ASC, therefore, developed a proactive sourcing strategy that eliminated the potential for SPP to be opportunistic and also facilitated the reduction of costs. The buyer (ASC) achieved this by proactively

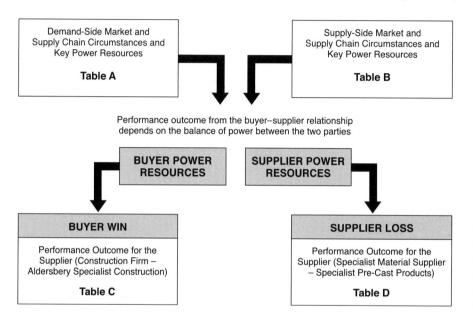

Figure 13.3 A summary of the dyad between the construction firm (ASC) and specialist supplier (SPP) and the performance outcome from the relationship

Table A Demand-Side Market and Supply Chain Circumstances and Key Power Resources

There are many construction firms acting as buyers from the multitude of concrete supply markets but fewer buyers for pre-cast structural concrete products in the car park construction market

Aldersbery Specialist Construction (ASC) has a low share of total construction market but a **higher share of the pre-cast concrete products market** for integration into car park projects with an annual expenditure of £120 million. Therefore, the supplier (SPP) has a **relatively low/medium dependency** on ASC for revenue

ASC has a **regular need** to source from the pre-cast concrete products market but there is **no absolute certainty/regularity** about requirements and volumes for specific products

The requirements of ASC are **relatively straightforward** (in terms of the products themselves) and are easily integrated into the project

ASC has **low/medium switching costs** because there are approximately only ten suppliers with the reputation and capability of providing very high quality and reliable pre-cast concrete products

ASC has a **relatively clear value proposition** – a high quality car park delivered on time and at an acceptable and predictable cost

The client and ASC are both aware of the potential scope for **standardisation** and **prefabrication** of specific component elements and have worked together to develop a specialised manufactured process. This was the case for key structural concrete elements that were commonly used in multi-storey car parks

ASC has **relatively low search costs**, as it has extensive knowledge and understanding about pre-cast structural concrete products and the strategies of the industry players

Almost every construction project requires concrete for the sub-structure (foundations) or structure (walls or floors). This may be in the form of standardised pre-cast elements

There are a small number of large suppliers in the pre-cast structural concrete products market but fewer suppliers operating in the region capable of delivering products to the required quality levels to tight timescales

The total contract value of the project was approximately £5.5 million of which £1.1 million was attributable to the pre-cast structural concrete elements

While this single contract accounts for a **relatively low share of the annual turnover** of Specialist Pre-Cast Products (SPP) (<1%), when one considers ASC's frequency of transaction and potential resulting annual workload (15–20 similar car parks per year) this expenditure accounts for a **medium share of SPP's annual turnover** (7.5%)

SPP has a **low/medium dependency** on ASC for this revenue, as there is a relatively high degree of certainty surrounding alternative contracts for similar products

SPP considers ASC's business to be **relatively attractive** as there are low costs associated with servicing the contract. SPP has also worked with ASC to create a highly specialised manufacturing process for its structural concrete components

SPP has relatively **high switching costs**

SPP's offerings are **relatively standardised** with **limited customisation** to the specific requirements of the client (and ASC)

SPP has a **very strong brand image** and **reputation** for delivering innovative products of a very high quality

SPP has **very limited information asymmetry** advantages over ASC

Table C Performance Outcome for the Construction Firm (ASC) – Buyer Win

In this relationship the construction firm, Aldersbery Specialist Construction (ASC), was faced with costs lower than original budget by £50 000. The original estimate for the precast concrete element was £1.1 million and final cost was £1.05 million

Functional expectations of client were met after remedial action by ASC to replace a number of defective elements

ASC fully covered the expense of this rework through claims against the material supplier (SPP)

Despite a very difficult site and the problems experienced, ASC delivered this project with minimal local disruption and in a programme period four weeks shorter than the client's schedule

The project enhanced the reputation of ASC in the industry

Table D Performance Outcome for the Specialist Material Supplier (SPP) – Supplier Loss

Specialist Pre-Cast Products (SPP) made a loss of £50 000 on this project. This was largely due to:
  The requirement to supply additional elements to replace incorrectly-sized ones
  Claims made against it by ASC due to the extra work required to overcome problems created by the supply of incorrect elements, poor workmanship and sub-standard materials

SPP damaged its reputation within the industry for delivering quality projects within time and cost constraints

Major industry players recognised that it was SPP's fault so it was expected to impact on future revenues

---

monitoring and benchmarking supplier performance. This work confirmed that the costs of the concrete elements could be reduced by £50 000 from the initial estimate of £1.1 million to £1.05 million. This cost reduction was achieved without compromising quality and functionality, or adversely impacting project duration. The cost saving was also obtained despite having to overcome a problem related to the supply of sub-standard components to part of the project.

The buyer (ASC)'s sourcing approach also meant that it was able to fully achieve its operational objectives in relation to maximising the functionality of the pre-cast concrete element within the multi-storey car park solution. Despite very difficult ground conditions on the site, this was facilitated by its considerable experience in the design and build of similar car parking facilities for other major car park operators and the development of a standardised design and specification for key prefabricated and pre-cast elements within these solutions.

The buyer (ASC) also obtained a number of other benefits. These included: reduced programme time from 40 weeks to 36; significantly reduced disruption on site; significantly reduced disruption to the city centre road network; and improved quality of building components. The final solution also provided FSU with a number of benefits including: reduced future maintenance; a high level of design flexibility that allowed the car park to be adapted, expanded or reduced in size in the future; and early opening leading to an increase in parking revenues. The buyer (ASC) also enhanced its reputation for the delivery of high quality and innovative solutions. The fact that ASC fully achieved its operational and commercial goals was attributable to its robust proactive approach to supply management. It received a high level of internal top management support that provided the required financial and technical resources to undertake the necessary collaborative sourcing activities (i.e. rigorous source planning, development of a clear standardised design and specification, robust supplier selection, and effective contract, risk and project management).

The supplier (SPP) made an overall loss of £50 000 by manufacturing, supplying and fitting the pre-cast concrete elements for this particular project. This loss, accounting for approximately 5% of the total contract value, was attributed to the supply of additional elements to replace incorrectly-sized concrete sections on part of the first floor of the car park (due to an error in its layout drawings showing an incorrect supporting structure), and the cost incurred by ASC to overcome the installation of sections of the wrong thickness on the second floor, poor grouting of other sections, and problems with the laying of the structural concrete topping to form a composite concrete floor.

On the second floor of the car park, SPP installed a number of pre-cast elements of the incorrect thickness. If ignored, this mistake could have led to a total collapse of the structure. To ensure that the structure could withstand the necessary loads placed upon by it by constant traffic flow SPP was faced with the difficult decision either to remove and replace the sections as they had done with a number of sections on the first floor and make changes to a number of the supporting structural steel beams to ensure they could support the extra loading, or to increase the thickness of the section by laying a thicker structural concrete topping around steel reinforcement. The supplier (SPP) eventually selected the latter option and agreed to pay ASC a sum of £25 000 to undertake the corrective works. The extra grouting and replacement of the structural concrete topping in other parts of the car park required a further payment of £25 000 to ASC. These costs (£50 000), along with the cost of replacing incorrectly-sized sections to part of the first floor (£50 000) effectively turned an anticipated profit of £50 000 into a loss for the same amount.

As a result of the problems, SPP damaged its reputation for delivering very high quality and cost-effective pre-cast structural concrete elements on time and to the client's (and SPP's) exact functional requirements. With reputation being a major consideration for many practitioners responsible for sourcing construction products and services, SPP anticipated that this would have an adverse effect on future revenue and returns. This was clearly a lose outcome from SPP's perspective.

13.5 Summary

The major finding from this case is that proactive sourcing approaches do not necessarily guarantee that both parties in the exchange relationship will always achieve a favourable outcome. In this case the client, FSU, and the main contractor, ASC, were both able to achieve a favourable outcome, in the sense that FSU achieved a partial win from ASC. This was because ASC did not pass on to FSU all of the value improvement it achieved from working with SPP but kept it for itself. This implies that ASC achieved a full win from its relationship with FSU.

In the context of the relationship between ASC and SPP, what might have been expected to result in a partial win–partial win outcome eventually resulted in a win–lose outcome favouring ASC. This was because ASC was able to use its value engineering skills to reduce the costs of the pre-cast elements by £50 000 and retain this for itself, while also having a successfully completed project, in which SPP had to pay for all of its own failures. This resulted, for SPP, in a lose

Table 13.1 *A summary of the relationship management approach and performance outcome*

Nature of Relationship Management Approach	ASC, with an ongoing portfolio of similar car park projects, was in a position to use its extensive knowledge and understanding of its external construction-related spend to develop robust and sophisticated procurement strategies with the objective of effectively leveraging upstream construction suppliers
	These strategies largely focused on the development of a proactive *supply chain management* relationship management approach with suppliers of key construction components
Nature of Buyer 'Win'	Costs were lower than original budget by £50 000. The original estimate for the pre-cast concrete element was £1.1 million and final cost was £1.05 million
	Despite a very difficult site and the problems experienced, ASC delivered this project four weeks earlier than programme and minimised the disruption on site and in the local area
	ASC enhanced its reputation and was also able to retain as additional profit the cost reductions it had engineered for itself
Nature of Supplier 'Loss'	SPP made a loss of £50 000 on this project. This was largely due to:
	The requirement to supply additional elements
	Claims made against it by the construction firm in relation to extra work required to overcome problems created by the supply of incorrect elements, sub-standard materials and poor workmanship
	SPP damaged its reputation within the industry for delivering quality projects within time and cost constraints
	Major industry players recognised that it was SPP's fault so it was expected to impact on future revenues
Conclusions	Proactive sourcing does not absolve the parties in the exchange relationship from the commercial consequences of their actions
	Both parties to a proactive sourcing relationship have to accept that commercial leverage and tension between them remains throughout the relationship
	The relative power of both players and their relative dependency on one another may, however, force one or both parties to accept some of the risk of failure if the consequence of not shouldering some of the risk leads to the collapse of the business model of the other
	In this case, as this problem did not arise, a lose outcome was forced upon the supplier by the buyer because the supplier was not likely to go out of business due to its failure on this specific project

outcome because it made a loss of £50 000 overall from the project and damaged its reputation in the market.

What follows from this is that just because two parties enter into a commitment to a long-term relationship this does not imply that the issue of risk disappears from the equation. While one way of dealing with the technical and operational problems that arose on this project might have been to share the costs of failure between the two parties, it does not follow that either party is obliged to adopt this approach when undertaking a long-term proactive relationship. Obviously, the buyer in this case would have to consider the consequences of the supplier's failure if this might lead to the collapse of the supplier's business, but in this case this problem did not arise. In this case the supplier was still able to operate and the buyer commercially took the view that, since the supplier had made the errors in construction, the supplier should be liable for the financial consequences. This is a salutary lesson for those who enter unthinkingly into proactive relationships based on partnering principles. The lesson is that financial and commercial considerations do not disappear for either party when long-term collaborative relationships are created.

Table 13.1 shows a summary of the relationship management approach and performance outcome.

The aerospace manufacturing facility case: proactive supplier development with a buyer partial win and supplier win outcome

14.1 Introduction

This case focuses on the procurement of a manufacturing facility by an aerospace company, Aerospace Manufacturing (AM), and its relationship with the main contractor, Platinum Construction Solutions (PCS). Despite having a regular need to source from the construction market for the creation of new facilities and refurbishment of existing facilities, AM did not have the necessary internal resource to be up-to-date with current leading-edge practice in construction. It knew, however, that the industry was highly competitive with few barriers to entry and that this provided huge potential power for a buyer with a high frequency and volume of demand.

This case demonstrates that a client with a continuous portfolio of capital expenditure projects is in a potentially powerful position to use its ability to consolidate its spend and develop a proactive approach to sourcing. A key element of such a strategy is the development of a long-term collaborative relationship management approach with a small number of first-tier construction suppliers. To avoid supply dependency and opportunism, AM's approach placed a considerable emphasis on the need for disciplined cost management and was, therefore, based on an open-book target costing approach overseen by an independent cost consultancy.

Prior to the implementation of this proactive *supplier development* approach, AM was not achieving its commercial and operational objectives and was receiving poor value for money. After adopting this approach, AM normally fully achieved its desired value proposition – a very high quality product delivered on time and at lowest feasible costs of ownership. In this case, however, AM only partially attained its objectives. This was because the independent cost consultancy discovered that further cost savings were possible if the proactive approach had been extended upstream to include suppliers of key components such as structural steelwork, pre-cast concrete flooring and M&E products and services.

Despite the balance of power favouring the client (AM), the construction firm (PCS) was in a position to fully attain its commercial and operational objectives, without having to face the uncertainties typically associated with a short-term adversarial arm's-length relationship management approach. The collaborative relationship management approach provided the mechanism by which it maximised revenues, while AM's target cost approach allowed it to earn high returns. This proactive relationship approach resulted, therefore, in a partial win–win outcome.

14.2 Background to the case: the construction of an aerospace manufacturing facility

Given the regular nature of its construction expenditure, the high value of the individual projects, the significant risks involved, and the strategic importance of the construction activity to its business, the client – Aerospace Manufacturing (AM) – recognised the need to develop a proactive approach to construction sourcing so that it could avoid adversarial and opportunistic supplier behaviour. With expert advice from professional services, AM implemented this proactive and collaborative sourcing approach. This facilitated the appointment of Platinum Construction Solutions (PCS), which was responsible for the management and integration of AM's requirements. The construction of a manufacturing facility for an aerospace company of this type requires the integration of a number of construction supply chains, as illustrated in Figure 14.1.

The analysis focuses on the relationship between AM and PCS. The project was part of an on-going relationship between AM and PCS for a number of related projects. This specific project involved the construction of a highly-specialised modern manufacturing facility on a brownfield site that had been semi-derelict for five years. The $30\,000\,\text{m}^2$ manufacturing plant, incorporating a large open manufacturing area with 20-metre-clear internal height for four overhead cranes, was designed according to the latest manufacturing thinking. The client (AM) wanted the leading-edge facility to provide the best possible production flow, from the arrival of raw material to the despatch of finished products, to ensure that it remained competitive in the global aerospace market. In addition to the main manufacturing area, the facility included a loading and storage area, a reception area, offices and meeting rooms on two floors, amenities and a control room for the complex M&E solution.

At the outset AM, in conjunction with a preferred design consultancy, developed a detailed design and specification against which PCS could deliver its solution. This contained a requirement to use a carbon-steel-fibre reinforced concrete slab, a structural steelwork building frame, a steelwork frame for the four internal cranes, roof lights, ventilation units, and a wall design using lightweight aerated blocks and external wall cladding. The client (AM) provided a detailed specification for the type of elements to use but it did not specify from which particular manufacturers and suppliers PCS had to source. This decision was left to the discretion of the contractor, who had to rely on its own knowledge and experience when attempting to deliver AM's requirements, at the same time as achieving its own commercial and operational objectives. It will be shown later that AM's failure to be more proactive in relation to the sourcing of components from upstream suppliers had a deleterious impact on the performance outcome for it in the relationship.

The buyer – Aerospace Manufacturing (AM)

The UK's aerospace industry is currently the second largest in the world with turnover in 2002 standing at £16.14 billion. While the aerospace industry in the

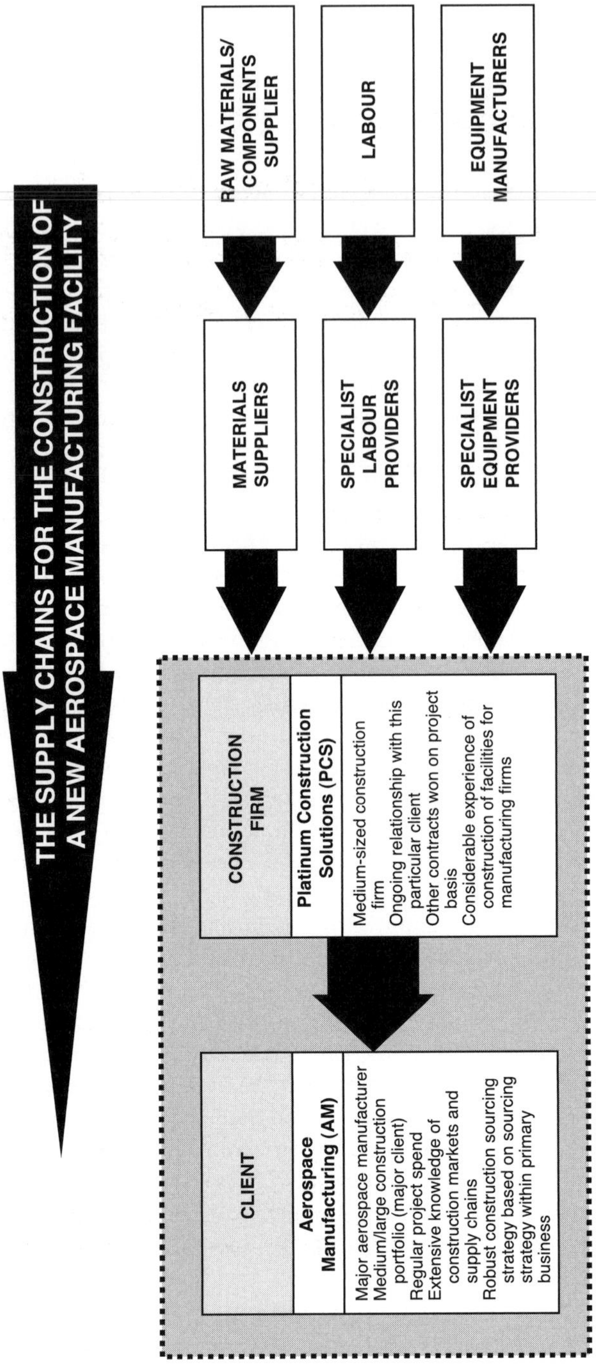

THE SUPPLY CHAINS FOR THE CONSTRUCTION OF A NEW AEROSPACE MANUFACTURING FACILITY

| RAW MATERIALS/ COMPONENTS SUPPLIER |
| LABOUR |
| EQUIPMENT MANUFACTURERS |

| MATERIALS SUPPLIERS |
| SPECIALIST LABOUR PROVIDERS |
| SPECIALIST EQUIPMENT PROVIDERS |

CONSTRUCTION FIRM

Platinum Construction Solutions (PCS)

- Medium-sized construction firm
- Ongoing relationship with this particular client
- Other contracts won on project basis
- Considerable experience of construction of facilities for manufacturing firms

CLIENT

Aerospace Manufacturing (AM)

- Major aerospace manufacturer
- Medium/large construction portfolio (major client)
- Regular project spend
- Extensive knowledge of construction markets and supply chains
- Robust construction sourcing strategy based on sourcing strategy within primary business

Figure 14.1 Construction supply chains for the construction of an aerospace manufacturing facility

UK has benefited from a long-term improvement in productivity, at the time of the project it was experiencing its worst downturn since the Second World War. As a result, the major players, including AM, were actively seeking ways to remain competitive by increasing operational efficiency and reducing costs whenever possible. In addition to the trend towards global consolidation of the industry with significant mergers and acquisition activity, firms are considering a wide range of strategies including the outsourcing of non-core activities to achieve these business objectives.

For AM the construction and refurbishment of its manufacturing facilities is a major activity that supports the sustainability of its primary business. Before the development and implementation of its current approach to construction relationship management the client was faced with significant difficulties. Construction projects were frequently delivered over-budget and late with major issues surrounding the quality of the final solution. Ineffective contract and project management meant that suppliers could be opportunistic and pursue claims and variations in an adversarial manner. As a result, lengthy and costly legal battles were commonplace.

In response to these problems, and the poor levels of value for money (in terms of high cost, poor quality and late delivery) that it was receiving when it procured its fragmented and relatively ill-defined construction requirements, the client acknowledged that it needed to reconfigure its whole approach to construction supply management to improve its efficiency and effectiveness. After an appraisal of its project management, design, engineering and procurement capabilities the client recognised that it needed to fundamentally re-engineer the project process.

To develop a more appropriate construction sourcing approach, AM realised that it had to base any relationship management decision on the analysis of key demand and supply information. The client (AM) recognised the need, therefore, to better understand the nature of its current and future construction requirements and the structure of the construction markets and supply chains through which they are delivered. With this understanding AM was able to think about which of the available supply management tools and techniques would best support its sourcing strategy and ability to maximise value for money.

The client (AM) acknowledged that it did not need an internal capability for the direct control of all parts of the project process, as it recognised that it could externally source professional services for the control and management of key activities. For example, design consultancies could complete the detailed design and an independent cost consultancy could undertake the cost management role. For the physical construction activity, AM recognised that construction firms, sourced in a coordinated manner, could manage the integration of the upstream construction supply chains more efficiently, and that control over supplier opportunism could be achieved through other mechanisms such as the promise of a continuous relationship.

In addition, AM recognised the inefficiency of going through the entire sourcing process and competitively tendering every construction project on an individual basis. Therefore, AM sought to develop longer-term relationships with construction firms based on collaborative ways of working. This was achieved by identifying a small number of competent 'preferred partners' that were willing to provide a continuous commitment to cost, quality and delivery improvement in return for regularity and certainty of demand (revenue) and profit (returns). This methodology also contained a number of safeguards to ensure that value for money could be attained. These safeguards included totally transparent open-book costing and the use of independent cost consultants to provide detailed costs models. The client (AM) was, therefore, able to procure its portfolio of construction projects using the leverage of its regular process spend, allied with what it believed was a detailed knowledge of its supply cost structures.

In the year in question, AM had a total construction budget of approximately £30 million. The size and regularity of this expenditure made it a major client in the construction industry. It normally allocates this high value workload to its preferred contractors on an equitable basis according to their capabilities. At the beginning of the project PCS provided AM with a target price of £16.25 million.

The supplier – Platinum Construction Solutions (PCS)

The supplier (PCS) provided a guaranteed target cost of £16.25 million to complete the manufacturing facility. To arrive at this figure, PCS was subject to a detailed and precise process by AM. The detailed scope of works, developed in conjunction with AM, was divided into a series of work packages for which competitive tenders were invited from an agreed list of suitable specialist subcontractors. Once these tenders had been analysed for technical and commercial compliance, the overall net cost of the construction work was established. To this figure PCS added agreed percentage on-costs for its design, construction and project management responsibilities as well as company overheads and profit.

The supplier (PCS) is a medium-sized player in the construction industry with an annual turnover of approximately £50 million. The company specialises in the design, construction and project management of industrial and commercial buildings for clients in the public and private sectors, including large distribution warehouses, major production facilities, large multi-storey structures and healthcare facilities. The firm maintains a strong reputation within the supply market for delivering high quality and innovative solutions to clients within high-risk industrial environments where high security and confidentiality are paramount. This reputation is also built on a track record of delivering client's precise functional needs, and completing projects on time and within costs constraints. This expertise also enables it to carry out site investigations, and feasibility and value engineering studies.

Construction firms typically face a very unpredictable future with no certainty of demand or returns. As a result, they are rarely in a position to make the necessary investments to develop and implement long-term preferred supplier relationships with clients. In this case, while the majority of clients in the industrial manufacturing sector only require major construction projects on a very infrequent basis, PCS was fortunate to have been selected by AM to be part of its long-term construction supply management framework. This provided the necessary volume and frequency of demand to incentivise PCS to work with the client to operationalise a proactive relationship management approach.

14.3 The buyer–supplier relationship management approach

In analysing the market, supply chain and power circumstances in this exchange relationship, it will become apparent that while AM had the potential power resources to leverage PCS aggressively it did not use these levers as effectively as it might have done. As a result, PCS was able to achieve a win outcome, with AM only receiving a partial win from its proactive sourcing approach. This case demonstrates, therefore, the fact that sometimes the supplier achieves more from the relationship under proactive sourcing than the buyer instigating the approach.

The client (AM) – construction firm (PCS) dyad

Clients with infrequent demand and a limited understanding of construction supply markets are unlikely to have effective control and leverage over their suppliers. Unless they employ professional services to gain some control, uninformed clients will also almost certainly face opportunistic suppliers, who leverage information asymmetries against them in pursuit of higher revenues and returns. Previous cases have highlighted, however, that the use of construction experts does not always eliminate the potential for supplier opportunism. This is because many professional advisers have only limited competence in the principles of commercial exchange. The client in this case, AM, recognised the need to develop a robust methodology for the delivery of its construction requirements. Fundamental to AM's approach was the possession of extensive information and understanding of key construction supply markets and the appropriateness of available technologies. This understanding enabled it to develop a robust proactive relationship management strategy at the first-tier with PCS.

In this case, the contract value (target cost) for the construction of the manufacturing facility was £16.25 million. With a programmed duration of 12 months the project accounted for approximately 32% of PCS's annual turnover. This provided AM with a significant power resource because this project accounted for a very high share of PCS's annual turnover. Also, the fact that AM had an annual expenditure of £30 million for the construction and refurbishment of similar manufacturing facilities (shared equitably between its three preferred construction firms) meant that it possessed a high frequency of demand. The client (AM)'s power leverage was further strengthened by the fact it used its understanding of the products and services that needed to be integrated by PCS and the supply markets from where these were to be sourced to develop a relatively standardised design and specification for key elements (e.g. structural steelwork, reinforced concrete slab, external cladding and M&E components) that required limited customisation across projects. As a result, PCS saw this particular project and the relationship with AM as highly attractive.

It is also necessary to consider the scarcity of AM's business (i.e. the availability of equivalent alternative contracts for PCS). In the construction industry the majority of construction firms have to operate within a highly competitive and adversarial environment, with no guarantee of alternative contracts because they are faced with irregular client demand. The ability to offer PCS a guaranteed average annual workload of £8–12 million strengthened AM's relative power in this case. The fact that there was a paucity of equivalent ongoing collaborative contracts for PCS increased the difficulty for it to exit from this relationship. This difficulty was exacerbated by the high switching costs that were created by AM's investment in an IT infrastructure at the offices of PCS.

The client (AM)'s possession of these power resources, particularly the high volume and frequency of a relatively standardised demand, enabled it to incentivise PCS to undertake the necessary dedicated investments and relationship-specific adaptations to make collaboration and proactive relationship management work in the long-term. In this relationship, these investments included the development of a dedicated in-house cost, project and risk management capability using the latest IT technology to ensure the delivery of cost-effective solutions to programme. Unfortunately, AM only had sufficient resources to develop and implement this *supplier development* approach with PCS, and could not extend it further upstream. Despite this, AM felt that if this proactive approach was undertaken in a robust and professional manner it could still maximise value for money.

On the supply-side of this relationship, the critical power resources for PCS relate to the scarcity and utility of its own supply offering for AM and its ability to use information asymmetries against the client. In so far as scarcity is concerned, the majority of construction firms typically operate within highly contested markets and find it extremely difficult to restrict the level of competition or create high switching costs for clients. In this particular case, however, the level of contestation was reduced for two reasons. First, AM was only prepared to work with a restricted number of competent and congruent construction suppliers. Second, there were a limited number of construction firms willing **and** capable of delivering the required solutions in a collaborative manner (using open-book costing) to the very strict deadlines and high quality levels demanded by AM. Although these two factors made the market less competitive, this did not provide the conditions that would allow PCS and its other preferred suppliers to close the market completely and premium price their supply offerings.

Given this analysis, it is reasonable to argue that the power situation between AM and PCS was one of *buyer dominance*. This arose primarily because AM had an attractive level of demand, with many potential suppliers all of which found the relationship attractive because of a paucity of equivalent customers. Given this *buyer dominance*, one would expect AM to gain more from the relationship in commercial and operational terms. The actual performance outcome demonstrates, however, that rather than a nonzero-sum outcome with a win–partial win in favour of the buyer (AM), the actual outcome was in fact a nonzero-sum outcome with a win–partial win favouring the supplier (PCS).

14.4 Performance outcome from the buyer–supplier relationship

In this project, AM was attempting operationally to maximise the functionality of the final manufacturing facility and commercially to minimise the total costs of ownership so that it could maximise value for money. The supplier (PCS), in contrast, was attempting to increase revenue and returns. In theory, AM ought to have been able to achieve a full win from this relationship because it possessed a level of demand characterised by high volume and frequency that was highly attractive to PCS. The client (AM)'s power position was also strengthened because PCS was effectively locked into a long-term relationship due to the relatively high switching costs created by the dedicated IT investment. Faced with this dependence PCS was deterred from acting opportunistically *ex ante* (pre-contractually). The client (AM) also further reduced the potential for opportunistic supplier behaviour by employing independent costs consultants to monitor supplier performance, audit cost information and ensure open-book accountability.

Despite this apparent situation of structural power favouring the buyer, AM failed to achieve its ideal performance outcome and maximise value for money.

Although AM attained some costs savings, its failure to achieve the maximum
feasible reduction in the total costs of ownership and maximise the functionality
of the solution meant that it only partially achieved its commercial and operational
objectives. Ironically, despite this partial win by the client. PCS was able to record a
full win from the relationship.

Figure 14.2 has a summary of the dyad between AM and PCS and the performance outcome from the relationship.

The client (AM) was reasonably satisfied with the outcome because it reduced the
total construction costs by £200 000 (from the initial target cost of £16.25 million to
£16.05 million) without compromising the quality of the solution or adversely

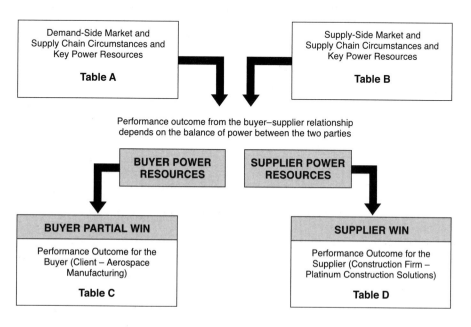

*Figure 14.2 A summary of
the dyad between the client
(AM) and construction
firm (PCS) and the
performance outcome from
the relationship*

Table A Demand-Side Market and Supply Chain Circumstances and Key Power Resources

There are many buyers in the total construction market for the construction of similar manufacturing facilities

Aerospace Manufacturing (AM) has a relatively low share of the total construction market but relatively **high share
of the local construction market** with an annual construction expenditure of £30 million. Therefore, the
construction firm (PCS) has a relatively high dependency on AM for revenue

AM has a **frequent need** to go to the construction market and ongoing plans for capital investment for new build
and refurbishment

The requirements of AM are **highly complex** (in terms of the project environment), **non-standardised** and require
considerable supplier expertise for their integration into the project

AM has **low switching costs** with a multitude of potential suppliers that would be keen to replace the current
preferred suppliers

AM, through the development of a robust construction sourcing strategy based on sourcing approaches for key
aerospace components, has a **very clear value proposition** – a high quality product delivered on time and at an
acceptable cost

AM is fully aware of the potential scope for **standardisation** of design and specification and **prefabrication** of key
components common across the project

AM has **low search costs**, because of its robust knowledge and understanding of construction products and services
and the strategies of the industry players. This minimises the scope for supplier opportunism

Table B Supply-Side Market and Supply Chain Circumstances and Key Power Resources

There are a very large number of suppliers in the total construction market with the required level of expertise to deliver this particular project

The value of the project, £16.25 million, accounts for a relatively **high share (32%) of the annual turnover** of Platinum Construction Solutions (PCS)

PCS is **highly dependent** on AM for revenue. As one of AM's three preferred suppliers for construction works it is guaranteed a level of revenue that accounts for between 25 and 45% of annual turnover

PCS considers AM's business to be **very attractive** as it has received significant dedicated investment from the client (e.g. an IT infrastructure facilitating leading-edge computer-aided design) and attained considerable knowledge and expertise related to delivering the required projects

PCS has relatively **high switching costs**

PCS's offerings are not commoditised and standardised but **highly customised** to the specific requirements of AM and working in an aerospace environment where health and safety are critical

PCS has a **very strong brand image** and reputation. This reputation has been strengthened by constantly delivering high quality projects on time and within financial budgets to a prestige client (AM)

Unlike relationships with other clients, PCS has **very limited information asymmetry** advantages over AM due to the open-book costing approach and the client's considerable knowledge and understanding of the construction industry

---

Table C Performance Outcome for the Client (AM) – Buyer Partial Win

The client, Aerospace Manufacturing (AM), was faced with costs lower than original budget by £200 000. The original estimate was £16.25 million and final construction cost was £16.05 million

The independent cost consultant benchmarked the performance of the construction firm (PCS). It was discovered that further cost savings might have been possible if PCS was more proactive in its approach with upstream suppliers of key components such as steelwork, M&E and ready-mixed concrete

AM's functional expectations fully met, but not exceeded

Delivery of project on time

Table D Performance Outcome for the Construction Firm (PCS) – Supplier Win

Platinum Construction Solutions (PCS) calculated that it made a profit of £750 000 on this project. This figure contained a basic profit, agreed in advance by AM, and an extra sum based on the savings identified by the independent cost consultant

PCS enhanced its reputation within the industry for delivering quality projects within time and cost constraints to a prestige client

This led to work with other manufacturing clients against whom it could leverage the knowledge and expertise acquired from working with this client to earn higher returns

---

affecting project duration. Cost information during the construction phase of the project was collected and audited by an independent cost consultant, which benchmarked this financial data against industry data to monitor supplier performance and support AM's contract and project management processes.

The possession of this detailed cost information, combined with its extensive knowledge of the industry, also enabled the cost consultant to discover that further reductions in total costs of ownership of the order of 8–15% might have been possible if the client had extended its proactive *supplier development* approach to include relationships with upstream suppliers of key components such as structural steelwork, cladding and M&E. This would have involved a move towards a proactive *supply chain management* approach. Despite this, while not fully attaining its commercial objectives in relation to reducing the total costs of ownership, AM was still able to achieve its operational objectives in relation to maximising the functionality of the manufacturing facility. This was made possible through the standardisation of design and specification and prefabrication and pre-assembly of key components. The client (AM) also received the finished project on time.

The supplier (PCS) made an overall profit of £750 000 on the project. This figure contained a basic profit of £650 000, agreed in advance by the client, and an extra payment of £100 000 based on the cost savings identified by the independent cost consultant. This additional figure was equal to 50% of the total reduction in total costs of ownership. Based on the sourcing of components in its aerospace business, AM had implemented a risk and reward mechanism as part of its target cost approach to further incentivise construction suppliers to minimise costs. The total profit of £750 000 received by PCS equated to a 5% return, which was substantially higher than PCS received from much of its other construction work. Given the open-book approach developed as part of the AM's collaborative sourcing framework, this level of return was accepted without challenge by the client.

In addition, the final solution was acknowledged by industry experts to be innovative in terms of design and construction allowing PCS to further enhance its reputation in the market for successfully delivering a very high quality and cost-effective solution, within very tight deadlines, and as part of an ongoing cost reduction programme to a major industrial client. This provided additional contracts for PCS from other major industrial clients. This was a full win for PCS.

14.5 Summary

The major finding from this case is that proactive sourcing can provide considerable improvement for clients, particularly if they are prepared to make the necessary dedicated investments in internal procurement capabilities. This normally requires the development of in-house competence in design and specification as well as in market and supply chain analysis. Despite this investment, it is clear that if the client limits its intervention to the first-tier of the supply chain, and if it pursues a non-adversarial collaborative approach, then additional savings may be lost for the client.

In this case it was the failure by the client (AM) to incentivise the first-tier supplier (PCS) to reduce its supply input costs, as well as its own failure to extend its approach into the supply chain beyond the first-tier that resulted in cost savings being forgone. The buyer (AM), while in many ways a model of proactive sourcing competence, was also at fault for developing a cosy relationship with the preferred supplier, PCS, due to its commercially non-adversarial approach to cost savings (50/50) and its guarantee of a reasonable profit margin (above what was normal for similar types of contracts with less proactive clients).

Given this, the lesson for clients pursuing proactive sourcing is that they must not only develop internal procurement capabilities but they must also look beyond the first-tier and incentivise first-tier suppliers to leverage upstream cost reduction opportunities as part of the relationship. In so far as this client (AM) failed to understand the scale of the opportunity available, it was guilty of engineering only a partial win outcome for itself when it could have achieved a full win. The supplier (PCS), on the other hand, was very pleased with an outcome in which a dominant client failed to impose aggressive commercial leverage on it, and allowed it to enhance its reputation and make relatively high returns.

Table 14.1 has a summary of the relationship management approach and performance outcome.

Table 14.1 A summary of the relationship management approach and performance outcome

Nature of Relationship Management Approach	The client, with an ongoing portfolio of projects valued at approximately £30 million, was in a position to develop long-term collaborative supply management strategies with the objective of leveraging upstream suppliers to maximise value for money
	These strategies focused on the development of a proactive *supplier development* relationship management approach with a small number of competent and congruent first-tier construction firms
	This involved the development of an open-book and target cost approach with a 50/50 sharing of cost savings achieved through target cost reductions
Nature of Buyer 'Partial Win'	The total construction cost was lower than original budget estimates by £200 000. The original estimate was £16.25 million and final construction cost was £16.05 million, although £100 000 was an additional cost because it was provided to the supplier as a bonus, making the final cost £16.15 million
	In benchmarking the performance of the construction firm and auditing the costs of the solution, the independent cost consultant discovered that further cost savings were possible if the client's proactive sourcing approach had encompassed upstream suppliers of key components
	The client received the level of functionality as laid out in the design and specification
	Project delivered to the client on the projected completion date
Nature of Supplier 'Win'	PCS made a profit of £750 000 on this project. This figure contained a basic profit of £650 000, agreed in advance by the client, and an extra sum (£100 000) based on the cost savings identified by the independent cost consultant
	PCS made a return close to 5%
	PCS also enhanced its reputation within the industry for delivering high quality and cost effective projects within time constraints to a major industrial client
	This led to work with other industrial and manufacturing clients
Conclusions	Proactive sourcing can result in asymmetric outcomes that favour the supplier rather than the buyer
	This occurs in circumstances where the buyer does not optimise the leverage available to it
	In this case it was the failure to look beyond the first-tier to leverage upstream suppliers or force the first-tier supplier to focus on this issue that was the basis for the buyer (the client) only receiving a partial win outcome
	In such circumstances, suppliers, especially if they are managed using a relatively non-adversarial and overly generous relationship management approach, can achieve a full win even when the buyer does not

The residential, office and entertainment complex case: proactive supplier development with a buyer partial win and supplier partial win outcome

15.1 Introduction

This case focuses on a key relationship within a project for the construction of a major residential, office and entertainment complex. In particular it focuses on the procurement of a critical sub-component, the pre-cast architectural cladding products, by a construction firm, Building & Engineering (BE). The main contractor (BE) was selected by the property developer, Urban Developments (UD), to design and build the complex. The primary sourcing relationship in the case is, however, between BE and Critical Cladding Services (CCS) the supplier of the specialist pre-cast architectural cladding products. These two parties have considerable experience of working together on a long-term and proactive sourcing basis on similar prestigious projects.

The proactive sourcing approach developed by BE focused, whenever possible, on the standardisation of design and specification of specific critical elements, off-site prefabrication and other 'best practices' transferred from an industrial manufacturing environment. In a fiercely competitive industry, BE anticipated that the successful implementation of this approach, which necessitated long-term supplier development relationships with key suppliers, would enable it to fully achieve its goals (i.e. achieve a full win outcome). In this case, however, BE was only able to achieve a partial win outcome that was matched by a partial win outcome for the supplier. This is a classic example of a stand-off in buyer and supplier power and leverage due to the relative equivalence of power resources available to both parties. In such circumstances, the normal outcome is a power situation of interdependence and a relatively balanced nonzero-sum outcome of partial wins for both parties.

15.2 Background to the case: the construction of a residential, office and entertainment complex

The project involved the design and construction of a major residential, office and entertainment complex. As with any construction project this required the integration of a large number of construction supply chains. The supply chain for the pre-cast architectural cladding elements required for the complex is shown in Figure 15.1.

The client in this case, Urban Developments (UD), is a major property developer with considerable experience of turning dilapidated buildings into highly sought-after office, retail, leisure and/or industrial developments. For this particular project, UD had acquired a major derelict industrial complex on the banks of the River Alpha very close to a major city centre with the intention of creating a large multi-use complex. The client (UD) hoped that the use of contemporary architecture could fundamentally change the character of this run-down industrial area by creating high quality housing, office space, retail facilities and a riverside entertainment complex.

This demanding design and build contract involved the transformation of a dilapidated industrial manufacturing complex into a distinctive $75\,000\,\text{m}^2$ innovative multi-use development. The new complex included $200\,000\,\text{ft}^2$ ($18\,600\,\text{m}^2$) of office space, 175 rooftop and riverside apartments, a new hotel, 40 retail outlets, 20 waterside restaurants and bars, a large basement car park and large landscaped public spaces.

The prominence of the scheme, its importance as an extension to the city centre, and the potential for regeneration on a large scale meant that the local planning authority was involved in the project early on at feasibility stage. As a result, planning permission was granted after just 24 weeks. Once this had been obtained UD sourced the project through a two-stage tendering route (an increasingly popular procurement strategy for clients whereby the first contract with the main contractor is for buildability, design and tendering assistance, and the second contract for the construction work on site). The construction firm (BE) 'won' the first-stage competition due to its track record for innovative, high quality and cost-effective solutions, as well as its open approach to collaborative relationships and its ability to work closely with UD's designers and professional advisers.

Working together, UD and BE considered the whole life cycle of the building during the development of the detailed design and specification. This resulted in a need for an external cladding system that could be installed with minimal disruption to the works and which would require minimal future maintenance. After considering the benefits of pre-cast concrete cladding products – increased durability, faster programme times, improved buildability, and consistently high quality standards – BE designed a cladding solution with a mixture of pre-cast concrete panels, natural stone-faced pre-cast panels, acid-etched reconstructed stone pre-cast panels and glass-reinforced cement (GRC) pre-cast panels. These were to be used on different elevations of the complex to ensure that a high quality but cost-effective effect was achieved.

To provide the 10 000 square metres of pre-cast cladding BE selected Critical Cladding Services (CCS), which had preferred supplier status with BE after working successfully with it on many similar projects. The selection of CCS also enabled BE to improve the efficiency of the construction process due to its ability to link the actual construction with the timing of the prefabrication work. The supplier (CCS) started manufacturing the panels four months before the site work commenced. In this way a stockpile of completed cladding panels was established that were inspected prior to being delivered to site. Then, with the just-in-time delivery of these panels, the frame was rapidly enclosed to produce a watertight envelope in which internal fitting-out could continue rapidly, thereby

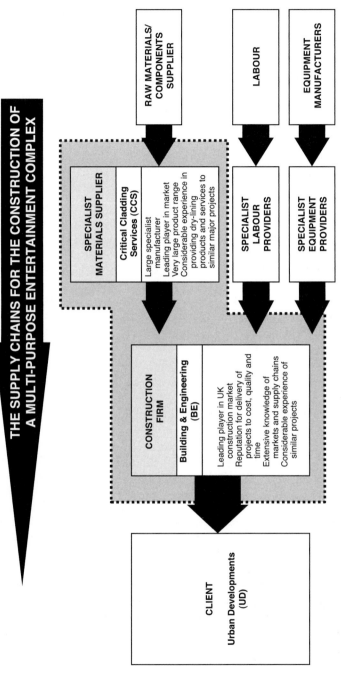

Figure 15.1 Construction supply chains for the construction of a residential, office and entertainment complex

reducing total construction time. The supplier (CCS) also worked closely with the steel frame and in-situ concrete contractors in the development of the detailed design, and spent considerable time on value engineering in the early stages reducing very large panels into more easily manoeuvrable units.

The buyer – Building & Engineering Plc (BE)

The client (UD) had considered the concept design to be critical and had employed architects and structural engineers to complete this task. This concept design was the basis upon which the first-stage of the tendering process was conducted and the construction firm, BE, was selected. After detailed development of this design, lengthy negotiations and the tendering of the work packages (the second-stage of the tendering process), the design and build contract for the residential, office and entertainment complex, with a guaranteed maximum price of £45 million, was signed by BE. The buyer (BE) has had considerable experience of working with property developers to design and build similar multi-purpose complexes, for which it has received a richly deserved reputation for innovation and quality, and the delivery of major projects on time and to budget. It has a turnover close to £1 billion for work related to the provision of design, civil and other specialist engineering, construction and management services.

In the second-stage of the tendering process BE worked with UD and its advisers to develop a detailed integrated design for key work packages including the cladding solution, the structural frame and key services[1]. From this design, a detailed specification was produced to solicit tenders from specialist suppliers. During this process UD wanted costs minimised but BE hoped that all potential risks could be managed, because the contract sum was fixed at £45 million and it would bear the full cost of any overruns. This meant that BE was not only interested in price but also on any specialist material supplier's knowledge and experience of working in a collaborative manner on similar prestigious projects. The major selection criteria used by BE, therefore, were cost, quality, an ability to supply the cladding panels within a just-in-time framework, and a history of expertise in installing panels on a site with restricted access.

The total cost of the pre-cast architectural cladding solution was initially estimated to be £1.85 million. After working with the client's advisers and developing the initial concept into a more detailed design and specification (as part of the two-stage tendering process), BE obtained prices from specialist suppliers for the cladding element ranging from £1.7 million to £2.1 million. The supplier (CCS) was eventually awarded the contract on the basis of a bid of £1.7 million. In addition to providing the lowest price, CCS was selected because of its extensive experience of delivering similar high quality solutions, on time and using highly innovative products.

Furthermore, the external appearance of this complex was regarded as critical and this made the issue of quality paramount. Structural cladding products can deteriorate in quality and appearance when subject to harsh weather conditions.

---

[1] The development of the integrated design from the earliest concept stage was critical to the attainment of benefits related to the interface of structure, cladding and services. For example, brackets and fixings for the cladding and services were incorporated when the steel was fabricated not added on later. Not only was this more logical, it also saved time and money – drilling a hole in the manufacturer's workshop cost around £1, whereas doing it later on-site would have cost £8. Total savings can be considerable on a large building with thousands of drilled holes and fixings.

The main reason, therefore, for CCS being granted a 'preferred supplier' status by BE was its highly innovative manufacturing processes (that provided cladding panels with superior structural properties to other manufacturers) and considerable project and materials management expertise. The buyer (BE)'s extensive knowledge of the supply market for pre-cast cladding products, combined with its ability to offer suppliers a relatively high volume and frequent level of demand, meant that it could establish preferred supplier relationships based on a proactive relationship management approach.

The supplier – Critical Cladding Services (CCS)

Cladding is placed over the building's structural frame to provide a barrier to outside elements. The main consideration in cladding any building is the desire to stop water penetration, as any moisture entering the building will cause problems for structural elements, resulting in large repair bills. Cladding also eliminates wind penetration, maintains internal temperatures through the control of heat gain and loss, reduces noise pollution, and can also improve aesthetic appearance. The cladding form must also, however, meet the needs of construction. Therefore, in deciding which cladding solution to adopt BE considered the individual character- istics and performance advantages and disadvantages of each alternative.

Given the nature of the project, BE recognised that the buildability of the solution was a key factor. On a purely practical level, the site had very little space to store bricks, stone or mortar and was in very close proximity to surrounding buildings. The just-in-time delivery to site of factory-finished com- ponents meant the site could be kept clean, tidy and quiet, and the easy craneage of the elements into place minimised the disruption in the surrounding area.

The choice of a pre-cast solution also provided BE with certainty of quality, programme and cost. In terms of quality, stringent production control and skilled factory-based craftsmen produced consistently high quality units with as close as possible to 'zero defects'. On this project, the window contractor claimed never to have worked before on a job where the openings were so accurate. The certainty of programme was ensured as production could be carefully controlled in the factory environment, and was not held up by the vagaries of the weather or labour shortages. The pre-cast components also made building quicker and easier. In one day, CCS's own erection team were able to install panels that covered an area that would have taken bricklayers 2–3 weeks to complete. In addition, the fact that on-site construction and off-site manufacture could be overlapped further reduced overall construction time by 10%.

Due to the controlled production environment, pre-casting gives certainty of cost, since the price quoted was the price paid, unlike the usual scenario in which the price tendered very seldom equals the out-turn cost. Furthermore, value for money was improved because pre-casting supported speedier construction (with less reliance on on-site labour and no requirement for scaffolding) and also contributed directly to cost savings. The fact that finished components were lifted directly from the delivery vehicle into position on-site also reduced the potential for accidents and the risk of hand-setting stone or brickwork in potentially hazardous locations.

The supplier (CCS) is a specialist pre-cast concrete contractor, producing high quality bespoke architectural cladding solutions from detailed design development, through manufacture in a factory environment, to on-site erection using its own teams. It has ongoing collaborative relationships with leading developers and specifiers to ensure that their projects gain maximum benefit from prefabrication. The supplier (CCS)'s precast solutions make a major contribution to improved quality, certainty, sustainability, safety and efficiency in the industry. The company has worked on many prestigious projects and the quality of its work is consistently recognised. It has an annual turnover of over £250 million, with net operating profits of between 6% and 7%.

15.3 The buyer–supplier relationship management approach

In analysing the market and supply chain circumstances surrounding the transaction and relationship management approach used by BE, it is clear that both parties had some, but not all, of the key power resources to enable them to leverage the other. Given that neither party had all of the cards in their hands meant that a stand-off occurred in power terms. In this power situation of *buyer–supplier inter-dependence* both parties were able to partially achieve some of their ideal commercial and operational goals, but not all of them. The outcome was, therefore, nonzero-sum with a partial win for both parties.

The construction firm (BE) – specialist material supplier (CCS) dyad

Given the nature of demand and supply in the industry, construction firms frequently have to enter into relationships with suppliers that they know will act opportunistically. Furthermore, construction firms may not always be in a position to stop supplier opportunism. For example, when a client specifies a particular product that can only be provided by one supplier it effectively eliminates competition in the supply market and opens the door to opportunism. Fortunately, this was not the case for BE in this project as the contract was for design and build (JCT 98 Two Stage Design & Build), which meant that it had control over the detailed design and specification and was not prevented from developing an effective sourcing strategy by the specifying actions of its client (UD).

In this case, BE was also able to avoid the most common cause for opportunistic behaviour in buyer–supplier relationships – the presence of information asymmetries between contractual parties. The construction firm (BE) had a comprehensive understanding of the nature of demand and the characteristics of the construction supply markets from which it sourced, as well as of the appropriateness of available technologies from upstream suppliers. Furthermore, while this single contract of £1.7 million was only a low share of CCS's total annual turnover (less than 1%), when one considers BE's *potential* annual requirement for similar cladding products, this expenditure accounts for a much higher proportion of its turnover (5–10%). This made BE an extremely attractive account for CCS.

Unfortunately, this level of demand did not provide BE with a power resource with which to dominate the relationship and leverage CCS completely. The leverage problem for BE was one of frequency. It had a regular need to source from the architectural cladding products market but, with a diverse and unpredictable portfolio of projects, it had no absolute certainty regarding the future functional requirements from clients and, therefore, the demand for specific products. As a result, BE selected its preferred suppliers based on the technical specification, quality and price of specific products, but it could not provide them with an exact demand schedule for total expenditure on these products annually. The buyer (BE)'s inability to do so undermined its ability to impose proactive sourcing solutions onto its suppliers and forced them to look for outcomes that shared the benefits of working together relatively equally, rather than retaining most of them for itself.

The buyer (BE)'s inability to offer suppliers a guaranteed level of demand impacted on its relative power in another way. In response to the uncertainty over future revenue from particular firms, suppliers of key components normally ensure that they have a wide portfolio of other customers, both within the construction industry and in other industries whenever possible. This has the effect of reducing the scarcity of any particular construction firm's business and reduces the level of dependency on, and attractiveness of, particular customers.

Despite these limitations, BE did possess some significant power resources – its relatively high volume of demand for prestigious project work in particular – that enabled it to incentivise CCS to work within a proactive and highly collaborative sourcing approach (*supplier development*). This involved CCS in undertaking a number of dedicated investments and relationship-specific adaptations related to their project management capability, IT infrastructure and production processes.

On the supply-side of this relationship CCS was, however, not without power resources itself. In addition to the fact that it had many alternative actual and potential customers other than BE it also had highly differentiated products and services to offer and was, therefore, able to close the market to many of its potential competitors. Furthermore, most of its potential competitors were unwilling to make the level of investments necessary to support a proactive relationship management approach. Finally, not all potential competitors were willing to accept the level of transparency (using open-book costing), very tight deadlines and high quality levels demanded by BE. These factors assisted CCS in closing the market, but not so completely that it could dominate the relationship with BE.

As a result, the power situation was one in which both parties needed one another and neither was able to totally dominate or leverage the other. A power situation of interdependence, in which both parties have high power resources against one another, pertained. Given this *buyer–supplier interdependence*, it was not surprising that the resulting performance outcome saw both parties gain partially, if not fully, from the relationship in commercial and operational terms.

15.4 Performance outcome from the buyer–supplier relationship

The buyer (BE) wanted to enhance its reputation for delivering projects on time and to high quality standards, while also reducing the total cost of ownership to the lowest levels feasible – this would have clear implications for the profits that CCS could earn. The buyer (BE) wanted also to have the highest possible functionality from the pre-cast structural cladding products so that it did not adversely impact the external appearance of the new development. On the other hand, the ideal outcome for CCS was to create a similar reputation for quality and timeliness so that this would close the market to competitors and increase the scope for additional revenue from BE and other potential customers. At the same time, CCS wanted to maximise its returns (to double digit levels if at all possible) from the transaction with BE.

The problem for both parties in this case was that neither of them possessed the power resources to impose its ideal solution on the other party. Although BE did not have absolute certainty about its future demand for specific cladding products, for this specific project it had a relatively high volume of demand that was very attractive to CCS because of the limited complexity required to fulfil the contract and lack of alternative prestigious contracts of an equivalent size. In this relationship, BE also had detailed cost models that enabled it to develop a clear understanding of the true cost of operations for CCS in undertaking its work, and a promise to CCS that it would be a preferred supplier and receive future work if it worked with CCS in a transparent manner. These factors reduced the scope for opportunism by CCS in negotiations pre-contractually and in delivery post-contractually.

Despite this, CCS was not without its own levers. First, competition was restricted because there were only a small number of potential manufacturers capable of delivering the cladding products required that were also prepared to make the necessary investments for a collaborative approach without the guarantee of a regular revenue stream. Second, CCS had a very solid reputation for successfully providing high quality products on time to cost-effective solutions.

These supply chain and market circumstances, summarised in Figure 15.2, resulted in a power situation scenario of interdependence because neither party was able to engineer a position of dominance. As a result, both BE and CCS were able to partially achieve their ideal outcomes.

The buyer (BE) developed a robust construction supply management framework that resulted in a reduction in the total cost of the pre-cast architectural cladding. In adopting this open-book approach, BE collected detailed cost information related to the manufacture and supply of key components and also employed an independent cost consultant to benchmark this financial information against industry data to monitor supplier performance. The result was a reduction in cost from the initial estimate of £1.85 million to £1.7 million. This £150 000

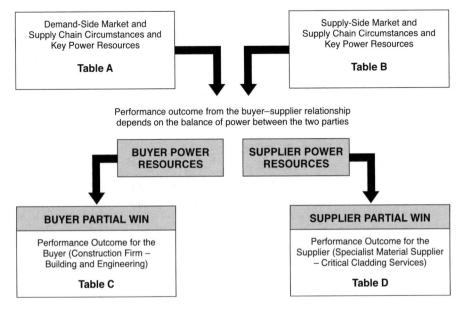

Figure 15.2 A summary of the dyad between the construction firm (BE) and specialist supplier (CCS) and the performance outcome from the relationship

Table A Demand-Side Market and Supply Chain Circumstances and Key Power Resources

There are many construction firms acting as buyers from the multitude of construction supply markets but fewer buyers for architectural cladding products

Building & Engineering (BE) has a low share of the total construction market but a **higher share of the architectural cladding products market** with an annual expenditure of £15 million. Therefore, the material supplier (CCS) has a relatively **low/medium dependency** on BE for revenue

BE has a **regular need** to source from the architectural cladding products market but there is **no absolute certainty/regularity** about requirements and volumes for specific products

The requirements of BE are **relatively straightforward** (in terms of the products themselves) and are easily integrated into the project without the need for scaffolding or heavy lifting equipment

BE has **low switching costs** as there are many suppliers with the capability of providing very high quality cladding products

BE has a **very clear value proposition** – a very high quality cladding product that does not require ongoing maintenance delivered on time and at an acceptable cost

BE and the client (UD) are both fully aware of the potential scope for **standardisation** of design and specification and **prefabrication** of key components common across the project. This was the case for the architectural cladding products used on this project

BE has **very low search costs**, as it has extensive knowledge and understanding about architectural cladding products and the strategies of the industry players supplying them

---

Table B Supply-Side Market and Supply Chain Circumstances and Key Power Resources

There are many suppliers in the total construction market but fewer suppliers capable of delivering products to the required quality levels to tight timescales

The total contract value of the project was £45 million of which £1.85 million was attributable to architectural cladding products

While this single project accounts for a relatively low share of the annual turnover (<1%) of Critical Cladding Services (CCS), when one considers BE's potential annual requirement for similar cladding products this expenditure may account for a **medium share of the annual turnover of CCS** (5–10%)

CCS has a **low/medium dependency** on BE for this revenue, as there is a relatively high degree of certainty surrounding alternative contracts for similar products

CCS considers the business from BE to be **relatively attractive** as it is relatively easy to service and it has considerable knowledge and expertise related to similar projects

CCS has relatively **low switching costs**

The products and services provided by CCS are **relatively standardised** with **limited customisation** to the specific requirements of the client (and BE)

CCS has a **very strong brand image** and reputation. This reputation has been strengthened by constantly delivering innovative products of a very high quality often within very tight timescales

CCS has **very limited information asymmetry** advantages over BE due to the construction firm's extensive knowledge of the marketplace

---

Table C Performance Outcome for the Construction Firm (BE) – Buyer Partial Win

On completion of the project the construction firm, Building & Engineering (BE), was faced with costs of architectural cladding products lower than original budget by £150 000. The original estimate for the cladding products was £1.85 million and final cost was £1.7 million

Functional expectations of the client (and BE) fully met but not exceeded

Delivery of project on time (assisted by the speed with which the cladding could be integrated into the solution)

Cladding solution has lower maintenance costs than expected

Potential cost reductions feasible but not achieved

Critical Cladding Services (CCS) made a profit of £150 000 or close to 9% return on this project
This level of profit was achieved despite the costs of installation being slightly higher than expected
CCS maintained its reputation within the industry for delivering innovative cladding projects of a very high quality
This led to work with other large construction firms in the future

reduction was achieved through greater efficiency by CCS in the manufacturing process and faster installation on-site, and it did not compromise the quality and functionality of the products or adversely impact the duration of the project.

The possession of this detailed cost information, combined with extensive knowledge of the industry, also enabled BE to monitor, with the assistance of the cost consultant, the overall value for money being attained. On this project BE discovered that further reductions in costs would have been possible if it had extended its proactive *supplier development* approach to include relationships with suppliers of raw materials such as cement, steel reinforcement, aggregates and natural stones. This would have involved a move towards a proactive *supply chain management* approach.

In addition to not achieving the maximum feasible reduction in total costs of ownership, BE also failed to fully achieve its operational objectives in relation to maximising project functionality. The buyer (BE) only achieved levels of functionality as defined in the design and specification and, despite having a solid understanding of construction products and services, it failed to access all possible innovations from the supply market. On a positive note, BE did discover that the final cladding solution had lower maintenance costs than expected because the individual elements could be replaced very quickly without major disruption to the complex overall. Finally, BE also received the cladding solution on time (assisted by the speed with which the cladding could be integrated into the solution), which ensured that it could deliver the finished project to the client to programme.

This was only a partial win for BE because it could have reduced costs more effectively if it had extended its approach throughout the supply chain, and also because CCS was able to make very reasonable returns from supplying the required pre-cast architectural cladding products. The supplier (CCS) made a profit of £150 000 from supplying the cladding products on this particular project. This figure represented close to a 9% return on an overall contract value of £1.7 million. This return was extremely acceptable to CCS, and higher than the normal returns of 5% or less that it often earned from supplying its products to other similar major projects.

The supplier (CCS) was not able to achieve its own ideal of double-digit returns, but it did achieve other gains. It was able to enhance its reputation within the marketplace by successfully delivering a very high quality product to a major client's very strict deadlines on a prestigious project. This led directly to the award of other profitable work with BE and other construction firms. As a result, CCS achieved a partial win from its ability to convince BE to allow it to be a preferred supplier and stop BE from forcing it into a win–partial win outcome favouring the buyer. This was because CCS achieved higher than normal returns from the exchange.

15.5 Summary

The major finding from this case is that proactive sourcing approaches do not always result in nonzero-sum outcomes that favour the buyer. In this case both parties achieved a partial win outcome because both parties had significant power resources that created an interdependent power situation. In this circumstance the buyer received a quality product on time and to specified quality standards, and was also able to engineer some reductions in the total costs of ownership.

This might at first appear to be a complete win for the buyer, but it was not because the supplier was able to deliver these benefits to the buyer while also making very close to above normal returns in a market in which it normally made low or normal returns of 5% or less. In this circumstance the buyer could have found a more ideal outcome if it could have leveraged the supplier to reduce its costs by the difference between 9% and 5% or less returns.

Table 15.1 A summary of the relationship management approach and performance outcome

Nature of Relationship Management Approach	The buyer, with a high value prestigious project, was in a position to persuade the supplier to work within a collaborative relationship management framework and create a dedicated project management capability, IT infrastructure and production processes
	As a result, the buyer was able to develop and implement a proactive relationship management approach (*supplier development*)
	This approach was undertaken in a power circumstance of interdependence because both parties had significant power resources to lever against the other
	In this circumstance the performance outcome was a partial win for both parties
Nature of Buyer 'Partial Win'	The costs of architectural cladding products were lower than original budget by £150 000
	Functional expectations, as set out in design and specification, were fully met but not exceeded
	Delivery of project on time (assisted by the speed with which the cladding could be integrated into the solution)
	The cladding solution has lower maintenance costs than anticipated
Nature of Supplier 'Partial Win'	A profit of £150 000 was made on this project, with a more than acceptable return of 9%
	This level of profit was achieved despite the costs of installation being slightly higher than expected
	The supplier maintained its reputation within the industry for delivering innovative cladding projects of a very high quality
	The return was somewhat higher than the supplier normally achieved from similar projects with other customers
Conclusions	Nonzero-sum outcomes can result in partial win outcomes for both parties
	Despite this, there is always tension in the relationship because, for both parties, there are always superior performance outcomes than a partial win
	Both the buyer and the supplier would ideally prefer to achieve a full win if suitable exchange partners, who are willing to accept a win–partial win outcome in favour of the other, could be found
	Nevertheless, when the power situation is one of interdependence the best that can be achieved is normally a partial win for both parties
	This does not resolve the conflict and tension in the relationship but merely reflects the stand-off in power terms between the two parties

Unfortunately, the buyer was not able to achieve this, nor was BE able to take advantage of its power resources with second- and third-tier suppliers. If it could have done so it could have significantly reduced its overall costs of ownership to much lower levels than it did achieve. Even if this had been achieved, however, if it did not also impact directly on the returns being made by CSS, it would not have significantly changed the partial win outcome for both parties in the BE and CCS relationship. This indicates that, even when both parties receive something of value from an exchange, there are always better (more ideal) performance outcomes for both parties if they can be engineered. This demonstrates the inherent tension endemic even when both parties receive partial win outcomes.

Table 15.1 shows a summary of the relationship management approach and performance outcome.

The high street public house case: proactive supplier development with a buyer partial win and supplier lose outcome

16.1 Introduction

This case focuses on the procurement of refurbishment services by a company, High Street Inns (HSI), which runs a chain of public houses. The case analyses the buyer–supplier relationship between the client (HSI) and a construction firm that specialises in refurbishment projects – Premier Quality Refurbishments (PQR). This single project forms part of a collaborative and proactive relationship between these two firms for an ongoing programme of construction work.

This case demonstrates that a client, with a continuous portfolio of similar major refurbishment projects, is in a position to consolidate its demand requirements and develop a proactive approach to construction sourcing. Within this approach HSI developed a long-term collaborative relationship management approach with two first-tier construction suppliers, but to avoid supply dependency and opportunism recognised the need for disciplined cost management based on an open-book target costing approach, overseen by an independent cost consultancy.

The client (HSI) anticipated that the implementation of its proactive sourcing approach, combined with its position of buyer dominance, would enable it to leverage PQR so that it could maximise value for money and achieve a full win outcome for itself, while only allowing PQR to achieve a partial win outcome predicated on the achievement of low or normal returns. In this case, however, HSI failed to attain all of its commercial and operational goals – the highest quality solution delivered on time and at the lowest feasible costs of ownership. This was because the independent cost consultancy discovered that further cost savings were possible if the proactive approach had been extended upstream to include suppliers of key components. This failure to achieve the desired outcome was not confined to the client. A number of problems arose during the project, which meant that PQR failed to achieve any of its goals and experienced a lose performance outcome.

16.2 Background to the case: the refurbishment of a high street public house

The refurbishment of a high street pub-retail property requires the integration of a number of supply chains, as shown in Figure 16.1. This process is highly complex and requires considerable expertise, particularly from the client whose demand initiates the project. Given the regular nature of its construction refurbishment requirements, the relatively high value of the individual projects, and the strategic importance of the refurbishment of the properties to its business, the client in this case recognised the need to develop a more sophisticated approach to construction sourcing so that it could avoid adversarial and opportunistic supplier behaviour and consistently attain value for money. Therefore, with expert advice from professional services, High Street Inns (HSI) decided to develop a proactive sourcing approach based on collaboration for the delivery of its new property refurbishment programme.

The client (HSI), a large owner and operator of public houses on the high street, had considerable experience of sourcing from construction supply markets for the refurbishment of its new properties. It used this experience, in conjunction with external construction professionals, to develop a detailed design and specification for its refurbishment requirements for this particular project. However, HSI did not have to use this documentation within a lengthy, reactive and arm's-length supplier selection process. As part of its proactive sourcing framework, HSI had already identified two construction firms, including Premier Quality Refurbishments (PQR), capable of delivering its new property refurbishment programme (approximately 25 properties per year). The client (HSI) awarded its annual spend equitably between the two preferred suppliers, and then leveraged them to maximise value for money (i.e. provide the highest level of functionality at the lowest total costs of ownership feasible).

Having worked successfully together on a number of very similar contracts, HSI selected PQR to undertake this particular project. It involved the major refurbishment of a high street bank into a public house. The total contract value for the project, based on the target cost provided by PQR, was estimated initially at £250 000. For this investment, HSI wanted a property of the highest quality that portrayed the same brand image as its other properties. To turn these commercial and operational requirements into reality, PQR had to manage and coordinate a large number of providers of construction products and services while also ensuring it adhered to a very tight programme of works of 12 weeks.

The detailed design and specification, provided by HSI, was relatively straightforward. It included basic functional requirements for air conditioning, brickwork, carpentry, electrical work, false ceilings, flooring (tiles and carpets), furnishings, glazing, heating, lighting, mechanical work, painting, partitioning, plastering, plumbing, ventilation and wall covering (tiles and wallpaper). However, as the project involved the refurbishment of a bank there was a higher level of complexity associated with the structural work within the basement where the safes had been housed. In the construction of new toilets PQR also had to knock holes out of very thick reinforced concrete walls for doorways and services.

The buyer – High Street Inns (HSI)

High Street Inns (HSI) operates within a highly competitive and challenging marketplace. The major competitive battle in the marketplace is between

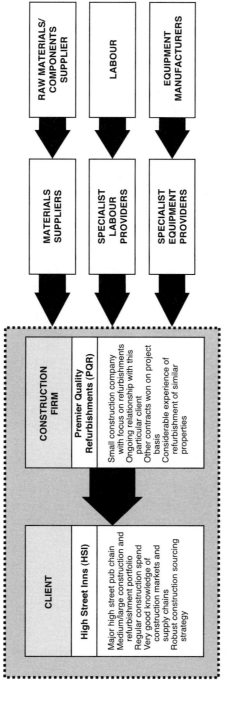

Figure 16.1 Construction supply chains for the refurbishment of a high street public house

brewers' tied houses and free houses. Traditionally, the vast majority of public houses were owned or controlled as brewers' tied estates, usually operated on a regional basis. That is, each brewer controlled most of the pubs in a radius around the brewery and acted as its main beer supplier. These pubs, whether managed, tenanted or leased, were required to take their supply of beer from the brewer. The exceptions to this general rule (and remainder of the market) are free houses. These outlets are free to obtain supplies of beer from any brewer. Brewers' tied estates of pubs once predominated, but laws restricting this traditional system of vertical integration forced the break-up of the national pub estates during the 1990s. Although regional brewers continue to own thousands of tied pubs (14% of the total in the UK), these laws enabled non-brewing pub companies (or Pubcos) to acquire large parcels of pubs from the national brewers.

Non-brewing pub companies subdivide into two types. The largest Pubcos, in terms of pubs under their control, are the owners of thousands of pubs that are tenanted or leased to individual publicans. Unlike the brewers which used to own and supply these pubs, the new owners are effectively either property management companies or financial investment vehicles as they offer little, or no, branding or conventional building of multiple concepts. The second type of Pubco is the managed group, which brings together an estate of large, profitable pubs under close management control. This type of Pubco, of which HSI is one, has perpetuated the tied system by owning large estates of branded pubs, but are still supplied by a single brewer or beer wholesaler (rather than sourcing freely on the market as free houses).

In 2004, the total UK public houses market was worth approximately £15 billion and consisted of over 40 000 companies, although only 190 of these firms had an annual turnover above £5 million. In this year, High Street Inns had an annual turnover of £650 million, pre-tax profits of £40 million and a portfolio of 500 properties. However, this current position of strength has been constantly challenged over the last decade. With supermarkets forcing prices downwards and encouraging take-home drinking, HSI realised that it had to develop business strategies with the objective of increasing market share and increasing the profitability of its properties. With a portfolio of properties increasing in number by 25 per year, HSI hoped for an increase in market share, but accepted that this could not be taken for granted. To achieve this increase HSI acknowledged the criticality of the location, but also recognised the importance of the actual refurbishment of its new properties, as this was directly linked to the creation of an attractive drinking environment.

High Street Inns (HSI) decided to develop a proactive construction sourcing approach to ensure certainty over the quality, cost and timely delivery of the final refurbished property. It also hoped that this proactive approach would enable it to leverage its relatively high volume and regular demand to improve the efficiency and effectiveness of its construction supply chain management activities to minimise project durations so that revenues could be earned as soon as possible, and reduce construction costs to their lowest feasible figure so that more refurbishments could take place. To implement these approaches successfully, however, it had to acquire a much more detailed understanding of construction markets and supply chains. This was achieved in conjunction with professional service providers.

In the development of its new proactive construction sourcing approach, HSI decided to separate the refurbishment of its new properties and the refurbishment of its existing properties. While the refurbishment of its existing properties only involves minor building works and redecoration, the refurbishment of its new properties (accounting for approximately 40% of HSI's annual construction expenditure of £16.25 million) usually involves major structural changes and complex construction work that requires a higher level of competence and capability on the part of the contractor. For the former, HSI decided to rely on competition within the local supply market, but for the latter HSI decided to develop very close collaborative relationships with two construction firms for all of its requirements. The client (HSI) decided to incentivise these contractors with a long-term guarantee of profitable work, but only if they were prepared to work with it on improving value for money (decreasing total costs of owner-ship, increasing functionality and quality and decreasing project durations) in a transparent manner, using open-book costing and independent cost consultants.

High Street Inns (HSI) selected PQR to undertake this particular refurbishment project, as it provided the lowest target cost from the two preferred contractors. The construction firm (PQR) was also selected due to its experience in delivering very similar projects – the refurbishment of eight separate high street banks – to a very high quality and within tight timescales. This specific project was PQR's fortieth for HSI.

The supplier – Premier Quality Refurbishments (PQR)

Premier Quality Refurbishments (PQR) provided a guaranteed target cost of £250 000 to refurbish a branch of a major bank into a high street public house. It divided the detailed design and specification, provided by HSI, into a series of work packages for which competitive tenders were obtained from an agreed list of specialist subcontractors and material suppliers. Once these tenders had been analysed for functional and commercial compliance, the overall total cost of the refurbishment was established. To this figure PQR added an agreed percentage on-cost for its management responsibilities, administrative overheads and company profit.

The supplier (PQR) is a small to medium-sized player in the construction industry with a turnover of approximately £6.25 million and an operating profit of £375 000 (6% return) in 2004. The company has the construction capability and experience to tackle a wide range of solutions from minor building alterations and fitting-out of building shells to major refurbishment projects covering all aspects of building, carpentry, roofing, mechanical, electrical, plumbing and ventilation work. However, it only has the financial ability to work on contracts up to a value of £1 million.

The firm maintains a strong reputation within the supply market for delivering high quality and cost-effective solutions to blue chip clients within very strict time deadlines. This reputation is built on a track record of consistently delivering client's functional needs, and completing difficult projects on time so that clients can move into its refurbished facilities (whether a pub, bank, retail outlet or corporate office) as planned. This reputation was a consideration in HSI's selection of PQR as one of its preferred refurbishment contractors within its long-term construction supply management framework. With a promise of 12 projects per year if performance was acceptable, this enabled PQR to avoid the situation that confronts the majority of construction firms – a very unpredictable future with no certainty of future revenues and returns.

16.3 The buyer–supplier relationship management approach

In analysing the appropriateness of the relationship management approach adopted between the client, High Street Inns (HSI), and the construction firm, Premier Quality Refurbishments (PQR), the key buyer and supplier power resources and market and supply chain circumstances are discussed. The analysis focuses on whether either HSI was in a position to maximise value for money or PQR was in a position to maximise value from supply. As we shall see, both parties achieved an outcome that was less than they might have expected given the balance of power and the proactive approach agreed upon.

The client (HSI) – construction firm (PQR) dyad

When one analyses client–contractor relationships in the construction industry the issue of adversarial and opportunistic supplier behaviour is often evident. Clients with infrequent demand and a limited understanding of construction supply markets are unlikely to have effective control and leverage over their suppliers. Unless they employ professional services to gain some control, uninformed clients will also almost certainly face opportunistic suppliers, which leverage information asymmetries against them in pursuit of higher revenues and returns.

However, the client in this case, HSI, with its ongoing portfolio of new build and refurbishment construction projects, understood the basic principles of commercial exchange and recognised the need to develop a robust methodology for the delivery of these requirements. Developed in conjunction with construction experts and professional advisers, HSI's approach was based on the possession of extensive information and understanding of key construction supply markets and the appropriateness of available products and services. This understanding enabled it to develop a robust proactive relationship management strategy (*supplier development*) at the first-tier with PQR.

In this case, the contract value (target cost) for the refurbishment of the new high street public house was £250 000, with a programmed duration of four months. While this particular project accounted for a relatively low share of PQR's total annual turnover (4%), when one considers the frequency with which HSI and PQR transact and resulting annual workload (12 similar refurbishment projects), this expenditure accounts in total for a very high share (48%) of PQR's annual turnover. The guarantee of an equitable share (50%) of HSI's major construction refurbishment spend is highly attractive to PQR and provides HSI with a key power lever in this relationship.

The buyer (HSI)'s power leverage was further strengthened by the fact that the design and specification for specific components (e.g. wall coverings, etched internal and external glazing, air conditioning and ventilation system, and ceramic floor tiles with HSI's logo) was relatively standardised and required limited customisation across refurbishment projects. As a result, HSI fully understood the construction products and services that needed to be integrated by PQR and the first-tier supply markets from where they were sourced. The supplier (PQR) also regarded this particular project and the on-going relationship with HSI as extremely attractive.

In considering the scarcity of HSI's business (i.e. the availability of equivalent alternative contracts for the construction firm), it is important to recognise that the majority of construction firms have to operate within a highly competitive and adversarial environment, with no guarantee of alternative contracts because they are faced with irregular client demand. As a result, the ability of HSI to offer PQR a guaranteed average annual workload of approximately £6.5 million augmented HSI's power in the relationship. This was because PQR would find it very difficult to find equivalent levels of guaranteed volume from other potential customers. This difficulty was increased by the high switching costs that were created by HSI's investment in an information infrastructure to support bilateral communications in the relationship.

The buyer (HSI)'s possession of these power levers, particularly its high volume and frequent level of fairly standardised demand, enabled it to incentivise PQR to become a preferred supplier within a long-term collaborative and proactive relationship management approach. Surprisingly, HSI only developed and implemented this *supplier development* approach with first-tier construction firms (such as PQR) and selected professional services suppliers. The buyer (HSI) felt that its proactive approach at the first-tier, if undertaken in a robust and professional manner, was sufficient to ensure the maximisation of its own value for money goals.

On the supply-side, the critical power resources for PQR were the relative scarcity and utility of its own supply offering for HSI, and its ability to use information asymmetries against the client. Unfortunately, PQR had no information asymmetry advantages over HSI and this meant that PQR were unable to use misinformation, branding or reputation to increase the client's perception of value (enhance the utility of the transaction for the client) or decrease the client's perception of contestation (create an impression of supply market scarcity) to achieve higher revenues and returns.

Despite this, there were two factors that enabled PQR to slightly restrict the level of competition in the supply market and increase the switching costs for HSI. First, even though many firms within the supply market were competent and capable of delivering its major refurbishment projects, HSI did not want to carry on competitively tendering each project as it considered this process to be inefficient. Instead it wanted to work with two construction firms to deliver its major refurbishment projects and use other mechanisms (e.g. an independent cost consultant) to ensure value for money was being obtained. Once selected, therefore, PQR had an advantage as the competition in the supply market was effectively reduced. Second, there were fewer construction firms willing and capable of delivering the required solutions in a collaborative manner (using open book costing) to the very strict deadlines and high quality levels demanded by HSI. Although these two factors made the market marginally less competitive it did not allow PQR and the other preferred suppliers to premium price their supply offerings.

Given the demand and supply circumstances in this particular transaction, the power situation between HSI and PQR was still one of *buyer dominance*. This asymmetrical position of power arose primarily because HSI had a very attractive level of demand and was faced with a highly competitive supply market, with only limited switching costs favouring the supplier. Any of the large number of potential contractors within this marketplace would have considered a long-term relationship attractive because of a lack of equivalent customers. Furthermore, PQR was deterred from acting opportunistically pre-contractually because of the promise of a regular demand and the ability of HSI to compare suppliers, and post-contractually because of HSI's robust understanding of the supply market and employment of a professional services provider to monitor the supplier's performance. Given this position of buyer dominance, one would expect HSI to gain more from the relationship in commercial and operational terms than PQR. The actual performance outcome supports this contention. However, rather than an expected nonzero-sum outcome with a win–partial win in favour of the buyer, the actual outcome was in fact worse for both parties – a zero-sum outcome with a partial win–lose favouring the buyer.

16.4 Performance outcome from the buyer–supplier relationship

Often in buyer and supplier exchange there is a competitive tension at the start of a relationship over what each party wants from the relationship, which continues throughout the project. Typically, the buyer attempts, operationally, to maximise functionality and, commercially, to minimise the total costs of ownership of what is purchased; while the supplier attempts to maximise revenue and returns from the buyer. In this particular case, this tension had been significantly reduced and the client, HSI, and construction firm, PQR, had developed aligned operational and commercial goals.

The supplier (PQR) had over time, recognising its dependency on HSI, come to accept that the best it could achieve would be a partial win, in which it received regular work in return for a low but guaranteed profit margin. On the other hand, HSI ought normally to have been able to use its position of *buyer dominance* to achieve its ideal goals of maximising the functionality of the supply offering and reducing the total costs of ownership of the final refurbished asset, while limiting the supplier's returns. Unfortunately, as Figure 16.2 demonstrates, failures on both sides of the relationship meant that HSI was only partially successful in its attempt to maximise the value for money it received from PQR, while PQR failed to achieve any of its goals and received a lose performance outcome.

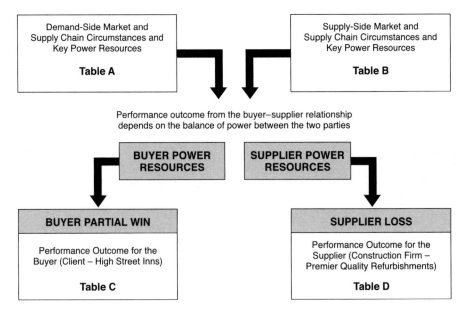

Figure 16.2 A summary of the dyad between the client (HSI) and construction firm (PQR) and the performance outcome from the relationship

Table A Demand-Side Market and Supply Chain Circumstances and Key Power Resources

There are many buyers (clients) in the construction market but fewer buyers with a regular demand for refurbishment projects

High Street Inns (HSI) has a low share of total construction market but a **higher share of the construction and refurbishment market** with an annual construction spend £16.25 million of which 40% (£6.5 million) is attributable to the refurbishment of 25 'high street' properties into new public houses per year. The remainder relates to the refurbishment and redecoration of existing properties

HSI has a **regular need** to source from the general construction market for the refurbishment of new properties, but there is **limited certainty/regularity** about specific construction requirements and location

The functional requirements of HSI are **relatively simple** (despite the design and specification changing across projects), but there is **medium complexity** associated with certain elements that require considerable supplier knowledge and expertise to integrate into the project

HSI has **medium switching costs** with a relatively large number of competent suppliers able to provide a high quality offering

The client, HSI, after working in conjunction with professional services, has a **relatively clear value proposition** – a high quality solution delivered on time and at an acceptable cost

HSI has not developed strategies for the **standardisation** and **prefabrication** of specific construction elements because it cannot predict the nature of its new properties (properties that need to be refurbished range from banks to churches) and it tailors the specification to the old building

HSI has **very low search costs**, as it has extensive knowledge and understanding about construction products and services and the strategies of the industry players. This eliminates the scope for supplier opportunism

---

Table B Supply-Side Market and Supply Chain Circumstances and Key Power Resources

There are a large number of construction firms in the construction market capable of delivering specialised refurbishment solutions

The total contract value of the project, approximately £250 000, accounts for a relatively **low share (4%) of the annual turnover** of Premier Quality Refurbishments (PQR). However, when one considers its share of the annual refurbishment requirements of High Street Inns' new properties (12 per year) this workload accounts for a **higher share of PQR's annual turnover** (48%)

PQR has a **very high dependency** on HSI for revenue, as there is a high degree of **uncertainty** surrounding alternative contracts (of equivalent size)

In addition to the volume and frequency, PQR considers HSI's business to be **very attractive** as there are low costs associated with servicing the contract

PQR has **medium switching costs**

PQR's offerings are not commoditised and standardised but **customised** to the specific requirements of the client (HSI)

PQR has a **good image** and **reputation** for delivering cost-effective refurbishment solutions to very high quality levels and within strict time constraints

PQR has **no information asymmetry advantages** over HSI and HSI's investment in PQR's information infrastructure ensures that communications are timely and all relevant project information is collected for the open-book costing approach

---

Table C Performance Outcome for the Client (HSI) – Buyer Partial Win

Costs were lower than original budget by £10 000. The original target cost was £250 000 and final contract value (refurbishment cost) was £240 000

The client, High Street Inns (HSI), employed an independent cost consultant to audit the performance of the construction firm (PQR)

It was discovered that further cost savings might have been possible if HSI had extended its proactive approach beyond PQR to include upstream suppliers of key components such as M&E and specialist woodwork

Functional expectations of HSI only met after remedial action by PQR to correct poor workmanship

Despite many problems, the project was delivered to HSI on time

---

Premier Quality Refurbishments (PQR) made a loss of £10 000 on this project. This was largely due to:
   Costs to overcome problems with poor workmanship related to the fitting of the bar counter
   Costs associated with the replacement of incorrectly installed materials and the need to pay a premium for their
      delivery to very short timescales (to avoid extensive liquidated damages)
PQR damaged its reputation within the industry for delivering high quality solutions to very tight programmes
Major industry players recognised that it was PQR's fault so it was expected to impact future revenues

In this case HSI wanted a very high quality solution delivered to a very tight programme. Using its extensive knowledge of construction products and services and working in conjunction with professional services, HSI developed a detailed design and specification. During this process HSI was also very much aware of the true costs of construction. This transparency of costs continued through the project because HSI implemented an open-book costing approach.

This approach, based on total transparency of cost information, facilitated the reduction of total construction costs by £10 000 (from the initial target cost of £250 000 to £240 000) without affecting the quality or delivery of the final solution. The detailed cost information was collected and audited by an independent cost consultant, who benchmarked it against industry data to monitor supplier performance and support HSI's contract and project management processes. This financial information, combined with extensive knowledge of the industry, also enabled the cost consultant to discover that further reductions in total costs of ownership in the region of 10% (£25 000) might have been possible if HSI had extended its proactive *supplier development* approach to include relationships with upstream suppliers of key standardised components (such as etched internal and external glazing, and ceramic floor tiles with HSI's logo), or used prefabrication and pre-assembly when appropriate (e.g. toilet modules). This would have involved a move towards a proactive *supply chain management* approach.

In addition to failing to attain its commercial objectives in relation to reducing cost to its absolute minimum, HSI was also unable to achieve its operational objectives in relation to maximising the functionality of the M&E solution. As shown earlier, the lack of proactive strategies focused on the standardisation of design and specification, prefabrication and pre-assembly of key components resulted in a lack of innovation in the upstream stages of the construction supply chains integrated by PQR. As a result, and despite the problems experienced by PQR, HSI only achieved levels of functionality as defined in the design and specification and missed out on improvements that would have been possible if it had worked collaboratively with upstream supply chain players. Despite this, the final refurbished public house that HSI received still provided patrons with the required ambience and supported its high quality brand identity. The project was also completed on time. This was, therefore, a partial win for HSI rather than the full win that was attainable if a *supply chain management* approach had been implemented.

Despite the ongoing collaborative relationship with HSI, on this particular project PQR made an overall loss of £10 000. This loss, accounting for 4% of the total contract value (original target cost), was attributed to the costs incurred by PQR to overcome poor workmanship in relation to the installation and fitting of the solid wood bar counter, the costs associated with the supply of additional specialised floor tiles to replace some that had been installed incorrectly, and the need to pay a premium for their delivery to very short timescales (to avoid extensive liquidated damages).

For the non-carpeted areas within all of its properties HSI specified very high quality ceramic floor tiles with its logo imprinted to aid the creation of a common brand image. In this particular project, however, a major problem arose after PQR installed these tiles onto a poorly prepared floor surface. On other projects PQR had applied a thin floor screed onto the concrete floors to ensure a level surface onto which the tiles could be laid. The supplier (PQR) did not think it needed to apply a screed to the floors in this case; a decision that was to prove very costly. After the tiles had been laid it soon became evident that large sections of the floor surface were very uneven and a number of the tiles cracked as heavy loadings were applied to the floor. The problems that this caused for PQR were increased as it only had three weeks to correct the problem before the property had to be open for business.

The company that supplied the specialist tiles only manufactured them to order and stated a lead-time of four weeks. To acquire the tiles within this timescale, and avoid the financial impact of the liquidated damages clause set in the contract, PQR agreed to pay the full market price for the tiles without their usual discount. Despite the additional cost implications of £15000, PQR identified this as the best option as it enabled PQR to avoid the liquidated damages clause and deliver the project on time. The tiles were on site within one week, which allowed PQR to avoid any delay to subsequent trades.

The supplier (PQR) also encountered a problem with the installation of the woodwork that formed the structure for the bar counter. The team of carpenters with the responsibility of forming the structure misinterpreted the plans and built it 3 metres too long and this needed to be corrected to meet fire regulations. The remedial works to correct this problem required a range of trades: carpenters to shorten the wooden bar counter; carpet fitters and tilers to patch up the floor; painters and decorators to patch up the wall; and, an electrical contractor to reposition the overhead lights. The cost of this remedial work (£5000), along with the cost of replacing the floor tiles (£15000), effectively turned an anticipated profit of £10000 (and a return of 4% on the project) into a loss for the same amount.

As a result of these problems PQR also damaged its reputation for delivering very high quality, functional and cost-effective refurbishment solutions, to a very tight programme, within HSI's collaborative sourcing framework. This caused PQR major problems after the project. With a large number of potential suppliers offering similar refurbishment services from which to choose, other practitioners responsible for sourcing construction products and services steered away from PQR because of its poor reputation. Therefore, in addition to having a major impact on the profitability of this project, PQR experienced a significant decline in its revenue from HSI and other potential customers post-contractually.

16.5 Summary

The major finding from this case is that proactive sourcing approaches can actually result in a lose outcome for the supplier, but they can also be less than ideal for the buyer. In this case HSI achieved only a partial win. Ironically, it could have achieved a much better outcome if it had managed its demand across all of its refurbishment projects for new (and existing) properties in such a way that it could standardise its specification for key common components and, thereby, leverage the second or third-tier suppliers of these products and services, as effectively as it had been able to leverage PQR in the past.

The lesson for PQR as a supplier was that simply because a long-term collaborative and proactive sourcing relationship is in place does not mean that a beneficial performance outcome is guaranteed. In this relationship PQR accepted that it could not achieve a full win and that a partial win, with low to normal returns and guaranteed volumes of work in the future, was the best that could be hoped for. Unfortunately, because PQR failed to manage its own responsibilities effectively it had to accept the liability for the cost of making good poor workmanship. This ensured that on this project a financial loss was made. Unfortunately for PQR, this also had the knock-on effect of damaging its reputation with HSI and other customers. This was a clear lose outcome for the supplier.

Table 16.1 A summary of the relationship management approach and performance outcome

Nature of Relationship Management Approach	The client, with an ongoing portfolio of projects valued at approximately £16 million, was in a position to develop long-term collaborative supply management strategies with the objective of leveraging upstream suppliers to maximise value for money
	Despite a highly contested supply market, HSI recognised that proactive collaboration might provide additional benefits that an arm's-length and reactive approach would not
	This strategy focused on the development of a proactive *supplier development* relationship management approach with two construction firms for the provision of major refurbishment projects
	This involved the development of a totally transparent open-book cost approach
Nature of Buyer 'Partial Win'	Costs were lower than original budget by £10 000. The original estimate (target cost) was £250 000 and final contract value (construction cost) was £240 000
	The independent cost consultant audited the performance of the construction firm. It was discovered that further cost savings would have been possible if the proactive approach had been extended to include standardisation of key components
	Functional expectations were only met after remedial action by PQR to correct poor workmanship
	Despite the problems, the project was delivered to HSI on time
Nature of Supplier 'Loss'	PQR made a loss of £10 000 on this project
	This was largely due to the costs associated with overcoming poor workmanship, the need to replace incorrectly installed materials, and the need to pay a premium for the timely delivery of additional materials
	PQR damaged its reputation within the industry for delivering high quality solutions to very tight programmes. This impacted directly on future revenues and returns
Conclusions	This case demonstrates that nothing is guaranteed, either for the buyer or the supplier, just because they both agree to adopt a proactive approach to relationship management
	The power situation of buyer dominance in this case ought to have provided a win–partial win performance outcome favouring the buyer
	Unfortunately, the buyer's failure to understand the scope for additional leverage at the second and third-tiers of the supply chain resulted in a sub-optimal partial win outcome for it
	On the other hand, the supplier's failure to operate in a professional and competent manner resulted in a complete loss for it – both financially and to its reputation
	Competence in discharging roles and responsibilities effectively is still a prerequisite for both parties, even when they are operating within a proactive relationship framework

This case demonstrates, therefore, that buyers and suppliers will not achieve either their ideal or optimal outcome from proactive sourcing if they are not competent in discharging their responsibilities respectively. In the buyer's case the failure to understand the scope for leverage through the adoption of a *supply chain management* approach resulted in opportunities for additional cost reduction being foregone. In the supplier's case the failure to monitor workmanship effectively resulted in the work costing more than it had anticipated and the loss of its reputation. This was a partial win–lose outcome favouring the buyer that was clearly sub-optimal for both parties.

Table 16.1 gives a summary of the relationship management approach and performance outcome.

The housing development case: proactive supplier development with a buyer lose and supplier win outcome

17.1 Introduction

This case focuses on the procurement of a housing development by a specialist housebuilding firm, Luxury Housebuilders (LH), and a specialist manufacturer of timber frames, Nationwide Timber Frames (NTF). These firms both have extensive knowledge of the supply chains and markets in the construction industry and considerable experience of working together in a collaborative manner to deliver similar projects. The analysis shows that proactively managed buyer–supplier relationships based on collaboration can sometimes result in a loss for the buyer initiating them and a win for the supplier. Furthermore, the ability to achieve commercial and operational objectives may also be adversely affected by unexpected events such as changes to government legislation.

In this case, LH developed a proactive and collaborative procurement strategy. The strategy focused on the standardisation of design and specification of common elements, off-site prefabrication and other best practices transferred from an industrial manufacturing environment. In a fiercely competitive market, LH antici- pated that the successful implementation of this approach would enable it to achieve significant cost savings, increased functionality and improved programme time across its entire portfolio of projects. Unfortunately, unexpected changes to the original layout and design of the housing development resulted in LH failing to achieve any of these objectives.

The proactive sourcing approach developed by LH provided its preferred suppliers with a guaranteed revenue stream and relatively high profit levels for the construction industry. This provided these suppliers, including NTF, with the necessary incentives to make dedicated investments in the collaborative approach. It also provided them with the opportunity to achieve their commercial objectives without having to face the uncertainties typically associated with a short-term adversarial arm's-length relationship management approach. In this particular transaction, NTF was able to achieve a win outcome even though LH experienced a lose outcome.

17.2 Background to the case: the construction of a major new housing development

The construction of a major new housing development requires the integration of a large number of supply chains. Although the supply chain for the prefabricated timber frames, as shown in Figure 17.1, is similar to many construction products and services, the role of the construction firm (LH) may extend to more than the 'integrator'. For the majority of new housing developments the construction firm is also the client and sponsor of the project.

Government policy in the UK focuses on reducing the deficit in affordable housing by increasing the output of rented accommodation, shared ownership, key worker accommodation, low cost home ownership schemes and open market housing. These different types of housing are provided to the market by different organisations. Within this housing development case, LH was effectively the client for all of the properties except the affordable housing that had to be included to obtain planning permission. For these properties LH formed a collaborative relationship with a Housing Association, which as the Registered Social Landlord (RSL) provided the finance for the project.

Luxury Housebuilders (LH) developed a detailed design and specification for the products and services that they required from the upstream supply markets. Instead of sourcing in a reactive and non-collaborative manner, LH had developed a proactive and collaborative approach that involved the standardisation of design and specification before working with a small number of preferred suppliers. Unfortunately, the project was affected by a number of extraneous actors. First, there were restrictions related to the availability of land for development. The Government was attempting to ensure that the majority of new housebuilding occurred on brownfield land in urban areas. It was also seeking to ensure that a sequential approach to new development was adopted, that is brownfield sites should be developed before greenfield sites. Once it had identified a potential site, LH had to understand the likely return on investment so that it could decide whether to purchase the land. This was not a simple task because without a detailed design and specification (and full planning permission) the costs of construction and revenues were based on high levels of uncertainty.

Second, despite LH wanting to maximise its return on the investment, the decision regarding the physical configuration of the site was not solely dictated by commercial considerations. The planning process required all details of the development, such as layouts, designs, materials, external finishes and landscaping, to be approved by the local planning authority. In order to reduce the land required for new housing, the Government was also trying to increase the density of new developments to include between 12 and 20 dwellings per acre. To build at these densities meant that there would be more emphasis on terraced dwellings and less emphasis on detached properties.

The buyer (LH), therefore, had to work closely with the local planning authority to agree an appropriate mix of house types and sizes, which met the housing requirements of the local community, but was also consistent with the character of the wider area. The planning authority also tried to ensure that proposals for all new housing developments of a substantial scale (over fifteen dwellings) contained a proportion of affordable housing. For a site with over fifteen properties, the failure to provide this affordable housing as part of a proposed development, along with unsatisfactory layouts, designs, materials, external finishes and landscaping, would

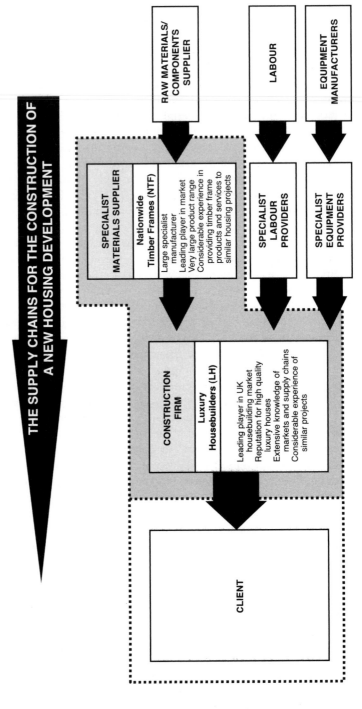

Figure 17.1 Construction supply chains for the construction of a new housing development

result in the refusal of the required full planning permission. A problem with obtaining full planning permission is often the reason for what can be a lengthy period between the site being acquired and the actual construction starting. For this project, changes to the original plan (the basis for the outline planning permission) that had to be made to obtain full planning permission led to a delay for the project and problems for the timber manufacturer (NTF).

The final factor impacting on LH's design and specification process was the adoption of innovative solutions for housebuilding and the use of industry best practices. Major players in the industry have recently been developing and testing new component systems and production processes in demonstration projects, as well as introducing partnering arrangements with their suppliers. The major firms have also brought in board-level expertise from manufacturing industry in order to implement lean supply chain management techniques.

As a result, the use of prefabrication and pre-assembly has become more prevalent within the housebuilding industry. The degree of prefabrication can take many forms as shown in Table 12.1. Many volume housebuilders have standardised their product by using standard plan forms built from bulk-purchased parts. The standard house types are regularly re-engineered by product development teams in response to feedback from customers. Research into what the customer wants is assessed continually and value for different types of end customer is defined in terms of price, locality and number of rooms, appearance and quality of construction. Modular industrialised housing systems are also being tested by a number of clients and contractors to reduce the cost and time of construction and provide tight quality control. Investment in R&D to develop better component systems to speed up construction can deliver housing with zero defects on-site, removing the need for expensive and time-consuming 'snagging'.

This case focuses on the supply of the timber frame components required for the construction of the houses on the development. These components were manufactured to a high quality and tolerance in a controlled factory environment and delivered to site for final assembly. The relationship between LH and NTF on this particular project is part of an ongoing collaborative relationship. The timber manufacturer (NTF) is one of two preferred suppliers that provide timber frames to LH's portfolio of projects.

The project involved the construction of a housing development on a brownfield site in an urban area. The original proposed plan was for 46 properties that consisted of a range of 2-, 3-, 4- and 5-bedroom detached houses, costing between £175 000 and £475 000, and a limited number of 2- and 3-bedroom terraced properties classified as affordable houses (to be managed by a Housing Association). After lengthy negotiations with the local authority it was agreed that for LH to obtain full planning permission the site would have to consist of 50 properties with a greater number of affordable properties:

- 16 affordable properties (8 two-bedroom and 8 three-bedroom properties within four separate terrace blocks)
- 8 two-bedroom properties (within two separate terrace blocks)
- 8 three-bedroom properties (4 detached and 4 semi-detached)
- 12 four-bedroom properties (8 detached and 4 semi-detached)
- 6 five-bedroom properties (all detached).

During the planning process LH was careful to ensure design strategies were compatible with local needs and that the residential environment would reflect

Front Elevation

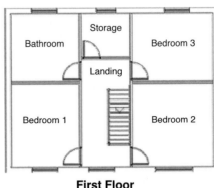

First Floor

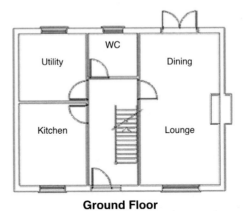

*Figure 17.2 The floor
layout of a typical three-
bedroom timber-framed
detached property*

Ground Floor

the true character of the area. This was achieved by using a range of materials and architectural details within the individual properties, as shown in the three-bedroom property in Figure 17.2. With the selection of special architectural features and special brick and timber products, including prefabricated timber frames, the challenge for LH was to provide high quality properties, at the lowest cost and within tight deadlines.

The buyer – Luxury Housebuilders (LH)

The buyer (LH) currently builds more than 4000 homes per annum, the majority being for open market sale. The firm is also actively involved in the delivery of affordable and social housing. In the fiercely competitive housebuilding market three factors determine whether a housebuilder makes a return on its investment. First, the early identification of the right opportunities is critical to business success. The buyer (LH)'s excellent regional knowledge and local research, combined with strong relationships with land agents and owners, ensures that the company maintains an ongoing supply of sites. At any one time LH is involved in the acquisition, pre-development and construction of over 250 individual projects.

The second factor relates to the ability of LH to understand and adhere to Local and Central Government policy. Once a site is acquired a decision has to be made in relation to the most profitable use of the land, but this has to take into account the many restrictions placed upon it by regulations. The buyer (LH) has considerable understanding of these factors as it had encountered few major difficulties in having major urban developments on brownfield sites approved in the past. The final factor relates to the ability of LH to implement appropriate industry best practices aimed at improved process efficiency and higher quality solutions. Five years previously, LH recognised that it was not obtaining value for money from its regular demand for construction. Problems with the supply of components and raw materials meant that projects were frequently delivered late, with defects and escalating costs. Subsequent claims led to long delays and LH recognised that its approach to supply management had to be changed.

In response to this poor performance, LH recognised the need to improve the efficiency and effectiveness of the project process through standardisation of design and specification for key inputs and the use of prefabrication and pre-assembly where appropriate. It became apparent, however, that for this 'innovative' strategy to be successfully implemented it had to be accompanied by innovation in supply and the complete re-engineering of the supply chains for these components. To achieve this LH had to understand its portfolio of demand for current and future projects and the structure of its construction supply chains and markets.

In addition, LH decided it was inefficient to tender every project individually and decided to develop closer collaborative relationships with key suppliers. The first stage of this process focused on the rationalisation of the supply base and selection of a small number of preferred 'partners' for the provision of critical construction activities and the manufacture and supply of key components. This approach also contained a number of safeguards against supplier opportunism, including open-book costing and the use of independent cost consultants. The buyer (LH) also used its extensive knowledge of the supply market to identify possibilities for prefabrication and pre-assembly of key components. In relation to the sourcing of prefabricated timber frames for houses (the focus of this case), LH recognised that it had neither the expertise nor the resources to undertake timber frame development, manufacture and supply internally.

After a successful trial of the prefabrication approach, LH decided to implement this strategy across all of its housebuilding projects and develop very close collaborative relationships with two specialist suppliers – Nationwide Timber Frames (NTF) and Specialist Timber Frames (STF). These suppliers were selected on the basis of the following criteria: cost, quality, experience, recent track record, an ability to implement best practices, flexibility and an ability to supply required quantities on time. Another factor was the central location of manufacturing facilities, which minimised delivery costs – a potentially major component of cost. Two suppliers were selected to avoid the risks associated with single sourcing

Table 17.1 A breakdown of the cost of the timber frames

Type of frame	Frame cost	Number	Total frame cost
Terrace block containing two 2-bedroom properties and two 3-bedroom properties (Affordable Housing)	£40 000	2 (8 properties)	£80 000
Terrace block containing four 2-bedroom properties	£37 500	2 (8 properties)	£75 000
Semi-detached 3-bedroom property	£22 500	2 (4 properties)	£50 000
Detached 3-bedroom property	£13 625	4	£55 000
Semi-detached 4-bedroom property	£30 000	3 (6 properties)	£90 000
Detached 4-bedroom property	£20 000	6	£120 000
Detached 5-bedroom property	£25 000	10	£250 000
Initial Estimate of Frame Cost for Entire Project			**£720 000**

and to ensure the required number of frames (for 6000 properties) could be delivered.

Unfortunately, problems with insufficient affordable properties led to major delays in obtaining full planning permission. The resulting very late change in the layout of the development had a significant impact on the total cost and profitability of the project. At the outset of the project NTF provided an initial price of £720 000 for the supply and erection of the timber frames for the entire development, as shown in Table 17.1.

The supplier – Nationwide Timber Frames (NTF)

Timber frame house construction, in its present form, has been used in the UK for hundreds of years. While timber-framed buildings still exist from the 12th century, nowadays, frames have the benefit of superior timber, modern preservatives and advanced building practices. The only difference between timber frame and conventional block and mortar constructions is simply that the internal leaf of block work is replaced by a timber frame structure. After the internal plasterboard finish the final appearance is no different to its masonry counterpart.

Timber-framed houses also have many advantages compared with houses manufactured using traditional methods. The components that make up a timber frame building are manufactured to the highest specifications and tolerances, using advanced methods and the latest equipment in a controlled factory environment. All the structural timbers are kiln dried and treated to protect them from insect attack and decay. Structural timbers are regularised (planed) for accuracy and ease of handling and, as a result, an average timber framed house (three-bedrooms) can be erected to a watertight shell within 48 hours of delivery. This speed of construction is achieved as the components are substantially completed in the factory and require only final assembly on-site. With such rapid construction the building is rapidly made watertight eliminating the ingress of moisture thereby reducing the chance of 'drying out' movement and shrinkage so often seen in traditional buildings.

By achieving a watertight and secure shell at such an early stage in the construction programme, the overall construction period is also substantially reduced and not affected by the weather. Bricklaying is taken off the critical path so that the internal fit-out can progress while the external cladding and site work is completed. Effective project management of these activities can enable the construction firm to reduce a contract programme by up to 50% compared to traditional building methods, and have the house occupied only five weeks after the structural frame delivery. Given these advantages it is surprising that only 10% of new homes use this technology.

Figure 17.3 shows how NTF re-engineered their design, engineering and manufacturing processes to reduce the time between order placement and completion of the manufacturing process from six to four weeks for regular customers. This enables them to build a new timber-framed house in a total of 6–8 weeks. This is significantly faster than the total programme time for a traditional brick and mortar property, which can take between 16–20 weeks to complete. The fact that timber-framed houses are quick to construct also has significant financial benefits including reduced site preparation costs, improved cash-flow, increased cost effectiveness, lower construction costs and improved profit margins.

The market for prefabricated and pre-assembled timber building frames is fragmented with a relatively large number of suppliers all holding low market shares. There is no single dominant player in the market. The supplier in this case, NTF, has a market share of around 15%. The market is also fragmented on the demand-side with a large number of potential end users with different needs and requirements in terms of size and appearance. Although timber frames can be used within the commercial, hotel, leisure, educational and healthcare sectors, the majority of the customers operate within the housebuilding market.

As a leading player, NTF has a strong financial base that allows it to invest heavily in the latest production technology and manufacturing techniques to remain at the forefront of design and innovation. In developing a sophisticated design and engineering capability, combined with its state-of-the-art manufacturing facilities for the just-in-time manufacture of alternative 'house types', the company is able to offer a value proposition based on enhancing the speed and quality of the build process, and improving the cost effectiveness of the final

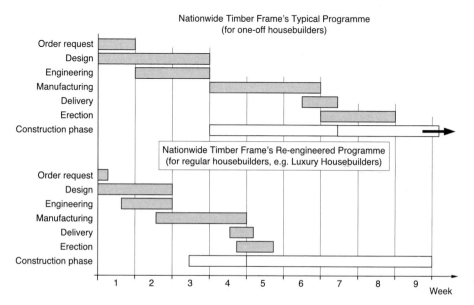

Figure 17.3 Nationwide timber frames re-engineered programme for regular customers

solution. Its continuous association with major housebuilding companies further strengthens the firm's strong financial position. The supplier (NTF) has worked with LH for twelve years and now manufactures timber-framed houses at a rate of 80 every working day in the dedicated production facility to meet the customer's current annual requirement of 2000 frames (for 3000 properties). In addition to the dedicated production facility, NTF has a focus on the efficiency of manufacturing and cost effectiveness through value engineering.

17.3 The buyer–supplier relationship management approach

In analysing the market and supply chain circumstances, and the buyer and supplier power resources, it is clear in this particular transaction that a power situation of *buyer–supplier interdependence* was evident. This balance of power ought to have resulted in a performance outcome of a buyer partial win and supplier partial win, but it actually resulted in a lose–win outcome favouring the supplier.

The construction firm (LH) – specialist material supplier (NTF) dyad

Construction firms are frequently faced with opportunistic behaviour from upstream suppliers, but this should not have been the case in this supply chain. The construction firm (LH) had extensive information, knowledge and understanding regarding the salience and nature of their external construction spend, the nature of the construction supply market and the appropriateness of available technologies from upstream suppliers. This understanding ought to have enabled LH to develop robust proactive supply strategies that resulted in the selection (and subsequent control and leverage) of competent and congruent upstream suppliers.

The construction firm's ability to leverage the specialist supplier is dependent, however, on market and supply chain circumstances and its possession of the key power resources within the relationship. In this case, the initial estimate for the total construction costs for the project was approximately £8 million of which £720 000 was attributable to the prefabricated timber frames. This single contract equated to a low share of NTF's total annual turnover (less than 1%) and may be considered to be of low importance, but when one considers the frequency of the transaction and resulting annual workload (2000 timber frames for 3000 properties) this expenditure accounted for a higher proportion of NTF's turnover (20%) and was seen as highly attractive by NTF. In terms of revenue and investment in internal processes LH was NTF's most important single customer.

The construction firm (LH)'s favourable position of relative power from the possession of high volume and frequent demand was further enhanced by the standardised nature of its design and specification that significantly reduced the level of complexity for both parties. In addition, the fact that there are a relatively limited number of equivalent customers in housebuilding also effectively limits the availability of alternative contracts and increased the difficulty for the supplier to switch. These switching costs were increased by the dedicated investments (dedicated manufacturing process) that NTF had made at its manufacturing plant to support LH's long-term collaborative and proactive sourcing approach.

In analysing the power resources of NTF it is important to acknowledge that the prefabricated timber frame manufacturer is operating within a fragmented market that has relatively high levels of contestation because there are many suppliers all with a relatively low market share. In such competitive markets, firms are usually unable to fully, or even partially, close the market to competition. The high level of contestation decreased within this supply market, however, as there was only a small number of manufacturers capable of supplying the required number of frames in a collaborative manner (using open-book costing) to the very strict deadlines and high quality levels demanded by LH.

The level of supplier scarcity is increased if any supplier has a relative superior competence in the manufacture of timber frames. With sufficient resources for investment in production processes and technology, the leading players (including NTF) are able to manufacture products that are either objectively superior in terms of their functional performance than those offered by their competitors, or that are perceived to be better as a result of the firms' reputations. This enables a firm to partially close the market, at least temporarily, and gain a higher share of the market than would otherwise have been possible.

In these circumstances, the power relationship between LH and NTF ought to have been one of *interdependence* and the performance outcome ought to have been one of partial win–partial win. Despite this, because LH faced difficulties in receiving full planning permission, and because NTF could create higher returns than LH assumed it would through the use of information asymmetry, a lose–win outcome occurred despite the buyer initiating the proactive (*supplier development*) sourcing approach.

17.4 Performance outcome from the buyer–supplier relationship

At the outset of the project LH was attempting operationally to maximise the functionality of all the elements of the finished houses and to ensure its reputation for selling very high quality houses was maintained. The construction firm (LH) was also attempting commercially to minimise the total costs of these elements (timber frames) and contract duration so that it could maximise the value for money it received from the supplier. This assumed a reasonable rather than exceptional rate of return for the supplier. In direct contrast, the objective of NTF was to increase or sustain the revenues and returns received from LH.

The construction firm (LH) ought to have been in a position to achieve most of its goals. It possessed a level of demand characterised by high volume and high frequency that was very attractive to NTF. Its relative power was also enhanced because the supplier was effectively locked into a long-term relationship because of the relatively high switching costs created by the dedicated investments and the buyer's understanding of the available technologies. The supplier (NTF) ought to have been deterred from acting opportunistically pre-contractually because of the promise of a regular demand, and post-contractually because of the threat of exit and relatively high switching costs created by the contract award and the establishment of a dedicated manufacturing facility. The buyer (LH) also attempted to minimise the potential for opportunistic behaviour by employing an independent cost consultant to examine the books of suppliers and monitor their performance.

On the other hand, NTF was not totally leveraged by LH and was also in a position to at least partially achieve its business objectives. First, the number of potential suppliers was restricted because there were only a small number of manufacturers capable of supplying the number of frames demanded by LH. Second, NTF had a very solid reputation for successfully delivering high quality products within a just-in-time manufacturing approach. Fundamental to retaining this reputation was NTF's ability to invest heavily in leading edge manufacturing technology, which ensured that it remained at the forefront of design and innovation. The buyer (LH) was NTF's single largest source of revenue and had invested in its manufacturing facility, but NTF was not totally dependent on LH because it had many other customers within a range of industries.

A summary of the dyad between LH and NTF and the performance outcome from the relationship is shown in Figure 17.4.

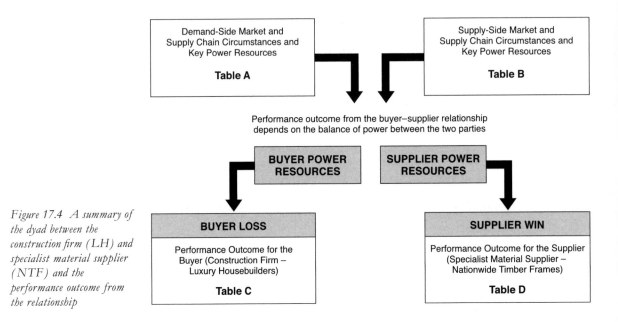

Figure 17.4 A summary of the dyad between the construction firm (LH) and specialist material supplier (NTF) and the performance outcome from the relationship

Table A Demand-Side Market and Supply Chain Circumstances and Key Power Resources

There are many construction firms acting as buyers from the multitude of construction supply markets, but significantly fewer buyers for prefabricated timber frames in the housebuilding sector

Luxury Housebuilders (LH) has a relatively low share of total ongoing projects to the value of £750 million. Therefore, the supplier in this case (NTF) has a **high dependency** on LH for revenue

LH has a regular need to source from the timber frame market, but there is **no current certainty/regularity** about specific requirements and volumes in specific areas of the UK

The requirements of LH are **relatively simple** (because of the standardisation of design and specification), but require supplier knowledge and expertise to manufacture

LH has **medium switching costs**, as although there are a large number of suppliers few have the same reputation for providing very high quality timber products

LH has a **relatively clear value proposition** – a house incorporating high quality elements, delivered on time and at an acceptable cost

LH is fully aware of the potential scope for **standardisation** of design and specification and **prefabrication** of key components common across the project. The use of timber frames manufactured off-site is an example of this

LH has **relatively low search costs**, as it has extensive knowledge and understanding about construction products and services, including timber frames, and the strategies of the industry players

Table B Supply-Side Market and Supply Chain Circumstances and Key Power Resources

There are many suppliers in the total construction market but fewer suppliers capable of providing prefabricated timber-framed solutions to the client's requirements

In this case, the initial contract value (total construction costs) for the project was approximately £8 million of which £720 000 was originally attributable to the prefabricated timber frames. This contract value rose to £800 000 when the construction firm (LH) had to change the design and configuration of the site

While this single project accounts for a **relatively low share (<1%) of the annual turnover of NTF** when one considers the annual workload from this particular construction firm (in total 2000 frames for 3000 properties accounting for approximately £35 million of revenue), this expenditure accounts for a relatively **high share of NTF's annual turnover** (approximately 20%). NTF is therefore **relatively highly dependent** on LH for this revenue

In addition to the guaranteed revenue, NTF considers LH's business to be **relatively attractive** as there are low costs associated with servicing the contract

NTF has **low/medium switching costs**

NTF's offerings (taken as a whole) are **relatively standardised** but there is **very limited customisation** to the specific requirements of LH

NTF has a **very strong brand image** and **reputation** for delivering innovative products of a very high quality

NTF has **very limited information asymmetry** advantages over LH

Table C Performance Outcome for the Construction Firm (LH) – Buyer Loss

Development costs for the construction firm, Luxury Housebuilders (LH), higher than original budget by 5% (£400 000). The original estimate was £8 million and final cost was £8.4 million

The extra cost was attributable to the numerous changes to the original design and specification that had to be made to overcome planning problems

A major element within this extra cost was the timber frames. Their cost was higher than original budget by 11% (£80 000). The original estimate was £720 000 and final cost £900 000. This figure also contained £100 000 of unused frames

Delivery of project late because of delays associated with:

    Requirement to get new planning approvals as minor configuration of site changed the number of affordable properties

    Lead-time on alternative larger timber frames

Functional expectations of client (and LH) not fully met after supply of alternative frames made from inferior materials

---

Table D Performance Outcome for the Specialist Manufacturer (NTF) – Supplier Win

Nationwide Timber Frames (NTF) made a visible profit of £55 000 or 6% on this project, but was able to make a real return of 10% due to efficiencies that were not passed on to LH due to the incompetence of LH's cost consultants

This figure included extra revenues from the client in relation to the supply of extra timber frames to overcome the numerous changes to the client's original design and specification. These were made during the construction phase

NTF enhanced its reputation within the industry for delivering high quality innovative projects to a prestige client

The reputation for innovation and cost-effective solutions and an ability to work in a collaborative manner enabled NTF to generate additional revenue from other major housebuilders against whom it could leverage the knowledge and expertise acquired from working with this client to earn high returns

---

This indicates that LH and NTF both possessed significant power resources and one might expect both of them only to be able to partially achieve their commercial and operational objectives. This is the normal outcome that one would expect from an interdependent power situation. In this case, however, LH failed to achieve any of its business objectives while NTF fully achieved its objectives.

Table 17.2 *A revised breakdown of the cost of the timber frames*

Type of frame	Frame cost	Number	Total frame cost
Terrace block containing two 2-bedroom properties and two 3-bedroom properties (Affordable Housing)	£40 000	2 (8 properties)	£80 000
Terrace block containing four 2-bedroom properties	£37 500	2 (8 properties)	£75 000
Semi-detached 3-bedroom property	£22 500	2 (4 properties)	£50 000
Detached 3-bedroom property	£13 625	4	£55 000
Semi-detached 4-bedroom property	£30 000	3 (6 properties)	£90 000
Detached 4-bedroom property	£20 000	6	£120 000
Detached 5-bedroom property	£25 000	10	£250 000
Initial Estimate of Frame Cost for Entire Project			**£720 000**
ADDITIONS TO ORIGINAL ORDER			
Terrace block containing two 2-bedroom properties and two 3-bedroom properties (Affordable Housing)	£40 000	2 (8 properties)	£80 000
Total Frame Cost for Entire Project			**£800 000**
FRAMES NOT REQUIRED			
Detached 5-bedroom property	£25 000	4	£100 000
Total Cost of Unused Frames			**£100 000**

In terms of final cost, LH was faced with an increased and unanticipated level of expenditure on replacement timber frames that significantly exceeded its original estimate. At the outset of the project, it was estimated (based on the outline planning permission) that the total costs of prefabricated timber frames was £720 000. After lengthy negotiations with the local authority this figure rose to £800 000, as shown in Table 17.2. The reason for the increase was the requirement for LH to change the original plans for the development to meet the local authority's guidelines for affordable housing. An additional eight affordable properties (4 two-bedroom and 4 three-bedroom properties within two terrace blocks) were included at the expense of four five-bedroom properties. This also meant that the final total contract value for the timber frames (£800 000) included four unused frames worth £100 000. This meant that the cost for timber frames escalated to £900 000, which substantially reduced the profitability of the project.

The late changes to the plans of the development and the specification provided to the supplier were necessary to overcome incorrect assumptions regarding full planning permission made by LH. In addition to the cost implications, the late placement of the order for the additional frames led to delays to the contract programme. The larger timber frames were subject to considerably longer lead-times. To reduce this lead-time to an absolute minimum, and minimise the impact on the internal fit-out of the properties, LH diverted similar frames from another project. These frames were made of slightly inferior materials (structural softwood rather than layers of structural grade pine laminated together). The buyer (LH) experienced a number of problems with the assembly of the inferior quality frames that further delayed the internal and external completion of these properties.

On this particular project, NTF made an overall visible profit of £55 000 for all the timber frames that it supplied to the construction firm at a total cost (including unused frames) of £900 000. This equated to a 6% return for the project as a whole. Given the open-book approach, this level of profit was accepted as reasonable by LH and benchmarked by the independent cost consultancy. This was not, however, the overall profit made by NTF. The cost consultant used on the project failed to understand the manufacturing efficiencies that NTF had been able to engineer and did not fully monitor the commercial gains that were made in new production processes internally and value and process optimisation strategies with NTF's own suppliers. This allowed NTF to achieve a full win outcome of 10% returns, which it did not communicate to LH.

In addition, the frames were acknowledged by industry experts to be very innovative in terms of design and integration into the construction process, and NTF was also able to enhance its reputation in the market by successfully delivering a very high quality product, in a very flexible manner, within very strict deadlines and as part of an ongoing cost reduction programme. This assisted NTF to win a number of contracts in the future. The supplier (NTF), therefore, maximised its returns from the relationship with LH and was also in a position to increase profitable revenues from other customers.

17.5 Summary

The major finding from this case is that buyers developing a proactive approach to sourcing may not always achieve a nonzero-sum outcome if they are faced with unexpected changes in the environment that destroy their own commercial and operational business model. In such circumstances the proactive buyer may have to shoulder the additional costs of any changes as these costs may not be retrieved from the preferred suppliers (or passed on to the downstream players in the supply chain).

In this case the situation facing the buyer was extreme. The local government planning changes forced the housebuilder (LH) into unexpected changes that caused a major increase in the costs of timber frames from £720 000 to £900 000, which meant that it was faced with a significant loss for the transaction. The supplier (NTF), on the other hand, was able to generate a full win for itself – in the form of double-digit returns – by declaring only a 6% return and then hiding the additional benefits it had been able to generate for itself through implementing the learning from working with the buyer.

The primary reason for this zero-sum outcome with a win–lose favouring the supplier was the relative incompetence of the cost consultants employed by LH. While employing cost consultants is one of the tactics developed by proactive buyers, especially when they lack the capabilities internally themselves, there is always the problem for the buyer that it is then at the mercy of the competence of its cost consultancy suppliers. In this case the proactive buyer was let down by its cost consultants and was forced (without knowing it) to allow its supplier to make above normal returns.

A summary of the relationship management approach and performance outcome is shown in Table 17.3.

Table 17.3 A summary of the relationship management approach and performance outcome

Nature of Relationship Management Approach	The construction firm, with a continuous portfolio of new housing developments, was in a position to use its extensive knowledge and understanding of its construction requirements to develop collaborative and proactive sourcing strategies with the objective of leveraging upstream construction suppliers to maximise value for money These strategies focused on the development of long-term proactive sourcing relationships with key first-tier suppliers (*supplier development*)

Nature of Buyer 'Loss'	The construction firm was faced with extra costs as a result of the numerous changes to the original design and specification that had to be made to overcome planning problems
	
	The cost of the timber frames was higher than original budget by 11% (£80 000). The original estimate was £720 000 and final cost £900 000 when unused frames are factored into the equation
	
	Functional expectations of construction firm not met after supply of alternative frames made from inferior materials
	
	Delivery of project late because of delays associated with:
	    Requirement to get new planning approvals as minor configuration of site changed the number of affordable properties
	    Lead-time on alternative larger timber frames

Nature of Supplier 'Win'	The supplier made a visible profit of £55 000 on this project but its real return was much higher at 10% rather than 6% because it was able to hide additional profits due to the incompetence of the buyer's cost consultant This figure included extra revenues from the supply of extra timber frames to overcome the numerous changes to the original design and specification The supplier also enhanced its reputation within the industry for delivering high quality innovative projects to a prestige client This led to additional revenue from other major housebuilders against whom it could leverage the knowledge and expertise acquired from working with this client to earn higher returns
Conclusions	Proactive buyers have to be careful about how they educate and monitor their preferred suppliers Despite educating their suppliers to undertake proactive sourcing approaches, if buyers fail to effectively monitor their behaviour post-contractually there will still be scope for post-contractual opportunism This is particularly a risk if the buyer and its cost consultants do not understand how the supplier is able to make improvements to its operational processes and generate higher returns from doing so When this occurs the risks of nonzero-sum outcomes favouring the buyer turning into zero-sum outcomes favouring the supplier are high

The petrol filling station case: proactive supply chain management with a buyer lose and supplier partial win outcome

18.1 Introduction

This case focuses on the procurement and supply management of a new petrol filling station facility by a petrochemical company, Performance Petrol (PP), and a first-tier construction firm, First-Class Forecourt Developments (FFD), a specialist design and build provider of petrol forecourt solutions. Both firms have considerable experience of working together to deliver similar projects. In this case, the client (PP) was able to use its regular and high-volume demand, combined with its extensive knowledge and understanding of construction supply chains and markets, to restructure its construction expenditure and develop a proactive relationship management approach.

The approach started with *supplier development*, and the thinking was then extended into the supply chain as a whole to create a *supply chain management* approach including key component suppliers. To enhance the level of value for money received, this approach relied on the effective use by PP of its power resources as a buyer to leverage construction suppliers. Within this long-term collaborative sourcing framework PP dominated its preferred construction firms, who were willing supplicants in the relationship. The construction firms were leveraged most of all by PP's regular and high-volume portfolio of standardised projects which made them a highly attractive and relatively simple account to service. Performance Petrol's commercial position was further enhanced by the use of off-site prefabrication for key elements of its projects and open-book cost management.

Despite the generally favourable power position that PP had been able to engineer for itself with these structural power resources, in this particular case they failed to achieve a positive performance outcome from its relationship with FFD. Unexpected problems with ground conditions led to major problems with the installation of the tanks contained within the original forecourt design. A late change was required to the number, capacity and layout of the tanks that led to a situation in which PP failed to achieve any of its objectives in relation to cost, quality and delivery. The fact that the problems were totally attributable to PP's actions meant that FFD was still able to partially attain its commercial and operational objectives. The contractor (FFD) was, however, not able to fully achieve its ideal goals because of the leverage still available to PP given the nature of the long-term collaborative relationship, so that the structural power resources still tended to favour the buyer.

18.2 Background to the case: the construction of a petrol filling station

The construction of a new petrol filling station requires the management of a number of supply chains, as illustrated in Figure 18.1. Instead of using a reactive and arm's-length approach, the client (PP) had developed a more proactive and collaborative approach to construction supply management. After developing an outline functional specification, in conjunction with internal and external professional services, it selects one of its preferred contractors and works with that contractor to develop the detailed specification. At this stage PP involved not only the construction firm (FFD in this case) but also the preferred specialist suppliers of key components. As will be discussed later, PP's proactive construction sourcing approach was based on a high degree of standardisation and prefabrication of these components.

The need to regularly replace its petrol storage tanks at its filling stations creates a commercial dilemma for PP. The excavation, removal and replacement of these tanks is both a lengthy and an expensive task that can interrupt the operation of the filling station for up to six months. Given the costs involved, the impact it has on revenue flow and the need to maintain a strong brand image within the highly competitive marketplace, PP normally combines the renewal of the tanks with the reconstruction of the entire site.

The case analyses the relationship between PP and FFD in a project for the reconstruction of a large filling station. As part of PP's ongoing construction programme, the project required: the dismantling of the existing canopy, demolition of old structures, excavation and removal of the old tanks, installation of new tanks and pipeworks, construction of the new forecourt building, and erection of the new portal frame canopy. The project also included all the associated external works including: new access roads, a reinforced concrete pavement and landscaping of adjoining land.

At the outset of the project PP provided FFD with an outline functional specification for the proposed solution. In conjunction with external professional advisers and specialist material suppliers, both parties used this outline document as the basis for the collaborative development of the detailed design and specification. All parties were able to draw on their own knowledge and experience of working in a highly specialised and regulated environment to develop a solution to meet PP's commercial and operational objectives – lowest feasible total cost of ownership and highest feasible level of functionality. Before the construction activity started the target cost for the project was £500 000.

The buyer – Performance Petrol (PP)

The buyer (PP) had an annual capital expenditure budget of between £20 million and £25 million for the reconstruction of petrol filling stations with petrol tanks in need of replacement. The average construction costs (including removal of old

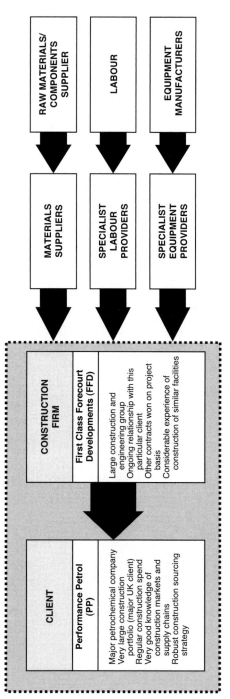

Figure 18.1 Construction supply chains for the construction of a petrol filling station

tanks and demolition of existing facilities) for the reconstruction of a petrol station was estimated to be approximately £480 000. This level of regular expenditure enabled PP to redevelop approximately 50 sites per annum. The size and regularity of this expenditure meant that PP was a major client (or customer) in the construction industry, and especially for those construction firms wishing to participate in forecourt modular design and build work. Its level of annual expenditure on the repair and refurbishment of other facilities further enhanced PP's standing within the industry.

A fundamental business driver for PP was the need to operate its combined petrol station and retail sites to their full commercial potential. To achieve this, and support its primary business of selling petrol, the planned reconstruction of its portfolio of forecourts was seen as a critical activity. In the past PP had not always dedicated the required resources to construction procurement to achieve value for money. Prior to the development of its proactive sourcing approach, PP was not receiving optimal value for money because individual projects were frequently delivered late, with considerable uncertainty over final costs, and the quality of the final solution was often unacceptable. Subsequent claims took a long time to be settled leading PP to recognise that it had to re-engineer its reactive approach to construction management.

Performance Petrol eventually recognised that it could fundamentally improve the efficiency and effectiveness of its management of its construction supply chains if it leveraged its relatively high volume and regular demand and adopted a more proactive approach. It understood that this required it to minimise project cycle time so that revenue could be earned as soon as possible, while also reducing construction costs to their lowest feasible figure so as to maximise the number of filling stations that could be built for the same level of capital expenditure. To achieve this, PP opted for the standardisation of design and specification of key inputs and the use of prefabricated modular components whenever appropriate. It also recognised that for this approach to be implemented effectively a much more detailed understanding of construction markets and supply chains would be necessary.

In the development of this proactive approach, PP decided to incentivise a number of preferred contractors with a long-term commitment to work and guaranteed margins. This offer was contingent, however, on the suppliers being prepared to work with it on construction efficiencies in a transparent manner, using open-book costing, and with the intervention of independent cost consultants for the development of detailed target costing models. After the initial offer to suppliers, PP chose to develop very close collaborative relationships with three construction firms. Three construction providers were selected to avoid the risks associated with single sourcing and to ensure that the competitive tension guaranteed high quality cost-effective solutions were delivered on time. Performance Petrol (PP) also played an active role in the procurement of specific supply inputs to guard against supplier dependency and opportunism. It then allocated its workload to its preferred contractors (and specialist suppliers) on a fairly equitable basis according to their supply capabilities. Performance Petrol anticipated that this would allow it to dominate the relationship and achieve a full win outcome for itself, with only a partial win for the preferred suppliers.

In this case, PP selected First Class Forecourt Developments (FFD) from its list of preferred contractors. The supplier (FFD) was selected because of its experience in delivering projects to a very high quality and within tight timescales. This specific project was its seventy-fifth for PP.

The supplier – First Class Forecourt Developments (FFD)

The supplier (FFD) provided a target cost of £500 000 to reconstruct the petrol filling station. To arrive at this figure FFD divided the detailed scope of works, developed in conjunction with PP, into a series of work packages for which competitive tenders were obtained from an agreed list of specialist sub-contractors and material suppliers. Once these tenders had been analysed for technical and commercial compliance, the overall net cost of the construction work was established. To this figure, PP added an agreed percentage on-cost for its construction and project management responsibilities, company overheads and profit.

The supplier (FFD) is a medium-sized player in the construction industry with an annual turnover of between £40 million and £45 million. The company specialises in the excavation, removal, replacement and decommissioning of petrol tanks and the demolition and reconstruction of the facilities on the forecourt. The supplier (FFD) has the construction and civil engineering capability and the experience to tackle any size of petrol station or forecourt contract. This provides FFD with a high level of control over any project, and particularly its timing. As a result, the only occasion when projects exceed their programmed time is when it encounters serious ground pollution problems that have not been identified in the ground investigation (as in this case).

The firm has a solid reputation within the supply market for delivering high quality and innovative solutions to clients within high-risk industrial environments where health and safety (and adherence to Construction (Design and Management) regulations) is paramount. This reputation is also built on a track record of delivering client's precise functional needs, and completing projects on time and within costs constraints.

18.3 The buyer–supplier relationship management approach

In analysing the relationship between PP and FFD the key buyer and supplier power resources available to both parties are discussed. The analysis shows that even in a proactive sourcing approach the buyer can sometimes lose when post-contractual circumstances conspire against it. On the other hand, when a long-term collaborative relationship is in place, the supplier can sometimes receive a partial win even when the buyer loses.

The client (PP) – construction firm (FFD) dyad

The client (PP)'s ability to leverage FFD was dependent on its possession of key power resources and its ability to monitor FFD to reduce the scope for opportunism pre- and post-contractually. In this case, PP had a regular and relatively high volume of demand and was supported by external professional services. This gave PP the opportunity to develop its proactive sourcing approach.

The initial target price for the project was £500 000, with a programmed duration of four months. This project provided, therefore, a low share of FFD's total annual turnover (less than 1%) and, if considered alone, would have been of limited attractiveness to its business. The potential and actual frequency of demand from PP, however, provided an annual workload of 15 to 20 of the 50 filling stations reconstructed by PP. This meant that the PP account was extremely attractive because it accounted for a high proportion of FFD's annual turnover. The client (PP) was FFD's major source of revenue and a key account.

The client (PP)'s relative dominance in the relationship was also enhanced by the standardised nature of its design and specification of key components. As a result, PP understood in detail the construction products and services it required and the supply market from which they were to be sourced. In addition, the fact that there were a limited number of equivalent petrochemical companies requiring new filling stations increased the attractiveness of the PP account. The problem of switching to alternative customers was exacerbated by the dedicated investments (a specialised project management application for PP project work) that FFD had made for PP on its internal IT infrastructure.

The client (PP)'s possession of these power resources enabled it to incentivise FFD (and two other first-tier construction providers), as well as a number of professional service providers and key second-tier specialist material suppliers, to work in a highly collaborative and open-book manner that was based on supply chain management principles. On the supply-side of this relationship, FFD was in a relatively weak position and was forced to accept PP's leverage of its position. This was largely a result of the fact that it was operating in a highly contested market with relatively low switching costs for the buyer (PP).

These factors nullified the fact that FFD was the largest provider of forecourt solutions to major petrochemical companies, and had a solid reputation for consistently delivering very high levels of value for money within a specialised and controlled environment. The client (PP) also understood the structure of the construction supply chains and markets through which its required products and services were created. Its possession of this key commercial and operational information prevented post-contractual opportunistic behaviour by FFD in the pursuit of higher returns.

This implied that PP ought to have been in a position to force FFD into accepting a win–partial win outcome favouring the buyer. Unfortunately for PP, despite its position of dominance over FFD and the use of a highly competent professional services provider to stop supplier opportunism, a number of un-anticipated problems during the construction of the petrol filling station meant that PP failed to achieve any of its basic commercial and operational goals. This meant that PP experienced a lose outcome even though the supplier, FFD, experienced a partial win outcome.

18.4 Performance outcome from the buyer–supplier relationship

Operationally, PP attempted to enhance the speed of project delivery, maximise the functionality of the completed petrol filling station and also ensure that its brand image was protected. Commercially, PP also expected to be able to minimise the total costs of ownership by limiting the returns of the supplier to a relatively low level, while also engineering cost reductions from key components in the supply chain. The supplier (FFD) was forced to accept this outcome because of the promise of additional work and because PP was its key account, with few similarly valuable customers available to it.

In practice, although PP ought to have been able to leverage FFD to achieve a full win from this relationship, a series of problems during the construction phase presented FFD with the opportunity to increase its revenue, which PP and its advisers could do little about. Furthermore, despite this situation of structural power favouring the buyer, PP failed to achieve its ideal performance outcome and ended up failing completely to achieve its commercial and operational objectives. Due to unforeseen ground conditions, the poor condition of the existing petrol storage tanks and problems in supplying alternatives, PP could not prevent the costs of ownership from increasing and the functionality of the solution from decreasing. Ironically, despite the collaborative relationship between PP and FFD, the fact that PP carried the risk meant that FFD was still able to achieve a partial win from the relationship, even though PP lost out in the end.

A summary of the dyad between PP and FFD and the performance outcome from the relationship is shown in Figure 18.2.

Due to unexpected problems that occurred during the excavation and removal of the old, and in the installation of the new, petrol tanks, PP was faced with an increased level of expenditure on earthworks, soil treatment and alternative petrol tanks. This meant that the total costs for the project significantly exceeded its original estimate. Initially, it had been estimated that the total cost for the filling station would be £500 000. This figure rose by 20% to £600 000 after PP had to change the position of the petrol tanks to avoid underground power cables of which it had been unaware, and FFD had to procure tanks of a completely different dimension and thickness to replace those originally specified.

The changes to the design and specification were made as a direct result of the failure by PP to commission a full site ground survey and environmental soil report. As part of its proactive strategy for construction supply management, PP had standardised the design of key components in the pursuit of lower input costs. This included the petrol tanks for all its new filling stations. During the excavation and removal of the existing tanks on this project a problem arose that meant that the proposed tanks would be unsuitable. The soil surrounding the tanks was contaminated and with the tanks being removed by 'hot cutting' it was necessary for FFD to excavate significantly more material than anticipated.

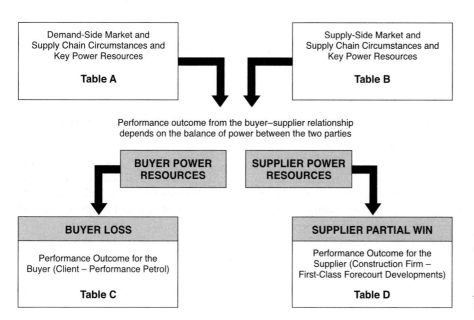

Figure 18.2 A summary of the dyad between the client (PP) and construction firm (FFD) and the performance outcome from the relationship

Table A Demand-Side Market and Supply Chain Circumstances and Key Power Resources

There are many buyers in the total construction market but fewer buyers for specialist solutions for petrol filling stations (especially prestige clients with a regular construction portfolio)

If this project is taken on its own, Performance Petrol (PP) has a relatively low share of the total construction market with a project value of £500 000. If this single project is taken in isolation the supplier (FFD) has a **low dependency** on PP for revenue

PP has a **regular need** to source from the construction market with an annual requirement for the reconstruction of approximately 50 filling stations. Therefore, with this ongoing requirement FFD has a **potentially high dependency** on PP for revenue

The requirements of PP are **relatively simple** (because of the standardisation of design and specification for common elements), but the hazardous environment requires considerable supplier knowledge and expertise

PP has **medium/high switching costs** as although there are a large number of construction firms, few have the same competence and capability as FFD for delivering very high quality projects within very tight deadlines

The client, PP, through the development of a robust sourcing strategy, has a **very clear value proposition** – a high quality project delivered to very strict deadlines and at an acceptable cost. However, there are minor problems with this value proposition as there is a slight over-emphasis on quality with over-specification and gold-plating of components that directly impact on safety

With an ongoing construction portfolio for similar projects, PP is fully aware of the potential scope for **standardisation** of design and specification and **prefabrication** for key components common across the projects

PP has **relatively low search costs**, as it has extensive knowledge and understanding about construction products and services and the strategies of the leading industry players

Table B Supply-Side Market and Supply Chain Circumstances and Key Power Resources

There are many suppliers in the total construction market but fewer suppliers capable of providing high quality solutions to the client's requirements and with the necessary expertise and experience to operate within a highly specialised and controlled environment

In this case, the contract value for the project was approximately £500 000. This figure equated to an average project for the construction firm, First Class Forecourt Developments (FFD)

While this single project accounts for a **relatively low share of FFD's annual turnover** (<1%), when one considers the frequency of the transaction and resulting annual workload (15–20 similar filling stations), this expenditure accounts for a relatively **high share of FFD's annual turnover**

Given this workload, FFD is relatively **highly dependent** on the client, Performance Petrol (PP), for this revenue

In addition to the guaranteed revenue, FFD considers PP's business to be **relatively attractive** as there are low costs associated with servicing the contract and it has considerable experience with similar projects in the petrochemical market

FFD has **medium/high switching costs**

FFD's offerings are relatively **standardised** to the specific requirements of PP and delivered to strict imposed time deadlines

FFD has a **very strong brand image** and **reputation**. This reputation has been strengthened by constantly delivering high quality projects on time, within financial budgets to a prestige client

Unlike relationships with other clients, FFD has very limited **information asymmetry** advantages over PP due to the open-book costing approach

Despite careful examination of client and utility company plans and the possession of a certificate from the electricity company guaranteeing that the power to the site had been shut off, FFD still managed, during the excavation of this additional material, to uncover two live 11 kV electricity cables that were not supplying the site, but simply passing under it. This 'hidden electricity line' presented an extremely dangerous situation, given the potentially explosive fuel/air mixture in the tanks and the thousands of volts of electricity.

Table C Performance Outcome for the Client (PP) – Buyer Loss

The cost of the project was higher for the client, Performance Petrol (PP), than budget by 20%. The original estimate was £500 000 and final cost was £600 000

The £100 000 of extra cost was due to:

Extra groundworks and soil decontamination (£35 000)

Extra costs incurred by the construction firm (FFD) to ensure the timely delivery of critical path activities (£40 000)

A premium for the delivery of the larger capacity tanks and pipes to very short timescales (£25 000)

Despite the problems the project was delivered on time. However, without the agreement the late change to the design and specification would have led to a significant delay

Original functional expectations not met. The change to the design (number, capacity and layout of tanks) meant that only 12 petrol pumps could be installed into the final solution instead of the 16 planned

Table D Performance Outcome for the Construction Firm (FFD) – Supplier Partial Win

First Class Forecourt Developments (FFD) made a normal profit of £20 000 (a 4% return) on this project

This figure was boosted by the extra payments received to cover additional costs (e.g. extra labour) to ensure delivery of the project on time

FFD maintained its reputation within the industry for delivering quality solutions within very strict time deadlines and an ongoing collaboration framework

This did not damage its ability to win other work from other major clients within the same industrial sector – petrochemicals

FFD was also considering using its expertise in tank installation, removal and decommissioning to acquire work in other sectors such as chemicals and water

Construction work had to stop while PP and FFD considered the alternatives, as it is illegal to run electric lines over, under or in close proximity to tanks. After careful consideration of the issues and cost implications (identified through the open-book approach), it was decided to move the location of the tanks to another part of the site, but this meant that smaller-diameter tanks had to be used to cope with the higher loads to be exerted on the tanks by the planned traffic running above it. In addition to the cost of the extra groundworks and soil decontamination (£35 000) and the cost of FFD expediting subsequent critical path activities (£40 000), the sourcing of these alternative tanks caused further problems in relation to the cost, functionality and delivery of the final solution.

To ensure the project was still delivered on time, and to minimise the commercial impact on PP of failing to have revenue flows on schedule, FFD agreed to pay the full market price for the tanks and extra pipework without its usual discount. The supplier (FFD) was unconcerned with this additional cost as the problem arose from PP's failure to conduct a thorough ground investigation – which was PP's duty within the collaborative framework – and it knew that it would be fully recovered on completion of the project. The buyer (PP) accepted the additional cost implications of £25 000 (on top of the extra £75 000), because it identified this as the best option and knew that it would be more than offset by the returns on the extra fuel sold through the pumps. The tanks were on site within one week, which meant that the project was delivered on time.

The change to the design, specification and location of the tanks had a significant impact on the functionality of the filling station. Given the space restraints, the use of smaller-diameter tanks meant that the total volumetric capacity for the four tanks was reduced by 25%. This meant that the forecourt could only have 12 petrol pumps instead of the 16 originally planned. The buyer (PP) accepted this fact, but acknowledged that it would lead to delays for customers and impact on future revenues. Given the problems outlined previously, therefore, PP received a completed solution that was sub-optimal, that affected its reputation with its customers, and at a higher cost than it should have done. This was a lose performance outcome for PP.

On the other hand, FFD made an overall profit of £20 000 on this particular project. This represented a 4% return on an overall contract value with PP of £500 000. Given the open-book approach, this level of profit (normal returns) was acceptable to PP and was verified and benchmarked by the independent cost consultancy as consistent with the level of returns that were normally achieved by FFD when operating on PP projects. This return meant that FFD was able to achieve the partial win outcome from the relationships that was normal, that is it made a normal profit and did not damage its own reputation within the industry for delivering high quality and cost-effective solutions within very strict time deadlines, and as part of an ongoing collaborative and proactive relationship management framework.

18.5 Summary

The major finding from this case is that proactive sourcing does not always ensure that the buyer will achieve a favourable nonzero-sum outcome. In this case, the buyer failed to achieve any of its basic operational and commercial objectives – although it did receive a completed petrol station capable of servicing its customers. In receiving this completed project the buyer had to pay more than anticipated for what was a sub-optimal solution. This was clearly a lose outcome from the buyer's point of view.

Since the problems on the project arose as a result of the buyer's failure to undertake the necessary groundwork analysis, the sub-optimal outcome could not be blamed on the supplier who, in this case, had behaved in an exemplary manner under the terms of the collaborative sourcing framework agreed upon by both parties. In this circumstance the supplier was still able to achieve the partial win outcome that had been agreed between the buyer and supplier before the project commenced. The case demonstrates, therefore, that just because a proactive approach is agreed upon – with a win–partial win nonzero-sum outcome expected – this does not mean that this will always occur in practice.

Since uncertainty and risk still exist, even in proactively managed construction projects, which firm carries the risk and uncertainty is still a significant issue for both parties. This case demonstrates that buyers adopting a proactive sourcing approach with suppliers may in fact suffer a loss of leverage. This is because they cannot seek to blame their supplier or pass risk on to the supplier unfairly if they are operating in a repeat game sourcing relationship based on agreed principles. In this case, because the buyer was principled, it was forced to accept the costs of its own incompetence. As a result, it experienced a lose outcome, while having to accept that the supplier was entitled to the partial win outcome that was the norm in the long-term principled relationship established over time by both parties.

A summary of the relationship management approach and performance outcome is given in Table 18.1.

Table 18.1 A summary of the relationship management approach and performance outcome

Nature of Relationship Management Approach	PP, with an annual need to reconstruct 50 similar filling stations, was in a position to use its extensive knowledge and understanding of its construction expenditure to develop a proactive sourcing approach with the objective of effectively leveraging upstream construction suppliers
	This strategy focused on the development of a proactive *supply chain management* relationship management approach with key first- and second-tier construction suppliers
	The relationship with the supplier in this case (FFD) was principled and had been in place for a number of years, with over 75 similar projects having been completed between the two parties
Nature of Buyer 'Loss'	The final cost of the solution was higher than original budget by 20% (£100 000)
	The additional costs were attributable to the extra groundworks and soil decontamination costs incurred by FFD to ensure the timely delivery of critical path activities, as well as a premium incurred for the delivery of larger than expected capacity tanks and pipes to very short timescales
	The fact that the final solution had fewer pumps meant that the solution did not meet the original functional expectations of PP
Nature of Supplier 'Partial Win'	FFD made a profit of £20 000 (a return of 4%) on this project. This was agreed through an open-book approach
	This was similar to the average return for FFD from the construction of other similar facilities
	FFD maintained its reputation within the industry for delivering high quality cost-effective solutions within very strict time deadlines and an ongoing collaborative framework
Conclusions	The case demonstrates that problems of risk and uncertainty do not disappear just because buyers and suppliers enter into long-term proactive sourcing relationships
	In this case, the buyer (PP) failed to undertake the necessary analysis of ground conditions to enable a proper design and specification of requirements
	As a result it was the buyer (PP) that was forced, because of the principled approach it had adopted with FFD in its long-term proactive relationship approach, to carry the full costs of its own incompetence
	This demonstrates that adopting a proactive sourcing strategy does not ensure that buyers will always achieve either a full or a partial win outcome
	In some circumstances it can be the buyer that loses under proactive sourcing and the supplier that achieves a full or, as in this case, a partial win outcome

19

The leisure and sports complex case: proactive supplier development with a buyer lose and supplier lose outcome

19.1 Introduction

This case focuses on the procurement of a leisure and sports complex by a city council, Major City Council (MCC). After providing a short background to the supply chains required for the project the case analyses the buyer–supplier relationship between the construction firm, Business Facilities Contractors (BFC), and a specialist supplier of painting and decoration services, Top Quality Decoration Services (TQDS). This single project forms part of a collaborative and proactive relationship between BFC and TQDS for an ongoing programme of construction work.

As one of MCC's preferred construction providers BFC had adopted a collaborative and proactive relationship management approach with its own first-tier suppliers. This approach was facilitated by BFC's ability to engineer a regular level of demand for common elements across MCC's construction requirements. This included painting and decoration for which the supplier in this case (TQDS) was sourced through a collaborative framework agreement.

The case demonstrates how a relatively minor problem in the relationship between BFC and TQDS escalated into a major contractual issue and legal dispute that also involved the client's design team and the upstream raw material supplier – Paints Direct (PD). This problem had significant cost implications for BFC, a major impact on TQDS's returns and, as a result, a detrimental impact on the ability of both parties to achieve their overall commercial and operational objectives.

In the pursuit of lower costs, BFC specified a new paint that had recently come onto the market from a major manufacturer (PD). At the start of the project, the highly experienced specialist supplier (TQDS), selected to provide the painting and decoration services, informed BFC and PD that the paint specified was unsuitable for the corrosive swimming pool area within the sports centre. The contractor (BFC) ignored this advice and relied on the advice provided by the paint manufacturer. The subsequent failure of the paint to adhere fully and adequately to the wall and floor surfaces led to an adversarial legal battle involving all of the supply chain players, which resulted in a situation in which both the buyer (BFC) and supplier (TQDS) in this case failed to attain any of their commercial and

operational objectives. This lose–lose outcome was surprising given the collaborative relationship in existence between the two firms.

**The leisure and
sports complex case**

19.2 Background to the case: the construction of a leisure and sports complex

The construction of a major leisure and sports complex requires the integration of a
number of supply chains. The supply chain for the painting and decoration element
of the project, as shown in Figure 19.1, is similar to that for many construction
products and services. In such a supply chain, the construction firm effectively
acts as a procurement gatekeeper to the upstream tier of material suppliers (or
trade subcontractors), which in turn act as gatekeepers to the raw materials
suppliers operating at the third-tier.

The client, MCC, had considerable experience of sourcing from construction
supply markets for its leisure, education, entertainment, housing and health facilities. Using in-house construction professionals, MCC develops either a concept
or detailed design and specification for its construction requirements. A detailed
version is produced only if MCC is very clear about its requirements, is not faced
with any uncertainty and does not require any innovation from the supply market.

Historically, MCC had rejected adversarial arm's-length sourcing in favour of a
more proactive and collaborative approach, based on selecting a limited number of
preferred construction suppliers. The client (MCC) normally awards its annual
construction spend relatively equitably among these preferred suppliers. This
practice provides each preferred construction firm with a level of demand that is
characterised by high frequency and high volume.

The project analysed in this case required the construction and fit-out of a major
state-of-the-art leisure and sports complex. The complex was to be located on a
former landfill site and the scheme involved the construction of an innovative
structure housing: two indoor swimming pools (a full size 25 m swimming pool
with a hydraulic floor to allow depth changes and a 10 m children's pool); a spa,
sauna and steam room; a water purification plant; two squash courts; a multi-
purpose sports hall; a fully equipped gymnasium; and administration facilities.
The project value (target cost) of the works was estimated at approximately
£9.5 million and the contract duration was anticipated to be 52 weeks.

The client (MCC) selected BFC to work with it to develop a very detailed design
and then deliver the entire construction package. The development of the detailed
design and specification for this landmark building was straightforward because
MCC had already produced relatively detailed documents. There was, however,
still considerable scope for BFC to utilise its extensive knowledge of upstream
supply markets to impact on MCC's initial design and specification. In particular,
BFC exerted considerable influence on MCC over the specification of the paint to
be used within the swimming pool environment.

The quality of construction and subsequent painting and decoration of this
pool area was critical in meeting MCC's requirement for a low maintenance
leisure facility. In achieving this a number of factors had to be considered. Most
important in the context of this case was the fact that concrete and other structures,
particularly related to water, operate in a harsh corrosive environment and
corrosion of concrete and steel reinforcement may occur as a result of carbonation
and the presence of high levels of chloride and other corrosive substances. To

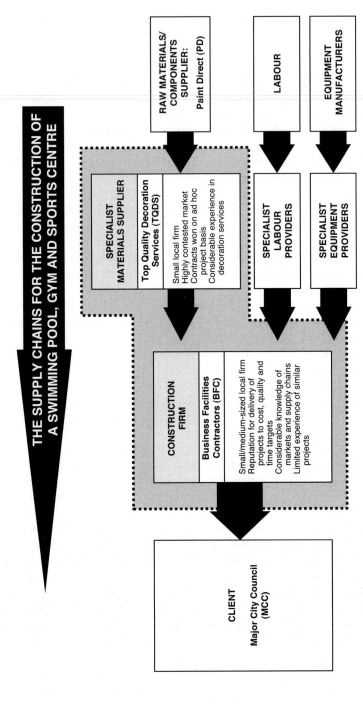

THE SUPPLY CHAINS FOR THE CONSTRUCTION OF
A SWIMMING POOL, GYM AND SPORTS CENTRE

RAW MATERIALS/ COMPONENTS SUPPLIER: Paint Direct (PD)

LABOUR

EQUIPMENT MANUFACTURERS

SPECIALIST MATERIALS SUPPLIER

Top Quality Decoration Services (TQDS)

Small local firm
Highly contested market
Contracts won on ad hoc project basis
Considerable experience in decoration services

SPECIALIST LABOUR PROVIDERS

SPECIALIST EQUIPMENT PROVIDERS

CONSTRUCTION FIRM

Business Facilities Contractors (BFC)

Small/medium-sized local firm
Reputation for delivery of projects to cost, quality and time targets
Considerable knowledge of markets and supply chains
Limited experience of similar projects

CLIENT

Major City Council (MCC)

Figure 19.1 Construction supply chains for the construction of a leisure and sports complex

avoid such problems the protection of the structure through high quality painting is critical.

While the relationship between MCC and BFC was critical for the overall development of a proactive approach in this supply chain, the discussion in this case focuses specifically on the relationship between BFC and the specialist supplier of the painting and decoration services (TQDS).

The buyer – Business Facilities Contractors (BFC)

The client (MCC) awarded the design and build contract for the new sports and leisure complex, valued at £9.5 million, to BFC. This contract was the largest single project within MCC's collaborative partnering framework for its £50 million new-build construction programme. The client (MCC) selected BFC for this high value and prestigious contract from its preferred list of contractors because of its extensive experience of providing similar solutions on time and within budget.

This reputation, for delivering similar projects and meeting client's expectations, was gained from providing many of the construction requirements for major blue chip clients. The fact that a large percentage (80%) of the workload of BFC was repeat business provided it with the opportunity to acquire a comprehensive knowledge and understanding of key construction products and services, and of upstream suppliers. Furthermore, regular demand from its major clients provided BFC with a significant power resource that facilitated the development and implementation of proactive sourcing strategies with upstream suppliers throughout the supply chain.

In conjunction with MCC, BFC developed a very detailed engineering design for main elements of the project including the innovative structural steel building frame, reinforced concrete foundations and pool tank, ground slabs, suspended floors and pre-cast concrete stairs. Detailed specifications were produced to accompany these designs when tenders were sought from specialist suppliers. During the process it was anticipated that all potential risks would be isolated and removed. This was critical for BFC because the design and build contract was fixed-price, with the full cost of any unexpected events being borne by BFC. This case demonstrates, however, that, even though proactive sourcing normally requires the buyer to work closely with and listen to the advice of its specialist suppliers, BFC failed to eliminate all risks in this project by ignoring the advice of TQDS. It will be shown that this had disastrous operational and commercial consequences for both parties.

The design and construction of the reinforced concrete pool tank and surrounding structure was a critical element within the project that involved considerable complexity. The swimming pool had a floating floor at one end that was capable of being raised and lowered to change the depth of the water. In addition to systems for the prevention of corrosion of the steel reinforcement bars within the concrete and the effective filtration and chemical treatment of the water, the pool area also required a complicated mechanical, electrical, heating and ventilation system to deal with the highly corrosive environment. Although these complex systems were integrated into the solution without any difficulty the relatively straightforward application of the paint to the concrete surfaces had significant cost implications for BFC.

At the outset of the project the total cost of the painting and decoration was estimated to be approximately £25 000. This figure was confirmed when BFC put the package of work out to tender and received prices ranging from £25 000 to £27 500. After consideration of the tenders, BFC selected TQDS, which submitted a price of exactly £25 000. The supplier (TQDS) submitted the lowest tender offer but it was primarily selected because of its long-term working relationship with BFC and its track record for delivering similar projects to a very high quality and within timescales.

The supplier (TQDS) tendered the lowest price on the basis of BFC's specification but, from its experience, it felt that quality issues might arise if the specified paint was used on the project. In the pursuit of lower costs to win the original contract from MCC, BFC had specified a new paint that had just come onto the market from a major manufacturer (PD). The supplier (TQDS) informed BFC and PD that the paint was unsuitable for the corrosive swimming pool area within the sports centre. The buyer (BFC) chose to ignore this advice and relied on the counter-advice from PD. In this way the benefits of adopting a proactive and collaborative sourcing approach were lost.

The supplier – Top Quality Decoration Services (TQDS)

The supplier (TQDS) specialises in providing high quality and professional painting and decoration services to major construction firms, property development companies, local authorities and other blue chip businesses. The firm has worked on projects of all sizes from small high street banks to large hotel and office complexes. It also offers a wealth of experience in the field of protective coatings and corrosion control for buildings and structures in environments where chemicals can damage integrity. The highly corrosive nature of the swimming pool area meant that BFC needed this service.

The supplier (TQDS) acknowledged that working in a collaborative manner with major construction firms, specialist material suppliers and public and private sector clients facilitates the development of comprehensive specifications using cost-effective methods and materials of the highest quality and appropriateness to ensure that client objectives are fully met. The firm's success in implementing proactive and collaborative partnering approaches had been reinforced by a high level of repeat business from major construction firms, such as BFC, for high profile projects.

The supplier (TQDS) had an annual turnover of £1.25 million in the year of the contract award. The supply of painting and decoration services accounted for three-quarters of this turnover (£0.95 million), with the supply of specialist coatings and corrosion control accounting for 25% (£0.3 million). For this particular project the contract value for the painting and decoration services including limited protective coatings and corrosion control was a relatively low figure of £25 000.

19.3 The buyer–supplier relationship management approach

In analysing the relationship between BFC and TQDS the power resources available to both parties are discussed, as well as the broader supply chain and market circumstances at play at the time. The case shows that, due to the incompetence of BFC both it and TQDS failed to achieve their operational and commercial goals. As a result, a lose–lose performance outcome occurred even though both parties were involved in a proactive sourcing relationship that had been in place for a number of years.

The construction firm (BFC) – specialist supplier (TQDS) dyad

The long-term collaborative relationship between a client and a construction firm is the key factor that allows a construction firm to engineer a regular demand and adopt proactive sourcing strategies in its relationships with upstream suppliers. The collaboration in the client–contractor and contractor–specialist supplier relationships is, however, dependent on the effective flow and transparency of key operational and commercial information. In this extended supply chain relationship management approach, even though a client may have extensive information, knowledge and understanding about how to leverage its own demand and the supply markets from which it sources, it normally has to rely on the construction firm's knowledge and understanding of the appropriateness of available technologies and solutions from upstream suppliers. If the construction firm makes serious errors in its sourcing approach then this will undermine the *supply chain management* approach as a whole.

Despite the apparent level of trust and commitment in the relationship between BFC and TQDS there is always an issue about which of them retains most of the value from the relationship even when a proactive and collaborative relationship management approach is adopted. The buyer (BFC)'s ability to control and leverage TQDS in order to maximise its own value for money was dependent on its capacity to obtain key power resources within the relationship, and also to effectively monitor TQDS in order to reduce the scope for supplier opportunism.

The contract value for the project was approximately £9.5 million of which £25 000 was attributable to the painting and decoration of the complex. This single contract was a relatively low share of the total annual turnover of TQDS (approximately 2%) and might be considered to be of low criticality (and importance) for it. When one considers, however, the frequency of transactions between the two parties and the resulting annual workload (approximately £400 000), this accounts for around a third of the turnover of TQDS. This makes the relationship highly attractive. As a result, BFC is the largest single customer for TQDS, which is willing to accept this high level of dependency on BFC in order to avoid uncertainty about future workload and retain its high quality directly employed workforce.

In addition to a high volume and frequent demand, BFC's power position was further enhanced by the fact that the design and specification for painting and decoration was relatively standardised and required limited customisation across projects. Typically, the only differences occur in the type of paint to be applied, the surface that has to be prepared and the surface area to be covered. As a result, BFC thought that it fully understood the product offering and the supply market and was in a relatively dominant position in which it could dictate the terms of the exchange to TQDS.

On the supply-side, the critical power resources for TQDS relate to the scarcity and utility of what it offers to BFC, relative to what other potential suppliers can offer in competition. The supplier (TQDS) operates in a very fragmented market that has high levels of contestation. In such highly competitive markets with a multitude of firms, all of which have very low market shares, firms are usually unable to close the market to competition and create a high degree of supplier scarcity. In this case, however, the high level of contestation was reduced by the fact that many of the potential suppliers were unwilling to provide their services within a framework approach that leads to such a high dependency on a single construction firm for revenue. This fact augmented the leverage of TQDS with BFC slightly more than one might have expected from a highly contested supply market.

The supplier (TQDS) had also attempted to differentiate its offer and increase its reputation by offering corrosion control and protection services on top of the normal commoditised painting and decorating services. By developing a brand associated with high quality and cost-effective services, TQDS anticipated that this would create a reputation for innovation that would enable it to gain and sustain, at least temporarily, a higher share of the market than would otherwise have been possible. This provided a power resource relative to other players in the market and allowed it to win regular repeat business from BFC.

Despite these levers for TQDS, the overall power relationship still favoured BFC and a buyer dominant position was in operation, with TQDS merely a willing supplicant. In this circumstance one might expect that the performance outcome would be a nonzero-sum win–partial win favouring the buyer. This outcome ought to have occurred through BFC's ability to obtain operational competence from TQDS, while still retaining control of the commercial aspects of the exchange. Unfortunately, the failure by BFC to listen to the advice offered by TQDS led to significant difficulties that resulted in a negative-sum outcome in which both parties experienced a lose outcome.

19.4 Performance outcome from the buyer–supplier relationship

The buyer (BFC) and TQDS ought to have had aligned operational and commercial goals in this case. This was because TQDS accepted its dependency on BFC and accepted that the best it could achieve would be a partial win involving regular work in return for a low but guaranteed profit margin. The buyer (BFC) ought to have been able to achieve its own ideal goals of improving the functionality of the supply offering and reducing the total costs of ownership, while limiting the supplier's returns. Unfortunately, as Figure 19.2 demonstrates, if the buyer in a proactive sourcing relationship ignores the technical advice of its suppliers then both parties can lose from the exchange.

In the pursuit of lower costs, BFC decided to standardise its painting requirements and specified a single paint finish for the internal walls for the entire complex. The selected paint had just come onto the market from a major paint manufacturer (PD) and was advertised in the trade press as an extremely hard-wearing and durable solution. At the start of the project, TQDS informed both BFC and PD that, while this paint was suitable for the majority of the walls, it was unsuitable for the corrosive swimming pool area.

Despite BFC demanding the open exchange of commercial information from all suppliers within its collaborative sourcing approach, it chose to ignore this 'expert' advice and relied on its own interpretation of the paint manufacturer's literature. This decision to keep to the original specification was to prove very costly, as the paint failed to adhere fully and adequately to the wall and floor surfaces throughout the swimming pool area.

When the problem first became evident, rather than attributing it to their incorrect specification, BFC looked for a scapegoat. The buyer (BFC) eventually blamed TQDS arguing that the problem was due to:

- inadequately prepared substrate surfaces, including the possibility for condensate and other moisture on the concrete surfaces;
- application of the paint in cold conditions and/or onto cold surfaces;
- the use of incorrect multiple thin layer coating techniques; and
- contamination of the paint surfaces between layers.

The supplier (TQDS) denied these claims, arguing that from the outset of the project it had foreseen the problems and had informed BFC that the paint it had selected to achieve a cost saving was unproven with a high risk of failure. It

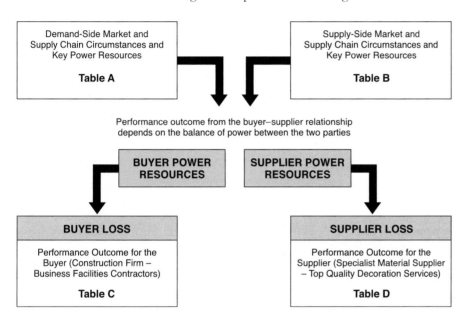

Figure 19.2 A summary of the dyad between the construction firm (BFC) and specialist supplier (TQDS) and the performance outcome from the relationship

Table A Demand-Side Market and Supply Chain Circumstances and Key Power Resources

There are many construction firms acting as buyers in the total construction market for decoration services

Business Facilities Contractors (BFC) has a very low share of the total construction market but a **slightly higher share of the construction market for leisure facilities** with an estimated project value of £9.5 million

BFC has a regular need to source from the supply market for decoration services but there is **limited current certainty/regularity** about requirements for specific products and services

The requirements of the client (and BFC) are **relatively simple** (in terms of the project environment and to a lesser extent the products themselves) and require limited supplier expertise for their integration into the project

BFC has **low/medium switching costs**, as although there are a very large number of suppliers a smaller number have the same reputation for providing very high quality products

The client (MCC) has a **relatively clear value proposition** – a high quality product delivered on time and at an acceptable cost. However, serious problems arose after BFC issued the supplier (TQDS) a specification for a paint for the swimming pool area that on application failed to adhere to the concrete surfaces

BFC is aware of the potential **scope for standardisation** of specific component elements. Despite 'expert' advice from TQDS, it selected a single paint finish for all internal walls

BFC has **relatively low search costs**, as it has extensive knowledge and understanding about painting and decoration products and services and the strategies of the industry players

Table B Supply-Side Market and Supply Chain Circumstances and Key Power Resources

There are many suppliers in the painting and decoration market but slightly fewer suppliers able to provide services of a very high quality and with the necessary experience of working within a highly specialised environment

The total contract value of the painting and decoration services for this project, approx. £25 000, accounts for a relatively **low share (2%) of the annual turnover** of Top Quality Decoration Services (TQDS). However, when one considers the regularity with which the construction firm (BFC) sources similar services from TQDS (approx. £400 000 per year), this workload accounts for a **higher share of the supplier's annual turnover (32%)**

TQDS is therefore **relatively highly dependent** on BFC for this revenue. This dependency is increased further as there is a high degree of uncertainty surrounding alternative contracts

TQDS considers the business of BFC to be **relatively attractive** as there are low costs associated with servicing the contract

TQDS has **low/medium switching costs** on this particular project

The offerings of TQDS (taken as a whole) are commoditised and standardised and there is **very limited customisation** to the specific requirements of the client (and BFC) and working in a highly corrosive environment

TQDS has a **solid reputation** for delivering its services to a very high quality

TQDS has **limited information asymmetry advantages** over BFC. However, an issue arose when BFC ignored the advice of TQDS with regard to the specific paint to be used within the swimming pool area

---

Table C Performance Outcome for the Construction Firm (BFC) – Buyer Loss

Painting and decoration costs three times higher than original budget. The original estimate was £25 000 and final cost was £75 000

The extra cost (£50 000) was attributable to the dispute surrounding the problems with the paint, as it included all the legal costs to overcome the problem

Delivery of project three months late because of delays associated with:

Communication problems between contractual parties related to appropriateness of paint within the specification

Delay by the construction firm, Business Facilities Contractors (BFC), acknowledging there was a problem. Initial repainting of poolside areas led to occurrence of same problem

Removal of paint to investigate cause of problem

Arguments surrounding whether peeling paint was due to poor application and workmanship or incorrect specification

Functional expectations of client only met after remedial action by BFC

Table D Performance Outcome for the Specialist Material Supplier (TQDS) – Supplier Loss

Top Quality Decoration Services (TQDS) calculated that they made a loss of £2500 on this project

This was largely due to the legal battle between the two parties regarding which of them was to blame for the problems with the paintwork in the swimming pool area

In winning the legal battle, and proving the paint was inappropriate for the surfaces and corrosive environment, the supplier managed to recover the majority of its legal fees

The expenditure on legal services and the failure to get paid on time for this project led to significant financial problems that threatened the survival of TQDS

TQDS also significantly damaged its reputation within the industry for delivering high quality services within time and cost constraints

Uncertainty within the marketplace as to whether the problems were the fault of TQDS was expected to adversely impact on future revenues

contended that the properties of the paint made the paint totally inappropriate for use in a corrosive swimming pool environment. It also countered the claims of BFC that it had not followed the manufacturer's guidelines for application precisely. This brought the paint manufacturer (PD) into the dispute because there was an issue now about whether or not PD had provided 'appropriate advice' for the paint's application and preparation of the pool's surfaces.

With no party willing to take the responsibility for the failure of the paint to adhere to the wall surfaces a costly and lengthy legal battle between BFC, TQDS and PD ensued. This dispute was surprisingly adversarial given the high level of collaboration between BFC and TQDS on previous projects. It ended with the Court of Appeal upholding the original court order that the specified paint was not 'fit for the intended purpose', but did not place any blame on the workmanship of TQDS or PD (the literature of which had in fact suggested that alternative – although more expensive – products might be more suitable for an environment with high levels of chlorine). This decision required BFC to provide TQDS with additional payments and extensions of time to remove and reinstate the paint finishes within the pool area.

In terms of final cost, BFC was faced with a significantly increased bill for painting and decoration services that could not be reimbursed from the client. At the start of the project, it was estimated that the total costs of decoration was £25 000. This figure increased by three times to £75 000 after further payments of £12 500 were made to the supplier to remedy the problem, liquidated damages of £7500 were paid to the client, and legal costs of £30 000 were included. This final figure included 90% of the legal costs of TQDS and PD.

The buyer (BFC)'s failure to fully, or even partially, attain value for money was further demonstrated by its inability to achieve other objectives. The functionality of the solution only met the client's expectations after the remedial work to correct the problem with the paint in the pool area was undertaken by TQDS. The lengthy legal battle to determine which party should pay for the corrective work also resulted in a delay of sixteen weeks to the programming of the painting and decoration. This had a knock-on effect for the entire project and despite concurrent programming of subsequent works, BFC delivered the sports and leisure complex to the client (MCC) three months after the scheduled delivery date. This seriously damaged BFC's reputation in the industry and contributed to a lose outcome for it.

The supplier (TQDS) also made an overall loss of £2500 by supplying the painting and decoration services to this particular project. This loss, accounting for approximately 10% of the original total contract value, was attributable to the legal costs that were not recovered when the ruling was made (£1500) and the costs associated with the management resource that initially attempted to resolve the problem through negotiation. The expenditure on legal services and the failure to be paid on time for this project led to significant financial problems that actually threatened the survival of the supplier.

Although TQDS was ultimately found not to be at fault for the defective paint-work, the lengthy legal process damaged its reputation within the industry for delivering high quality and cost-effective solutions. With reputation and brand image a major consideration for many practitioners responsible for sourcing construction products and services, TQDS expected the problems experienced on this project to adversely impact on future revenues and returns. This was particularly problematic for it because the relationship with its major customer had also broken down irretrievably as a consequence of this dispute. This was clearly a lose outcome for TQDS even though it had operated within the logic of a proactive sourcing approach.

19.5 Summary

The major finding from this case is that partnership sourcing does not guarantee a nonzero-sum outcome for both parties to the exchange. In this case the fact that win–partial win outcomes favouring the buyer had historically been achieved between BFC and TQDS did not mean that this was inevitable in the future.

Table 19.1 A summary of the relationship management approach and performance outcome

Nature of Relationship Management Approach	The construction firm, with a regular and continuous portfolio of projects with major clients, was in a position of *buyer dominance*
	This allowed it to develop long-term collaborative and proactive supply management strategies with the objective of leveraging upstream suppliers to maximise value for money
	These strategies focused on the development of a proactive relationship management approach (*supplier development*) with key construction suppliers in the upstream tier of the supply chain
	Unfortunately, the construction firm failed to listen to its expert supplier because it wanted to reduce the total costs of ownership
	This resulted in a failure of the paintwork and a costly legal dispute that affected both parties adversely
Nature of Buyer 'Loss'	Painting and decoration costs were three times higher than original budget. The original estimate was £25 000 and final cost was £75 000
	The extra cost was attributable to the dispute surrounding the problems with the paint, as it included all legal costs to remedy the problem
	Delivery of project was three months late because of delays associated with: Communication problems between contractual parties Delay by construction firm acknowledging there was a problem Arguments surrounding whether problem was due to poor workmanship or incorrect specification
	The original paint did not meet the functional expectations of client, and were only met after remedial action had been undertaken by the contractor
Nature of Supplier 'Loss'	TQDS made a loss of £2500 on this project. This was largely due to the lengthy legal battle
	The expenditure on legal services and the failure to be paid on time for this project led to significant financial problems that threatened the survival of the supplier
	TQDS also significantly damaged its reputation within the industry for delivering high quality services within time and cost constraints. This was expected to adversely impact on future revenues
Conclusions	Proactive sourcing does not guarantee a nonzero-sum outcome for both parties
	In this case the buyer ought to have been able to achieve a win–partial win outcome in its favour due to its power resources
	That it did not and a lose–lose outcome occurred is directly attributable to its desire to pursue cost reductions against the advice of its expert supply partner
	The case reinforces the conclusion that buyers receive what they pay for. Unfortunately, in this case, the supplier, who operated in a principled manner using the logic of partnership relationships, was also penalised by the intransigence of the buyer

This was because the buyer in this case, in pursuit of lower total costs of ownership, chose to ignore the advice of its relationship partner despite the fact that TQDS had far more expertise in this area than BFC.

The consequence of this unwillingness to accept a more costly solution on the advice of the supplier often occurs in sourcing relationships (both reactive and proactive). This is either because the buyer assumes that it knows best or because it fears that the supplier is only suggesting a more expensive option in order to achieve higher returns. The problem in this case is that these types of error ought not to be made in proactive sourcing relationships in which transparency and high levels of trust are expected. If trust and transparency are present then the buyer should normally accept the superior expertise of the supplier.

In this case the buyer was unwilling to accept the advice of its expert suppliers and this implies that the proactive sourcing approach being adopted by BFC was sub-optimal. This demonstrates that when undertaking proactive sourcing relationships, it is more than possible for one or both parties to fail to understand how to work together effectively. In these circumstances, as the legal dispute in this case demonstrates, both parties can lose from the exchange. This reinforces the point that choosing reactive or proactive approaches does not ensure success in implementation. For successful implementation to occur it requires that both parties adopt appropriate relationship management styles. The buyer (BFC) did not and this led to a lose–lose outcome for both parties.

Table 19.1 shows a summary of the relationship management approach and performance outcome for this case.

Part C

Conclusions

Beyond win–win: understanding relationship and performance management options for buyers and suppliers in construction

20.1 Introduction

In this final chapter the themes developed in this book are drawn together and a framework is provided for thinking about relationship and performance management choices. The discussion focuses, first, on a reiteration of the key theoretical and practical arguments. This involves, primarily, the need for buyers and suppliers in construction to think carefully about the appropriateness of their relationship and performance management strategies, particularly in the light of the fact that win–win outcomes – that simultaneously allow both parties in an exchange to achieve their objectively ideal outcome – are not achievable, whatever individuals may believe subjectively.

Given this understanding, which is supported by the case material presented here, it becomes clear that buyers and suppliers in construction supply chains and markets have to think carefully about which types of relationship management approach are more or less appropriate to adopt, in order to achieve performance optimisation for themselves, first, and their exchange partners, second. In this light both buyers and suppliers have to recognise that there is no single relationship management approach that is always the most appropriate for them to use to achieve their performance goals in all circumstances. On the contrary, both buyers and suppliers have to recognise that sometimes reactive and sometimes proactive relationship management approaches – based respectively on opportunism and on principled ways of working – will be the most appropriate means by which to achieve particular performance outcomes under specific supply chain and market circumstances.

It is, therefore, essential that buyers and suppliers understand the circumstances under which reactive and proactive relationship management strategies are more or less appropriate. But there is an even more important issue that the case material in this book forces us to address. This is the problem of competence in the effective management of reactive and/or proactive relationship approaches. It will be obvious by now that the cases presented here demonstrate that competence flows not only from knowing how to choose the most appropriate relationship option given the power and leverage circumstance, but also from understanding how to implement any such approach effectively. In the cases presented here there is considerable evidence that, even when the parties to an exchange understood which approach is the most appropriate to implement, one or both parties may not be fully competent in executing a chosen relationship management strategy.

It follows, therefore, that if construction managers – whether acting as buyers or as suppliers – are to be successful in the future they must understand that best practice arises from the recognition of the demand and supply, as well as power and leverage, circumstances that exist within particular construction supply chains and markets. It also requires the ability to select and implement appropriate relationship management options given these specific circumstances.

20.2 Appropriateness in relationship management and the problem of non-commensurable performance outcomes

Based on deductive logic, and the sixteen empirical case studies presented here, there appears to be a number of key issues that must be addressed by organisations operating within construction supply chains and markets. The first is the need to understand which relationship management approach is the most appropriate to adopt. Many managers appear to believe that proactive sourcing approaches are always more appropriate than reactive sourcing approaches. This failure is often couched by managers in phrases such as: 'traditional leveraged contracting is old school' or that 'we should stop being adversarial and be more collaborative'.

As we saw, these types of comment tend to demonstrate a complete failure by managers to understand that there is nothing 'old school' about trying to be commercially adversarial – it is in fact the basis of all good business practice. Furthermore, recourse to false dichotomies is not the basis for rigorous or robust thinking. A moment's reflection demonstrates that being collaborative is not the opposite of being adversarial. The opposite of collaborative is arm's-length ways of working, and the opposite of being adversarial is to be non-adversarial commercially (Cox, 1999a).

To be able to understand, therefore, which relationship management approach is the most appropriate to adopt under any given circumstance it is necessary for managers (whether acting as buyers or suppliers) to have three competencies.

- First, they must understand what is the full range of relationship management approaches available for any supply requirement.
- Second, they must understand what is the current (and future) power and leverage situation under which the exchange relationship will operate.
- Third, and most important of all, they must understand which of the relationship management approaches available leads them to the most favourable performance outcome feasible, given these power and leverage circumstances.

It is important when developing this competence that managers recognise, as we argued at length in Chapter 3, that they must not seek win–win (*positive-sum* outcomes). This is because these outcomes are unattainable in dyadic buyer–supplier relationships, if not in other forms of business exchange (Cox, 2004b). Rather than seeking a win–win managers must, therefore, seek those *nonzero-sum* and *zero-sum* performance outcomes that maximise their interests either in the short-term (if the relationship is a *one-off game*) or in both the short- and long-term (if it is a *repeat game*). This implies that both reactive and proactive relationship management options, as well as *nonzero-sum* and *zero-sum* performance outcomes, may be desirable maximisation choices for buyers and suppliers under specific power and leverage circumstances.

Competence for buyers and suppliers resides, therefore, in their ability to select the most appropriate reactive or proactive relationship management approach in order to achieve the performance outcome that best maximises the buyer's or supplier's interests now, and (but only if this second issue is relevant) in the future. The problem for competent management in construction supply chains and markets is that only some, but not all, managers have this competence. This is because many managers do not fully understand all of the sourcing options available to them, and even fewer have a methodology (i.e. strategic source planning or strategic marketing planning) through which it is possible to understand the power and leverage circumstances that operate now, and in the future, for any particular exchange relationships into which they might enter.

In the discussion here a way of thinking about selecting appropriate relationship management and performance outcomes has been outlined theoretically. To assist managers it is necessary, however, to link the theory with some practical guidance on how to link the relationship management options available in construction with changing (or contingent) circumstances. In doing so, we start with the nature of the demand and supply characteristics that have to be managed, and then link these to the power and leverage circumstances that exist now and in the future. Only in this way is it possible for managers in construction to understand the full range of circumstances that have to be managed when they undertake CAPEX (capital expenditure on projects) and OPEX (operational expenditure on the operation, repair and maintenance of the facilities that have been constructed).

The first consideration, as outlined in Figure 20.1, is to segment the type of expenditure that is required (whether CAPEX or OPEX) in terms of the nature

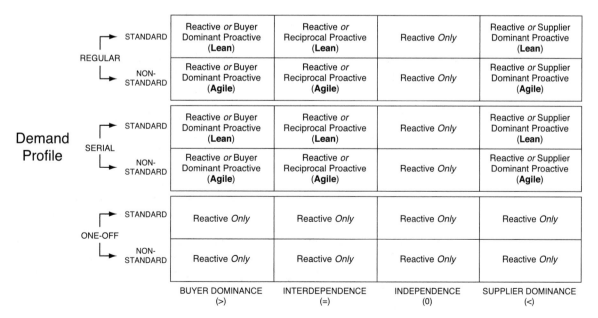

Figure 20.1 *Segmenting reactive and proactive relationship management options*

of its demand profile. By demand profile we mean the frequency of the particular demand requirement (i.e. is it a *regular* or a *one-off* requirement or is it in between, in the sense that it is not regular or one-off, but sufficiently episodic to constitute a *serial* requirement). Linked to this one must also be aware of the capability to standardise the design and specification of the requirement. In this sense demand can be either *standardised* or *non-standardised*. These two major aspects constitute the key aspects of the demand profile for CAPEX and OPEX expenditure under all circumstances, and not just in construction. This means that demand can be: regular, but standard or non-standard; serial, but standard or non-standard; or one-off, but standard or non-standard.

This provides a useful way of segmenting the demand profile for construction activities, but to properly understand the nature of the choices available to them, managers also have to be cognisant of the power and leverage circumstances that exist in the relationship between buyers and suppliers in the markets and supply chains for particular categories of demand. This requires an understanding of power and leverage both at the dyadic level, and also within the supply chain power regime for particular categories of demand and supply. It is a complex subject that was discussed at some length in Chapter 2, and which is explained in far more detail elsewhere (Cox, 1999b, 2004a; Cox *et al.*, 2000, 2002, 2003, 2004).

The essential features that must be analysed to understand the power and leverage circumstances that exist between buyers and suppliers are threefold: the relative *scarcity* and *utility* of the exchange transaction for both parties, and the level of *information asymmetry* for both parties about what is done operationally and with what commercial consequences. When these factors are analysed in the round, with due attention being paid to the scope for these variables to change over time, it is possible to determine what the power and leverage circumstance is in any exchange transaction at the dyadic (buyer and supplier) level. The four potential outcomes that can arise are, as follows:

- *Buyer dominance* (>): the buyer controls the relationship and can be expected to appropriate a dominant share of the value from the exchange, in the form of increased functionality and reduced total costs of ownership, with suppliers earning nothing or only low or normal returns.
- *Interdependence* (=): the buyer and supplier have countervailing power resources such that neither party can control the relationship and they must share the value from exchange, with the buyer expecting improvements in functionality and reduced total costs of ownership, but with the supplier earning above normal returns.
- *Independence* (0): neither the buyer nor the supplier have strong power levers and exchange is determined by market forces, with the buyer receiving the functionality and total costs of ownership benefits that flow from market contestation, with the supplier earning only low or normal returns and constantly having to innovate.
- *Supplier dominance* (<): the buyer is a price and quality receiver and the supplier controls the relationship and determines the level of functionality and the total costs of ownership that the buyer receives, while earning above normal returns or super normal profits.

These power and leverage circumstances can now be linked with the demand profile circumstances that have to be managed to create, as in Figure 20.1, a decision matrix for thinking about relationship management options. In selecting between different options it is essential to keep in mind that there are *reactive* and *proactive* options, but that some options are more appropriate in some circumstances than others.

Reactive options involve commitments by both parties only to *one-off games* – that is short-term relationships that are governed by tight comprehensive clause contracts, in which costs and benefits and risks are tightly defined before the commencement of the relationship. In *one-off-games* the two parties can expect to be opportunistic about operational and commercial trade-offs both pre- and post-contractually, and both parties may have to have recourse to legal claims if the other party attempts to behave opportunistically post-contractually. This is because neither party expects to be involved in a relationship with the other party beyond the terms of the current short-term relationship.

Proactive options normally are very different, and this is because they can only be operationalised in circumstances where both parties expect to be involved in *repeat games* in which bilateral dependency – a continuous need to work together operationally – is anticipated. In repeat games both parties have to accept that costs, benefits and risks cannot be fully defined because circumstances may change over the term of the relationship in ways that are currently unknowable. In such circumstances of foreseeable bilateral dependency it is essential for relationships to be governed by general clause, rather than comprehensive clause, contracts. In these types of relationship it is essential for both parties to make credible commitments to guard against post-contractual opportunism, and to find ways of agreeing at the commencement of the relationship how currently unforeseeable operational outcomes will be dealt with commercially in the future (Williamson, 1985, 1996).

In *repeat games* there are two broad types of proactive relationship and performance management. The first type, which draws its lineage from the automotive and manufacturing industries, is *lean*. Lean relationship management practices are predicated on the adoption of close working relationships focused on optimising value and process efficiencies and effectiveness. This normally requires a continuous working relationship to optimise value from the customer's perspective, while driving out all unnecessary waste and inefficiency from systems and processes, such that the customer experiences a continuous improvement in functionality and reduction in the total costs of ownership. This type of approach works well for highly standardised goods and/or services, where design and specification can be standardised and the processes and systems to deliver finished products and/or services can be clearly specified in advance. This type of approach works well, therefore, when construction requirements can be standardised at the design and specification stage, and where there is a continuous demand for such requirements.

There is, however, a second proactive or *repeat game* approach known as *agile*. Agile relationships are focused on a continuous commitment by two parties to work together in order to deliver goods and/or services that are partly knowable, but which cannot be specified exactly in advance. In such circumstances, both parties can commit to a relationship and to working together operationally over time, but they cannot always specify clearly exactly what it is that must be delivered. In this sense both parties must be responsive to changing volume and design and specification requirements, even though the basic operational infrastructure for delivery stays the same. These types of relationship approaches are normally essential in fast moving consumer goods markets, such as the fashion industry

271

or publishing. They may also work well in construction relationships where the basic delivery mechanism is the same but the exact operational requirements can vary widely and unexpectedly. In these circumstances general clause principles can provide certainty for the relationship, so that unforeseen events have a framework within which they can be managed efficiently and effectively.

Given this discussion, the segmentation approach suggested in Figure 20.1 should now become apparent. As the figure demonstrates, by linking together the demand profile with the power and leverage circumstances, and then plotting the reactive and proactive relationship management approaches within the matrix, the scope for proactive and reactive sourcing becomes self-evident. Thus, when demand is one-off and either standard or non-standard, and irrespective of the power and leverage situation between the buyer and the supplier, only reactive sourcing approaches (using comprehensive clause contracting) are possible. In such circumstances the scope for, and the risks from, pre- and post-contractual opportunism must be accepted and planned for by both parties in the relationship.

Similarly, even if demand is serial or regular, and irrespective of whether or not design and specification can be standard or non-standard, reactive sourcing will always be required under power and leverage circumstances of *independence*. The reason for this is self-evident. In these power and leverage circumstances the buyer cannot provide any incentives for the supplier to enter into a long-term relationship because of the *ad hoc* and low volume nature of its demand. Furthermore, a buyer entering the market on a one-off basis with low volume would normally be interested only in working with whichever supplier could offer it the best current value for money deal, given the level of contestation in the supply market at that time.

Choices for buyers and suppliers are far more complex, however, when demand is serial or regular and power and leverage situations of *buyer dominance*, *interdependence* and *supplier dominance* occur. When buyer dominance occurs and demand is regular and standardised a buyer might decide that, since it lacks the internal competence or resources to develop a proactive approach, that a reactive short-term bidding approach is most appropriate. While this might be a sensible decision, given the lack of internal competence or resources, it is feasible in this situation (if the internal competence could be developed and a willing supply partner located) for the buyer to select a proactive relationship approach based on lean management principles. If this was achieved it would result in a *buyer dominant proactive (lean) approach* being implemented. In this scenario the bulk of the value from the relationship would flow to the buyer rather than the supplier.

Conversely, in circumstances of regular demand with standard requirements, but where there is an *interdependence* power and leverage situation, both parties to an exchange could operate the relationship reactively as a one-off game, but they could also choose to operate a *reciprocal proactive (lean) approach*. In such an approach both parties would share relatively equally in the value created from the exchange. Similarly, when there is regular and standard demand but *supplier dominance* occurs, the supplier could elect to pursue a reactive short-term approach, but it could also encourage a buyer to work closely with it on a *supplier dominant proactive (lean) approach*. In this circumstance, the bulk of any value created would flow to the supplier not to the buyer.

Similar principles apply when demand is regular but non-standard. In all of the power and leverage circumstances possible with this type of demand profile the buyer and supplier could elect to operate reactively, especially if they do not possess the internal competencies to operate proactively. On the other hand, they could also adopt proactive approaches, but these would now be based on *agile* rather than *lean* principles, with the bulk of any enhanced value flowing either to the buyer in *buyer dominance*, being shared equally in *interdependence* and to the supplier in *supplier dominance* situations. The reason why *agile* rather than *lean* principles of proactive relationship management would be required in this scenario is because, with demand being non-standard but regular, the basic infrastructure can be specified and a long-term relationship created, but the exact requirements cannot be precisely specified, and both parties must operate responsively to changing requirements.

When considering situations of serial (or episodic) demand, where requirements can be standardised, it is clear that the same principles as for regular standardised demand pertain. In all three situations of *buyer dominance*, *interdependence* and *supplier dominance* the parties can elect to operate reactively if they do not possess the internal competencies or resources to manage a proactive approach. Assuming that the competencies exist and willing partners can be found it is, however, possible for a dominant buyer to create a *lean* proactive approach to appropriate the bulk of the value from serial and standardised demand requirements, or for this to be shared under *interdependence*, or to flow mainly to a dominant supplier. Relatedly, when demand is serial but non-standard it is feasible for buyers and suppliers to operate reactively, but now (whether the flow of commercial value is to the buyer, shared or to the supplier) the appropriate proactive sourcing approach operationally is to be *agile* rather than *lean*.

As the discussion above has shown, and as Figure 20.1 demonstrates, however, the selection of options is not always as straightforward as this discussion implies. This is because sometimes, depending on the internal competencies and resources of the two parties to the exchange, a proactive approach will not be possible in practice, even though it is feasible in theory. This is because sometimes one or both parties lack the competence or resources to undertake a particular approach (Cox *et al.*, 2003). In these circumstances it is sensible for the buyer or supplier to adopt only a reactive approach until the skills and capabilities to operate pro-actively have been put in place.

Nevertheless, by segmenting demand and supply characteristics effectively, and linking these with power and leverage circumstances, the appropriateness of particular relationship management choices becomes apparent for buyers and suppliers. There are, however, two additional problems with appropriateness for managers operating in construction supply chains and markets. There is a CAPEX and OPEX problem and there is also a multiplicity of supply chains problem. The CAPEX and OPEX problem arises because, while there is always a need to understand the appropriateness of a particular relationship approach in the context of the very different demand and supply and power and leverage characteristics that impact on CAPEX and OPEX decisions, there is also a need to understand how decisions taken at the CAPEX stage of a project may have significant effects on power and leverage in the very different demand and supply circumstances that pertain at the OPEX stage. If these two issues are not considered together, before the CAPEX stage is commenced, it is normal for the buyer to discover that OPEX performance is sub-optimal.

The multiplicity of supply chains problem is inherent within construction supply chains and markets whether one discusses the CAPEX or the OPEX stage. As the case studies in this book demonstrate, although it is possible to single out a particular dyadic exchange relationship from within a particular project and analyse the appropriateness of a particular relationship management approach and performance outcome, CAPEX projects and OPEX delivery activities are made up of a multiplicity of very different supply chains, each of which has its own unique demand and supply, as well as power and leverage, characteristics. This means that competence in construction management requires managers to have a sophisticated understanding of the myriad of supply chains that constitute a complex CAPEX project and OPEX delivery process, as well as the ability to map the current and future state of the power regimes that flow within them. Only by understanding how to manage this myriad of power regimes appropriately, in the context of an overall CAPEX project and OPEX delivery process, is it possible for managers in construction to become fully competent. Appropriateness can then become extremely complex. This is because managers within a particular CAPEX and/or OPEX activity may have to manage simultaneously some of their relationships reactively and some proactively and *lean*, while others may need to be managed proactively but *agile*.

The segmentation approach adopted here is useful in one further additional respect when considering the issue of competence. There has been considerable discussion in recent years about the need for everyone in construction to adopt the *proactive lean approach* that is prevalent in the automotive industry. The segmentation methodology used here provides a useful corrective for this overly simplistic thinking. When managers in construction think carefully about the demand and supply, and power and leverage, circumstances within which they operate, it will soon become apparent that, for the vast majority, proactive sourcing is a non-starter. The primary reason for this is because their demand profile (if they are the buyer) or the client's engagement (if they are the supplier) is one-off and non-standard, or at best one-off and standard.

In these circumstances it is impossible for the buyer or supplier to adopt a proactive relationship and only a reactive approach – with all of the concomitant risks of pre- and post-contractual opportunism for both parties – is feasible. In such circumstances managers are encouraged to accept this fact of life and use the principles of comprehensive clause contracting to manage opportunism pre- and post-contractually as effectively as they are able. The same is true when demand is serial or regular, and power circumstances have *independence* characteristics. Unfortunately, for most buyers and suppliers operating in the construction industry this is the circumstance they normally find themselves in most of the time. As a result, developing reactive relationship management skills is a necessity for competence in the industry. This must be achieved, therefore, before anyone considers developing a proactive sourcing competence. This is a point often forgotten in recent industry reports and recommendations.

Nevertheless, even though the industry must recognise that it has only a limited number of opportunities for proactive relationships to be developed between buyers and suppliers in the chain, it must not be forgotten that *proactive* management principles can still be applied internally within *all* organisations. Construction managers should not, therefore, miss these internal opportunities to develop proactive approaches, even when they have to implement reactive sourcing approaches externally. While the principles of competence internally in proactivity and competence externally in reactivity are a requirement for everyone, there are a number of fortunate players in the industry that do have the potential to operate with (or create supply chain structures that have) regular and serial demand

profiles. In these supply chain and market circumstances there is clearly scope for
the adoption of proactive relationships based either on *lean* (if demand is standard)
or *agile* (if demand is non-standard) management principles.

For these proactive approaches to work, and for them to be superior options
compared with the more traditional reactive approaches, it is essential that the
buyers and suppliers adopting them understand that any necessary investment in
these competencies, plus any additional costs and risks that must be borne in
implementing them, must be outweighed by the benefits that are likely to arise
from operating them (Cox et al., 2003, 2005). If the investment decision is positive
and a proactive approach is feasible then it is clear, for those fortunate few in
construction who (because of a high volume and regular process spend) are in a
position to take advantage of this way of working, that the scope for value
improvement in construction supply chains and markets is very high indeed, as
some companies have demonstrated in the past (Cox and Townsend, 1998).

Unfortunately, even though managers in construction may develop the competence to segment their demand and supply, and power and leverage, circumstances
effectively, and understand the full range of relationship and performance
management options available to them, there is one final competence that has to
be developed for relationships to be managed effectively such that performance is
optimised. This is the development of an implementation competence for each of
the feasible relationship management options.

As the sixteen case studies presented here demonstrate, even when an appropriate relationship management approach has been adopted implementation can
be variable. This means that relationship management and performance outcomes
can be *ideal* (the buyer or supplier understands not only the appropriateness of the
relationship option but also how to implement it effectively, so as to achieve
the ideal win outcome for themselves); *optimal* (the buyer or supplier understands
appropriateness but is only able to achieve a partial win outcome due to non-
conducive power and leverage circumstances, even though it is fully competent
at implementation); or *sub-optimal* (the buyer or supplier understand appropriateness but must accept a lose outcome because power and leverage circumstances
give it no alternative, or it individually or collectively chooses the wrong option
or, having selected the appropriate option, cannot implement the option successfully because it is incompetent at implementation). When this latter outcome
occurs this normally means that one or both parties achieves a lose, or a partial
win, outcome even though a superior partial win, or full win, alternative would
have been achievable.

As Figures 20.2 and 20.3 show, while win–win (*positive-sum*) outcomes are not
feasible, *nonzero-sum*, *zero-sum* and *negative-sum* outcomes can all occur in construction supply chains and markets, under both reactive and proactive relationship
management approaches. Thus, as the case studies discussed here reveal, in both
nonzero-sum and *zero-sum* outcomes one of the parties can select an appropriate
relationship management option and achieve its *ideal* performance outcome,
even though its exchange partner cannot. These *ideal* outcomes occurred for the
buyer in the reactive win–partial win Logistics Warehouse Case (Chapter 4) and
the win–lose Sports Stadium Case (Chapter 5) and, proactively, for the buyer in
the win–partial win Prefabricated Restaurant Case (Chapter 12) and the win–lose
Multi-Storey Car Park Case (Chapter 13). It also occurred for the supplier, reactively, in the partial win–win Corporate Office Facility Case (Chapter 6) and the
lose–win Heavy Engineering Facility Case (Chapter 9), and proactively for the

supplier in the partial win–win Aerospace Manufacturing Facility Case (Chapter 14) and the lose–win Housing Development Case (Chapter 17).

In other cases the buyer or the supplier individually, or in some cases simultaneously, was only able to achieve an *optimal* rather than *ideal* performance outcome. These types of outcome occur in both *nonzero-sum* as well as *zero-sum* performance outcomes. An *optimal* rather than *ideal* performance outcome occurred for the buyer, reactively, in the partial win–win Corporate Office Facility Case (Chapter 6) and the partial win–lose Motorway Case (Chapter 8) and, proactively, in the partial win–win Aerospace Manufacturing Facility Case (Chapter 14) and the partial win–lose High Street Pub Case (Chapter 16). A similar *optimal* rather than *ideal* outcome occurred for the supplier, reactively, in the win–partial win Logistics Warehouse Case (Chapter 4) and in the lose–partial win Water Pipeline Case (Chapter 10) and, proactively, in the win–partial win Prefabricated Restaurant Case (Chapter 12) and the lose–partial win Petrol Station Case (Chapter 18). Finally, both the buyer and the supplier were able to record an *optimal* rather than ideal performance outcome, reactively, in the partial win–partial win Health Facility Case (Chapter 7) and, proactively, in the Office and Entertainment Complex Case (Chapter 15).

The case studies also demonstrate that it is possible for buyers and suppliers (individually or collectively) to achieve performance outcomes that are *suboptimal*. These outcomes can occur, as we saw above, because the buyer or supplier is forced by circumstances to accept a lose outcome, or because it is forced to accept a partial win outcome when – if it had been more competent – a win

WIN–LOSE (ZERO-SUM)	WIN–PARTIAL WIN (NONZERO-SUM)	WIN–WIN (POSITIVE-SUM)
THE SPORTS STADIUM CASE (Chapter 5) Buyer achieved ideal outcome with project delivered on time and to budget Supplier made a loss due to incorrect design and specification causing buyer to make claims against it **Buyer competent/supplier incompetent**	**THE LOGISTICS FACILITY CASE (Chapter 4)** Buyer achieved ideal outcome with project delivered early and to budget Supplier achieved an acceptable (optimal) outcome of normal returns **Buyer competent/supplier competent**	**Not Feasible**
PARTIAL WIN–LOSE (ZERO-SUM)	**PARTIAL WIN–PARTIAL WIN (NONZERO-SUM)**	**PARTIAL WIN–WIN (NONZERO-SUM)**
THE MOTORWAY CASE (Chapter 8) Buyer achieved an acceptable (optimal) outcome, but could have achieved more if it had understood supplier cost base better Supplier made a loss due to sub-standard product causing buyer to make claims against it **Buyer partially competent/supplier incompetent**	**THE HEALTH FACILITY CASE (Chapter 7)** Buyer achieved an acceptable (optimal) outcome, but could have achieved more if it had understood supplier cost base better Supplier achieved an acceptable (optimal) outcome and increased returns **Buyer partially competent/supplier competent**	**THE CORPORATE FACILITY CASE (Chapter 6)** Buyer attained an acceptable (optimal) outcome but could have obtained more if it had understood supplier cost base better Supplier made above normal return and achieved ideal outcome **Buyer partially competent/supplier competent**
LOSE–LOSE (NEGATIVE-SUM)	**LOSE–PARTIAL WIN (ZERO-SUM)**	**LOSE–WIN (ZERO-SUM)**
THE MANUFACTURING EXTENSION CASE (Chapter 11) Buyer paid more for a building that was delivered late and not to original specification Supplier made a loss and damaged its reputation in supply market **Buyer incompetent/supplier incompetent**	**THE WATER PIPELINE CASE (Chapter 10)** Buyer made design errors and paid more than expected for a late solution that damaged its reputation Supplier made a reasonable return and an optimal outcome with its reputation intact **Buyer incompetent/supplier competent**	**THE HEAVY ENGINEERING FACILITY CASE (Chapter 9)** Buyer made design and build errors causing delay in project and extra costs Supplier had an ideal outcome – made an above normal return and enhanced its reputation **Buyer incompetent/supplier competent**

Figure 20.2 Performance outcomes from reactive relationship management

might have been possible, or it was forced to accept a lose outcome when a partial win was feasible. Before discussing these cases it is important to recognise, however, that there can be circumstances when a lose outcome may demonstrate competence. This would occur if a supplier, for example, decided to provide a 'loss leader' to a buyer in order to win more lucrative business later, or to win more lucrative business from other buyers due to the reputation gained from working with the original buyer. The initial relationship would appear as a lose outcome technically but would in fact demonstrate competence overall. This did not occur in the cases discussed here because in all of the cases studied for this book the lose outcomes reported were a demonstration of incompetence in implementation by either the buyer or the supplier individually, or by both at the same time.

In the cases discussed here, due to individual organisational incompetence, the buyer, reactively, received a lose outcome in the lose–partial win Water Pipeline Case (Chapter 10) and in the lose–win Heavy Engineering Case (Chapter 9), and, proactively, in the lose–partial win Petrol Station Case (Chapter 18) and in the lose–win Housing Development Case (Chapter 17). Similarly, the supplier was incompetent, reactively, in the Sports Stadium Case (Chapter 5) and in the Motorway Case (Chapter 8), and, proactively, in the win–lose Multi-Storey Car Park Case (Chapter 13) and the partial win–lose High Street Pub Case (Chapter 16). Finally, both the buyer and the supplier were simultaneously incompetent, reactively, in the Manufacturing Extension Case (Chapter 11) and, proactively, in the Leisure

WIN–LOSE (ZERO-SUM)	WIN–PARTIAL WIN (NONZERO-SUM)	WIN–WIN (POSITIVE-SUM)
THE MULTI-STOREY CAR PARK CASE (Chapter 13) Buyer achieved an ideal outcome with project early and with lower costs than anticipated Supplier made a loss due to design and build errors, damaging its reputation **Buyer competent/supplier incompetent**	**THE PREFABRICATED RESTAURANT CASE (Chapter 12)** Buyer achieved the ideal of continuous cost reduction with project on time Supplier made an acceptable (optimal) normal return and enhanced its reputation **Buyer competent/supplier competent**	**Not Feasible**
PARTIAL WIN–LOSE (ZERO-SUM)	**PARTIAL WIN–PARTIAL WIN (NONZERO-SUM)**	**PARTIAL WIN–WIN (NONZERO-SUM)**
THE HIGH STREET PUB CASE (Chapter 16) Buyer achieved an acceptable (optimal) outcome with project delivered on time and with some cost reductions, but these cost savings could have been larger Supplier made a loss due to its poor workmanship and damaged its reputation **Buyer partially competent/supplier incompetent**	**THE OFFICE AND ENTERTAINMENT COMPLEX CASE (Chapter 15)** Buyer achieved project at lower cost and on time but could have achieved more significant cost savings Supplier made acceptable if not ideal return and maintained its reputation **Buyer partially competent/supplier competent**	**THE AEROSPACE MANUFACTURING FACILITY CASE (Chapter 14)** Buyer received project on time and to specification and with lower costs, but these cost savings could have been larger Supplier made an above normal return for its type of work and enhanced its reputation **Buyer partially competent/supplier competent**
LOSE–LOSE (NEGATIVE-SUM)	**LOSE–PARTIAL WIN (ZERO-SUM)**	**LOSE–WIN (ZERO-SUM)**
THE LEISURE CENTRE CASE (Chapter 19) Buyer completed the project late with much higher costs and damaged its reputation Supplier made a loss and experienced serious long-term reputational consequences impacting on survival of the company **Buyer incompetent/supplier incompetent**	**THE PETROL STATION CASE (Chapter 18)** Buyer achieved the project on time but with higher costs and lower functionality than specified due to its design failures Supplier made a normal return and maintained its reputation **Buyer incompetent/supplier competent**	**THE HOUSING DEVELOPMENT CASE (Chapter 17)** Buyer had to make numerous design changes and project delivered late at extra cost and with less functionality Supplier made above normal returns and enhanced its reputation **Buyer incompetent/supplier competent**

Figure 20.3 Performance outcomes from proactive relationship management

Centre Case (Chapter 19). In these latter two cases a *negative-sum* outcome was achieved. Such outcomes are the apotheosis of incompetence because both parties are incapable of implementing the appropriate strategy effectively.

Despite this, there are some circumstances where a buyer or a supplier does not receive a lose outcome but is still guilty of a degree of incompetence because it does not achieve all that it could have given the prevailing power and leverage circumstances that existed at the time. In such circumstances it achieves a partial win outcome when it could have achieved a win or a somewhat better partial win outcome than that which was actually achieved. This occurred for the buyer, reactively, in the partial win–lose Motorway Case (Chapter 8), in the partial win–partial win Health Facility Case (Chapter 7) and the partial win–win Corporate Facility Case (Chapter 6). It also occurred, proactively, for the buyer in the partial win–lose High Street Pub Case (Chapter 16), the partial win–partial win Office and Entertainment Complex Case (Chapter 15) and the partial win–win Aerospace Manufacturing Case (Chapter 14).

What this demonstrates is that both buyers and suppliers cannot be successful unless they understand appropriateness in their selection of reactive and proactive relationship management options. It also shows, however, that they must also know how to implement reactive and proactive relationship management approaches effectively once they have selected an appropriate relationship approach. If they do not, then incompetence in implementation can turn what should have been an *ideal* or an *optimal* into a seriously *sub-optimal* performance outcome. On the basis of the evidence presented here, while buyers and suppliers both appear to be guilty of failing to implement reactive and proactive approaches effectively, it is buyers who are often the most guilty of sub-optimality when implementing reactive or proactive relationship options.

20.3 A contingency approach to effectiveness in construction management

The discussion above has, hopefully, demonstrated that what is *ideal* or *optimal* for a buyer may not be *ideal* or *optimal* for a supplier, and also that any attempt to search for win–win outcomes is a waste of everyone's time and effort, whether in construction or in any other types of supply chain or market. In order for buyers or suppliers to achieve the best performance outcome that is available to them it is, therefore, necessary for both of them to recognise first of all that *positive-sum* outcomes are not achievable in buyer and supplier exchange. Furthermore, it may well be the case that even when *nonzero-sum* outcomes are available to either party *zero-sum* outcomes may, in some circumstances, be the most appropriate choice. This is because *zero-sum* outcomes may provide a way of maximising returns for one party at the expense of the other when there is no need for a *repeat game* to be played between the two parties. In such circumstances a *one-off game* may allow one (normally the dominant) party to behave opportunistically against the other and achieve, thereby, more than it could have if it had selected a *nonzero-sum* outcome.

This means that what is the appropriate thing to do can never be defined completely in advance of an analysis of the changing (contingent) circumstances that confront a buyer or a supplier in any specific exchange relationship. It is, therefore, a mistake to argue that proactive approaches to relationship management are always superior to reactive approaches, or that *nonzero-sum* outcomes are always preferable to *zero-sum* outcomes. Clearly, what is or is not the most appropriate thing to do in all circumstances depends on the types of exchange relationship (games) that buyers and suppliers are engaged in, and the options that are available to either party to maximise its goals.

Nevertheless, although there can be no categorical statements about appropriateness, some general rules can still be discerned for the selection of appropriate relationship management approaches for buyers and suppliers in construction supply chains and markets. In *one-off games* where there is no need for the buyer or supplier to work together over time then it is normally preferable to adopt reactive rather than proactive relationship management approaches. The primary reason for this is self-evident. Since neither party expects to work with the other in the future – which is often the case for major clients and their major contractors in construction supply chains and markets – then pursuing short-term pre- and post-contractual opportunism is likely to be the preferred route for both parties.

In such circumstances buyers are advised to design and specify their requirements tightly, and have clear terms and conditions in place contractually that are managed through well-defined comprehensive clause contracts that define, as closely as is possible, how all of the potential risks, costs and benefits that may occur will be managed within the relationship. In doing this sensible buyers, who do not engage with the industry regularly, will normally have to employ competent professional design, engineering, project management, sourcing and cost consulting services to ensure that they tender and manage their projects effectively. Suppliers, on the other hand, can be expected to take advantage pre- and post-contractually of buyers who do not understand these rules of the game, and try to drive performance outcomes away from *nonzero-sum* as far in the direction of *zero-sum* as their need for a reputation requires.

If this provides general guidance for buyers and suppliers in *one-off games* it is clear that buyers and suppliers may use the same general principles in *repeat games*, or they may choose instead to adopt more proactive relationship management approaches. When deciding whether or not to adopt a proactive approach buyers and suppliers must, first, pay attention to the demand and supply circumstances to ensure that these provide a suitable environment for adopting such an approach. Such an analysis will also provide an opportunity to understand whether a *lean* or *agile* (or indeed *leagile*) approach will be required. It is also necessary to understand the prevailing power and leverage circumstances so that the appropriate approach to commercial exchange can be put in place. Once it is clear that this external environment is conducive and that both parties wish to work together in an aligned way, it is then necessary for both parties to ensure that they have the internal resources to fund this highly resource intensive activity, and that they have developed the necessary internal competencies to ensure that implementation is likely to be successful.

Our experience of consulting with organisations that have tried to implement proactive sourcing both in construction and in other industries is that they rarely adopt this benign path to effective implementation. All too often experience shows that buyers fail to understand that proactive sourcing involves more than simply providing a long-term contractual commitment to a supplier. Most buyers who believe they are being proactive do not appear to understand that there are very different approaches for different demand and supply and power and leverage circumstances, or that they are supposed to do far more in driving improvement in the relationship than just awarding contracts and expecting suppliers to innovate. On the supplier side of the relationship similar levels of ignorance also occur on a regular basis. It is all too apparent that most suppliers in construction sign up to proactive sourcing as nothing more than a marketing ploy. When involved in these types of relationship it is all too apparent that most suppliers have no real internal understanding of how to implement a proactive approach, or how to drive it through their own business, or through their input supply chains.

For these reasons, virtually all of the proactive relationship approaches that the authors have witnessed in construction have tended to be sub-optimal until the principles enunciated here have been understood and implemented. The recent fashion in favour of *project partnering* demonstrates the truth of this insight. *Project partnering* has been touted as the way in which to introduce proactive relationship management principles into construction. Unfortunately, proponents of this way of thinking often demonstrate that they singularly fail to understand the demand and supply, as well as power and leverage, conditions that must be in place to support a proactive relationship and performance management approach. If a project is *one-off* no amount of exhortation by buyers or suppliers to work proactively can overcome the lack of incentive for either party to make the necessary investments in the relationship for it to work effectively (Cannon and Perreault, 1999). In these circumstances, while it is possible to undertake proactive relationship and performance management in projects (i.e. when there is a serial and regular need for them) it is not feasible to partner on a *one-off project*.

One final word about appropriateness is perhaps in order. It will be plain to anyone who has reached this stage in our discussion that we believe that, given the right circumstances, both reactive and proactive relationship approaches can be appropriate ways of managing relationships. Furthermore, it should also be clear that we do not accept the feasibility of win–win outcomes in which both parties simultaneously achieve their objectively ideal performance outcomes, whether reactive or proactive approaches are used. This is as true in construction supply chains and markets as it is in all other industries in which buyers and suppliers interact (Cox, 2004b).

Despite this general conclusion, and the realisation that while a *positive-sum* outcome is not feasible all other forms of *nonzero-sum*, *zero-sum* and *negative-sum* outcome are, it is possible that some readers may still believe that there is an outcome that is better than any other for managing construction relationships. Many managers and commentators may still believe (even if this cannot mean a true win–win) that mutuality – in the form of a *nonzero-sum* outcome in which both parties simultaneously achieve a partial win – is the best way of managing relationships, whether these be reactively or proactively managed. In this line of reasoning it is often argued that if both parties achieve a partial win then they have satisficed rather than maximised their interests, and allowed the other exchange partner to attain something that they valued. This, it is often argued, is the best way of sustaining relationships over time because it is demonstrably fair, or equitable, to both sides in the exchange.

This is an appealing idea, and one that many readers may wish to support. It is worth stressing however that, while it may be appealing, when one analyses the potential operational and commercial outcomes that can occur in a partial win–partial win performance outcome in some detail, it soon becomes apparent that this apparently mutually beneficial outcome is far more complex than may at first appear. It has been argued elsewhere, and demonstrated in Figure 20.4, that

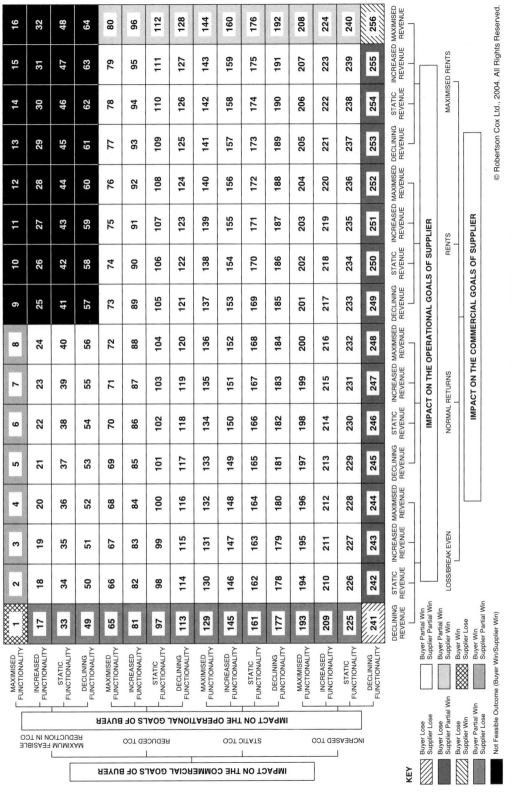

Figure 20.4 Feasible commercial and operational outcomes in buyer and supplier exchange (Source: Cox (2004b) p. 140)

when one links together the potential operational and commercial forms of exchange between buyers and suppliers 224 performance outcomes are feasible in practice (Cox, 2004b).

Figure 20.4 also shows that, when buyers and suppliers undertake transactions, when both operational and commercial factors are considered in detail, far more partial win–partial win (*nonzero-sum*) outcomes are feasible than any other. There are fully 175 potential performance outcomes under *nonzero-sum* partial win–partial win outcomes, with only 49 potential performance outcomes for all of the other *nonzero-sum*, *zero-sum* and *negative-sum* outcomes that are feasible. What this implies is that when managers say that they think that partial win–partial win outcomes are the best way of managing relationships they are actually stating a fact of life – namely, that most buyer and supplier relationships, and especially those that must be sustained over time as *repeat games*, normally occur under conditions of *nonzero-sum* partial win–partial win.

Despite this, it has to be said that, while it is one thing to recognise that many relationships result in partial win–partial win performance outcomes, this does not mean that it is the best choice for either the buyer or supplier. The logic of what has been argued here is that, even when a partial win–partial win outcome is feasible, there is nearly always a better alternative for the buyer or the supplier if it could find an alternative exchange partner (or induce its current partner) to provide such an outcome for it. Thus, other things being equal, when a buyer is operating in a *one-off game* there are always three outcomes that are preferable to a partial win–partial win outcome. These are the win–partial win, win–lose and partial win–lose outcomes. Similarly, even when the buyer is operating in a *repeat game* there is always at least one outcome that is preferable to a partial win–partial win and this is a win–partial win. Conversely, using the same logic, a supplier, in a *one-off game* in which reputation is not important, would always prefer a lose–win, lose–partial win, or partial win–win outcome to a partial win–partial win outcome. In *repeat games* a supplier would always prefer a partial win–win to a partial win–partial win outcome. This is because buyer and supplier exchange is always contested due to the non-commensurability of their objective interests (Cox, 2004b, c, 2005).

This conclusion is reinforced when one considers the 175 commercial and operational performance outcomes that occur in the partial win–partial win arena. When buyers and suppliers negotiate relationship outcomes operationally and commercially in the partial win–partial win arena it is obvious that some outcomes are more favourable to one party than to the other. Furthermore, there is no midpoint in which both parties achieve the same performance outcome. This is because the two parties in the exchange are, in fact, pursuing very different goals that are never fully commensurable. Operationally the buyer seeks to maximise functionality and reduce the total costs of ownership, while the supplier seeks to increase revenue and returns.

Given this lack of commensurability of interests, it is axiomatic that at whatever point in the partial win–partial win cell a buyer and supplier agree to operate, there is always a superior performance outcome for both of them than the position they have currently settled upon. This is because, even if the buyer attains an outcome in Cell 18 of Figure 20.4, or the supplier attains an outcome in Cell 239, there is always a superior performance possibility for both parties outside of the partial win–partial win framework if it could be achieved. More importantly perhaps, even if the buyer or supplier cannot currently operate outside the partial win–

partial win framework, any position within it that is not in Cell 18 for the buyer, or Cell 239 for the supplier, is a sub-optimal solution for each of them, within the partial win–partial win arena. Given this, buyers and suppliers have to accept that exchange is always contested, even when they are accepting *nonzero-sum* outcomes that are a partial win–partial win for both parties.

It seems sensible, therefore, to suggest to buyers and suppliers in construction supply chains and markets that they should consider their own interests first and those of their exchange partners second. This means that that, while they may have to accept *nonzero-sum* outcomes as the basis for sustaining *repeat games*, they do not have to do so if they are involved in *one-off games*. Furthermore, even in *repeat games*, if they can find partners who are prepared to provide 'loss leaders', (i.e. *zero-sum* outcomes that are objectively a lose outcome in the short-term) to them, in order to achieve some other highly valued outcome outside of the immediate relationship, these may be preferable to all of the other *nonzero-sum* outcomes available. For buyers and suppliers to think, first, about their exchange partners' interests is nearly always a recipe for sub-optimality. Incompetence in implementing reactive and proactive relationship management approaches is also a certain recipe for sub-optimality in performance.

The reason for writing this book was to provide buyers and suppliers in construction supply chains and markets with a useful way of thinking about the relationship and performance management choices available to them, and how to maximise their interests under contingent circumstances. It is our view that it is always a mistake to believe that there is one single best way of managing all construction relationships. Furthermore, we believe that reactive and proactive approaches can both be appropriate ways of working in particular supply chain and market circumstances. Despite this, even though there is no single best way of managing relationships to achieve the maximum feasible benefits for one's own interests, there are – in our view at least – better ways of thinking about the problem of appropriateness under changing circumstances. If this book provides some useful questions and a framework that allows managers to think about the choices available to them when they strive to maximise their interests in *one-off* and *repeat games* then it will have served its purpose.

References

Cannon, J. P. and Perreault, W. D. (1999), 'Buyer and seller relationships in business markets', *Journal of Marketing Research*, **36**(4), pp. 439–460.

Cox, A. (1999a), 'Improving procurement and supply competence: on the appropriate use of reactive and proactive tools and techniques in the public and private sectors', in Lamming, R. and Cox, A. (eds.), *Strategic Procurement Management: Concepts and Cases*, Earlsgate Press, Stratford-upon-Avon.

Cox, A. (1999b), 'Power, value and supply chain management', *Supply Chain Management: An International Journal*, **4**(4), pp. 167–175.

Cox, A. (2004a), 'The art of the possible: relationship management in power regimes and supply chains', *Supply Chain Management: An International Journal*, **9**(5), pp. 346–356.

Cox, A. (2004b), *Win–Win? The Paradox of Value and Interests in Business Relationships*, Earlsgate Press, Stratford-upon-Avon.

Cox, A. (2004c), 'Business relationship alignment: on the commensurability of value capture and mutuality in buyer and supplier exchange', *Supply Chain Management: An International Journal*, **9**(5), pp. 410–420.

Cox, A. (2005), 'The problem with win–win', *CPO Agenda*, **1**(3), Autumn, pp. 38–42.

Managing in construction supply chains and markets

Cox, A., Ireland, P., Lonsdale, C., Sanderson, J. and Watson, G. (2002), *Supply Chains, Markets and Power: Mapping Buyer and Supplier Power Regimes*, Routledge, London.

Cox A., Ireland, P., Lonsdale, C., Sanderson, J. and Watson, G. (2003), *Supply Chain Management: A Guide to Best Practice*, Financial Times-Prentice Hall, London.

Cox, A., Lonsdale, C., Sanderson, J. and Watson, G. (2004), *Business Relationships for Competitive Advantage: Managing Alignment and Misalignment in Buyer and Supplier Transactions*, Palgrave Macmillan, Basingstoke.

Cox, A., Lonsdale, C., Watson, G. and Wu, Y. (2005), 'Supplier relationship management as an investment: evidence from a UK study', *Journal of General Management*, **30**(4), Summer, pp. 27–42.

Cox, A., Sanderson, J. and Watson, G. (2000), *Power Regimes: Mapping the DNA of Business and Supply Chain Relationships*, Earlsgate Press, Stratford-upon-Avon.

Cox, A. and Townsend, M. (1998), *Strategic Procurement in Construction*, Thomas Telford, London.

Williamson, O. E. (1985), *The Economic Institutions of Capitalism: Firms, Markets, Relational Contracting*, Free Press, New York, NY, USA.

Williamson, O. E. (1996), *The Mechanisms of Governance*, Oxford University Press, Oxford.

Index

Page numbers in italics refer to charts and diagrams. The suffix 'n' indicates a reference to a footnote.